TESTING TO FAILURE

DESIGN AND RESEARCH IN MIT'S DEPARTMENT OF ARCHITECTURE

SARAH M. HIRSCHMAN, EDITOR
SA+P PRESS 2011

EDITOR:

Sarah M. Hirschman

ASSISTANTS:

Jonathan Crisman

Curtis Roth

Nadya Volicer

Kyle Barker

Introductions to research projects and studios were provided by the instructor of the class or studio, and in the case of theses, by the thesis student. Image captions were provided by the designer, where applicable. Transcripts of symposia were shortened significantly.

GRAPHIC DESIGN:

Lindsay Anmuth

COVER DESIGN:

Curtis Roth, art by Carl Lostritto

"Diffusion" and more of Lostritto's work can be found on page 372.

PUBLISHER:

SA+P Press

Cambridge, MA 2011

PRINTER:

Oddi Printing

Printed in Iceland

CONTACT:

SA+P Press

Room 7-337, MIT

77 Massachusetts Avenue

Cambridge, MA 02139-2307

ISBN

978-0-9836654-0-3

Copyright 2011

TABLE OF CONTENTS

EXTRA-LARGE

NUMERICS

GLOBAL

ARCHIVE

SURVIVAL

MISUSE

SUPPORT

THE UTILITY OF AN ARCHITECTURAL HYPOCHONDRIA

Sarah Hirschman and Arindam Dutta

A good department of architecture could be a little bit like a gestalt–the whole is greater than the sum of its parts. Of course, there have been schools of architecture that have flourished by circling wagons around the pedagogy of singular, charismatic individuals. At MIT, however, one tends to see several, not one, strong threads represented. We are very far from the days when we could conceive–and teach on the premise–of architects as representing a singular professional profile or catering to one dominant category of object. Architects are today being called in to advise, and deliver on, a staggering range of questions, from problems of branding, to addressing social equity, to reversing global warming, to push the frontiers of technological capability, not least to test given cultural imaginaries. At the same time, architecture's success in the world today presents new challenges for schools of architecture. More architects are being employed globally, more buildings are being built today with visible architectural flourishes than ever before. More technology goes into buildings: buildings self-diagnose how they breathe and cool down, who's inside them, what people inside might be doing. The complexity of building surfaces sometimes makes them more expensive, per square foot, than a luxury car. One corollary of these developments has been a heightened emphasis on quantitative performance, posing architectural questions that often appear better answered by technologists and industry. If society no longer belongs to homo faber, we are no longer practitioners what the twelfth century Hugh of St. Victor called ars legendi, "an ascetic discipline focused on a technical object."[1]

Architecture today is a sumptuous, talkative, collaborative, remote-controlled, imagistic, process-laden art. At the same time, it is not as if other intransigencies have subsided. Mortgage agencies appear to have–as we have learned–no problem making huge, ruinous gambles; they only appear unwilling to gamble on better architecture. The construction industry remains wedded to standardized operations. In this situation, an obdurate insistence on limiting the set of conversations–of architectural plays– seems only to lose the game. Schools of architecture are today confronted with transmitting both the abecedarium of the traditional skill-sets, in addition to considerably ramping up the situational constraints that the student can muster. Students today must master how different technologies work, learn to operate as cultural critics, acquire familiarity with different areas of the world, as well as confront the discursive mechanisms of the contemporary market.

One way of training good players is to play a lot, play with the largest variety of antagonists possible, such that a defined skill spills over into a knack for operating in unknown and unfamiliar terrain. This is what MIT is setting out to do. MIT is a small school with a very low student-teacher ratio, accepting only a select group of students every year. Its faculty comprises some very provocative, energetic and protean practitioners of their art whose brief is embedded within the context of one of the world's foremost research universities. Whether in the field of design, technology and computation, urbanism, history and theory, or in the realm of sustainability, MIT presents multiple areas of vertical integration, allowing undergraduate and masters' students to access researchers and teachers teaching at the doctoral level.

What MIT presents today is a closely-coordinated–and collegial–group of architects, historians, and technologists, actively engaged in educating a new generation of practitioners and theorists, having an intense discussion about what architecture does, and its place in the world. This is a moment of critical self-reflection for the discipline, and there is no better illustration of that than the many symposia, conferences, lectures, and discussions going on within MIT's many walls about pedagogy and the role of teaching. Rather than turning out typical MIT architects, the department serves as a enormously supportive and productive holding pen, a place to gain exposure to ideas and processes that don't yet have a fixed outcome. The role of the architect is hotly contested, and offered in a different light in every chapter of this book. From the resurrection of a Modernist sensibility towards monumental social infrastructure to a super-scientific interest in the molecular substance of building materials, architects here are biting off way more than they have ever chewed.

Grouping a community, when its very value is in its lack of singular agenda, seems counterproductive in a book like

this. The most exciting and intellectually rich moments are those where there is little agreement, where there are active debates and differences of opinion. Towards that end, we've found threads, tags even, that filter through projects and processes going on now that might help organize, if not effectively explain, focuses within the department and within the discipline. What is presented here in this book is a sequence of 'forums,' knots of discussion where the various threads that run through the department acquire heightened definition. When it comes to the question of technology, for instance, what is presented is less a lapse into technophilia than an absorption; tectonics, materiality, parametrics, sensoria, these represent contending strains of argument, as skeptical of technology as appreciative of its power, détourning its elements to produce surprising outcomes whether in the realm of practice or theory. Inspecting our work to find truths is a project of fiction, and it results in a kind of architectural hypochondria. Are we this? Are we that? Is this an infection? What's this bug that we can't shake? Architects understand the world as much as polemical drama as a global museum space, as much as a production line to be subverted and obtruded into as a call or invitation to a public.

Maybe it's the faulty economics of architecture that's bringing about this new attitude, maybe it's the dramatic technological shifts that are changing everything in the design process, maybe it's a restlessness with increased specialization and a seeming pigeon-holing of the architect. Today, the architect's role seems to be more expansive and imperial than it ever was, on the other hand, one could argue that various schools, in a desperate gambit for 'relevance' are chasing the dissipating colors of a disciplinary rainbow. There is a quite a fever of new programs and units that appear to respond to new impetuses; schools of architecture are today announcing specializations in geography, curatorship, politics, cultural studies, even economics. Whether this dissipation of resources is tantamount to a capitulation or the symptom of some new strength, it is today hard to say. At MIT, where all these fields are nonetheless covered, strategies for their combination and use remain in contention. For sure, there is no lack of thought and discussion about it, no dearth of opinions.

1   Ivan Illich, *In the Vineyard of the Text* (Chicago: University of Chicago Press, 1996), 5.

INTRODUCTION:
BEYOND A HIPPOCRATIC OATH, THE NECESSITY FOR CRITICAL SPECIFICATION

Nader Tehrani
Head, Department of Architecture

The nature of the architectural discipline has shifted quite radically in the last twenty years; much can be disputed about what constitutes 'discipline,' but there is little doubt that developments in the media around which design revolves have constituted nothing less than a game-change. Much of this is due to technology and the accompanying redistribution of power, knowledge and access to which this digital era has given rise. There is little doubt that the expanded population of practitioners and critics that this access allows is a positive development. But there are implications that attend the rise of a super-technical class of designers, and no simple analogs can be made to generations that came before.

For those who witnessed and participated in the transition from pencil to mouse, it involved the iterative task of perpetual "catching up" with emerging software while also helping to rethink some of the fundamental paradigmatic shifts that it involved. How form is conceived, how fabrication processes are rethought, who authors what, how accountability shifts from one hand to another, the new relations between process and product, these are only a few among a range of factors impacted by this powerful disciplinary shift. It also involves a certain degree of paranoia, an acceptance of the impossibility of constant relevance.

A simultaneous transformation has acted upon schools of thought. Where once we could easily identify the authorities of Rossi, Rowe, Hejduk and Koolhaas, in turn, we could also identify the institutions that were the breeding grounds of their speculations, techniques, and processes. Notwithstanding the headcount of those who have departed, this generation was also the last to have the luxury of maintaining the hegemonic link between persona, institution, and the idea of a school of thought. Of them, Koolhaas is the exception and the only one to survive the fallout and shakedown of the academy in the late 1990s. He mastered the transition from centralized authority to a distributed power of authorship and pedagogy, as is evident in the many practices and academic voices to which he has given birth. More than any singular design, Koolhaas's focus on rhetoric, communication and the ability to speak to current and developing culture must be underlined as a strategic contribution to a discourse in flux. With his prescient engagement with emerging markets, he staked out new territory, finding relevancy creating academic, financial, and technical spaces within which to operate. Koolhaas's innovation in this regard extends beyond his own practices – what he created was a precondition that permits others to innovate in new modes and fields.

For hundreds of years, there have been adjustments, variations, tweaks to style and building culture, few totally radical moments of change and disorientation. The moment of Modernism, with the conspiring technical advances of steel, concrete, and glass construction, as well as mass production, affected such a rupture - a unique turning point where modes of operation needed to be relearned, and values reinterpreted for a new era. We find ourselves again at such a moment, not only because of the changes to technique described above, but because the expanded breadth of the discipline has admitted so many more to it, with such varying profiles. The demographics have shown young practices from all cultural denominations flourishing outside of the loci of power that were once centers of culture.

The various fronts on which the digital era has operated have been well enumerated: the speed of communication, the simultaneity of production by way of BIM platforms, visualization techniques from the real to the pornographic, the versioning potentials of parametrics, optimization and performance modeling, mass customization, and the sheer power that the medium has given single individuals to produce what once took teams to accomplish. But what is most remarkable is the way in which education, knowledge and information have all become aligned, flattened even, a phenomenon that is as liberating as it is problematic. What was once reserved for books, elite colleges, and higher levels of education has now become accessible to anyone with an Internet hookup, wherever they may be—the impact this has had on formerly disenfranchised economies cannot be understated. But the knowledge has changed too, as a result. The moving target of disciplinary knowledge has never shifted so rapidly as now.

Some of this data is indeed the articles, curricula and pedagogical models that once required tuition to access, but a vast store of it is contained in the gradient range

from erudite critical texts all the way down to the smut of daily blogs that critique and editorialize the production of architecture minute by minute. The rigor and methods that characterize traditional history, theory and criticism practice were once lodged in the patience of time and tenure. Verification of data, analysis of findings, and strategic retrieval of archival information were all consolidated in the hyper-educated scholar working at a steady clip.

Modes now promote an immediate digestion, a constant churning of opinion, an impatience in waiting for the next journal or upload submission cycle. For this reason, standards are tested constantly and traditional research methods are pit against the endless stream of information flowing out of the Internet; the intellectual culture of the blog offers new ways for scholarship to reach the public, sometimes controversially so, platforms that were once not available outside of the elite presses of university publications. Practice will not tolerate the slow because in emerging economies, speed becomes the mediating agency by which 'success' is measured, forcing foundations to be poured prior to the completion of working drawings. What was once a classical and organic work of architecture, with all parts-to-whole thought through, is now conceived of in a more temporally layered way, with improvisation and the invocation of new rules at every benchmark. Changes in the way we communicate have affected great shifts beyond just the rarefied landscape of the academy.

While the failed economies of the advanced world tease out the intellectual implications of the most recent architectural obsessions, it is the remote developing economies that can afford to and do build out the risk of these speculative experiments, an honor once only bestowed to the few. The translation of ideas from one culture to another, not to mention the practices of building and communicating with fabricators, necessarily brings about reinterpretations of the most productive variety. In the new eyes on old ideas we see a resurgence of disciplinary excitement and invention, a redirection of course. Necessarily, the stakes are higher: the "scale" at which these experiments are undertaken, whether in the hands of the avant-garde in Beijing or the real estate gamblers in Macau, displays a gravity that architecture never could before. With cities' growth visible in real time, and the environmental damage of mismanaged expansion breaching regional boundaries, the implications become less abstract every day.

To be clear, the predicaments of the current condition are not straightforward: the potentials and dangers tempt each other at every turn. What is critical, though, is the significance of this shift in the role of architecture, design, and its relationship to the world. For those who said that architecture was dead, we know it is not only alive and well, but in fact expanding its domain and conquering others. For those who see everything as business-as-usual, the potential for architecture's status, instruments, agency and modalities to open up new avenues for practice and research have been wasted.

How to engage the current predicament is, of course, a challenge that many leaderships have addressed. Our own culture at MIT has encountered a variety of tendencies over the past two decades, most of which remain current and hold the same gravity today as they did when first elaborated. Among them, a strong value has been instilled on not just the product of architecture, but also its process. The importance of debates revolving around tectonic expression, the elaboration of light and inhabitation, the process of building community, the identification of cultural differences, the place of architecture in the city and its urbanistic implications, the role of the landscape within urban discourses, the imperatives of sustainability and the emergence of the virtual environment as the basis of speculation have all formed a complex web of discussions over the years.

The danger of attempting to satisfy any punch-list is readily evident in its insufficiency: we should imagine, much like in the medical field, that as architects we would have a Hippocratic Oath to a range of issues and requirements, knowing fully well that by fulfilling them, we have still not addressed the surplus that architecture requires. For instance, sustainability in architecture may need to be an ethic the same way zoning and other code requirements have come to serve as measures for health and safety, but never a headline or a singular directive. Architecture, instead, needs to be defined as a process of building knowledge, of inventing ways in which the discipline is transformed and will be transformed by challenging its values.

Returning back to the question of authority, it is unique and of this time that the power to transform culture is located with students. Students' reign over technology, information, access to knowledge and the mastery of different media within an interdisciplinary context makes them able to take on projects that exceed the theoretical: they do involve theoretical challenges, but also are weighted by mandates of delivery and implementation that cannot be addressed by those with ancient overheads. All of this does not lessen the authority of Rem, but the newly distributed power of a generation of emerging voices, some of which have hardly broken thirty, is having astounding effects on the ways we practice, learn, teach and collaborate.

At MIT, we don't produce the classic architect, if there is such a thing. We harbor intensification, specification, and the many microscopic views that form the leading edges of the discipline. The many extremities of views, as focused through the Department's discipline groups, allow intensive research on the one hand, but permit a higher-level collaboration and intersection with others similarly inclined towards rigor on the other. The notion of a critical type of specification, then, is not one that limits interests – it instead calls for an awareness of how they are strategically deployed.

Practice as we know it is on the verge of obsolescence, rightly so, and it is futile to prepare students for it. Instead, the student of architecture should be challenged to rethink what it means to practice, the conceptual ground on which the profession is based need not be hallowed. The 'what' is not always interesting, even if necessary, but the 'how' and the 'why' are what is most critical in our pedagogy, especially at a time when the 'what' can come about with such ease and so few critical obstacles. To this end, there is an inevitable link between techniques and ideas: both are important, both change over time. To fortify those new to the discipline with the critical judgment required to strategically operate on a shifting field is the task – software changes, formal obsessions wax and wane, but a conceptually rich understanding of the project and processes of architectural intent serves well through all weathers. The only way to know if we've done it right is if we go too far, if we test to failure and have to come back.

STRATEGY

UNSOLICITED

There are routine ways that architectural contracts are born: competitions, articles, word of mouth. Professional practice leaves little leeway for architects to reconsider, even interrogate, programmatic briefs set by clients. Teaching studios and workshops allows for greater exploration beyond the hurly-burly of satisfying clients. Each profession considers itself premised on some 'essential' core, professions only become of value to the extent that they are able to commit more and more conceptual and objective territories within their remit. Take the city for example: lawyers, economists, business associations, planners, engineers–each of these professions vie with one another to exercise control over the urban realm. To that extent, the briefs that architects receive from clients are only an effect of what they are able to represent as their legitimate claim.

Inevitably, cutting-edge architecture schools, as well as architecture offices, both need be sites of experiment, of unsolicited interventions that represent continuous rethinking, even breaking, of professional, disciplinary, and territorial boundaries. By necessity, these projects represent those that architects want to see in the world, without clear concern for constituency or client. Rather, they implicitly represent critiques of the way in which the built realm is inexorably received as if a given; they deconstruct the processes, typologies, and protocols of the normative. This riskier attitude situates the architect as a site of production not just of designs, but of the ideas behind them. The intervention is a conscious insertion into the world as it hums along, oblivious, a project taken on to have some greater social or interactive goal, and it is because of this charged context that it also becomes a sort of mouthpiece for the philosophies and priorities of a practice. This imagining of alternate worlds, of alternate modes

Images courtesy of J. Meejin Yoon / MY Studio / Höweler Yoon Architecture

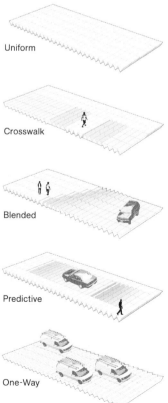

Uniform

Crosswalk

Blended

Predictive

One-Way

Public Works: Unsolicited Small Projects for the Big Dig, 2008—MY Studio/ J. Meejin Yoon and Meredith Miller

The vast sea of hardscape that covers the underground roadways of the Big Dig are reimagined as a transformable recreation and transportation space; one of many proposals put forth in J. Meejin Yoon and Meredith Miller's 2008 speculative book project combining original urban research with straightforward proposals for a variety of interventions.

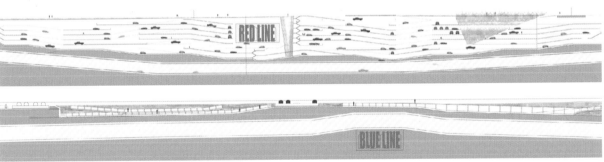

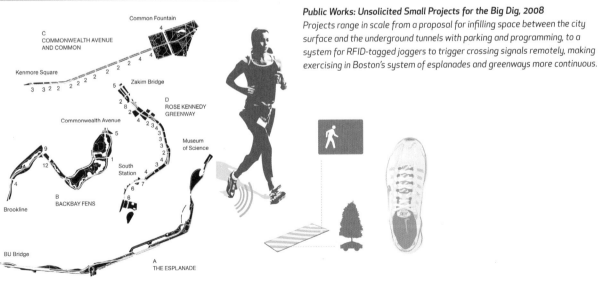

Public Works: Unsolicited Small Projects for the Big Dig, 2008

Projects range in scale from a proposal for infilling space between the city surface and the underground tunnels with parking and programming, to a system for RFID-tagged joggers to trigger crossing signals remotely, making exercising in Boston's system of esplanades and greenways more continuous.

White Noise / White Light—MY Studio
White Noise / White Light was one of nine tempo-
rary interactive urban installations commissioned
and installed for the Athens 2004 Olympics from
August 12–30, 2004 at the plaza entry to the
theater of Dionysus below the Acropolis as part
of the ATHENS 2004: Catch the Light Program.
Part of the programmed 'Listen to Athens' route,
the project inserted a luminous interactive
sound- and land-scape within an urban public
plaza to create a publicly choreographed field in
flux. Semi-flexible fiber-optic strands, arranged
in a fading grid, responded to the movement of
pedestrians through the field by emitting white
light and white noise. For 18 days, visitors walked
through and interacted with the sonic field of
chest-high end-emitting optics.

of built and lived existence, may appear at first glance as a remnant of idealism, the unsolicited conjurations and expressive fantasies of a profession all too-readily (and justly) associated with egoists. Certainly, architecture is not short on an illustrious history of utopianism, whose value is likewise misconstrued by that myriad cadre professing 'pragmatic' concerns. The architect's calling, if anything, must be as maker and destroyer of worlds. Nonetheless, within this august history of utopias, another name for which must be merely the unsolicited or the inopportune, there is also a more tempered, engaged conception of the unsolicited in the sense of the unsought or posed against the wholly expedient. For each utopia that premises a despotic client, there are equally numerous architectural propositions that emphasize democratic principles, engaging more astute politics and economics, For that matter, most projects that see their way into built realization represent less a pragmatism than an expression of powerful interests, the transfer of public resources to private preserves.

In that context, the intervention is not a purely speculative affair. It holds a kind of outsider status with the aim to change expectations and alter the course of history around it. MIT is today home to a number of practitioners–Meejin Yoon, Sheila Kennedy–who built agency into their practices with a series of unsolicited engagements with the built

White Noise / White Light

Activated by the passersby, the fiber optics transmit light from white LEDs while the speakers below the raised deck emit white noise. Just as white light is made of the full spectrum of light, white noise contains every frequency within the range of hearing in equal amounts. The white noise made for the project is based on a physical phenomenon called Johnson noise, where noise arises from the thermal motions of electrons in a resistor carrying current in an electronic circuit. This field of white noise creates a unique sound-scape in the city and masks out the noises from the immediate context, forming a place of sonic refuge within the bustling city.

realm. For both Kennedy and Yoon, the tremendous infrastructural transformation–America's most expensive highway project ever–of those proliferating trestles and yawning chasms of the 'Big Dig' or the Central Artery Project provided ample raw opportunities for unsolicited architectural thinking.

Do architects reserve the right to propose projects whose clients or subjects are only notional? Who decides how cities are built? Can messages be communicated through building and installation? Can the architect have a role in

White Noise / White Light

Each stalk unit contains its own passive infrared sensor and microprocessor, which uses a software differentiation algorithm to determine whether a body is passing by the stalk. If motion is detected, the white LED illumination grows brighter while the white noise increases in volume. Once motion is no longer detected, the microprocessor smoothly decreases the light and fades the sound to silence. The movement of pedestrians creates an afterglow effect in the form of a flickering wake of white light and white noise, trailing and tracing visitors as they cross the field. Depending on the time of day, number of people, and trajectories of movement, the project is constantly being choreographed by the cumulative interaction of the public. The field becomes an unpredictable aggregation of movement, light, and sound.

wider intellectual discourse, in the cultural life in which people construe their everyday existences? Unsolicited interventions represent ways in which architects can begin to take on a reflexive set of priorities and to project them into the world. In another light, the unsolicited represents ways in which architects bring the world–its hardships, its inexorable patterns, its normalizing tendencies–into their own preserve, untangle its tangled skeins, represent differently its inner workings. Such engagement mandates another level of architectural research thinking. The interventionist is, in this sense, more realist than the professional conservative. Like the flâneuse, she scours the streets, looking for opportunities, imagining new relationships with architecture's constituencies, different modes of voluntary imprisonment, engagement, pleasure, even resistance.

To say that a project is unsolicited is not to suggest that it just appears out of thin air. It's an imperative for action, it's an ideas competition with no deadline. It reflects a 'clearer', albeit paradoxically sullied landscape of how things actually are and how they could be. The unsolicited project is an interruption, a taking-of-the-floor by the architect who is promoting her own voice and agency in the creation of her

brief. It is also to assert that there is some kind of expertise unique to the architect, some kind of perspective that only they are able to offer the world. This practice also suggests that there is a project to be had, that there exist a set of priorities and interests for the designer separate from the specifics and details the client lays out, and this is where the unsolicited intervention becomes really powerful. It is, in effect, a declaration of concern. This is what is wrong with the city, these are the types of projects that it needs and that we would like to see in the world, this is an issue behind which a constituency can be gathered.

Public Works: Unsolicited Small Projects for the Big Dig, produced in 2008, is typical in light of Professor Meejin Yoon's teaching strategy as well as the operational logics of her firms Höweler+Yoon Architects and MY Studio. As a speculative book, *Public Works* was an undertaking that examined, on the firm's own private initiative and dime, the

Eco-Pods: Filene's Bioreactor—Höweler + Yoon Architecture

Algae Bioreactor Concept Proposal for Boston Globe Ideas Competition, Boston , MA, Höweler + Yoon Architecture and Squared Design Lab. Taking advantage of the stalled Filene's construction site at Downtown Crossing, Eco-Pod is a proposal to immediately stimulate the economy and the ecology of downtown Boston. Eco-Pod (Gen1) is a temporary vertical algae bioreactor and new public Commons built with custom prefabricated modules.

remnants of Boston's Big Dig and opportunities as a site for engagement. After the completion of the extensive infrastructural renovation of downtown Boston's roadway system, this book of projects proposes ways in which the underdeveloped residual public spaces left over might be reconfigured. Each section in the book combines extensive cataloging of the existing environment with proposals for how to bring the human scale experience back into massive urban infrastructure. The interventions reach towards speculative forms of architecture precisely in the way that all projects are before they are built; in other words, they are no different in terms of the technical or formal demands that most projects make upon a site or its infrastructure, only what they lack, what they simultaneously invite, is a constituency, an abstract clientele. They represent in essence a sort of architectural op-ed piece that speaks directly to those who make the RFPs.

Eco-Pods: Filene's Bioreactor

An on-site robotic armature (powered by the algae bio-fuel) is designed to reconfigure the modules to maximize algae growth conditions and to accommodate evolving spatial and programmatic conditions in real-time. As an open and reconfigurable structure, the voids between pods form a network of vertical public parks/ botanical gardens housing unique plant species–a new Uncommon for the Commons.

Eco-Pods: Filene's Bioreactor

Once the funding is in place for the original architectural proposal, the Eco-pods will be redistributed to various neighborhoods around Boston, to infill other empty sites and provide housing and locally harvested energy to local communities. The future dispersal is anticipated and designed for, making the Eco-pods pre-cyclable. A high density, locally productive and locally consuming, modular urban node, the Eco-Pod Pre-Cycling Downtown tower will have a net positive environmental impact.

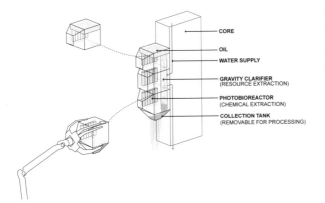

Eco-Pods: Filene's Bioreactor
Micro-algae is one of the most promising bio-fuel crops of today, yielding over thirty times more energy per acre than any other fuel crop. Unlike other crops, algae can grow vertically and on non-arable land, is biodegradable, and may be the only viable method by which we can produce enough automotive fuel to replace the world's current diesel usage.

Yoon uses *Public Works* to test ideas about the ability for architecture to effect social change: "these projects reclaim architecture's place as a primary conduit of information in the public realm. They investigate architecture as a mediating mechanism within the broader cultural phenomena of broadcast and spectacle, and understand architecture as a mass media capable of producing new publics that engage the structures of communication and transmission, transforming participant subjects from passive consumers into active agents."[1] As a folio, this set of interventions has something to say about the way that infrastructure, running through and around the city of Boston, can engage the human scale. Infrastructure projects, typically, are thought of at the aggregate and regional scale, far beyond the sensual ambit of the passers-by, the pedestrians, the commuters, the residents who abut their overdetermined scale. While Yoon's projects themselves illustrate ways that one might instantiate this type of thinking, Yoon furthers a broader philosophy in the process, one that might develop and shape future projects, solicited or not. She says: "these days what's more interesting than the orchestrated, choreographed effects of architecture is architecture's potential for inducing new atmospheres and behaviors, unscripted effects and unprogrammed events–a kind of re-examining and revisiting of architecture's potential to construct, as much as the requirement that it be constructed."[2] This is clear both in the way that *Public Works* took off as a project in itself, as

well as in the content of each landscape- and person-scale intervention contained within it.

Unsolicited interventions demand nimbleness. Projects are no longer defined by normative demands, rather by the imagination, so new talents, new skills, may be required in order to employ them strategically.

Research, the creation or assembly of new data, is also a hallmark of this mode of operation. Where the impetus of client demands seems to justify traditional projects, research and information gathering takes on that role in the unsolicited. In effect, it is just another way to find that solicitation. In the third chapter of *Public Works*, "Jetsam," an inventory of infrastructural objects present in the Big Dig's surrounds leads to the proposal of the project "Periscope," which draws light up and down from the Greenway surface into the car tunnels running below. Similarly, some projects, because of their experimental nature, become research in themselves. *White Noise White Light*, installed in Athens during the 2004 Olympics, was a contained piece, but at the same time served as a proving ground for certain types of technological advances. Once accomplished, the firm could then apply lessons to future projects, a benefit not unlike what one might expect from more traditional research.

(Bottom and opposite) **Periscope, from Public Works "Jetsam"**
Hybrid fixtures connect surface and sub-surface with visual access and lighting effects.

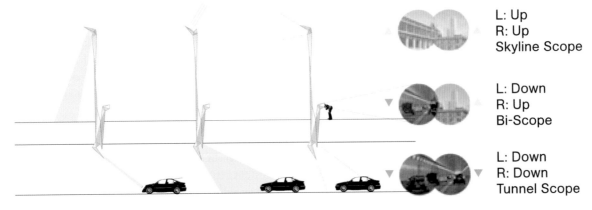

L: Up
R: Up
Skyline Scope

L: Down
R: Up
Bi-Scope

L: Down
R: Down
Tunnel Scope

Similarly, the *Interim Bridges Project*, by Professor Sheila Kennedy with her office Kennedy + Violich Architecture, takes on the truths of construction, the realities of the Big Dig, and uses them as turning points for an intervention. In this case, a temporary building was constructed as a way to focus public attention on the dramatic shifts and changes taking place in the excavation for the underground roadway. The building invites viewers to experience the details of the project, to focus on the very fact of construction.

Yoon brings her appetite for variety and belief in multi-platform research into her teaching. She has led workshops to Cambodia, pairing up with Building Technology Professors Ochsendorf and Andersen, collaboratively designed a floating pontoon dock, traveled with students to Taiwan to engage in fabrication/street art projects, and most recently has led a workshop to develop projects for MIT's 150th anniversary FAST project festival. The common thread between these is not medium or scale, nor is it a singular idea about something like technology or interactivity. What connects these is a belief in the stretch from one to another–the application of specialized knowledge from one field into places it has never been seen before. This is the natural outgrowth of the expanded practice, which aims to produce social and spatial effects of a certain interactive character, regardless of medium, place, or scale.

Shortly after she began teaching at MIT, Professor Yoon joined the popular Media Lab class *How To Make (Almost) Anything*, taught by Professor Neil Gershenfeld of the Center for Bits and Atoms. More than learning about designing and stuffing circuit boards, what Yoon credits to this class is her introduction to a particularly "MIT" brand of DIY ambition–it's about experimentation and figuring out, on a very basic level, how things work. The course's premise is that with the proper tools and a range of knowledge, you can figure out how to make just about anything. This isn't a disciplinary class, though all sorts of industrial design and electronic engineering knowledge goes into it; the CBA is interested in the making of *things*, not what things you make. Rather than a purely design-based mode, projects coming out of this class are developed to work first, and look good second. Projects involving LEDs, sensors, and interactivity were suddenly on the table for MY Studio and Höweler Yoon, and ideas about interactivity and embedded electronics were accessible. New tools don't change the nature of the project, though–Yoon and Höweler may sometimes be called artists, but they are always architects, occupied with architectural concerns. "These projects, whether installations, armatures, furniture, or buildings, are all architectures in the fullest sense of the word–they engage a material and spatial practice that is constructed, experienced, and perceived."[3]

With Höweler+Yoon Architecture, the multi-media dexterity of their projects provides a platform to theorize about a broader type of resistance to typical architectural modes of working. The office's monograph, *Expanded Practice*, takes on this very question. Part of Höweler and Yoon's discussion of the expanded practice notion is an intense focus on research, and in this it dovetails again with the culture at MIT. A research practice relies on its own ability to read the environment, to condense and clarify issues, and to find opportunities for action. Relieved from the finite demands of discrete projects, issues explored in a research project have the potential of becoming long-term pre-occupations, less a kind of 'signature' trait, more the honing of a sensibility. Ideas explored, for example, in Yoon's *Defensible Dress*, a project she began to develop in the *How to Make* class, make their way into her later interactive constructions. Having an eye towards research at all times means the building up of a practice's archive, the material from which one can continually draw. This contains not just documentary evidence of what exists, but also a range of responses and ideas that correspond, an archive for action.

What might begin as an interest in proximate sensing from a custom microcontroller in Athens might develop into a permanently installed instrument requiring custom two-sided LEDs in Washington, DC. The transition from temporary art installation to permanently installed client project is not insignificant either, as it shows how the practice is able to funnel their own interests into commercial success in a very strategic and intentional way. By valuing projects like *Public Works*, the team is able to declare a stake, an interest in the urban scale experience. "No project lies fallow even if it remains a prototype, every seed of an idea suggests another, and most have echoes in subsequent projects."[4] When opportunities arise for projects that aim to better integrate the public into urban infrastructure, Höweler+Yoon Architecture is prepared with a series of starting points, a set of ideas that describe the climate of potential projects they might undertake. The research of this book means that the firm has a ready roster of attitudes, sensibilities, a demonstrated agility at the urban scale, and that they are proactive in finding evidence in the urban environment to support the projects that excite them.

The ability to spot projects to work on opportunistically is intentionally developed. In *Expanded Practice*, Filip Tejchman uses the term 'superproducers' to describe Höweler and Yoon.[5] He adopts it from the music industry, where it refers to exceptional engineers and technicians who edit and mix recordings without actually creating the raw material themselves. This 'super-'vening characteristic comes from an extreme facility with the technology of production, such that they become implicated in the music itself. Think of Brian Eno. By increasing the number of platforms on which the practice can publicly think—fashion, industrial design, publications, buildings, installations, interactive artwork—they can begin to 'superproduce', to tell the story of their interests and researches without being beholden to any one medium. Design is here seized as a totalitarian, imperialistic activity, albeit from below,

professing a kind of viral outreach into the plenitude of objects. Important in this notion of the superproducer is the idea of raw material and specialization. Rather than the drive for unique knowledge and skills, the Höweler and Yoon (as well as the sort of *How To Make Almost Anything* ethos) practice operates by a type of curatorial and cultural triage. Highly conceptual responses to unique circumstances are their hallmark, and the convening of multiple experts from multiple fields to help them fabricate and materialize ideas is their method. This collaborationist attitude means that they are not limited by their own abilities, and the concept of practice remains ever-fungible, infinitely autodidactic. The interventionist mode feeds on ideas, possibilities, fractures within the normative condition.

In this light, MIT can be seen as a school for interventionists. Faculty and students typically identify themselves as investigators: they don't necessarily know how to accomplish everything on their long list, but they know where to seek out that knowledge, and it's available in abundance. There is little interest in designing for the status quo—everything undertaken within the studio sequences and the many workshops going on every semester has a reason, and more often than not, can be seen as an intervention.

Interventionism is a practice, a way of imagining projects in situations where none may be apparent, for which there may be little call. It's also a way of releveraging the agency of the architect, an assertion that the designer needn't just take cues from programs that are handed down to her, but reserves the wherewithal to move up the hierarchy of cultural and infrastructural control.

Interim Bridges Project—Sheila Kennedy / KVA
This project exposes the excavation work of the Big Dig by inviting the public into an intimate viewing platform.

1   J. Meejin Yoon, *Expanded Practice: Höweler + Yoon Architecture / MY Studio*. New York: Princeton Architectural Press, 2009, 169.

2   MY interview in Elite Kedan, Jon Dreyfous, and Craig Mutter, eds. *Provisional: Emerging Modes of Architectural Practice USA*. New York: Princeton Architectural Press, 2010, 181.

3   Yoon, *Expanded Practice*, 9.

4   Brooke Hodge, "Watching it Grow: The Interdisciplinary Project of Höweler+Yoon Architecture/MY Studio," *Expanded Practice*, 203.

5   Filip Tejchman, "The Superproducers," *Expanded Practice*, 196.

PECHA KUCHA: ARCHITECTURAL INSTALLATIONS AS PRACTICE AND GENRE [PANEL DISCUSSION] MIT150 TRANSCRIPT

TUESDAY, APRIL 26, 2011

Antón García Abril: Visiting Professor of Architecture, MIT
Skylar Tibbits: Professor of Architecture, MIT
William O'Brien Jr.: Professor of Architecture, MIT
Joel Lamere: Professor of Architecture, MIT
Phil Seaton (for Sheila Kennedy): MArch Student, MIT
Nick Gelpi: Professor of Architecture, MIT
J. Meejin Yoon: Professor of Architecture, MIT
Nader Tehrani: Professor, Head, Architecture Department, MIT
Gediminas Urbonas: Professor of Art, Culture, and Technology, MIT

This conversation has been edited for length and clarity..

Antón García Abril: I would like to introduce the first question, about this MIT spirit that we've just enjoyed in several expressions– from processes to more objective approaches, from systems to more abstract transformation of reality through different tools of the technology of expression. What's the objective of the installations, are they a contemporary type, where MIT is leading and offering it to the cultural world, or is it a tool, where the destiny of this tool is experiment, research, future actions, or systems in architecture? I don't want to point to anyone, so … Skylar?

Skylar Tibbits: I think personally they become pure research and experimentation, like you were saying. So given a scenario or a problem, and a commission to do an installation, then you're going to try and solve that in whatever capacity you can, and through the method of solving that issue, you find opportunities formally and materially, with machine techniques and processes and all of that. But I think then by focusing so consistently on installations and this pure research agenda, it becomes a type all its own, because the more you do of that, the more commissions you get to do more installations, and the more you get focused on the installation scale, and the more you know these processes and materials. I think it's both, it maybe started out on the experimentation/research side, and transitioned into a life of its own.

William O'Brien Jr.: I would add that it seems across the panel, there is a pretty clear divide between those that are interested in using installation as an extension of a pure body of research, whether that be a kind of structural endeavor or geometric enterprise, or one about sensors, and then there's another group who might be more interested in taking on the idiosyncrasies of the collaboration itself, and leveraging particularities of a certain site, or a certain strangeness to a collaboration as a way to give rise to a specific installation.

Antón García Abril: I would like to introduce another question. With a distant view of MIT as a whole, those slight and subtle differences that you are referring to are imperceptible. When a Spanish architect arrives here, he's struck immediately by how unique and how unitarian the full MIT community works in the same direction. So I understand that those, and that's part of the strength, but those subtle differences that you battle about, and will continue to battle, are seen in the research scene as part of the full MIT spirit, no? You are able to transfer into the installations all the knowledge that is collected through the school. But the question is, does that unity not obstruct personal expressiveness through installation? Does that unity of MIT not misuse the possibility of the mock-ups–the small research, the constructed research–to escape from the style. I'm

Image credit: George X. Lin

introducing the term. How can that be transferred to architecture? Should we push the site? Sheila?

Phil Seaton [standing in for Sheila Kennedy]: I think it's important to do both. I think the ambition of our installation in particular was that it not be pigeon-holed as pure research. We were trying to make something that could stand on its own. It would be an object for contemplation in terms of the type and style of the installation, but also would simultaneously advance the research. And I think it's less valuable as an installation, at least in our terms, if we don't succeed in doing both. To ignore all of the practicalities of enclosure, of trying to make things stand up, I think would be largely disappointing. So I would deny the premise, in a sense, and say that we aren't trying to use the research to escape type but that we're trying to do both at the same time.

Antón García Abril: You have insisted in your presentation that technology could substantially modify the way that we build. It's a general reflection in architecture that it seems in our materials and our basic ingredients, we haven't changed much in the last fifty years. On the contrary, the tools and the accessories we construct with have changed, and maybe this is the line of research by which architecture can advance. But I'm concerned that this advance is focused on this process of fabrication. You do models that are immediately constructed in mock-ups or installations. All this research has forgotten a little bit the traditional systems with which we build structures. We are trying to push the research through practical responses to today's needs without forgetting the avant-garde of the technology that we are incorporating. So where is the gap between what we have to do immediately tomorrow to build this research, and this strictly distant future, and today's standards of construction research?

Nick Gelpi: I think that the problem of fabrication on its own is that it's not serious enough. And I'm thinking of a quote that Gediminas projected that said, you know, "we don't play painting, but we play piano." Some of it's play, some of it's serious. And I think that perhaps a better question would be, is installation a type? What are the types of installation? What are the types that we're all doing? It seems like we're all doing different types. I kind of agree with Liam–there's a distinction between what we're doing that started as a kind

of collaboration between fabrication and computer science: Joel's is a kind of exegesis of space, Liam's is a collaboration, Meejin's is a kind of intervention in the space, and I guess my question would be if we're actually doing the same thing at all, if installation is anything other than just a kind of practice in a box.

[Questions from the Forum]
Unidentified Audience Questioner: In these presentations you talk about a lot of elements, some of them architectonic. But that's a fake materiality. Why aren't we talking about fake materialities?

Nick Gelpi: I think that's an interesting idea. To me, the Mies mock-up is about a fake materiality, the kind of questioning of the legitimacy of the tectonic without the correspondence to the material itself. So that is to put into brackets–it's something that interests me. I'm thinking back to the discussion last night about pedagogical practices and Hernan Diaz Alonso mentioned that there was a difference between just doing experiments as opposed to research. Whereas research is very precise, what is the problem that you are working on, what result might you want, working towards pushing the field in a certain direction, as opposed to just being playful, I would say.

Antón García Abril: It's not organized like this, but it seems like the table goes from a room to a pavilion, it goes up in scale–an urban intervention, and the full city. All these ranges of scale are included of course in the concept of installation. And that matches with all the interests of the architects, no? Going from the system to the full city. Meejin, maybe your interest is in interacting with social, wider scenarios and wider public spaces, with the same micro-element?

J. Meejin Yoon: I would agree, I would say that there is an interest in design at a micro scale, how that can impact a larger scale–more urban–and it skips, let's say, the architectural scale. I think I would agree with Skylar, it seems like it's both that we're talking about type and about tool. And the installations are an excuse to engage in that at an entry level that is do-able, affordable for a certain kind of practice. I think the more we practice in the United States, the more frustrating the construction systems in place become. It's more difficult to experiment. So the Johnson Wax column [that Nick showed earlier] is like a fantastic moment that represented when architects could experiment at the architectural scale, and I think that in a way we have lost that for, let's say, 99% of the practices in the United States at the moment. I think there are a few that manage to pull it off. And so the research is happening at one scale with the anticipation that it will have some productive architectural use, like in Sheila's project. But the reality of being able to produce it, manufacture it, warranty it, it's kind of daunting. And that's why this kind of playful experiments, or serious play, is critical to keep the spirit of the architect alive in terms of experimentation.

Antón García Abril: I have felt that spirit of time alive in Gediminas and Nader's installation, where the generative process of the form, at least, refers to a very distant idea of permeability through a portico system. Along with that, I am seeing an icon that refers to a full city. So the presence of time opens a new variable. It's not just a constructive matter.

J. Meejin Yoon: I would say that Nader and Gediminas's installation is an architectural scale project, unlike any of the other installations present. It's architectural in scale–it's structural, it's inhabitable. It itself is water-tight, so it has more aspects that I think a building, per se, might have. And I think because of that it's super exciting, because you want to inhabit it, you want to engage it like a portico, even though it will never be experienced like a portico because it's floating out on a barge.

Gediminas Urbonas: It was one of the challenges to really create an extension of Killian Court, to realize one of those scenarios that were projected back in '72, that were the future of the city space, closing Memorial Drive. At least now we can inhabit that. We got the permission for two days to close Memorial Drive. And that is an important act. Even though it's just for two days, but it's on the level of projection again for the future, you can produce something.

Nader Tehrani: I can introduce a couple of other variables to the discussion. One, just to piggy-back on last night's discussion. I think that maybe Hernan stopped short when he spoke about the experiment vs. research because probably if we were to expand our terrain and look at all the communities at MIT, there is actually a lot of work going on, but they never fit into the same definition or modality of play or research, or whatever you want to call it. But it

seems that there is a necessary play or experimentation without an a priori understanding of what the results are going to be, in order to do research. The idea of accident or circumstance is central to that. At the same time, and one of the reasons that I love Skylar's presentation, is that in retrospect, he can look back and begin to identify another element that came out of last night's conversation, and that's the idea of a project. There's an intellectual project that through many different proposals, designs, fabrications, and all of that, construct some kind of continuity and difficulty within the context of the discipline. The systemic ways in which a certain set of problematics are radicalized through an architectural project are easily decipherable and imaginable from, let's say, the way that Skylar is working, to the way in which it can be made more complex in an architectural project that deals with those kinds of things that Meejin, you are talking about. Questions of enclosure, waterproofing, circulation, and all of that, the sorts of contingencies of architectural merit. I think we need to help define what research can be at MIT, and how to expand it.

Skylar Tibbits: I'll pick up there–one of the things that you mentioned when you were talking about where there is the connection back to existing systems –existing systems of structure, I think it touches maybe the idea of research in general that research might be an opportunity to cross disciplines, and it's the opportunity to say, "look, if you're trying to challenge a notion of structure, you take an existing system and you take two steps forward that might be experimentation, that might be play." It's still an incremental improvement, and I think that's useful. In that scenario, you're never really going towards the way that we build, but you can have other useful collaborations in other disciplines and by going in a direction that is more pure research, you might have feeders that come back to the discipline further down the road.

Nick Gelpi: Can I ask a question, Skylar? I wonder if what you're saying is that cross-disciplinary collaborations–is it a case that allows you to not be burdened by the slow-moving problems of architecture, to operate outside of the field? What are the examples where pure external research came back on the discipline?

Skylar Tibbits: I think a good example, and something that Meejin pointed out, is the stubbornness of the construction industry.

And so in that sense, it is sort of running away—you find your own solutions and so by doing that, you then propose your own problems, and it's a sort of cycle of moving forward. I think within that you also find lots of incremental solutions, whether they're material connections or a new machine, that aren't necessarily architectural that could have huge implications architecturally. So, you know, are any of the projects that I showed directly applicable [to the architectural scale]? Probably not, but small instances in them would be extremely applicable.

Antón García Abril: When we talk about these links between different atoms that surround this practice, we always approach architecture to the length of infrastructure, let's say. MIT and the installations are very close to a very abstract notion of structure and space as a consequence. But it's closer technologically than conceptually, to other technologies related to mostly audio-visual automatic technologies. So isn't that something that would wrap and trap MIT into its own success, or, should installations merge and connect and meet a lot of disciplines that surround this school –Civil Engineering, Geology, all kinds of energies, arts, music. Or are we still fascinated about the atoms and the bits, and that's the only research that feeds our architecture, in terms of producing, in terms of representing?

J. Meejin Yoon: I can speak to that as someone who produced one of the installations, but also coordinated the installations between the participants and the Department of Architecture with the FAST committee, who may not be architects, and the Institute at large. At the beginning, I had to actually present these projects to the committee and convince the committee that these were really interesting works. They could not understand the value, let's say, of the architectural question that individuals were pursuing. But they could understand the more general idea, or its effect on the campus, or its other pragmatic qualities, like Nick's pavilion. Everyone was very excited because they needed some *shade*. It wasn't because of the research in the sandwich skin, etc., and I do think it was an interesting process for me because being involved in the discipline of architecture, I understand the relevance, and the critical importance of all the research topics. But in presenting it, it became very clear that to the rest of the Institute, this is a very narrow spectrum of research, and maybe from their perspective the criticism could be that we're not interdisciplinary enough.

Nader Tehrani: There was a humorous moment in our collaboration, because we worked for two or three months on a project that was summarily killed every week. And then, what you see up on the screen is actually the result of a two-minute discussion that was meant to be a two-hour meeting with your team. If I remember correctly, it was based on a verbal description. They said, "I love it, run with it!" But it addressed exactly what you say right now, that there seems to be, as in all advanced areas of study, a kind of autonomous set of disciplinary issues that we can only share with each other. That's a kind of advanced knowledge in very microscopic ways, but its position in the world, in the horizon of expectation, in terms of the reception of a wider audience, needs to at the end develop a different lens within which it can be situated. That was an apt lesson.

William O'Brien Jr.: I would guess that we all hope that there is a way to describe these projects that doesn't come off as a kind of autonomous technologically-centered set of work, but instead asks questions about what the cultural impact is. There are probably ways to present the work that position each of the projects within culture. I think that the architectural design group is uniquely positioned to leverage the robustness of the technological abilities here, but through a kind of cultural lens. So, establishing links, say, with the History, Theory, Criticism group [HTC] that enables some kind of translation of what fabrication is for, what it is about, what kind of message we are trying to give as a department, how do we translate it in some ways culturally, being culturally relevant.

Antón García Abril: I understand, and I agree. But there are several schools, in the United States, and in Europe, that are great manufacturers of technology. Several periods of history are more demanding of ideology or technology. I think now the demand is for technology. And that is the strength of this school. But, I don't know if our challenges, our social challenges now, should be in creating cultural constructs, while architecture has to solve enormous goals and challenges that we are immersed in now. I am referring to the weird urban situations we are going to have, the dramatic changes that have to be incorporated into architectural technologies, into a new religion. And that is the strength of having a school, with all of these infinite disciplines that are easily interchangeable. And that's the question–how the installations could refer to these goals on a smaller scale, as *pre-projects*. While cultural ideology has been necessary, maybe now technology is that which provides that advance in culture.

Arindam Dutta: What we are confronting here is the strangeness of objects. And what is most elusive is objecthood—somehow, objecthood is always other to thought. All your projects were very successful. My question is about installation quite rigorously as a genre. What we've seen here is a kind of intermediate moment between a sort of research and a sort of reflexive practice and a sort of future outside the work that will eventually become a sort of architecture, or produce architectural ideas. But my question is—how seriously then do you guys take the spectator? Is the spectator in this scenario simply being asked to go, "WOW, cool"? In which case, your work is perhaps something like a trade show. Because each of you produce shops. I'm thinking of someone like [György] Kepes, and one of the reasons that the engineers loved him was that he was very good at producing the *WOW* moment. That was his thing. Should architecture, should art—we know, but I want to throw this out there to see how you respond to it. It is a facet of questioning that we did not see presented today, with maybe a couple of exceptions. I just want to throw this back to you.

Joel Lamere: I think that the thing that distinguishes the trade show and exposition as spectacle from what we're up to in part centers on this question of research, because it's a thing that is a little bit beyond the salesmanship of a trade show. I think personally for our installation, the spectacle was always in service of a kind of a public awareness towards architecture. So, our project—I imagine that its absence will produce a kind of conscientiousness of the stair and the kind of remarkable architectural condition with its absence that is in service of a kind of spectacle as stair—maybe that's 'trade show' early on, but then becomes a kind of seeping consciousness which happens with the absence later on. That's my brief answer to that—with this question of objecthood that you brought up again.

Nick Gelpi: I'm just quickly reminded of the story which doesn't relate much to anything of the World's Fair—the Paris one with the Eiffel Tower, 1889—and then Chicago gets it in 1893 or 1894, whatever it is. And so it's Burnham, the White City, and they don't

have that *wow*, and they want the *wow*—it's just kind of architecture. And they're all really stressed out, with a few months to go, and they just accept that they're not going to be able to outdo the Eiffel Tower. I think there's an idea about wanting to produce something very contemporary—like *wow* with a contemporary flavor. At the last minute they get it—it was the Ferris Wheel. Certainly you can ride the Ferris Wheel, it's nice, but I don't think there was a kind of perception of the subject in the Ferris Wheel—it's just kind of a contemporary innovation that does *wow*. So I guess I kind of differ from these other panelists—I kind of shamelessly accept that to a certain extent, to be honest.

Michael Schwab: I just wanted to say when it comes to the question of research, that what I felt was maybe lacking from this panel was that I don't think that the making of things replaces the question of what research is transforming. In so many of the projects, I was trying to find out what actually you are transforming, outside of materials, and the kind of ambition you want to read of that kind of transformation. So, the cultural framework is one field of transformation. Culture is one field of transformation, but it need not be cultural. Technology, as you suggested, might be taken for granted as a field within which to operate. If you transform beyond technology, where would you go?

Nader Tehrani: I'll offer a closing response to that question. While it is undoubted that architecture is situated within a world of multiple audiences that it has to communicate to, it's also arguable that some of the most amazing inventions in architecture are so deeply rooted in the techniques and the functions that are internal to its discipline that they're vastly invisible to ninety-nine point nine percent of culture.

Antón García Abril: Perfect.

MONUMENTS+BITS: RECENT WORK BY KHOURY LEVIT FONG
NOTES ON RESEARCH AND PRACTICE

Rodolphe el-Khoury

The exhibition *Monuments + Bits* showed a number of uniquely developed technologies and originally authored software to create new modes of exhibiting architecture. Illuminated displays sensitive to touch triggered themed projections of architectural work. The exhibition explored *augmented reality* techniques: physical models, which visitors were invited to pick up and handle, were tracked by cameras enabling the mobile projection of information onto these same models. The apparatus for holding the physical elements of the technology–webcams, LCD projects, and LED lighting systems–were integrated into a parametrically designed physical environment. Shaped nets, hanging in the form of vaults were used to position projects and cameras.

The exhibition combines parametric modeling and fabrication techniques with emerging responsive media to present architecture and urban design projects in an interactive and digitally augmented environment.[1] The exhibition dramatizes the event of collective monuments and their tense relationship to the immediacy of individual experience. Conventions are recast through new parametric capacities in the production of architectural form, while current developments in interactive media refashion perceptions of the fixity of the built environment.

The design takes advantage of the different characters of the Eric Arthur Gallery's two main spaces to explore contrasting strategies for the integration of digital interactive technology and imagery into physical environments: while electronic and AV equipment is prominently displayed as part of a space-defining superstructure in one room (A), it is seamlessly embedded in the other (B).

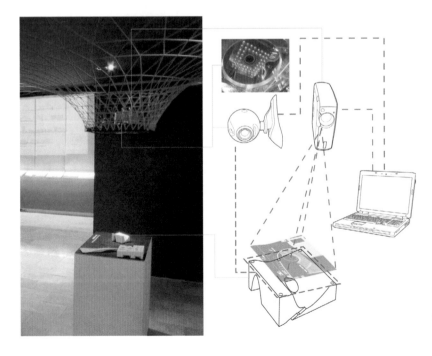

Diagram Showing Responsive Image Projection
Video tracking enables the projection of context-specific content in three possible scenarios.

Images courtesy of Rodolphe el-Khoury / Khoury Levit Fong

Roof Landscape
MUSEUM OF POLISH HISTORY

EXIT

Diagram Showing Responsive Image Projection
Video tracking enables the projection of context-specific content in three possible scenarios.

The exhibition is innovative in two significant ways:

1. It utilizes parametric modeling/fabrication techniques to facilitate the adaptation of the exhibition and its installation in different spaces.

2. The exhibition has responsive and interactive features that enhance the communication of the material and adapt the mode of presentation to better suit a variety of viewing conditions. For instance, video tracking enables the projection of context-specific content in variable scenarios:
—When only one visitor is in the room the projected image relates to the model that is closest to the visitor.
—When two visitors are in the room and looking at different models the projected images alternate between the two.
—When three or more visitors are in the room the projected content is randomized.

The exhibition demonstrates how emergent digital technology can be functionally and formally integrated into architectural projects.

Other interactive features include:
—Augmented Reality display–3-D printed massing models are augmented with animated images. The models are tagged with infrared reflectors that enable the system to identify them and lock on to them with a projection of precisely directed and dimensioned images and captions.
—Responsive displays–computer vision tracks the gestures of visitors allowing them to select images with a light touch for enlargement by means of digital projection.

Project Credits:
Design Team: Rodolphe el-Khoury and Robert Levit with James Dixon, Mike Fung, and Renée Leung.
Programming: James Dixon.

1   The exhibition opened at the Eric Arthur Gallery in Toronto on September 28 2009 for two months. The CMYK Gallery of the University of Michigan's A. Alfred Taubman College of Architecture and Urban Planning hosted it in January 2010 for one month.

SENTIENT ARCHITECTURES: AT HOME OPTION DESIGN STUDIO

FALL 2010

Instructor: **Rodolphe el-Khoury**
Teaching Assistant: **Moritz Philipp**

The migration of computing from dedicated appliances to physical environments, thanks to massively proliferating microchips and ever-expanding information networks, directly implicates and empowers architecture as a transformative agent and medium. The fact that objects can now sense, think, act and communicate with the help of embedded technology points to an architecture that is more closely aligned with the networked dynamics of living systems—a sentient architecture.

The studio addresses architectural questions posed by embedded computation i.e., the integration of miniaturized computing, sensing and actuating devices into the objects and spaces of everyday life. Architectural applications in the following areas or research and technology will be sought and implemented in working prototypes: responsive and interactive systems; augmented reality, embedded/situated technology, ambient intelligence, mobile computing, locative media.

The focus is on the domestic environment. The aim is to develop in design and research project some prototypes and ideas for improving the functionality, optimizing the environmental performance and enriching the experience of home with the digital enhancement of common building materials, components and technologies.

Nadya Volicer | MArch
Sentient Weather

This project is about weather, specifically a kind of third weather that is present within the home, located in the in-between spaces: panes of glass, wall cavities, even entire rooms in the case of the greenhouse and root cellar. These spaces are conditioned to have a weather distinct from the exterior and that of the domestic interior, whose comfort levels fall in a predictable middle range. If we examine these spaces as having a climatic condition all their own, how can we create third weathers that not only mediate between exterior and interior weathers, but also offer a potential physiological benefit to inhabitants, as well as a degree of spectacle for viewers both inside and out? And how can sentient technologies assist in the functioning of this new kind of all-weather house?

The Fog Block relies upon mist to serve as cloud cover to shield from solar gain and provide privacy. Maintaining the expected dimensions of the ubiquitous glass block, this unit is designed for plug and play capabilities and is hermetically sealed. In this way, Fog Block invites the weather into the intermediate zone of the house and uses it to mediate between the interior and exterior weathers. It also provides a spectacle both for the inhabitant and passersby.

Because exterior weathers affect areas of the site in varying ways, what other systems could be combined with the Fog Block in order to optimize performance? Revisiting precedents, it is clear that third weather conditions exist on numerous scales; from the hermetically sealed double paned window to the inhabitable solarium. Taking advantage of this range, one could image the home as a thickening wall, incorporating systems at several scales to the point at which the wall becomes the entire room; the third weather all-encompassing.

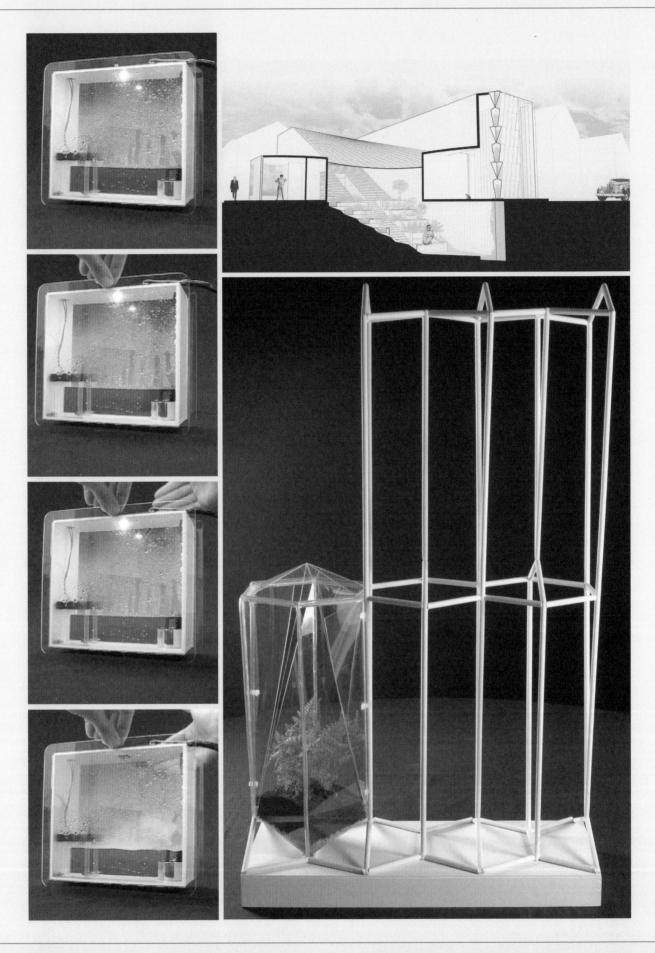

Chun Lun Otto Ng | ·MArch
WallBots

WALLBOTS are architecturally intelligent agents that are powered by electronic and kinetic systems to continuously reshape spatial boundaries and programmatic organization. In a swarm-like fashion, they reconfigure themselves in response to real-time information, including weather, social-network information and user behavior.

Wallbots can stretch from 1 meter to 1.5 meters by expanding their origami skin and kinetic skeleton. They can move and navigate freely; in coordination with each other, they form an ever-changing spatial boundary. Wallbots attach to each other with a simple electromagnetic mechanism and infrared positioning feedback.

Project WallBot liberates architecture from its static condition allowing space to be continuously shaped by the pressure of events — such as the shifting patterns of movement, and ever changing thermal requirements. WallBot assumes its ever shifting configurations by means of hepatic and graphic user interfaces or by responding to and learning from user habits and behavior.

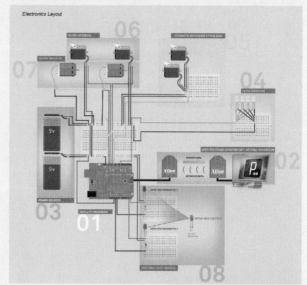

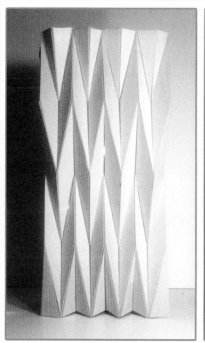

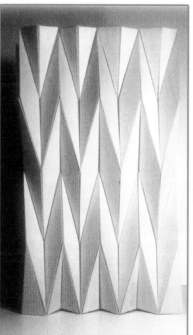

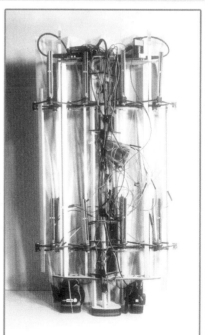

WIDTH = 100%　　　　　**WIDTH = 150%**　　　　　**NAKED**

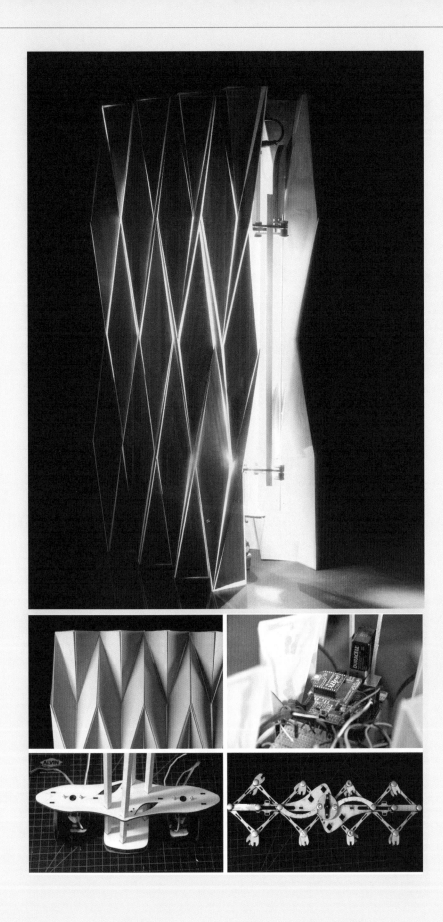

WHY ARCHITECTS SHOULD DESIGN A ROAD BRIDGE
NOTES ON COLLABORATION, UNPREDICTABILITY, AND FORM

Dr. Holger Falter (Engineer/Arup) **& Shih-Fu Peng** (Architect/heneghan peng architects)

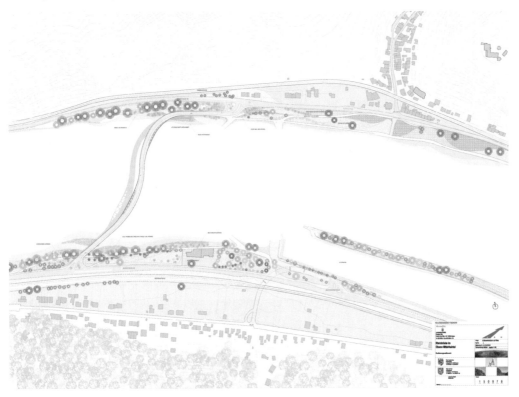

Site Plan
Showing landings of north and south ramps and the formation of a new landscaped park system along opposite banks.

A bit of clarification–the design must be a road bridge, not pedestrian–which in most cases is closer to architecture than infrastructure. Reason being that the structural constraints for a pedestrian bridge rarely limit architectural form. On a road bridge, they almost always do.

I once saw an episode of *Star Trek Voyager* where the holographic doctor, in order to remake himself as a new, more human, entity, gave himself the common cold to experience pain. This really did not work until the chief engineer rigged it so that the doctor was not in control of the on/off switch so that he no longer had the ability to turn off the cold when he felt like it.

We believe collaboration revolves around two issues: control (constraints) and the production of the new. The relative degree to which they engage each other results in different degrees of the new.

The bridge's structural profile minimizes intervention into the continuous void that shapes the Rhine River Valley.

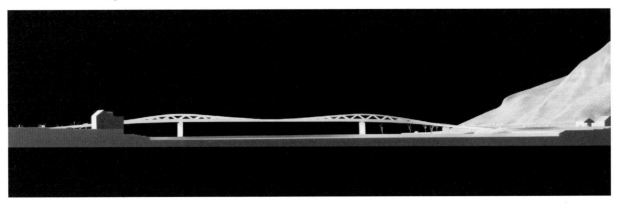

Images courtesy of Shih-Fu Peng / heneghan peng architects.

We will draw reference to a bridge Arup and heneghan peng architects designed in the UNESCO World Heritage-designated stretch of the Upper Middle Rhine River Valley where for several decades every attempt at bridging in order to sustain the local economy and prevent a continuing exodus of its inhabitants has failed, leaving this beautiful stretch bridgeless.

Siting:

A significant proportion of architectural competitions are won on site strategy; not just physical, but temporal, program, functional, not to mention socio-economic-political. Architectural site approaches are highly unpredictable and very often malleable. Infrastructure however, tends towards predictability, arriving at solutions via statistical data, precisely because it must contend with its sheer size tempered by its desire for invisibility. Road bridges fall very much in the latter, yet they occupy key positions within our visible environment.

The siting of a road bridge, a statistical and complex exercise, begins with a projective analysis of traffic flow, peaks and troughs. Locating the on/off ramp in the wrong direction will result in severe congestion. Unlike architecture, traffic flow can be simulated with high degrees of accuracy. The proposal, an s-shape, resulted from orienting the ramps in the direction of predominant traffic flow, east-west corresponding to south-north bank respectively. By curving both segments, each segment functions as a ramp reducing the overall bridge length and minimizing impact on the banks of the Valley.

The competition site boundaries landed the north-bank ramp directly inside the town of Sankt Goarshausen, resulting in a signalled junction, which in turn resulted in congestion. The decision to shift the entire bridge east by 300 meters eliminated this issue. Though the decision resulted directly from the traffic engineer auto-tracking at various locations along the bank, architecturally, the shift meant that the town, a protected UNESCO view corridor, no longer had to contend with an obstruction.

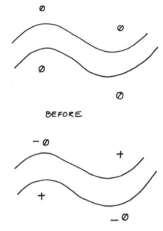

BEFORE

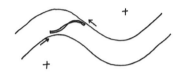

TRAFFIC CHANGE AFTER

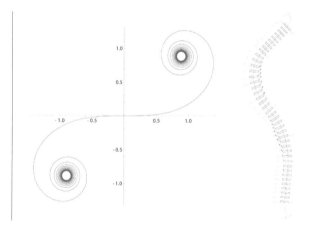

Both orientation & s-shape are generated from traffic flow data projections.

Clothoids use radii that change linearly along its path and are used in engineering roads.

Shift of bridge west of competition site boundary
Required competition view showing minimal obstruction to Sankt Goarshausen, note ramp on image left.

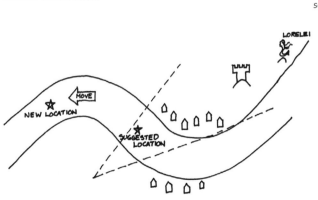

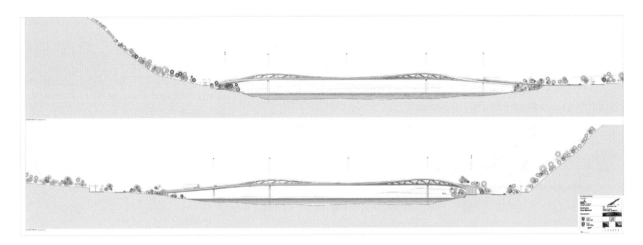

Cross-section showing the two torsion wings as they flip from side to side allowing unobstructed views up & down stream.

Form:

An architect may decide on a curved, angular, or orthogonal profile, or perhaps a parametric construct that defies formal categorization. This position may be intuitive, contextual, programmatic or otherwise. Regardless, this relies on the architect taking a position on form and its relation to site and performance. Though its logic can be evidenced, its rationalization remains contestable.

Vehicular trajectories, when transitioning between straight and curved segments, don't quite work at right angles, nor do they work well using circle radii. Curves used to describe vehicular paths are clothoids, curves with linearly changing radii along their paths, derived from deceleration into and acceleration out–a form based on rates of change. This results in precise determinable curves verifiable against performative values. The accuracy tolerance between form and its performance nears 0. Vertical rise is likewise track-able. The rise of ramps have ranges verifiable against visibility relative to speed. What we found challenging was working with forms derivative from parameters and logic specific to a discipline outside our field of vision.

The s-shape of our proposal is described using 2 clothoids against a speed range. This produces a sinuous curve minimizing impact, and blending into its surroundings. Architecturally, a diagonal path given the splendid views both up and down river, improves safety visibility, as people are less likely to be distracted turning heads whilst driving.

Structure: Columns & Spans

The archetypal architect's request to a structural engineer: "Could we shift that column over a bit?" We tried this during the early design process, however, unlike a building, the small movement of a column not only shifted a loading equivalent to 30 African elephants, but in turn collapsed the static system, the form.

The initial constraints that determine road bridge profiles are often quite straightforward. In our case, cargo ships had to clear both horizontally and vertically, positioning the 2 columns for the central span. Given clearance parameters, the columns are spaced far apart resulting in massive loads. One may initially observe that cars and trucks are not so heavy. In fact, parking structures have some of the lowest loading requirements of any building type.

Main span load distribution is achieved in torsion when combined with static loads from cross-section cantilever.

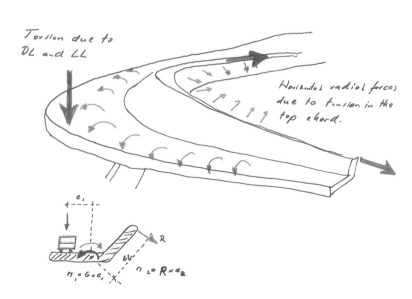

Bridges, however, understand loads relative to motion; a caravan of trucks loaded with concrete blocks, bumper-to-bumper, causes vertical static loads, but the same caravan of trucks traveling in one direction, on one side of the bridge, all braking in sync, due to deceleration of its mass, introduces horizontal dynamic loads significantly larger than the static load.

From these constraints–whether suspension, tension, box beam, truss–'form' emerges, falling under the heading of effective structural depth, which takes into account the accumulation of *all* loads.

Architecturally, our approach to the site given its UNESCO designation was to minimize visual obstruction within the valley void. The curvature of the 2 clothoids that form the s-shape meant effective depth for the main span over the river could achieve a load distribution in torsion (similar to the brim of a hat) when combined with the static loads resulting from the cross section working as a cantilever. Architecturally, this proved invaluable, as bending needed only to be taken on one side of the bridge for any one curve allowing for the unobstructed views along its length both up and down stream.

Further, shifting effective depth above the deck reduced the vertical rise the ramps needed to climb and in turn their length, the most destructive aspect of the bridge to the valley, as they carved their way through the landscape.

Views showing the blending of torsion 'wings' into deck plate.

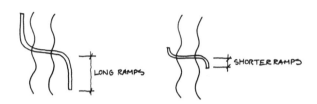

The most destructive aspect of bridges to the landscape at times is not the bridge, but rather its landing points, its ramps.

Flux vs. Stasis:

Structure must contend with finding stasis, if not only temporarily. Architecture, however tends towards movement and change, perhaps if not only to guard against its own obsolescence. Structure is more content with slowing down an object, finding equilibrium. Structural systems often do not see materiality, dimensionless matrices of forces. Architecture inevitably contends with the object, materiality, thickness, opacities, degrees of transparency, though at times in the sense of surface appearance only.

Unlike buildings, which are by nature largely static forms designed to allow movement and programmatic mixing, bridges begin with movement both programmatically and

Structural systems often do not see materiality, only dimensionless matrices of forces.

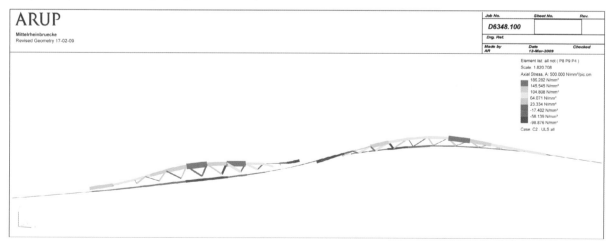

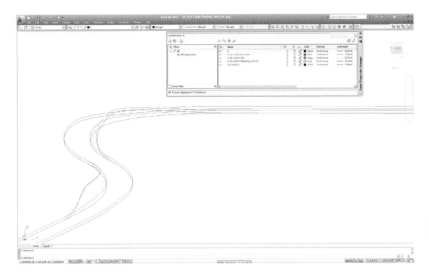

Eight lines, each composed of seven points at geometric centers was the only information exchanged between architect & engineer.

structurally. Architecture, through form and material, finds a way to hold this in place.

Methodology & Integration:

Though much of architecture today has shifted towards skin, a lot of the time this convergence is driven visually. This is as opposed to the classic Form [Skin] & Structure separation (i.e. the column grid went to the engineer whilst the architect worked on the envelope).

On a road bridge, the luxury of being able to control this overlap is no longer relevant. The structural imperatives and the magnitude of forces requires the entire structure to work together, which in turn does not allow form [architecture] and structure [engineering] to take separate paths, nor for structure to 'support' design in the more common scenario of building. Both systems move in extreme close proximity to each other. Furthermore, much of structure ends up supporting its own weight before a single vehicle arrives. This is not to say design is not possible. One possible way to capture this may be to say that the field of play or design comes with a precise set of transformative variables, framed (constrained) yet infinite.

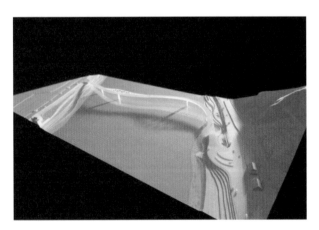

The parametric model quickly becomes a collaborative interface. Each operation in form or geometry immediately impacts the stability of the static system or diagram significantly. Unlike a building where forces can find minor routes through adjacent structure, bridges oftentimes have all but two columns. Our model was optimized on eight lines, each composed of seven points at geometric centers. No further piece of information was exchanged between the architect and engineer. On other bridges with Arup, information defining form has been further reduced to Excel tables, with no more than twenty-one cells (seven rows, three columns).

Collaboration:

So now back to the Doctor and his cold in Star Trek Voyager. We believe that only when the constraints, engineering in our case, have cohesion in themselves and are not selectable and controllable by the architect, can form achieve a high degree of unpredictability and the new—a kind of singularity through differentiation, as opposed to the one.

Collaboration probably is more likely a threshold, an inversion that is achieved in the design process, a tipping point perhaps, when the 'other' is so large that the architect no longer has the capacity to preempt or take view, and is forced to define form on the grounds of the 'other'. It is at this point that the process produces new form or enters the space of the unpredictable.

HIGHLY ACCELERATED LIFE TEST (HALT) OPTION DESIGN STUDIO

FALL 2010

Instructor: **Roisin Heneghan and Shih-Fu Peng**
Teaching Assistant: **Kathleen Dahlberg**

HALT presents an opportunity to test a product to find its maximum limitations and all possible failure modes.
How do we design for 2050 when:
The world's population is forecast to increase by 50%
66% of the world's population will live in cities
temperature could increase by 2-3 degrees centigrade
carbon emissions per m2 of occupation will need to decrease significantly

So, how might we live in 2050?
…..where the 'empty' site in the context of sustainable urban development is a dying species? Students must 'demolish' critically in order to construct their site, not identify vacant lots. The 'site' is Hong Kong Central, practically 100% built. Hong Kong limits sprawl, land reclamation has been stopped toward the water and in reverse, up the mountain, limiting horizontal expansion of the city.

As the average lifespan of a building is approximately 40 years, the possibility of reconfiguring the city grid & morphology at an urban level begins to be possible.

Curtis Roth | MArch
Pulp Preservations

As Hong Kong increasingly becomes imbedded within the unprecedented growth of the surrounding Pearl River Delta, it has sought to re-stake its unique identity (both urban and political) as an autonomous territory through the repackaging and commodification of its own histories, a relatively non-existent product in a multi-city metropolis whose oldest construction dates back to the 1970s. Hong Kong's highly orchestrated preservation movement entails a radical shift from a city of the always-new to a city which now moors its identity to the colonial history it once struggled to extricate itself from, and with it, the packaging of five key colonial sites through the iconic interventions of a predictable collection of western European architects. But the re-presentation of Hong Kong's highly-mediated history also gives rise to an alternate reading of its past, that of a city whose history of continual change lies in the perpetual erasure of architectural history itself. A history of architectural eradication through the permanent desires of maximum-value real estate scheming.

The Pulp Preservation movement argues for a new model of preservation for Hong Kong, operating not from a pre-determined catalog of colonial sites but a much more open-ended and perpetually updatable catalog of Hong Kong's histories which incorporates not merely the colonial, but the non-physical, the archaic, the strange and mundane narratives of Hong Kong as the impetus for constructing new urban scenarios from the pulp of its own erased, forgotten or unacknowledged histories.

As the first architectural proposal within the Pulp Preservation movement, the project operates with a double agency, proposed as an infrastructural system for updating the capacity for density around Hong Kong's colonial sites, it simultaneously navigates within Hong Kong's feverish vertical real estate economy, depositing a collection of highly conditioned internal environments in low value territories, serving as platforms for Pulp Preservations, allowing for a diverse group of shareholders within an open-ended infrastructural anti-icon.

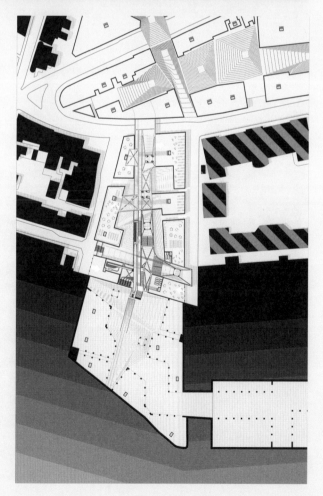

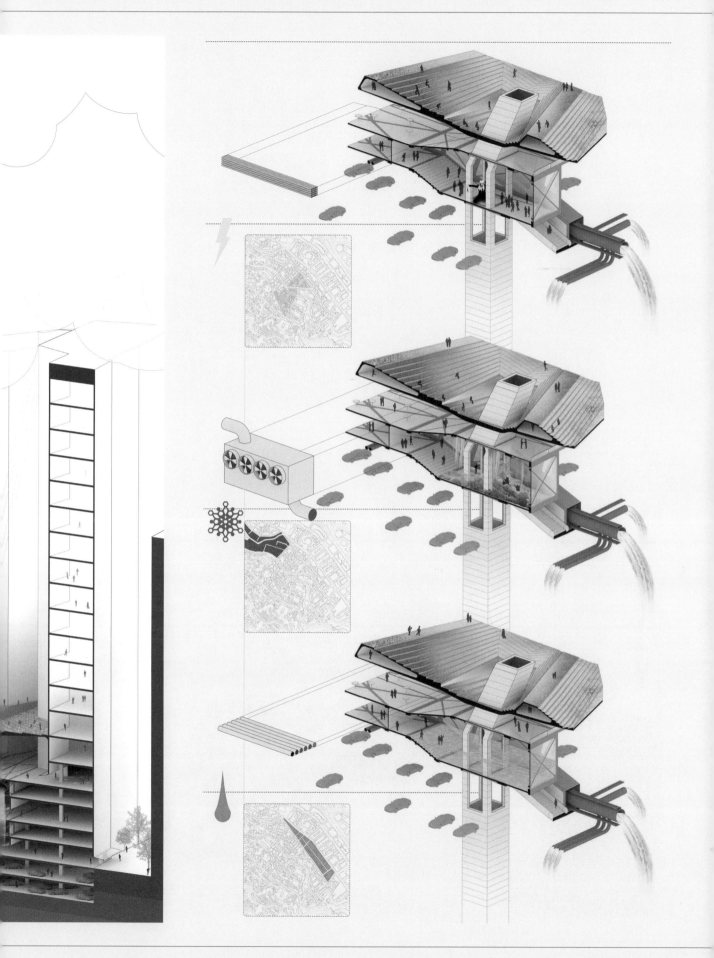

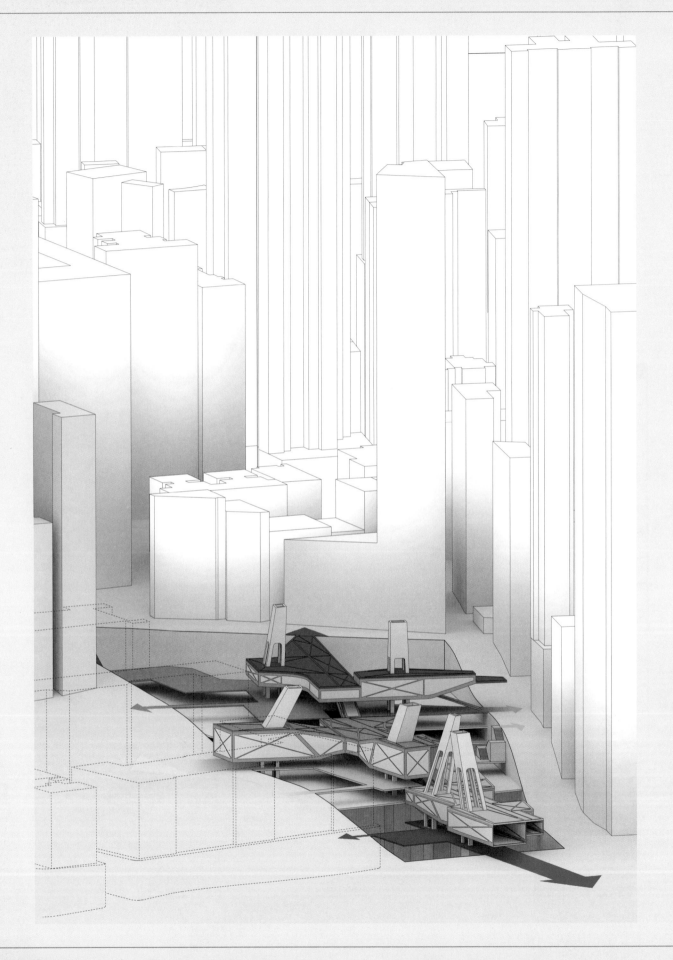

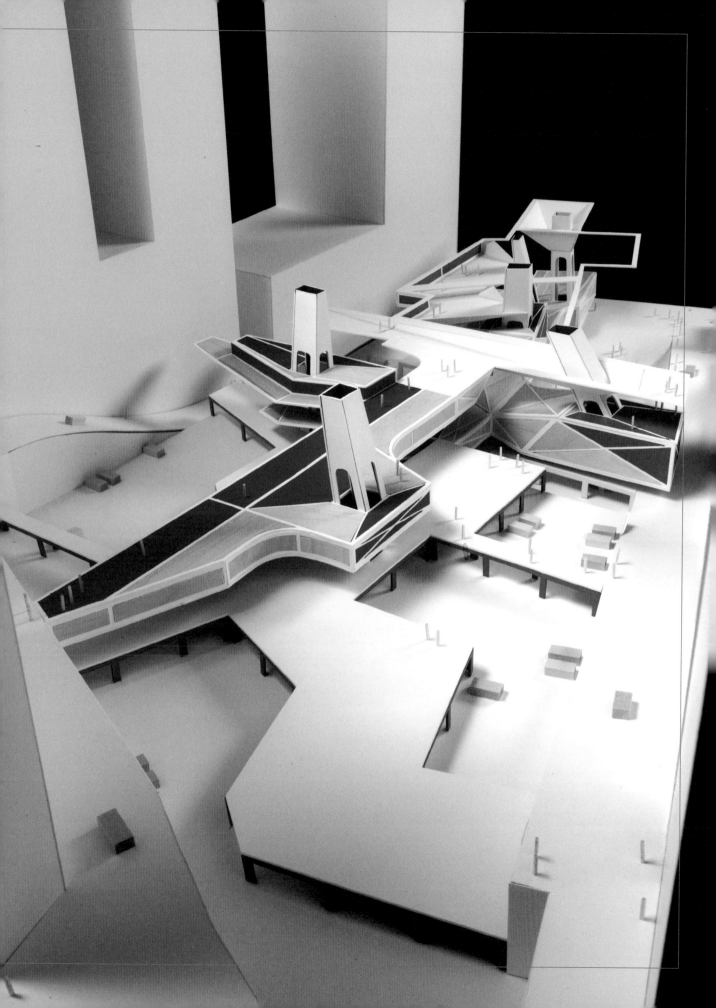

OVERLINER FAST [FESTIVAL OF ART SCIENCE AND TECHNOLOGY] PROJECT

Joel Lamere and Cynthia Gunadi

Where a stair confronts the exigencies of the ground, breaking away from the strict figural regularity of the repetitive system above, so too does 'Overliner' stretch from a liner into a broader canopy. Through a complex technique of curved folding, flat sheets of plastic become figured rigid beams, manifesting the deep textures latent in two-dimensional curved lines. The result is a lightweight and diaphanous kind of spatial origami suspended overhead, underscoring and overlining a quietly remarkable architectural condition.

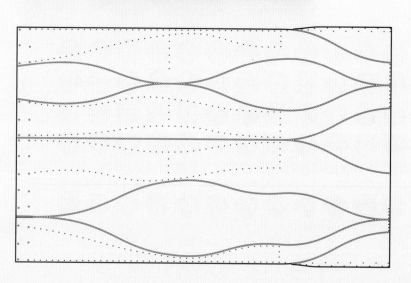

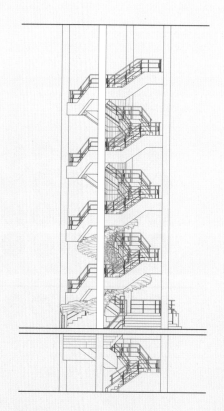

LIGHT DRIFT FAST [FESTIVAL OF ART SCIENCE AND TECHNOLOGY] PROJECT

J. Meejin Yoon

Light Drift is an interactive lighting installation that appeared along the Memorial Drive side of the Charles River and drew viewers into a playful engagement with the artwork, the river's edge, and each other. Ninety brightly glowing orbs in the river change color as they react to the presence of people along the shore.

The lighting elements are shaped like orbs or buoys and are equipped with electronics that allow them to respond to a viewer and to communicate with each other. The orbs on land use sensors to detect the presence of a person and relay a radio signal to the corresponding orbs in the water, allowing visitors to transform the array of orbs in the river. As viewers engage the orbs, the grid of lights in the water becomes an index of the activities on land. Multiple viewers can create intersections of linear patterns, encouraging viewers to "play" with each other. These orbs bring the community together by providing gathering spaces for watching the river turned into a flickering constellation of a field of lights and creating new connections on the river's edge.

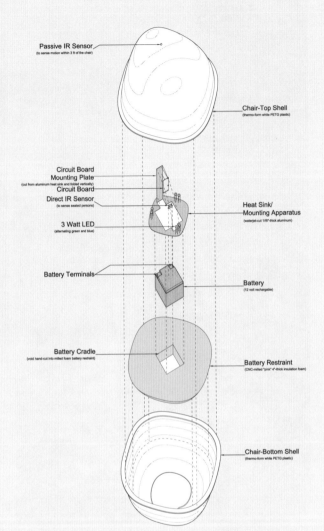

Passive IR Sensor
(to sense motion within 3 ft of the chair)

Chair-Top Shell
(thermo-form white PETG plastic)

Circuit Board Mounting Plate
(cut from aluminum heat sink and folded vertically)
Circuit Board
Direct IR Sensor
(to sense seated persons)

Heat Sink/ Mounting Apparatus
(waterjet-cut 1/8"-thick aluminum)

3 Watt LED
(alternating green and blue)

Battery Terminals

Battery
(12 volt rechargable)

Battery Cradle
(void hand-cut into milled foam battery restraint)

Battery Restraint
(CNC-milled "pink" 4"-thick insulation foam)

Chair-Bottom Shell
(thermo-form white PETG plastic)

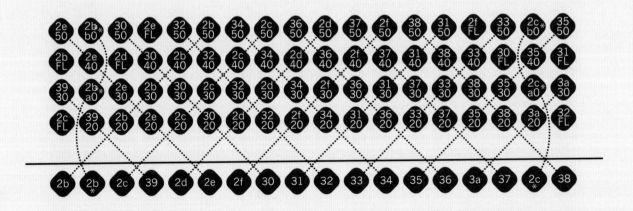

TWINS: HOUSES IN FIVE PARTS, UPSTATE NEW YORK 2009-2011
NOTES ON RESEARCH AND PRACTICE

William O'Brien Jr.

This design proposal for two vacation homes for two brothers and their families on one plot of land in upstate New York represents an examination of a curious part to whole relationship. The mathematical principle of "dissection" states that any two regular polygons with equal areas can be divided into sets of similar shapes; "minimal dissection" is the pursuit of the fewest number of subdivisions in each polygon. This scheme appropriates this principle as a solution to (1) general similarities in the programmatic requirements, and (2) distinctions in the desired relationships to the site, voiced by the two brothers for each of their homes.

A regular six-sided polygon and a regular four-sided polygon contain the same five shapes—each are made up of the same four trapezoids and one triangle. The adjacencies between the five shapes are different within each of the regular polygons, as are their orientations relative to the outer perimeters of the polygons.

Images courtesy of William O'Brien Jr.

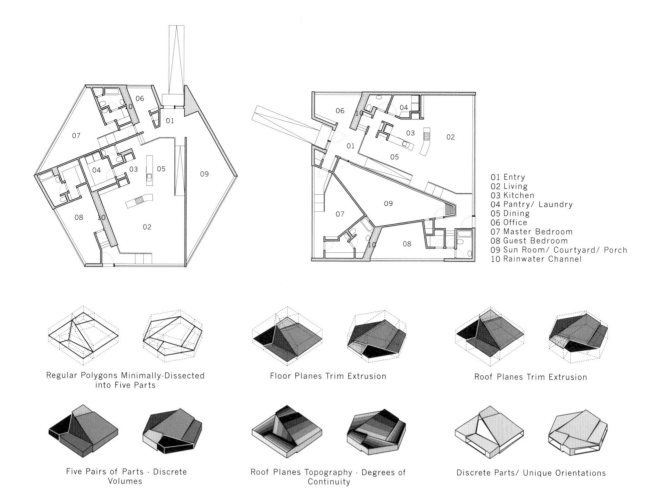

01 Entry
02 Living
03 Kitchen
04 Pantry/ Laundry
05 Dining
06 Office
07 Master Bedroom
08 Guest Bedroom
09 Sun Room/ Courtyard/ Porch
10 Rainwater Channel

Regular Polygons Minimally-Dissected
into Five Parts

Floor Planes Trim Extrusion

Roof Planes Trim Extrusion

Five Pairs of Parts · Discrete
Volumes

Roof Planes Topography · Degrees of
Continuity

Discrete Parts/ Unique Orientations

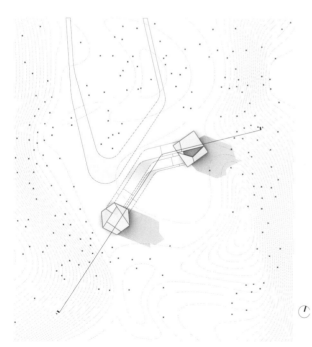

Translated into spatial divisions in an architectural plan, these static, fixed arrangements prompt sectional-flexibility. Conceptually, in section, the floor planes and the roof planes are configured in order to accommodate strategic micro-topographic continuities and discontinuities across the collective surfaces.

Flows in circulation of residents and water govern possible configurations of the floor-scapes and roof-scapes respectively. An overall articulation of the five volumes as discrete parts acts as a second ambition which directs the possible formal outcomes of the houses. Programmatically, the pairs of parts are used similarly between the two houses, although each programmatic piece utilizes its unique adjacencies; the triangular space is used as a vertically-oriented, sun room/open-air courtyard in the center of the square house, and as a landscape-oriented, screened-in porch in the hexagonal house. Siting of the houses privilege the visual linkage between each of the main living spaces and unique scenes of the upstate New York landscape; in the case of the square house, a wooded wetland frequented by many species of birds, and in the case of the hexagonal house, an open pasture bordered by a distant grove of trees.

Proximity of houses relative to one another is calibrated through the development of the agricultural usage of the interstitial land. Water collection from the two roofs is directed to a subterranean piping system between the houses. The agricultural development of the land between the two houses separates them visually (to varying degrees depending on season) while linking them inextricably, both infrastructurally and communally. Water dispersal stems from two pairs of "water channels" embedded in two walls in each house. The planometric dovetailing of four different crops, which oscillate in harvest seasons, accommodates different proximities of crops to each of the houses. Leaf vegetables, berries, wheat and corn are braided together in order to provide each house immediate access to each food type.

Materially, the houses remain abstract, to offer a reading of the forms as packages of discrete volumes with orientational differences made possible by the large apertures. There is a rubber roofing system that is used for the tops of the houses and dark, thick stucco that coats the sides and underbellies of the houses.

Project Team: Bhujon Kang
Visualization: Peter Guthrie

UNTITLED AFTER-EFFECTS
NOTES ON RESEARCH AND PRACTICE

Filip Tejchman

There are a few things that come to mind when someone mentions the Summer: road trips, air-conditioning and fire hydrants...

Besides its cultural imageability, the fire-hydrant is one of the most explicit and visible spatial mechanisms occupying the urban terrain: each hydrant owns a stretch of the curb, parking within its territorial borders is forbidden, any activity that challenges the function of the hydrant is essentially illegal. Hydrants are stand-ins for the invisible civic apparatus–the visible tip of an infrastructural iceberg.

During any week-long stretch of a New York City heat-wave, you will certainly find a hydrant in the city that has been hacked: disturbed and unscrewed, just enough to produce a misty spray of cool water, celebrating what the hydrant basically is: a high-pressure geyser of potable municipal water. With the valve loosened, the discrete spatial envelope that the hydrant had previously occupied, has been dissolved and become the space of an event. In true Situationist spirit, the détournement of this infrastructure has carved out a new space in the city, adapting secondary characteristics as the framework for programmatic invention.

These secondary characteristics, or after-effects, produced by the multitude of systems around us, represent a kind of waste–a by-product of the internal machinations and material / spatial transformations that are inherent to the maintenance of space. Waste in the sense that we do not use them or make them do work. Whether they are integral to the infrastructure that make modern life possible or an unplanned hack applied to an existing system or structure, after-effects challenge and de-stabilize the logic associated with the original and break down the terms in which we typically frame function and purpose–the after-effects are the infrastructure.

Situationist Tool-Kit

Hacked Infrastructure

Images courtesy Filip Tejchman.

Scent Diffusor

Friday Night Lights

is a networked sidewalk/street projection system proposed as part of a nation-wide retrofit of the ubiquitous Cobra-head street lamp, in which the mercury-vapor or incandescent lights are replaced with LED panels. Requiring far less space, these new lamps allow for the piggybacking of one device onto another–in this case an LCD projector. During various game nights– Superbowl, World Series, etc.–playing fields would be projected onto the streets and sidewalks of neighborhoods, creating a temporary public event space through the adaptation of an everyday system.

SoundFront

was a NYSCA installation proposal for an intervention at the scale of the sidewalk, using the scent dispersion technology employed by fast-food and retail establishments to brand the air in concert with commercially-available noise cancellation systems. With the ambient effects of scent and sound diminished, passers-by would enter into a virtual room, creating a cognitive disjunct from the surrounding city.

Air-conditioning is perhaps the most visible architectural infrastructure of waste. Not because its tangible excesses force many of us to carry a sweater or scarf to the movies during the sweltering heat of a New England summer, but because all we do is let it cool. Consider the diesel block of a Mack truck. For years, truck-drivers have been using the engine compartment of semi-trailers as an ad hoc mobile kitchen, wrapping food in foil and placing it near the exhaust manifold alongside cans of soup, beans and many other more regionally specific treats. After a few hours of driving, the trucker can stop and enjoy a freshly cooked meal. This was the subject of a conversation between Chris Maynard and Bill Scheller, during a more prosaic road trip, a not-very-long jaunt from Montreal to Boston, during which they began to speculate about similar possibilities, in which the after-effects of transportation were conjoined with the specificity of geography. This served as the inspiration for another kind of road novel: the geographic/anthropological cookbook, one that explored the after-effects of the car itself–the physicality of the machine, the noise, the heat–its living and breathing organicism. Manifold Destiny was the result. Part cookbook and part travel essay, it reveals a global culture that capitalizes on the energy released by a mechanism intrinsic to everyday life: the combustion engine. When an engine is running, what it is really doing, is trying to be as efficient as possible in converting the latent energy of burning fuel into motion. During the process, heat is produced–radiators, insulation, coolant, and heat sinks are an infrastructure designed to negate the after-effect, dissipating it into the surrounding environment. What Manifold Destiny revealed is the inherent value of after-effects, in providing a scaffold for programmatic and cultural production through the adaptation of mundane systems in non-normative ways.

The southern Ice House, a building typology whose cultural identity can be summed up as: cold beer+good food+great music, was born from the adaptation of an everyday and otherwise unremarkable typology. A heavily insulated and usually windowless building used for storing and distributing ice before the era of wide-spread domestic refrigeration, the Ice house offered an air-chilled oasis during summers, that over time added, groceries, a place to sit, eat and listen to music, to its list of other services provided. While fulfilling its intended purpose, the Ice House evolved through the symbiosis of one program with another–based on their performative effects and appropriation of associated environmental control systems–supporting the emergence of a new building type and program, eventually consuming the original. Like the engine block, the ice house demonstrates the possibilities of recontextualizing the after-effects of everyday infrastructures as a method for spatial and programmatic action.

While architecture culture often obsesses over the imagery that the Situationist project produced–fragmented maps and territories, traversed by diagrammatic lines of flight–the practice of Psycho-Geography and its methods are a precedent for the appropriation and drawing of space, by deploying mundane and everyday systems in non-normative ways–the benign violation of the normal. In their Rijksind installation proposal, the Situationists (Debord, Constant and others) envisioned individuals using walkie-talkies and tape decks to traverse the literal interior and exterior territory of the gallery–guided by a constellation of defamiliarizing effects that hacked the mechanisms of sensation and recognition, linking the experiential and spatial in unexpected ways and thus resurfacing the cognitive landscape of the city.

The Situationist strategies challenge the dominant discourse of adaptive reuse which, in its most populist sense, is the conversion of defunct industry into viable residential and commercial building/program types. The rehabilitation of former programmatic specificities is often limited to the eccentric detail or material palimpsest, but rarely the performative effect. By extending the critical frame of architectural adaptation beyond economic and social recovery and into the reformulation of after-effects as a productive programmatic infrastructure, we re-define terms like ambience, ambient transition and effect as outlined by the situationists, charting a performative dérive through the geography of

View of Chiller Pools With Canopy Above

View of Cold Water Return Showers

after-effects–the becoming energetic of the dérive. Harvesting and using the after-effect, the by-products of already existing systems–the evaporative steam cloud, exhaust stream, ambient glow of city lights and untuned background hum of building mechanical systems, proposes a practice that expands on the definition of commonwealth, in which water, air and nature also come to include after-effects, probing the shores and boundaries of public space, which in every sense move, Situationist-style, between interior and exterior. Each of these represent a spatial and material possibility for the direct and instrumental manipulation of energy and space, at the scale of architecture and within the limitations of the architectural discipline. After-effects are the unappropriated territory, a landscape of energy and the forgotten ambient poché.

The Chiller

is based on the existing Marley™ MS cooling tower system. A modular and scalable cooling system utilizing water and often concealed within decorative objects like public fountains or pool. We proposed adapting the same system, but rather than simply decorative, the waste heat would support the operation of a public bathhouse–a post-modern baths of Caracalla

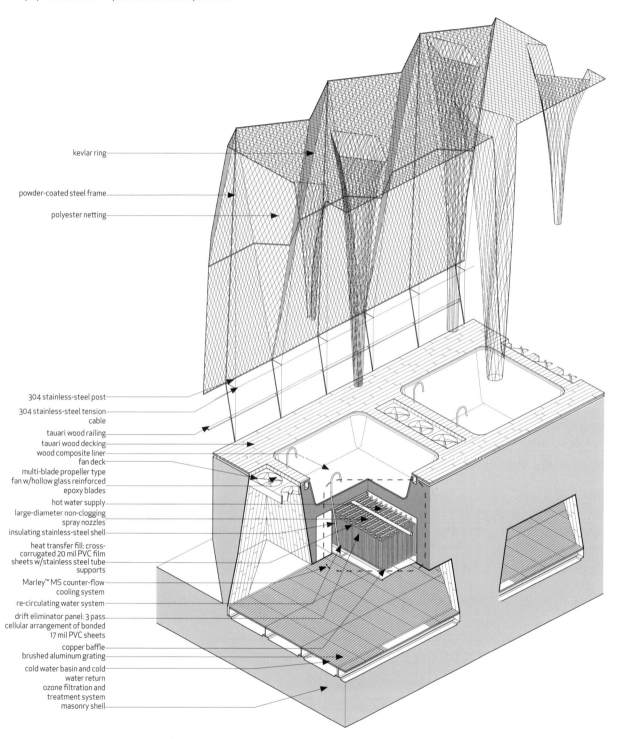

kevlar ring

powder-coated steel frame

polyester netting

304 stainless-steel post

304 stainless-steel tension cable

tauari wood railing

tauari wood decking

wood composite liner

fan deck

multi-blade propeller type fan w/hollow glass reinforced epoxy blades

hot water supply

large-diameter non-clogging spray nozzles

insulating stainless-steel shell

heat transfer fill: cross-corrugated 20 mil PVC film sheets w/stainless steel tube supports

Marley™ MS counter-flow cooling system

re-circulating water system

drift eliminator panel: 3 pass cellular arrangement of bonded 17 mil PVC sheets

copper baffle

brushed aluminum grating

cold water basin and cold water return

ozone filtration and treatment system

masonry shell

TRANSACT, TRANSPORT, TRANSFORM TAIPEI WORKSHOP

Instructors: **Adèle Naudé Santos, Ana Miljački, Leah Buechley, Joel Lamere**

Designers mine raw bits of tomorrow. They shape them for the present day. Designers act as gatekeepers between status quo objects and objects from the time to come.
– Bruce Sterling, Shaping Things

The city of Taipei is made up of many locally specific elements (vernacular architecture, cultures of night-markets and "stinky tofu," lively nightlife, commercial towers, recent metro lines, two rivers and many festivals), but it is also a city that resembles other cities close to its size. We designers like to believe that if we could implement decisions on an urban scale, Taipei could rush towards a beautiful, efficient, and generous future, a future better than one haphazardly determined by politics and commerce. We will approach our workshop as an occasion to explore design transformations that designers are uniquely capable of imagining.

We will focus especially on artifacts and activities that are created through individual agency yet give rise to complex collective patterns. Together, we will design and prototype urban interventions in the Dazhi district in three broad categories: transaction (concentrating on acts of exchange), transportation (dealing with transportation both in the abstract sense and in the concrete, with the new and projected metro infrastructures), and transformation (concentrating on the form of things).

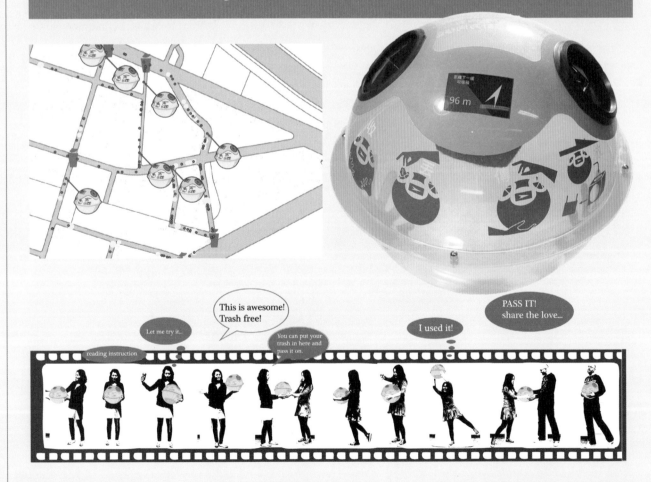

Bonifaz Kaufmann | Media Lab, **WaiKai Leslie Lok** | MArch, **Philip Robert Seaton** | MArch, **Ying Mei Cheng** | SCU, **Kimberly Lin** | SCU, **Tsia Chun Huang** | SCU, **John Wei** | SCU, **Yu Ting Yang** | SCU

Trashball!

You go to the carnival. You go to the night market. You buy a twinkie, or a chicken foot. You unwrap it. You eat it. You look for a trash can. Coney Island, you find one. In the Shilin Night Market, you don't. You put the trash in your pocket. Or in that other plastic baggie, in your other hand. You shop. You slip your trash into a shoe at the Birkenstock store, but guilt makes you fish it out. What if you could hand it to that guy across the way, the one leaving the market? What if you could do it without getting a bloody nose?

RECENT WORK
NOTES ON RESEARCH AND PRACTICE
Cristina Parreño

Chicago:

Infrastructure Recycling is a design challenge which aims to explore the concepts of "urban recycling" and "terrain vague" in the context of a rust belt city. In recent years, the "rust belt" concept has diffused internationally. In that sense, the aim of this project is not so much to focus on the particular concerns of one city, as to take Chicago as the object of a research that can have a broader scope and shared interests with other territories. *Infrastructure Recycling* approaches urban, social, architectural and environmental aspects through the architectural project.

THE SITE: Lake Shore East has an intense history, and the area has changed much throughout the years. By 2001, it had lost its activity and become one of those indeterminate zones that punctuate the urban landscape and that we now call "terrain vagues." Spaces that, in words of Saskia Sassen, "are part of the interiority of a city, yet lie outside of its organizing utility-driven logics and spatial frames . . . . They are under-used spaces, often characterized more by memory than current meaning." The "terrain vagues" can be seen as the representation of deterioration and abandonment that is opposed to the image of a prosperous city, but they can also be seen as spaces of freedom in an urban environment that is increasingly standardized and regulated.

THE INFRASTRUCTURES: The Chicago River's main branch was originally the heart of the city and the origin of an incipient industry. In 1920s, the double-decked belt road Wacker Drive was built, allowing a continuous flow of trucks transporting freight goods for the industry of the Loop. At the end of the 20th century, all the industry disappeared and the Loop was transformed into the business district. Wacker Drive became an ex-industrial infrastructure without a clear use, but clearly over-dimensioned.

THE PROJECT: The architecture that we propose for Lake Shore East is a structure that absorbs Wacker Drive allowing different activities to colonize the roads. The project is an urban intervention that starts from what exists and generates new interrelations and new ways of experiencing and discovering the city. The project doesn't intervene on Lake Shore East–it just recycles the infrastructures to the North of the site. And in doing so, the site is opened to a large spectrum of possible uses, occupations and experiences; its potential as "terrain vague" is exploited, offering new possibilities of interaction with the urban landscape. The project generates an architecture that enriches urbanity, proposing an alternative to that other, more static way of dealing with urban spaces in traditional approaches.

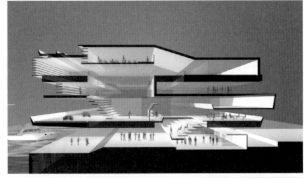
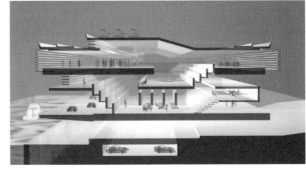

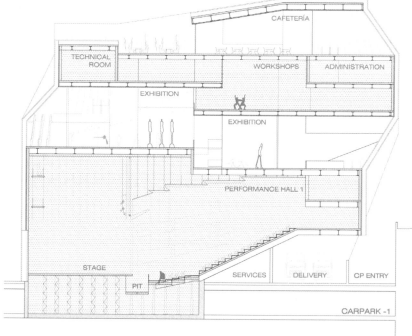

Beirut:

The *Project for the House of Arts and Culture* in Beirut aims to support the movement of free creativity that made this city play a leading cultural role in the region for a very long time. The fact that the arts and culture in Beirut were developed from grass-roots movements and processes that had to do more with the street and less with the institutions was the driving force of the project. The project starts from the idea of the souk as a typology, where the activity of commerce gets diluted and is merged with the space of circulation, and where the social interaction plays a fundamental role. The *Project for the House of Arts and Culture* in Beirut will perform like a vertical souk. The vertical circulation and the program will be mixed, allowing for improvised encounters among people, encouraging the type of interaction and relationships that were very much part of the art culture from Lebanon.

The complex program is divided in two parts:
1. The Cultural Boxes are the parts of the program that need to be enclosed. Their function is specific, and the form responds to their function. These rooms are detached from the general circulation of the building.
2. Circulation Voids are the parts of the program located in the space generated in between the boxes. The Circulation Voids are very open and their program can be mixed with the circulation of the building in one way or another.

The Boxes are piled vertically in such a way that a series of voids in between the boxes is created. These voids are connected, creating a vertical helicoid that will allocate the parts of the program that are more open and mixed with the vertical circulation. In the helicoid, communication amongst people will be most intense and the public activity is encouraged, allowing for exchange of ideas and social interaction.

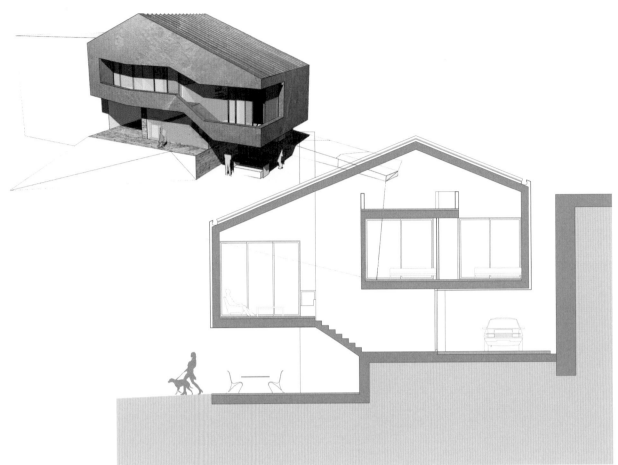

Gredos:

This project is a summer house for a family with three children. The conditions of the project and the site itself are charged with constraints, restrictions, and information. The project will be developed by dealing and responding to the forces that rule the site.

Access and Views: Access to the site is produced to the north. The house will have its entrance to this orientation with a very opaque façade that will provide privacy from the neighbors. The house on this side is totally aligned to the street, continuing the fabric of the village. The South of the site faces the views of the mountains and the river. The house will be more open to this orientation allowing a strong connection to the exterior.

Topography: The level of the plot is 1.5m below the level of the street. This condition dictates a game of split levels that will enrich the spatiality of the interiors and simultaneously will raise the living area and rooms allowing them to enjoy the views of the river to the south.

The Regulations: The site is constrained by severe urban regulations. The roof needs to have two planes which have to have a specific inclination of no more than 40º and no less than 30º. Simultaneously, the material of the house in the first level has to be the local stone and in the roof only Arabic tiles can be used. There are also restrictions on the height of the house which cannot be more than 6 meters, and no more than two floors. All these restrictions, combined with the topography, views, and client constraints, generate the system for the volume of the house.

A smaller but heavier volume of stone will connect the house with the earth and will hold a second volume of larger dimensions. The two volumes are merged in the interior providing a circulation system that progressively takes the user to the upper level in a promenade that follows the topography of the site.

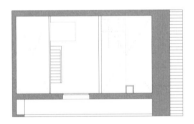

RETROFIT + SHRINK-WRAP DUBAI: AN URBAN RECOVERY PLAN
M.ARCH. THESIS
FALL 2009

Charles H. Curran
Supervisor: **Nasser Rabbat**
Readers: **Ana Miljački, Hashim Sarkis, Nader Tehrani**

The 2008 collapse of Dubai's high-end property market and subsequent population decline halted the unprecedented expansion of the city's built footprint. Dubai's economic engine, which quickly transformed huge amounts of capital into new architectural "bling," had come to a grinding halt, revealing the underlying instability of a city built on speculation rather than foresight. Large swathes of the city still remain incomplete and largely uninhabited, creating vast urban blights. Dubai risks damage to both its image and its ability to function. The city's decline, however, presents a unique opportunity for immediate and sweeping intervention against urban decay. My thesis proposes a dialectical planning process of retrofitting and shrink-wrapping Dubai.

The retrofit strategy engages stopped building projects crucial to Dubai's function and image. The technical goal is to generate corridors of urbanity that permit the city to operate while the population and economy recover. The theoretical aim is not to produce new models for planning, but to generate design proposals that overtly critique and improve upon the existing built environment. The shrink-wrap strategy repositions Dubai's vast oversupply of real estate as an investment for the future. This directive removes redundant buildings or even whole developments from the market and preserves them for eventual redeployment. The goal is to create an image of progressiveness and anticipation, while also physically maintaining these built assets to prevent further economic loses.

These strategies create a clearinghouse for Dubai's injured property market, improving or preserving individual buildings and simultaneously introducing comprehensive planning initiatives for transportation access and public amenities on the ground. The design interventions tested on the Dubai International Financial Center demonstrate a range of possibilities to induce economic and urban recovery within the development and its immediate context, and serve as a primer to retrofit & shrink-wrap other developments in this desert Emirate.

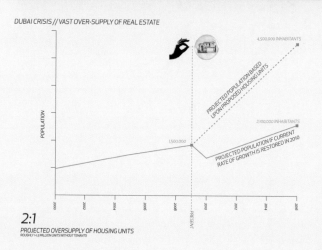

DUBAI CRISIS // VAST OVER-SUPPLY OF REAL ESTATE

2:1
PROJECTED OVERSUPPLY OF HOUSING UNITS
ROUGHLY >1.5 MILLION UNITS WITHOUT TENANTS

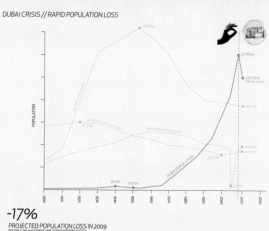

DUBAI CRISIS // RAPID POPULATION LOSS

-17%
PROJECTED POPULATION LOSS IN 2009
ROUGHLY 250,000 EXPATS AND GUEST WORKERS IN TOTAL

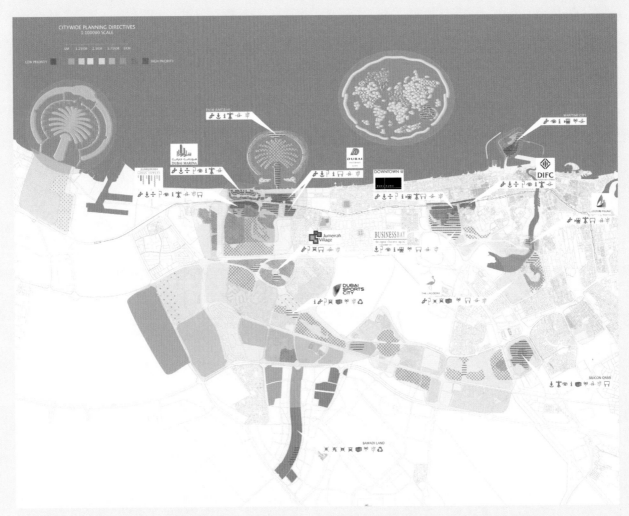

DUBAI CRISIS // SCALE OF STOPPED BUILDING PROJECTS

DUBAI CRISIS // STATUS OF HIGH-RISE PROJECTS COMMENCED SINCE 2007

	# OF PROJECTS	ESTIMATED VALUE
217 COMPLETED		USD 21 BILLION
336 ACTIVE		USD 76 BILLION
313 STOPPED		USD 113 BILLION
866 TOTAL		USD 210 BILLION

SOURCES: ZAWYA REAL ESTATE DATABASE, EMPORIS DATABASE, FIELD RESEARCH

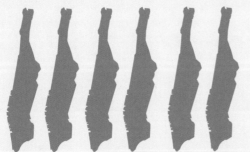

FLOOR AREA
EQUIVALENT OF

:

10 MANHATTANS CANCELLED OR ON HOLD
1 MANHATTAN CURRENTLY UNDER CONSTRUCTION
1.44 MANHATTANS COMPLETED SINCE 2006

1083 KM^2 TOTAL

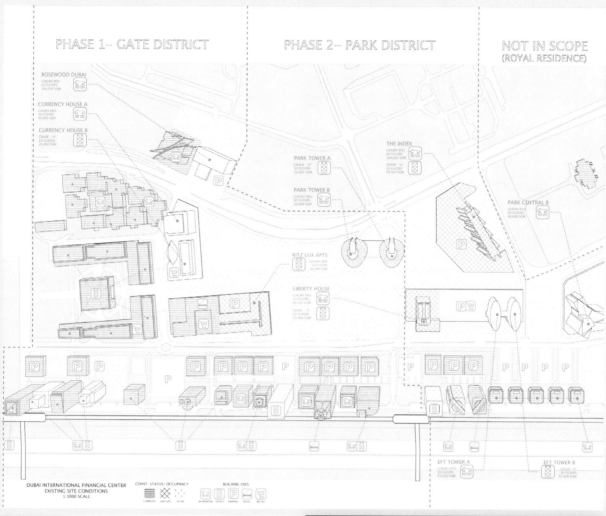

PHASE 1– GATE DISTRICT   PHASE 2– PARK DISTRICT   NOT IN SCOPE (ROYAL RESIDENCE)

ROSEWOOD DUBAI

CURRENCY HOUSE A

CURRENCY HOUSE B

PARK TOWER A

PARK TOWER B

THE INDEX

PARK CENTRAL B

RITZ LUX APTS

LIBERTY HOUSE

EFT TOWER A

EFT TOWER B

DUBAI INTERNATIONAL FINANCIAL CENTER
EXISTING SITE CONDITIONS
1:3000 SCALE

CONST. STATUS/ OCCUPANCY

BUILDING USES

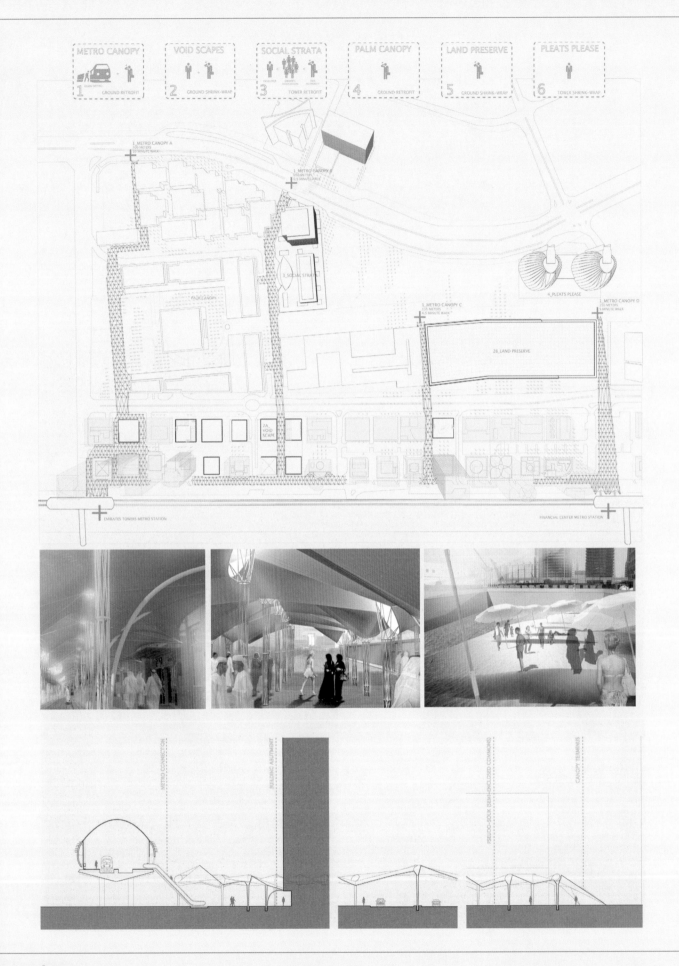

SHRINK-WRAP FACADE, PLEATING PLAN
1:500 SCALE

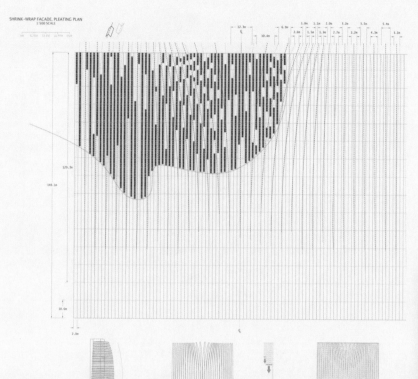

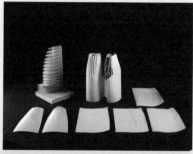

UNFOLD
SURFACE GEOMETRY OF INCOMPLETE TOWER

ALIGN
INITIAL LAYOUT FOR MATERIAL PATTERNING

OVERLAY
MATERIAL OF STANDARD WIDTH

PLEAT
EXCESS MATERIAL PATTERNED FOR FOLDING

EXTRA-LARGE

THE PUBLIC SPHERE, SIZE XL

Is the public realm forever lost to formal determination? Is the city no longer recuperable to architecture, frittered away as it were to the caviling of interest groups, the takeover by real estate cartels, the amorphous interests of consensus-building where actors with the lowest imaginations have the loudest voices? Is democracy its own greatest threat, in that it seems to warrant no institutional power greater than average opinion to lead itself? Is what is left to the city simply a raft of managerial and optimization tasks? The insertion of bike lanes, the regularization of bus schedules, the little 'green' solar-powered composting garbage bin that poses no challenge to the patterns of consumption?

Such a fate would indeed be doleful. Small-scale projects and community-level activism have their place, but in ignoring strong institutional intervention and essential physical and infrastructural supports that institutions provide, any theory of democracy threatens to undo its own premises. Grassroots movements work on a sort of last resort level of public engagement, but there is no reason to

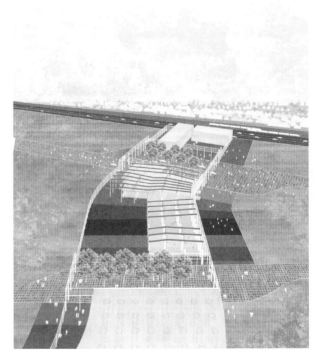

ASCO—ORG/ Alexander D'Hooghe
The landform is a collective, disurbanist form. This megastructure (building permit granted, CD's ready, construction to start late 2011) organizes a collection of independent public functions located in a suburban-sprawl setting. These institutions–fire station, police station, youth center, bus depot, etc.–each need built area, asphalt surfaces. The project arranges these linearly, separating them with 'public rooms' between each program, yet integrating them through a massive perimeter fence structure to define a potentially infinite linear form capable of defining a territorial order in contrast to the scattered suburban context beyond.

reject institutional power outright, especially if one has the ability to direct the institution. One advantage of working within a research institution like MIT is the number of forces that can be brought to bear on pressing current issues. With the robust resources of the Urban Design and Architecture faculties, complicated problems can be tackled from a number of angles.

To reduce the range on which we envision our plans is to preemptively limit the effectiveness of designers. Likewise, if democracy requires strong institutions–although strong institutions do not a democracy make–can cities do without monuments? Without institutional and formal presences–monuments, positive or negative–that tether the civic realm, give visible focus to the polis? If anything, both the older communitarian ethos or the new cultures of social networking appear to foreground even more the importance of physical congregation, of totemic structures or spaces that metastasize modernity's myths of the collective. Online shopping appears to be killing superbox retail, but Oxford Street, Fifth Avenue and Omotesando are flourishing more than ever. What would Facebook revolts be without a Tahrir square, a space that, prior to the so-called Arab Spring, was nothing more than a traffic interchange, a station from where buses left for the provinces? Why is it, then, that architecture has somehow given up thinking about monumental scales, about monuments? If the heady optimism of late Modernism has today dissolved into the cold ash of nostalgic retrospection, is there call to resurrect some new conception of the collective? Under what auspices is it to be convened? What form of monumentality would be adequate to it, responsive to it?

SOMA

This is an open-air market structure, built as a contemporary re-interpretation of the structure-infill system. The project introduces an endless grid of possibilities. These are organized into, initially, a 100x100m field. A series of square concrete panels, penetrated by different platonic forms to become porticos, establish the grid. A series of manipulations transform the generic infinite order of the platonic panel grid into the form of the market building in response to programmatic, contextual, and logistical specificities.

ASCO—ORG/ Alexander D'Hooghe

The exterior fence structure of the landform building lifts at points to enable access to the public room which houses multiple layers of public infrastructures (render farm: Animotion bvba).

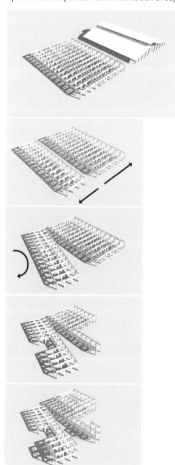

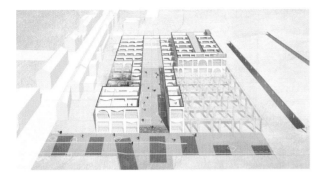

SOMA—ORG/ Alexander D'Hooghe

(left) The platonic panels structure the order of the in-filled program and surrounding public space.

(below) Public space extends into the interior of the market defining a continuous public surface ordered by the platonic panels.

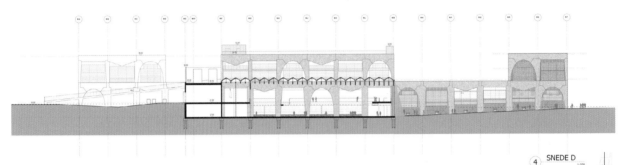

To hear Professor Alexander D'Hooghe tell it, urban design stalled somewhere in the early-mid nineteen-seventies, roughly parallel to the collapse of the 'grand narrative' of the welfare state, and it's this truncated future rescued from an abandoned past that becomes the scope of his recuperative investigation. Let others fritter away their talents and energies into contingent technical-managerial interventions in the au courant idioms of landscape urbanism or the techno-social hypotheses of so-called configurational studies. For D'Hooghe, there is only the large-scale synthetic gesture, where the disparate mechanisms of the city are recouped back into the formal definitions of architecture. D'Hooghe pushes a radically self-conscious reinterpretation of the role of the designer, one where the fear of stepping on toes and making controversial top-down decisions is replaced with a confident (and productive) grand-standing for liberal values. The argument here is that efforts at community-based design and bottom-up, grassroots planning are so distributed and seemingly transparent that they are in fact unable to muscle the difficult task of identifying public ideals. In this sense, D'Hooghe's focus is less on resurrecting a past than with exploring the future, a mission that aligns well with MIT's brief to itself.

D'Hooghe's interests offer a critical bridge between the School's two strong departments, Architecture and Urban Studies and Planning. He exemplifies the synergies obtained between the M.Arch. studio sequence, the specialized S.M.Arch.S. program, as well as the City Design and Development program, where architects and planners are re-engaging the lost debate surrounding the

formal implications of large scale intervention and the socioeconomic and technological complexities involved in city planning. With other faculty, such as Alan Berger and Eran Ben-Joseph, D'Hooghe's teaching and work address implications of architecture's relevance at the regional or urban planning level. His research group, Platform for a Permanent Modernity (PPM) consolidates these ideas spanning architecture and urbanism into a single entity that provides continuity across studios and semesters.

In D'Hooghe's practice, ORG Office for Permanent Modernity, which he runs with Natalie Seys in Massachusetts, and with Luk Peeters in Belgium, not all projects are of the massive and infrastructural variety. From the practice's website: "From the city to the couch: the principle of permanent modernity is valid at every scale level. Intelligence is a question of being able to zoom in and out in order to maximize the leverage small interventions may have on the bigger scale." Rather than isolated events, ORG's projects, even when small, carry forth the larger ambitions of the group, enforcing ideas about proactive infrastructures on every scale. Leverage is an important keyword for this practice, as it acknowledges the broader goals that accompany any design by the firm and their consistent adherence to a program of inscribing an architectural agenda onto what might, at first glance, seem to scale out of architecture's reach.

Implicit also within this project is the question of social justice, an issue that is approached from different angles throughout the planning and studio design sequences at MIT. The objective within PPM and ORG's work is driven by a social agenda certainly, one that addresses the precariousness of the contemporary middle class, as well as the financial structures that support this perpetual teetering on the brink. Given its exorbitant debt levels, most of the American 'middle class', for instance, stands to lapse into poverty within two to three months of unemployment, a constituency that D'Hooghe terms the 'prekariat'. How can architecture and planning begin to address that sort of large-scale demographic shift, especially in a country where housing and planning policy so privileges outrageous leveraging by the mortgage industry? In this way, a comprehensive notion of Urban Design is encouraged, and students work with large-scale causes and effects in the built environment that bring government, planning, and housing all together in concert.

Because this brand of thinking transcends politics, seeking out the underlying causes and effects of economic and social/spatial conditions, it can sometimes hit on an especially timely topic before others are aware of it. D'Hooghe's Option-level Urban Design studios like Towards a New Monumentality in Passaic (2006) and Projecting a Metropolitan Area: The Case of Long Island (how the other half lives) (2009) engage directly with very contemporary economic-planning conditions. Students are asked to think critically about typologies that are often discounted as architectural anachronisms and to engage in design thinking with broad strokes. Even before the recent economic crisis

ASCO—ORG/ Alexander D'Hooghe
The external skin is a steel colonnade built with I-beams and Lauffer frames. It unifies the different architectures and styles into one single form.

was full-blown, the Passaic Urban Design studio was actively immersed in the high-risk mortgage and precarious cash-flow situation that most of American suburbia is founded on. This team was able to identify very pressing economic conditions and to propose large-scale infrastructural responses to them, all before news of the housing crisis was widespread. Findings from this studio were published in a special issue of Volume, "Crisis? What Crisis? Suburbia After the Crash," in 2006, presented in the form of a white paper proposal to the government.

The premise of these studios is often disaster, self-inflicted disaster, the result of a society pulling itself apart at the seams, but ends up somehow hopeful. Like a self-cleaning oven, these ebbs and flows of economic and social disaster actually make way for new and revolutionary change in their wake. This is a mode of opportunity-finding that is in full effect at MIT. On the one hand, there are large-scale inevitabilities in play, and on the other a belief that any situation, when approached critically, can become a platform for change. D'Hooghe's project often lies in identifying these opportunities where change is immanent and positioning the designer as a kind of crow bar to dislodge the status quo. Design problems at MIT are not rote responses to unchangeable situations, they are dynamic in and of themselves. Allowing the student to participate in the construction of a social network to support her architectural ambitions promotes a broader type of design thinking that looks for opportunities in novel places and keeps responses flexible.

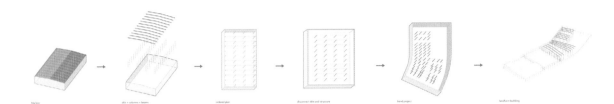

This type of thinking is best illustrated by D'Hooghe's interest in the Big Box typology, which pops up throughout ORG work, PPM research, and design studios, because it's often discounted as outside of architecture, non-architecture. Precisely because of this slippage to the outside does the Big Box become a site of radical architectural intervention. In D'Hooghe's words, it's a typology that is so reductivist and optimized, has so successfully engineered the architect out of architecture, that it begs the question of how the architect could then be reinserted. No longer complicit, the architect is unwittingly

ASCO—ORG/ Alexander D'Hooghe
The landform megastructure contains several institutions. Of only one–the fire station–is the Organization for Permanent Modernity effectively also the architectural designer. The building is a banal big box, of which the elements have been reshuffled. The ordered internal structure is decoupled from the skin of the building and the entire form is bent.

positioned as outside, and this, D'Hooghe urges, is actually a position of enormous power, if identified. So many assumptions go along with the Big Box–its efficiency, it's mundanity, its replicability–that it might actually provide a surprisingly effective way to communicate with the

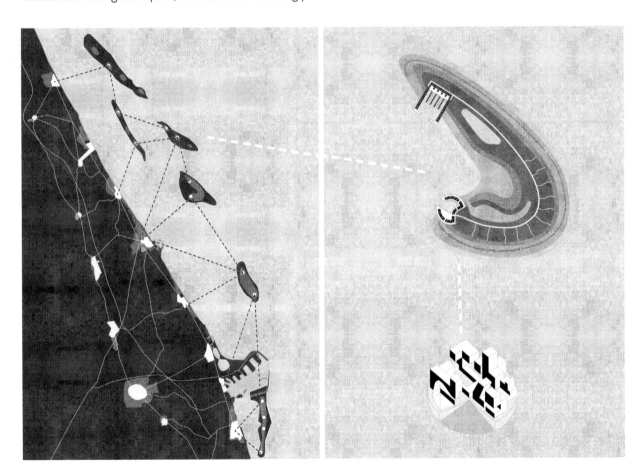

BESK—ORG/ Alexander D'Hooghe
This painting displays a project for a national defense of the coastline of Belgium in the North Sea. The plan foresees a chain of islands, between 6 and 20 kilometers out from the current coastline. These islands are radicalizations of the existing sand banks that structure the underwater topography of this part of the North Sea. Consisting of dynamic shifting dunes and beaches, they will largely absorb the energy of mega storms. Yet they will simultaneously define a national park North Sea, allowing for boats and visitors to dock on the various islands using small marinas. Settlements may take up to 5-10% of the new land. The instability of the land makes urban sprawl impossible. Architecture (as a matter of investment) cannot afford the degree of fluidity and change to characterize nation; its project is limited to a series of large concrete cylinders, within which building can occur. These drums are outposts of civilization; even when the last dune is washed away, they will stand.

public and to integrate new social services. If, for example, Big Box stores, following the infinite sameness of their construction, begin to form a new type of infrastructure across America, how might they be used to further a simultaneous hidden agenda?

Throughout all of these projects, students are encouraged to explore the implications of top-down design, of enormous infrastructural insertions into an existing patchwork landscape of strip malls and suburbs. D'Hooghe charges students with boldly envisioning a different future.

Alexander D'Hooghe inhabits a unique critical position as an urban designer and an architect eager to explore the transformative potentials of both fields. He sees these disciplines as lacking, as bereft of their historic power, and envisions a dramatic realignment of politics and design. He calls up the theories of Modernism in order to reinhabit the optimistic promise of the top-down, the confident imposition of social ideals through design. Rather than shying away from analogies to totalitarian or Fascist architectural precedents, D'Hooghe aims to mobilize their same tactics to different, but no less comprehensive, political ends—what he calls "macro-visions of social justice."[1] With an impassioned belief in the designer's social mandate, D'Hooghe pushes to renew interest in massive infrastructural insertions as politically progressive potentialities. To continue on the course presently charted is self-defeating. As he sees it, "the design professions will cease to actively participate in influencing social order."[2] That self-willed impotence has designers writing themselves out of a truly visionary job.

Three key concepts emerge from D'Hooghe's work, and are essential to understanding his priorities: the utopian, the liberal, and the infrastructural. Without a notion of utopia,

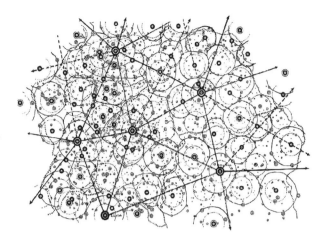

BESK–Cristaller reference
The concrete drums that may host buildings are placed seemingly randomly across the island. They are not; in fact, they correspond to an extension of the medieval settlement pattern characterizing the north of Flanders, out into the sea (where during the middle ages, monasteries and small fishing villages have in fact existed not too far from the proposed ones). This drawing by Walter Cristaller abstracts a proto-capitalist medieval settlement pattern in Southern Germany and illustrates Cristaller's theorization of the formal and geometrical properties of settlement order. Its distorted triangulation pattern is equally valid for most of the Low Countries.

or an imagined ideal future, he contends, designers are simply reflecting and replicating a current state, one that could indeed use some changing. As he writes, "the utopian promise is a prerequisite for social change," bringing to light his belief in the activist role of designers.[3] To abdicate this potentially revolutionary post is not only irresponsible on the part of the architect or urban designer, it is a way to write designers out of all equations, to foretell the death of a relevancy.

The liberal enters D'Hooghe's writing as an imperative. "Because it speaks on behalf of the collective, urban design is political."[4] To attempt to sidestep the responsibility of

Habraken Exhibit, Spring 2011
On the occasion of the MIT Architecture Department's celebrations of MIT150, the Organization for Permanent Modernity built an installation called 'Homage to Habraken.' This installation is an interpretation of John Habraken's concept of structure-infill. However, it also became a mock-up model of a potential new building system, an upgraded version of the historical structure-infill concept. The open market structure in Brussels will realize this mock-up in concrete, with elements about four times bigger than those of the art exhibit.

creating productive, challenging urban spaces, he writes, designers have simply stopped envisioning the big picture and left the massive-scale public works projects to engineers and managers. "We generally associate formalism with institutions, while we connect informality with grassroots democracy and community life."[5] The political aspect of urban design has long been negatively associated with oppressive régimes, but there is no reason, in D'Hooghe's view, why their same methods cannot be used in service of a liberal ideal. The informal grassroots distributed method has given us, since the nineteen seventies, only the gradual degradation of urban legibility. Better to take on the task of massive infrastructure with the socially progressive ideals of the designer to use this knowledge in a more deviant manner towards the deliberate staging of frictions and forms of coexistence, which from a traffic management point of view may make no sense, but from a public interest point of view are imperative.

Infrastructure becomes a vast platform for action in this new formulation, and a field of work to be recaptured for urban designers and architects. The shift towards engineers and policy makers as the principal designers of major infrastructural projects has robbed society of the grand optimistic gestures that once were embodied there.[6] Conceptual ambition and bold vision provided, infrastructural projects like transportation nodes could do a kind of social double duty, consciously creating spaces for interaction rather than simply optimizing movement. "The generational task of urban designers and architects graduating in America today will involve the radical re-conceptualization of infrastructure as a series of finite, concrete objects that are simultaneously places: in short, a series of discrete stages."[7]

Palace of Justice, Plan Existing and Proposed—ORG/ Alexander D'Hooghe
We propose to explode the palace and re-deploy its fragments on the ground. This results in dramatic plan changes that nevertheless maintain an internal consistency and order to each of the several building fragments. Instead of an eclectic order, we propose to radicalize the exposure of difference into an irreconcilable formal conflict.

What is clear throughout all of his writing is the desire to diagnose and to find treatments for the particularly contemporary condition that he terms, in *Volume*, 'grey goo'. He writes, "There is no better spatial deployment of the condition spawning mass estrangement than America's middle ring suburbs. Grey Goo, while borne out of a garden city dream, has developed asymptotically into an ever more vast asphalt tarmac, with scattered debris and remains of civilization."[8] In addition to publishing the results of his doctoral research at Berlage, *The Liberal Monument: Urban Design and the Late Modern Project* (2010), D'Hooghe writes regularly for important architecture and urban design periodicals like *Volume*, *New Geographies*, *Places*, *Hunch*, and *Projections*, expanding on different aspects of his thinking. Writing and contributing to disciplinary dialog fits perfectly with the zoom-in/zoom-out ethos of ORG and PPM because it operates on yet another scale of intellectual influence and allows the firm to promote its ideas beyond their own design contributions.

The narrative of resistance that guides D'Hooghe's scholarly production and logical arguments is not always immediately legible to those who aren't primed for it because he takes such obvious joy in the aesthetic of monumental technocracy. His drive towards the mega or the macro is constructed in opposition to what happened in the wake of Modernism, a collective backlash that was once revolutionary but has stagnated now into a straight-jacket of grass-roots workshopping and crowd-sourced design.

At first glance, this return to an era of huge industrial-scale complexes and conditions imposed from above sounds like the enemy; it sounds like Howard Roark and god-complexes, but that is exactly D'Hooghe's point.

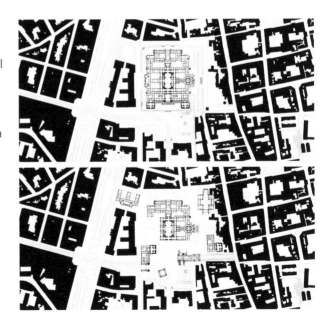

When formerly-effective strategies have been abandoned, essentially because of bad marketing, it opens up a platform to re-imagine their utility for the present. The antidote to the hulking physical manifestations of oppressive régimes is not dissolution into mass-mediated factions building piecemeal. Indeed, if the politics of historic monumentality are so legible in Modernist projects, a strong precedent exists for a liberal politics to be writ large across the city, ensuring developments of the positive kind.[9] It is difficult to overstate the import of this type of re-thinking the grand gesture. It returns power to the hands of the architect, and a confidence in form-making as well as a sort of designer's activism that has not been seen in recent decades.

Architecture doesn't stop at the boundaries of a building. It is the spatial organization of the world, and thinking on a mega or an extra-large scale allows priorities that are quite clear in one register to be translated for whole regions. D'Hooghe's work in urban design urges architects to recuperate the power they once held, to "rummage through old boxes," to find the techniques and strategies of the past that can be reactivated for the present condition and "hard-core contemporary design."[10] This is an exciting way to think forward about being socially effective and cohering a kind of disciplinary confidence boost, but it is also a huge responsibility worth taking on.

Palace of Justice Proposal—ORG/ Alexander D'Hooghe
The result produces almost no new form, but re-defines what exists as an assemblage of fragments into a latter-day Acropolis for the European Union. This exemplifies the political aesthetic developed in the book 'The Liberal Monument.'

1   Tali Hatuka and Alexander D'Hooghe, "After Postmodernism: Read dressing the Role of Utopia in Urban Design and Planning," in *Places* 19.2, 20.

2   Hatuka and D'Hooghe, 27.

3   Hatuka and D'Hooghe, 20.

4   Alexander D'Hooghe, *Hunch: The Berlage Institute Report*, no. 14 (2010), 95.

5   D'Hooghe, *Volume* 9 "Crisis! What Crisis? Suburbia After the Crash," (2006), 152.

6   Alexander D'Hooghe, *Projections: MIT Student Journal of Planning* "Designing for Growth and Change," (2011), 87.

7   D'Hooghe, *Projections*, 90.

8   D'Hooghe, *Volume*, 45+.

9   Alexander D'Hooghe, *AA Files: Annals of the Architectural Association School of Architecture*, no. 51 (2004), 17.

10   Interview with A. D'Hooghe, 1 April 2011.

STRUCTURE-INFILL; SAR, WITTGENSTEIN, AND OTHER MATTERS:
A CONVERSATION WITH JOHN HABRAKEN MIT150 TRANSCRIPT

MONDAY, APRIL 25, 2011

Arindam Dutta: Professor of History, Theory, and Criticism, MIT
John Habraken: Emeritus Professor, former Head, Department of Architecture, MIT
Alexander D'Hooghe: Professor of Architecture, MIT

This conversation has been edited for length and clarity.

Arindam Dutta:
[reading Habraken's, The Structure of the Ordinary]
"The house is in the town, the room is in the house, in the room is a chair. In the chair sits a person who speaks. The sight of an act is that part of physical reality in which the act is observed. For the observer, every act has a site. There is an unlimited number of sites because the unlimited number of objects that can be observed is without limit." The sentences read like architectural haiku, their meaning self-evident, but strung out, they seem to indicate some greater program, a script for the world.

And in John Habraken's world, architecture is troubled perpetually by its inability to fully comprehend the circumstances of its own making. This brings forth a push from the world of practice into the world of research, producing the trans-historical, the trans-cultural attempt at a scientific language, systematic attempts to delegate what varies in architectural production. One realizes that these haikus are in fact far from a poetics. Rather, in a syntactical sequence, they offer the prescriptive task of a grammar, propositions strung along what appears as a kind of magician's attempt at architectural discussion. In the realm of pedagogy and research, intervention is often simulated as different kinds of games, repetitive as games are, following the same sets of rules, and never repeating as games often do, each player presenting the possibility of an infinite variety within a finite formal framework.

Today it gives me great pleasure to bring back one of our very own. John Habraken was the founding director of the Stichting Architecten Research, or SAR, translated in English as Foundation for Architectural Research, a research body founded as a consortium of Dutch architectural firms in 1965. It supports an alternative to mass housing, a Dutch project that came out in 1962, a pamphlet in 1962 critical of the mass housing movement of post-war reconstruction that argued for greater choice afforded to occupants, culminating in Habraken's propositions for structure-infill combinations. As a research office, SAR was significantly influential within the world of Dutch architectural offices and the building industry, holding up for a while the prospect of potential collaboration between the two factions. Posters from the SAR 65 report, produced as polemical inserts within the marketplace, adorned most Dutch offices of the period. Habraken's own global reputation garnered followers for the SAR method across the Third World as well as the United States. In 1967, John Habraken was appointed professor at Eindhoven Technical University to set up its new Department of Architecture and serve as its first Chairman. He was appointed as Head of the Department of Architecture at MIT in 1975. His American phase was marked by interest in architectural practice as a variant of game or systems theory, manifested in his research in early computational paradigms.

The *Grundsveldt Variations*, a research publication carried out with MIT students is another influential work from this period. His book, *The Structure of the Ordinary* is an investigation of laws governing the built environment as we deal with patterns of transformation. He's the recipient of many awards including the 1988 Creative Achievement Award of the Association of Collegiate Schools of Architecture in the US. Some of Habraken's ideas are still present within MIT. It's sort of a deep DNA of MIT, I think, that we keep coming back to. But perhaps it's a deep DNA of architecture itself.

Alexander D'Hooghe: Let's go right to a question. So from the formative moments, especially of SAR, what stuck with me the most was the phrase: "I am a proponent of autonomy of the built environment." Not the autonomy of the built object, of the artfully designed, authored object, by the single intuitive architect genius, but the built environment as a complete system, as an anthropological system as a complete structure. From that, if I understand your work correctly, comes a reflection on the fact that architects' agency over the making of the building is, and in fact *should* be, limited. It should not be comprehensive because there are many other people that come into play in the construction of the city. However, it appears that the various constituents that guide the building process are the architects who do the construction, the industry, contractors, theorists, universities, but none of those were properly equipped as entities to deal with an autonomous structural field. And it seems that SAR perhaps was an attempt to construct an entity that could be responsible for the digging up of the autonomous built environment, of the structure that was deep underneath in there. Is that a correct assumption? Would it be possible for you to expand a bit on how SAR came about and what your role was?

John Habraken: You mentioned the autonomy of the built environment, and in retrospect that has become one of my major obsessions. To understand that, to see the built environment as something that has a life of itself, I've tried to introduce the idea of the field, because I think what we talk about is the built environment *and* the people in it. The two go together. And if you think of it as an organic autonomous thing, when the people leave, the built environment will disappear. And without the built environment, people can't live. So it's this total unity that's become more and more my interest. But of course that was not at the beginning. I only discovered that afterwards.

In the beginning, there was a very intuitive idea that there was something wrong with the way that we dealt with the built environment in the Netherlands. What was wrong was that the users, the inhabitants, had nothing to do with it anymore. And that led to the idea of a separation, because we had forgotten about the people inside, except in a narrow, functionalist way. They needed to be introduced as agents in that same process. I think that was the beginning, I tried to introduce this in my book about sports. It was also the result of everyone getting nervous about their role in the larger scheme of things. Throughout the rebuilding of the Dutch nation after the war, the developers, the builders, the manufacturers, the government, and the bureaucrats all took over, and the architects saw that they were sort of pushed aside. They came together to seek an opportunity. It was a very defensive move. But then somebody in the group announced the idea that if they were serious about it, they should put their money together and do something about it, make research about it. And they responded to that challenge, and then of course they said, "well the only person around here who has not been compromised by practice is John Habraken because he's only written, so let him do the research." And that's how we started.

Arindam Dutta: The situation is one that is quite unique. We are talking about ten offices agreeing to contribute fifteen thousand Guilders per year to fund a shared research office that will carry on this corrective activity. This is unique in the history of architecture, I think. It's not a government-funded body, it's private architects agreeing to do this because they seek a more informed and more involved role.

John Habraken: Well, there was a committee on housing by the architects, the equivalent of the AIA, and the Chairman of that committee was himself an architect who did a lot of housing, and he became concerned about the role of the architect. They felt that architects no longer had much to say about the future of the built environment. That was in a period in which all the professions, but particularly architects, felt a responsibility to push forward the culture, the future. They felt they had to shape the culture for the Dutch nation. It's hard to imagine that kind of attitude today, but it was genuine, with all the pragmatics that were involved. So this Chairman called together eight or nine of his colleagues who were all known as people heavily involved with housing projects to discuss the problem of how the architects would get more influence about the future of the built environment.

Alexander D'Hooghe: What is extremely striking is the attempt to construct across various egos, tastes, and agendas, this common platform. The reason the platform had to be common was because you were really after the discovery of innate, rational orders of

building. By rational, I mean inclusive of the various practices that people develop, that users develop when they are inside a built environment, rather than as you called it, the narrow, functional approach. As we see it today, you were after dimensional and configurational rules or parameters that would be shared in a post-war Dutch welfare state, but that wouldn't be more degraded for the individual than the ones that were, at this moment, being constructed.

John Habraken: The leading idea was that, if you look at history, the way built environments went about, basically there was a very close relationship between the house and the users, and that you could not separate these two. So it seemed to me that it was unnatural to do big projects in which the user has no say. Proposing that separation was a really pragmatic idea. "*Technically* it's possible, why don't we do it?" That was very naïve because it took me a long time to find out why it was so difficult to have it done. But we decided that our role was not to change everything, but to find out what the architect should be able to do in a new situation. So, how do you design when you make the circulation in order to support the infill? Because you have a problem–in those days, if you did a housing project, the first thing that had to be produced was the floorplan. Then the floorplan was multiplied so that you had an apartment building. And with the floorplan, everybody could act. The banker could figure out what it might cost, the builders could figure out where the columns would go, etc., so everybody could work. And what we were saying is that you can design everything *except* the floorplan! So it really pulled the rug from under the professional game. And that of course was the reason for all of the problems that we had to deal with in the political arena.

But technically we decided that there was a research area that we had to investigate. How do you make an open building with no floorplans in it, how can you explain to your client that this is the best possible type of a building that he can put his money in? So that was the problem of formal evaluation, or what, later on, was capacity. We didn't say, "what is the function of this building?" because that's what produces the floorplan. That was the research problem, which brought us to methodology. How do you figure out the capacity of such a building? And there was one little issue, which was: if one party builds the support building, and another produces

the infill, how do they coordinate their work? In those days, that was felt to be very important, towards mechanization, that was another technological issue.

Arindam Dutta: Just to clarify for the audience, your conception of support and infill is not to be equated with the idea of a skeleton and whatever kind of ancillary spaces that they might hold. You speak of support as what is in a way *infrastructural*, or *prior to* the building. This would include the utilities that private companies manage and bring up to the site, which are given site conditions in terms of legality, bylaws, and so forth. Today architects do their designs and they leave it later for certain people, so that they make sure that these things are worked out. But it's very clear that what you're asking for here in reevaluating the notion of support, as paying the consideration of this prior condition right at the outset of the project and of the research, and that's what would be transformed—the stuff that usually architects have no choice in.

John Habraken: Yes, I think that was the essence, that we defined the support as including everything that was communal to the users. And fit-out, or infill, was everything that the eventual user could control. So it was a *distinction of control*.

Alexander D'Hooghe: In hindsight, one of the several revolutionary statements that were you were making was to in fact explode architectural object-hood. The idea of the building as a single isolated object—that is just shot to pieces—and what is left instead is a series of layers with different life spans.

John Habraken: We used to have urban design and architecture. And architecture was doing the buildings in the context of urban design. If the building becomes bigger, it becomes the context itself for the infill. So in that sense, it is an organic development that will happen anyway. I think, intellectually speaking, the important thing afterwards turned out to be that we introduced the idea of time and change and control. Because different parties control it, the frequency of change of the infill is faster than the frequency of change of the communal. It's always the case. Architecture was always the defiance of time. We were to build the monument that would defy time. And here we said, *time is of essence in our designing*. So the control part was the political part, but the change, design part was of intellectual interest.

Arindam Dutta: SAR was quite instrumental in creating some kind of interaction between the building industry and the architects, even if, in the end, they didn't get along well at all. But SAR got some commissions from the building industry, correct?

John Habraken: Yes. The first few years, we were financed by those ten architectural firms and architects' offices, actually. There was an eleventh part which was the contribution of the organization which was the equivalent of the AIA. The President of that group was also on our board. But then some builders came our way, or manufacturers, and they said, "If you can manage to do what you propose to do, it's in our interest. We would love that because it would make our lives much easier." And so we said, "Why don't you pay us?" And so from then on, we had also builders and manufacturers who contributed to the research.

Alexander D'Hooghe: I had a question that pertains exactly to your move from Western Europe to the US–I find it so striking that in the SAR work, very much is driven by a desire to uncover dimensions,

structural dimensions, configural relations–not forms, parameters– that are not the invention of an architect. They are structural to an ordinary environment. So a lot of the work was to uncover these dimensional or configurative relations. It seemed to me also that when you were unearthing this, that you really believed, and perhaps still believe, that these dimensions are structural, are scientific, are true to the human species as a whole.

John Habraken: Well, if you do a methodology, and you believe that what you contribute is helpful for your colleague architects to use in their work if they want to solve certain problems, you don't want to preempt the architectural style–that's somebody else's decision. The simplest idea of methodology leading to a tool is that we have a measurement that's a methodological tool, by which we can communicate with each other about the size of things. Basically, if you look at the methodology that we proposed, there were two things that we were concerned with: how do you speak about dimension, and how do you speak about position? I still believe that the position of things and their dimensions are the two basic tools that every architect uses. So what we tried to do is to formalize that a little bit more in a sense that you can talk about the issue of capacity. How do I present or represent the space that is yet to be occupied? The concept of zones comes in as a positioning tool. Just like zones in urban design are positioning tools. In that sense it was a very straightforward idea.

Arindam Dutta: How do you distinguish your approach from, let's say, Christopher Alexander and his *Pattern Language*?

John Habraken: Well, I felt that what he was doing was close to what I was interested in. But there was also a very important difference, and that is the idea of patterns. In my eyes, a pattern is something that people follow because they agree about the value of it. It's basically an expression of what we are willing to share with each other. It's a product of consensus about form. You do not have to talk about the value of what it is. It's simply because you say, "that's what we like to do together." Chris Alexander, in the beginning particularly, very much tried to prove that the pattern was right and true, that there was a basic truth in patterns that you could unearth and formulate. That is something that may well be true about what he is saying, but I didn't think that it was very interesting. I think that patterns are interesting as a means of communication, a means of consensus. Built environment is the product of communal agreement, in my eyes.

Arindam Dutta: One of the first projects that SAR did was to create

an architectural Esperanto–they are quite amazing to look at, because it's an attempt to create an architecture-speak in script. But the communicative interest is throughout from the European context through to the American context. It seems to me that in the American context, you are not so hooked in with industry or architects–that your work and your research reflexively moves back more into methodology. I'm thinking of your NSF grant, for example. But your work seems to at that point adopt certain methodologies about communication. You are moving back into the work of philosophy, where now the question of intervention by the architect is becoming a kind of game, or a game theory-inflected set of rules. "You do A, I'll do B," et cetera. It seems to me that at that point methodologically, you are trying more and more to formalize the interactivity of the built environment, even as you are saying that it is autonomous. Would that be correct?

John Habraken: Yes. You mentioned two things–they may be connected, but different. My interest in philosophy was less about what they were saying about the world, but that you could say things in that way–a very disciplined way. I was interested in being that disciplined myself. It was not just logic–it was pattern, poetry. I think this is one part of my interest, to have a kind of discipline to say things as clearly as possible. The other part that you mentioned was the NSF grant. In the beginning of my understanding what I was dealing with was that architects work together, that the built environment is the result of many designers working in relationship with one another. We were living in a culture in which we totally ignored that, in which the individual expression of the designer was the only thing that anybody talked about. So I became interested in the idea that there are ways in which architects meet one another. And that's where the games came in.

Arindam Dutta: How do you think the world turned out? I mean, there are younger Dutch architects who have had a sort of great role on the world stage. What do you make of what came after, in the two decades following your retirement?

John Habraken: Well, I'm invited to give lectures from time to time. My impression is that the younger generation doesn't have the hang-ups that my colleagues had about these things. They take it very easily that there are different ways to work. They don't feel personally insulted. They are very pragmatic in the sense that *if there are tools that you can use, you use them.* So you can have a discussion about whether they are useful or not or whatever, or whether certain concepts are interesting or not, and I think that is great progress. That is the way things should be tested. Another development, of course, in those twenty years, is the so-called Open Building Network that has been developing internationally. It meets every year in another place in the world. We keep track of different Open Building projects, and in the last five or ten years, important projects have come about. It used to be that an Open Building project was always seen as a sort of experiment. The last ten years, the initiative of the really interesting projects comes from the clients who decide that they want this way of working because it is in their interests to do that and because there is a financial interest there. That is a real sea change.

[Questions from the forum]
Bill Porter: John, can you speculate on the implications for education of those people who in the profession might behave as expert infillers, bringing in a new generation of professionals who

could perform what you have envisioned? Is it technology, is it a question of values, is it specific areas of skill, patterns of education like the predominance of the design studio, should that be changed dramatically? Give us a hint.

John Habraken: Well, personally I think, what I would like to teach is what I did in my design course where you deal with how architects relate to one another although they each have their own responsibility in the design that they're working on. And I am right now working on another book on this issue, in which we have four times seven "plays." It's not an exercise because an exercise is rote training, and that's not what this is. It's not a game because games you can win and lose, and this is not something you can win and lose. ` Designing means that you do not know what the end result will be. It's a continuous change in the form that is developing, learning to deal with time. The second one is about horizontal relationships. When two architects work on the same street, sharing patterns, or type, or context. The same thing about the position–that's a horizontal relationship. The third one is vertical relationships. A relationship with the urban designer and the architect, which is the issue of the dominance and the hierarchy. And the final parts are about fields–when you learn to put together all the things you learned about in the first part to make continuous fields which we give as a start of seven different kinds of fields with different kinds of biases.

TORONTO PORTLANDS URBAN DESIGN STUDIO

Instructor: **Michael Dennis and Dan Chen**
Teaching Assistant: **Yashar Ghasemkhani**

The subject of this studio is the (re) development of the port lands in Toronto, a former industrial site of approximately 1200 acres on the waterfront. The project is to provide an urban design and guidelines for the development of the site, a landscape/open space design, and the architectural design of one building. In addition, the intent of the project should be described with illustrative drawings of the proposed urban, landscape, and architectural character. The purpose of the project is to explore the differences and interrelationships between architecture and urbanism.

Amrita Mahindroo | SMArchS Urbanism

PREMISE The Portlands site in Toronto presents an unusual situation in which a former industrial site is in such proximity to a rapidly expanding metropolitan centre. Hindered only by the polluted soil conditions on the site, the Portlands presents a lucrative opportunity for the future expansion of the city, with unsurpassed views of the Toronto skyline, from the island vantage point. The proposal assumes that the site's unusual disconnect from the existing city as a consequence of the Gardiner freeway and the larger grain industrial buffer, will gradually breakdown with increased urban renewal which will merge the fabric of the Portlands site with that of the existing city. The proposal seeks primarily to articulate an independent identity for the portlands site, placing an emphasis on it's mixed use, and thus creating a city fabric which provides enough diversity to accommodate multiple building typologies and parcel sizes, whilst maintaining a sense of control over the formal structure of the city.

RETENTION OF INDUSTRIAL LANDMARKS The Portlands site is a littered with very prominent industrial relics, 3 of which have been retained in the scheme and have formed the symbolic nodes for structuring the transportation axis across the site and providing the landmarks through which the identity of the site can be established.

STRUCTURE The spatial organization of the site has been based in part on the existing infrastructure and in part on the provision of primary streets and public transport routes which have been distributed according to 5min walking circles across the site. The primary street structure then provides the formal edges to the neighborhoods which result from the 5min walking circles.

WATER The existing site is essentially two peninsulas of land divided through the centre by the channel. In an attempt to bridge the scale of the channel, it's size was reduced to through land reclamation to create the primary boulevards across the site. In this fashion the path of canals and waterways, becomes the civic structure for the site, as the major boulevards culminate in landmarks or civic places such as the basin park.

GREEN SPACE The site is buffered along the lake edge by existing parklands and the beach. The city fabric has been dotted with additional neighborhood parks and linear soft landscaped recreational strips along the canal system, encouraging the use of the canals as civic spaces. These are complimented by the basin park which laces the edge between land and water, providing a vital resource to cleaning the site water run off, and improving the soil conditions on the site.

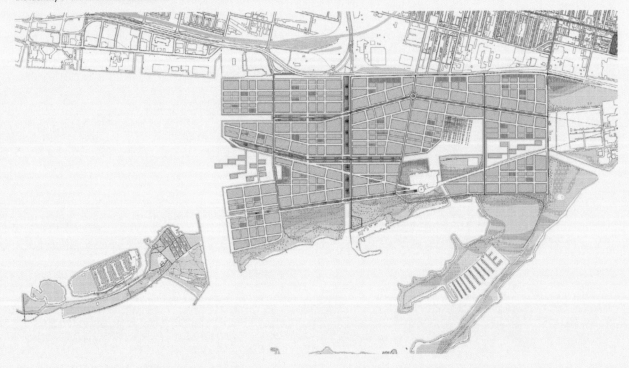

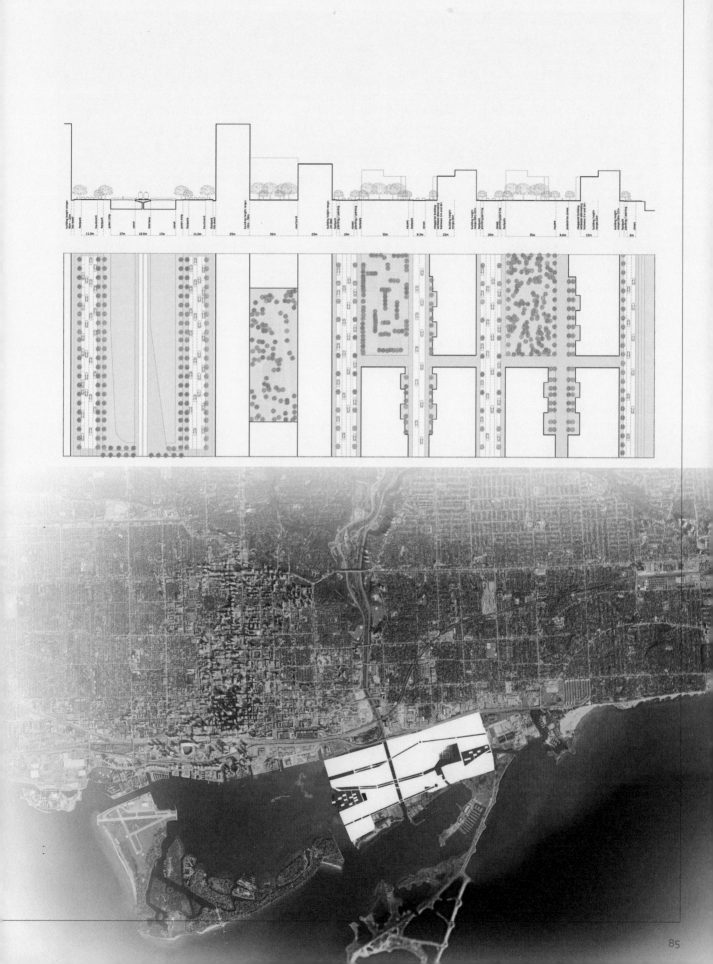

BILBAO URBAN DESIGN STUDIO

Instructor: **Alan Berger and Alexander D'Hooghe**
Teaching Assistant: **Ryan Maliszewski**

This studio will study design strategies for the area connecting the historic city of Bilbao to the Atlantic ocean through an elongated system of road, harbor and marine infrastructures.

The projects will cover different scales from the territorial to the architectural. Marine and landscape systems, as well as architectural infrastructures will be investigated in order to devise a strategy for the very large scale. Of course, the visit to Bilbao will allow visits to some of the recent masterpieces in architecture and infrastructure design. The Studio will run in conjunction with a studio at the CEU Madrid. The studio will be supported by Alan Berger's P-REX research group and D'Hooghe's Platform for a Permanent Modernity.

Jae K. Kim | MArch
Mahsan Mohsenin | SMArchS Urbanism
Dynamic System for the Total Ecology of the Valley

Ecological Process: Providing benefits only for Sestao is not the best solution in this project. We are proposing a Dynamic System along the river, which is working as an Economic Generator to benefit the whole waterfront and Sestao. As a result, this project will be able to protect the area from any recession or economic failure.

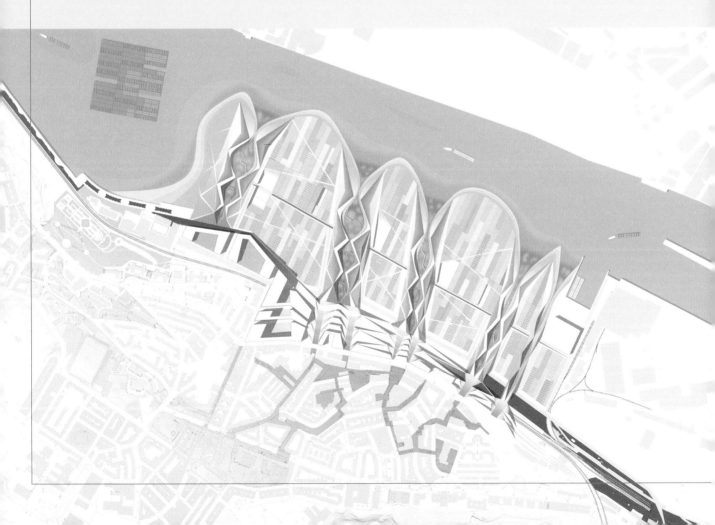

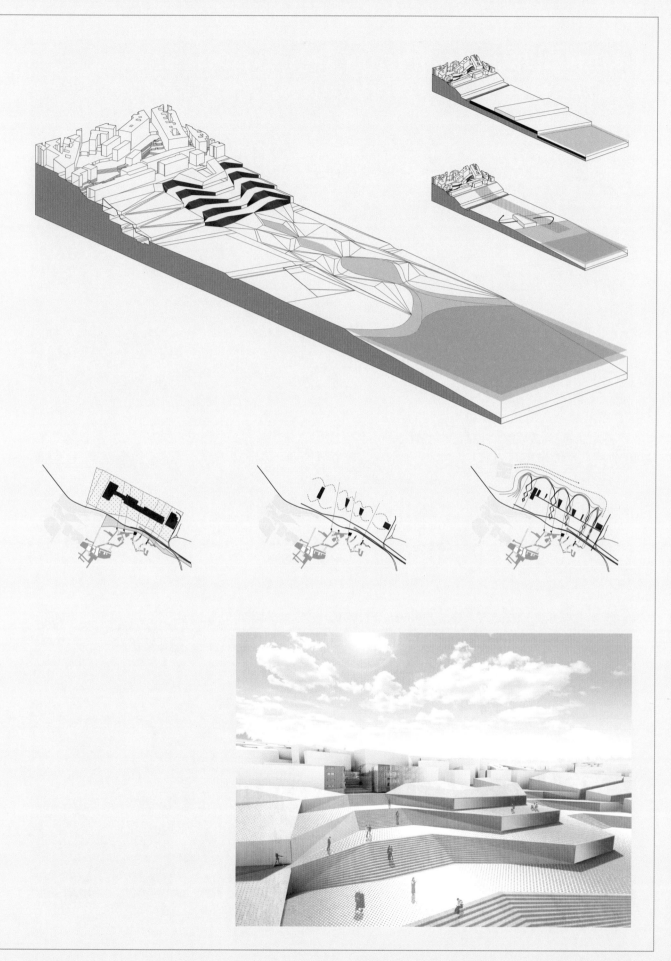

PROJECTING A METROPOLITAN AREA: THE CASE OF LONG ISLAND (HOW THE OTHER HALF LIVES) URBAN DESIGN STUDIO

Instructor: **Alexander D'Hooghe**
Teaching Assistant: **Michelle Petersen**

Formally, this studio assumes the possibility of an architectural conception of the scale of the territory or the region. That does not mean that buildings ought to be gigantic; but rather that a repertoire of formal thinking can be developed that can effect the legibility and formal clarity of the urbanizing region, thus providing with a civic sense of collective order.

Politically, the studio takes advantage of the opportunity presented to American cities in this time of crisis by using investments in infrastructure, education, and sustainable development in order to reframe the structural order of the American city.

Geographically, the studio chooses to locate itself in an half-urbanized area of middle ring suburbs: not urban centers, not exurbs, but the vast field between both. These suburbs have typically been built between the 1930s and the 1960s, and have by now lost a lot of their initial glamour and myth, furthermore suffering from a sustained lack of investment over the last 30 years. This year, the focus is on Long Island, east of Manhattan.

Sociologically, the studio aims to work on behalf of the American 'prekariat'. The 'prekariat' is a term borrowed from contemporary Germany. It describes a group that presents itself as middle class but lacks the financial stability to really be a middle class: the prekariat consists of families and individuals who are just surviving, but for whom a sudden interruption of the monthly paycheck would equal disaster, as they live on credit and lack any fall-back position.

Disciplinarily, the studio interrogates the possibility about the rise of a subfield called 'territorial design' or 'territorial architecture'. Just like 'urban design' and 'planning' were not 'disciplines' but rather highly particular, purposeful projects.... This subfield is based on the recognition that the conception of project on a territorial scale requires an instrumentarium and set of techniques that cannot be copied straight out of architecture, urban planning, or even 'urban design'. The studio is about establishing some of these techniques. These will include a synthetic mode of thinking that integrates infrastructural, civic, formal, landscape, programmatic, political and social thinking–to be channeled through a series of singular device: the actual interventions themselves.

Infrastructurally, the studio wants to revisit its 'form giving' potential. Infrastructure is historically a segregating device. We are historically far enough away now from the moment of trauma caused by Moses' parkway projects in Queens (which served to destroy existing flourishing ethnic communities), in order to revisit the premise that: infrastructure investment, when carefully approached, can constitute a measure of 'productive segregation'–a way of ordering the territory in a series of 'chambers' or districts, which give identity and clarity to the constitutive civilizational fragments of eastern NY metro area.

Ryan Maliszewski | MArch
Renewed City

Long Island's suburbanization is a monotonous mess. Within the mess, this project proposes an 'Ecocity' for a liberal democracy, which is bounded by existing infrastructure and connected to Manhattan by a studio proposed magnetic levitating train. The Ecocity triples the existing density, centralizes industry to promote car-free living and relies on renewable energy managed by a newly established Special Energy Zone in conjunction with an offshore wind farm.

The depth of design resolution varies according to the scale of intervention. This linearity enables the specifically designed renewable energy infrastructures to monumentalize a resource-conscious way of life within a loosely defined and fluctuating city form. The carefully designed monuments create a constellation of transit hubs, and arenas for social and civic collectivity. Ultimately, the Renewed City displaces the existing suburban condition and will be a model system for suburban reconciliation during an era of big government spending in green infrastructures.

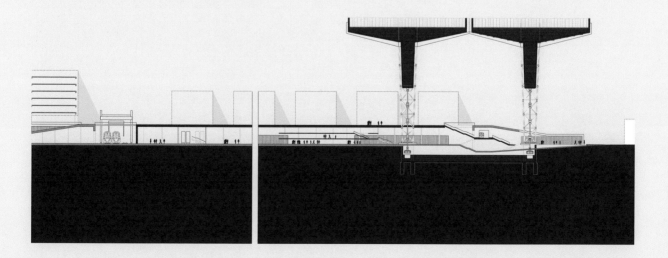

Haruka Horiuchi | MArch
Grid of Infrastructural Insertions: Sites of Opportunity in a Field of Decay

We are investing billions in infrastructure through the stimulus bill; we must carefully reconsider what kind of investments we are making for our future. Rather than simply building more highways, bridges and tunnels as we have done in the past, we should be injecting energy into the eroding urban areas of our cities. If the key to a sustainable future is through maintaining thriving, vibrant and densely populated metropolises, we must lay this groundwork now. The current foreclosure crisis has revealed badly corroding neighborhoods. These troubled sites are the ideal opportunity for architectural insertions of a civic nature, aimed at strengthening communities from the bottom up.

Background: I began by analyzing the economic stimulus bill to extract the vital needs and concerns of today, as framed by the government. The major themes point to infrastructural investment in the form of information and communication, social services, and health and recreation. In parallel, through an investigation of the whole of Long Island, dense pockets of foreclosure were discovered around the Bedford-Stuyvesant area of Brooklyn. Characterized by a history of poverty and violence, Bed-Stuy exists in the grey area between downtown and suburbia, and was attempting a comeback as a viable place to live until the foreclosure crisis. Now, with more than 500 foreclosures per square mile, boarded up windows and gaping empty lots are threatening to take over the identity of this neighborhood.

Territorial Strategy: Thinking of foreclosed lots as sites of opportunity, I propose a multi-pronged strategy to inject a new civic infrastructure into this area. By overlaying a 1/4 mile and 1 mile walking distance grid with a 500 ft communications grid, I have selected a small subset of the available sites to create a new infrastructural network to provide access to knowledge, social services and health.

This strategy intentionally leaves 9 million square feet of foreclosed space untouched for the moment–to gradually be turned over to a community land bank–a sort of holding pattern to prevent rash development until a wiser time for investment.

For those sites which fall into the new infrastructural network, 4 types of architectural insertions are proposed:
1. If no foreclosed lot exists at a grid point, then a communications tower will be inserted as a locally managed asset which strengthens the regional network.
2. If a grid point falls upon a foreclosed property that is not derelict or abandoned, government funding will save the property with the caveat of inserting a civic program, as well as a communications tower.
3. The third type of insertion addresses the crumbling corners of the urban block. Surprisingly many corner buildings are being foreclosed–a clear architectural strategy of rethinking the urban building prototype is proposed.
4. Finally, areas with an agglomeration of many or large foreclosed plots will be used to maximize recreational program for the surrounding area. Literally all of the Park's Department's currently offered recreational facilities could be offered in one complex.

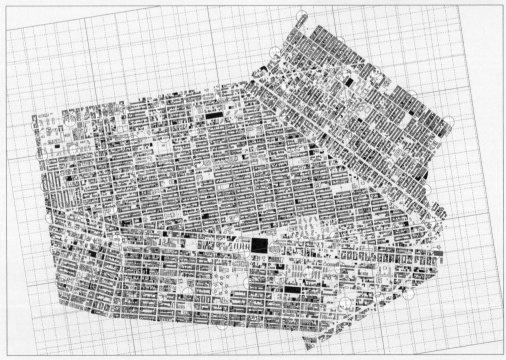

Zachary Lamb | MArch
Perpendicular Urbanism_Jetty City_Groin

Perpendicular Urbanism is a proposal for the south coast of Long Island that links the logic of coastal real estate development to the imperative for increased coastal protection infrastructure.

The edge where Long Island meets the North Atlantic is a violent and dynamic landscape in which wind and water continually form and reform the land. Over the last half century, this edge has been hardened in efforts to protect ever-spreading suburban communities. The very hardening intended to protect the landscape has now left Long Island more vulnerable to the threats of sea level rise and global climate change.

Perpendicular Urbanism is an alternative to the conventional binary of continually rebuilding along suburban modes after disaster and the outright retreat. A series of urbanized jetties along the barrier islands on the eastern end of Long Island are proposed to catch and retain sediment carried in the littoral drift which moves massive amounts of sand west to east along the coast. Currently, these sediments are deposited in the navigation channel for the port of New York and New Jersey, and must be dredged and dumped offshore to allow large vessel navigation. The proposed jetties will reduce the need for dredging and provide a site for spoils disposal upstream of the jetties. Gradually, the jetties will accumulate both natural and dredged sediments, building up the barrier islands and the defenses against storm surges.

To offset some of the public costs of developing such a protection infrastructure, the jetties are designed as sites for urban development. Throughout the world, dynamic and volatile landscapes are valuable real estate. This project captures this value to subsidize coastal protection infrastructure for the good of the heavily populated Long Island coast.

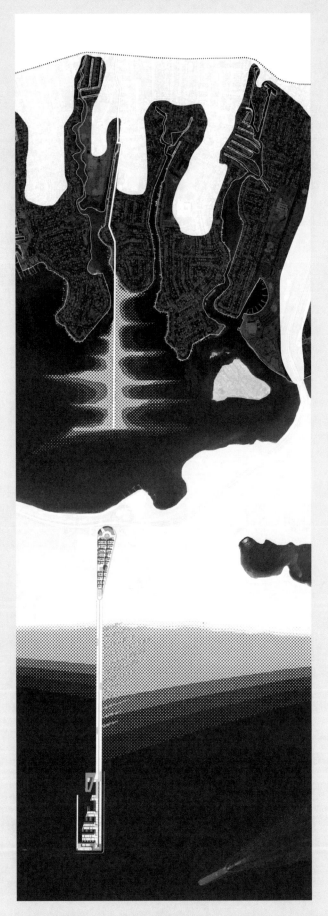

Lisa Pauli | MArch
Sub_Urban Refuge: Long Island Disaster Shelter for 50K

Long Island is America. The sprawling shag of sub_suburban development gives it its only shape with frequent infrastructural divisions between the banal and the ordinary. A wider lens nods to Long Island's class gradient that sweeps from the financially secure northern green to the southern, dissolving beaches. Very few points connect Long Island to the rest of America and the paths to these are often in embedded in storm surge zones. Among these characteristics runs a common thread: Long Island is a potential death trap.

This project is a manifesto; the scale of the proposition rejects contemporary visions and scales of architecture. It is a critique both of American sprawl and of the government's preparedness strategies in time of disaster. Recent catastrophic events throughout the world have begged the question of "what if?" My proposed solution answers these questions taking as precedent the current stimulus package and a recent history of federal funding to states that facilitate national security through infrastructure.

Long Island's eight million residents access the rest of the world through a bottle-necked array of bridges and tunnels on the south-western tip of the island, 118 miles from its extremity. The designated coastal evacuation routes on the southern edge of the island and most of its airports would be destroyed by a category 4 hurricane. Long Island needs a landmark; it needs a safe-haven. The Shelter provides refuge in time of disaster and secures infrastructural supplies and leisure activities the other 99% of the time.

CYCLES: GEOLOGICAL AND CULTURAL RESONANCES ALONG ICELAND'S GOLDEN CIRCLE OPTION DESIGN STUDIO

Instructor: **William O'Brien Jr.**
Teaching Assistant: **Adela Kalenja**

This traveling studio, *Cycles*, acknowledges a paradigm shift; a significant departure from the dichotomous depiction of landscape architecture as a dynamic series of regenerative processes, and architecture as a static accumulation of constructive phases. Rather, with attention directed toward recent advancements in technologies that provide innovative visualizations of patterns of transformation within our environment, *Cycles* aims to induce architectural design tactics which establish a mutually-dependent relationship between 'life-cycles' of buildings and 'cycles of life' in landscapes.

Cycles operates with the awareness that increasingly architectural design can be understood as the management of interrelations between multiple dynamic systems—those which occur naturally and those which are designed and implemented synthetically. The greater site of the studios' investigation is Iceland, which presents itself as a prime laboratory for extreme ecological change, geological transformation, biological development and meteorological activity. The specific sites of the studios' design research occur along The Golden Circle, an ecotourism route which outlines a myriad of geological phenomena including volatile displays of hydrological, volcanic, and geothermal activities. The design problem posed in Cycles requires the design of an interrelated network of ecotourism outposts along The Golden Circle, and the planning of its corresponding infrastructure for the potential of future sustainable development. The studio's broader ambition is to propose design strategies which suggest alternative resonances between the inevitability of geological transformation and the necessity of cultural development.

The combination of the volatile geological conditions of Iceland and its rapidly shifting developmental status produces a scenario which acts as an augmented representation of similar circumstances in many parts of the world. Faced with the mandate of developing a more robust ecotourism infrastructure, architectural designers are being charged with the challenge of amending seemingly contradictory systems—those which are driven by ecological processes and those which are driven by processes of urbanization. *Cycles* aims to establish interstices between existing and invented organizational systems by (1) privileging a conceptualization of 'site' as dynamic, ever-transforming and time-based processes, while (2) developing 'design' relationally, conditionally and tactically.

Prior to departure, students researched the current developmental ambitions of Iceland by identifying recent international design competitions sponsored by Iceland officials. These include the 2005 Vision Akureyri International Design Competition for Northern Iceland which looked to relink the environmental features of Eyjafjordur, Iceland's longest fjord, with the cultural prospects of urbanization, as well as the more recent Vatnsmýri International Design Competition which focused on redevelopment opportunities of defunct airport landing strips. Also during this preparatory phase, collective student research was directed toward the creation of provisional codification techniques for the

Laki volcanic fissure system located in Skaftafell National Park
Part of a volcanic fissure system that abides by a cycle of activity that causes a string of eruptions approximately every 850 years. The last eruption, which occurred in 1783, had catastrophic effects in Iceland and its impact was harshly felt throughout Europe for several years. It has been regarded as one of the most significant socially- and culturally-repercussive events of the last millennium causing substantial population depletion in Europe due to famine—a result of the unusually high levels of sulfur dioxide. "The meteorological impact of Laki resonated on, contributing significantly to several years of extreme weather in Europe. In France a sequence of extremes included a surplus harvest in 1785 that caused poverty for rural workers, accompanied by droughts, bad winters and summers, including a violent hailstorm in 1788 that destroyed crops. This in turn contributed significantly to the build-up of poverty and famine that triggered the French Revolution in 1789."
—Richard H. Grove, Nature 393 (1998).

site's ecological, geological, biological, meteorological systems. Building from existing maps and current geographic information systems, students invented synoptic mapping methods—simulations—highlighting changing conditions over several different scales of time.

Travel within Iceland's The Golden Circle exposed students to the tangible implications of its geological variation and volatility on processes of infrastructural development and urbanization. One portion of the trip provided an introductory and historic ecotour including time at Iceland's major geological features; Thermal Baths at Blue Lagoon, Thingvellir National Park, Oxararar River, Thingvellir Lake, the Lava Fields, and Gulfoss. Students further articulated analytical mapping techniques begun prior to departure based on in-field verification. The second portion of the trip was spent at several sites along The Golden Circle empirically documenting the specific sites of the studio. During this portion of the trip, students were asked to formulate a position regarding the potential role of ecotourism as a foundational organizational strategy for the future sustainable development in Iceland.

Upon their return, students designed parametric models which reference specific 'cycles'—documented temporal characteristics—such as ecological, geological, biological, and meteorological systems. These relational models formed the basis of the organizational potential of a masterplan for architectural interventions that line The Golden Circle. The models developed were to be responsive to changing field conditions and were to privilege architectural strategies that register time-based processes. Students invented novel systems of organization at the intersection of visual and spatial fields, with the promise of eliciting new formations capable of providing diverse urban ecologies and alternative architecturally-performative characteristics. At its core, the studio explored flexible part-to-whole relationships that were able to differentiate to produce adaptive architectural organizations.

Cycles Studio: Composite Terrains

Students designed parametric models which reference specific 'cycles'–
documented temporal characteristics–such as ecological, geological,
biological, and meteorological systems. These relational models formed
the basis of the organizational potential of a masterplan for architectural
interventions that line The Golden Circle.

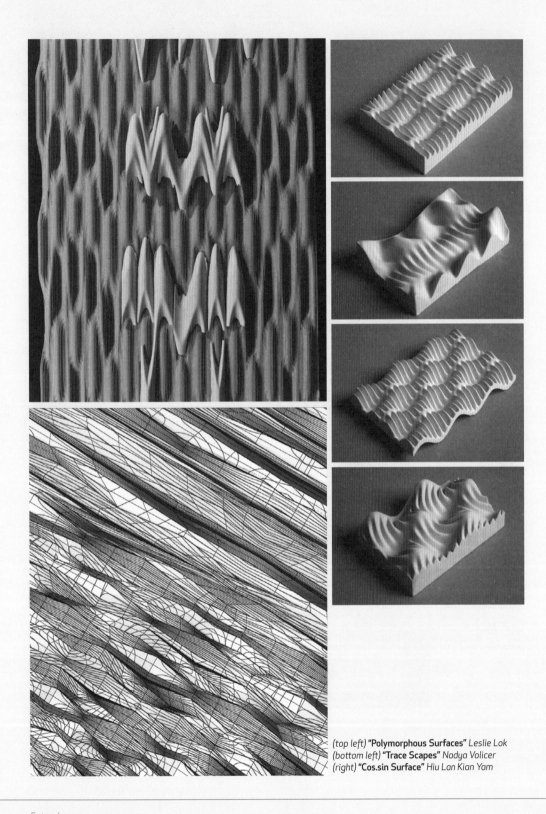

(top left) **"Polymorphous Surfaces"** *Leslie Lok*
(bottom left) **"Trace Scapes"** *Nadya Volicer*
(right) **"Cos.sin Surface"** *Hiu Lan Kian Yam*

(top) **"De_Orchestrated Landscape"** *Sasa Zivkovic*
(bottom) **"Composite Systems"** *Lisa Hedstrom*

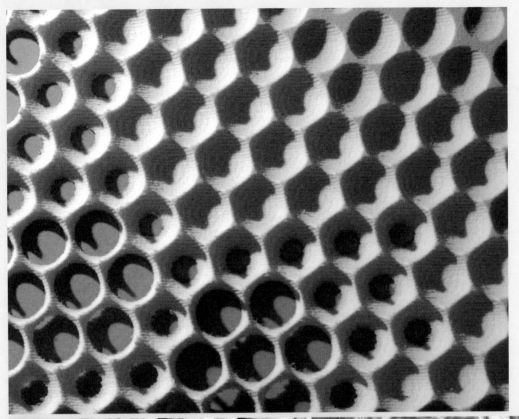

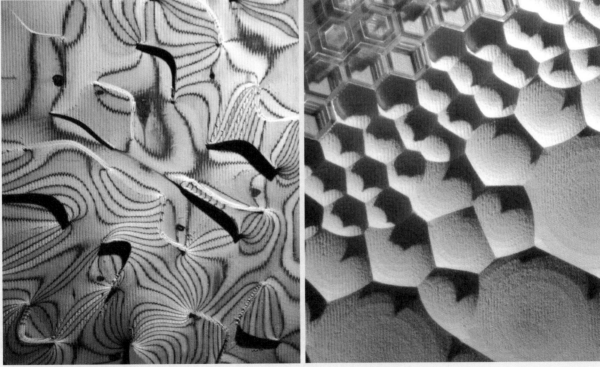

(top, bottom right) **"Composite Systems"**
Ella Peinovich
(bottom left) **"Slicing Continuity"**
Yushiro Okamoto

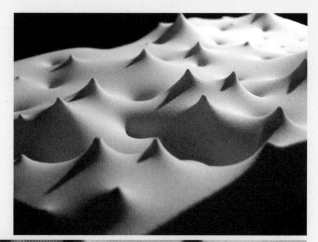

(top) **"Composite Systems"** *Lisa Hedstrom*
(bottom) **"Slicing Continuity"** *Yushiro Okamoto*

Sasa Zivkovic | MArch
Geoformer

Geoformer operates on the edge between the artificial (man-made, synthetic_ and the natural (organic) within ordering systems in landscapes. Because of the relatively young landscape in Iceland, the man-made collides with nature very directly and sometimes brutally. Interestingly, out of these collisions between two systems a third order emerges that occupies the 'in-between': a domestic landscape layer that lies in the realm of both the synthetic and the organic. Geoformer is trying to operate within this 'third condition', which is mostly created under the influence of geothermal energy, and is aiming to create a geothermal domestic landscape layer.

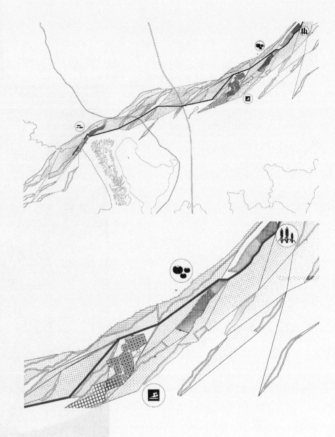

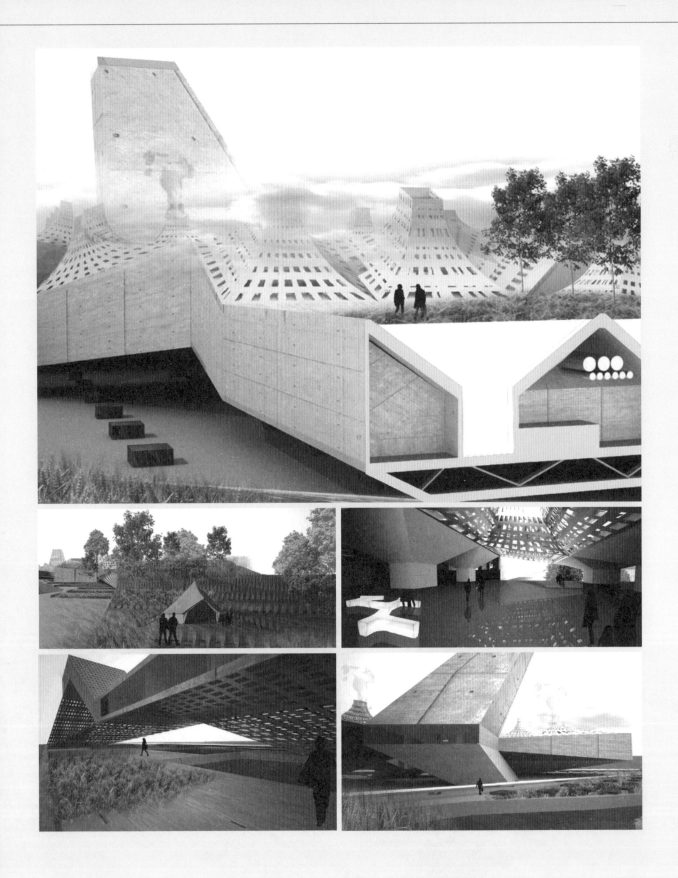

Ella Peinovich | MArch
Ecotourism Post: Hydrology

The proposal for education and research within the desert station is centralized around the understanding of braided rivers. According to the Institute for the Study of Continents, Department for Geological Sciences as Cornell University, efforts to characterize river flows for most glacierized basins have been severely restricted by a paucity of discharge observations. This problem is due to a combination of (1) harsh weather conditions and low accessibility, (2) high costs associated with maintaining stream gauges in these remote areas, and (3) widely shifting systems are virtually impossible to gauge using traditional stage-recording devices. They believe that defining the complex hydrologic and sedimentologic processes that interact to form a braided channel configuration are crucial in understanding the relationship among climate, glacier mass balance, and hydrology.

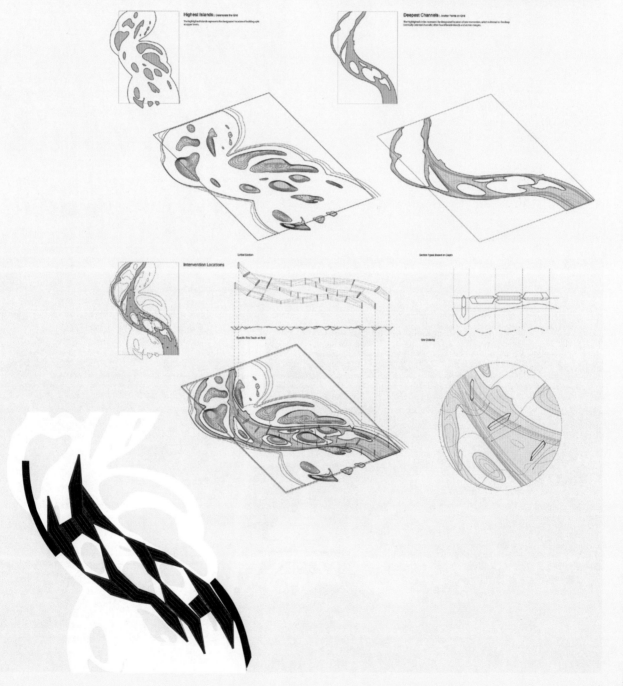

SKY EVENT FAST [FESTIVAL OF ART SCIENCE AND TECHNOLOGY] PROJECT

Otto Piene, Emeritus Professor of Architecture

Rising above the Great Dome of MIT, immense inflatable stars soared over Killian Court on the evening of May 7 during FAST Light, the culminating event of the MIT150 Festival of Art, Science and Technology. The sculptures celebrated–and incorporated–the distinctive symbiosis among artists, scientists and engineers that emerged at MIT during the 1960s with the founding of the Center for Advanced Visual Studies and continues today throughout the Institute. This event began in the afternoon as the sculptures were arrayed on the ground and–with the help of a crew of students and alumni–started to inflate. The stars launched at dusk and were fully illuminated at 9:00 pm, floating overhead while members of the crew and the audience kept them tethered to the earth. This participatory event was a collaborative art process leading to luminous images against the canvas of the night sky.

Photographs copyright Andy Ryan. Drawing courtesy of Otto Piene.

MEGAFORM: A FRAME OF OPPOSITION M.ARCH. THESIS

John T. Pugh
Supervisor: **Alexander D'Hooghe**
Readers: **Rahul Mehrotra, John Ochsendorf**

The contemporary city is a wasteland of generic strip malls, big boxes and cookie-cutter housing. Its urban form has largely been shaped by its most popular means of transportation, the internal combustion vehicle. Architecture as a profession has struggled to discover a means to create a substantial impact within this infinite urban plane. However, one urban building typology capable of producing these effects has evolved over the past century, largely ignored by our profession: the megaform. This typology provides the framework for architects to profoundly influence their cities. Alternatives, such as the suburban shopping mall and the new urbanist town center exist all across the United States. These historicized non-spaces are lost within the sprawl of the metropolitan area due to their genericness, lack of cultural or civic programming and their inherent spatial and social rigidity. This project is a critique of these interventions and provides an alternative proposition. This proposition accepts that urban form is strongly influenced by its modes of transportation and speculates about the development of an urban realm made possible by the electric vehicle. This infrastructural proposition integrates a transportation network for the electric vehicle with the megaform typology to create an urban nexus within the space endlessness of the contemporary city.

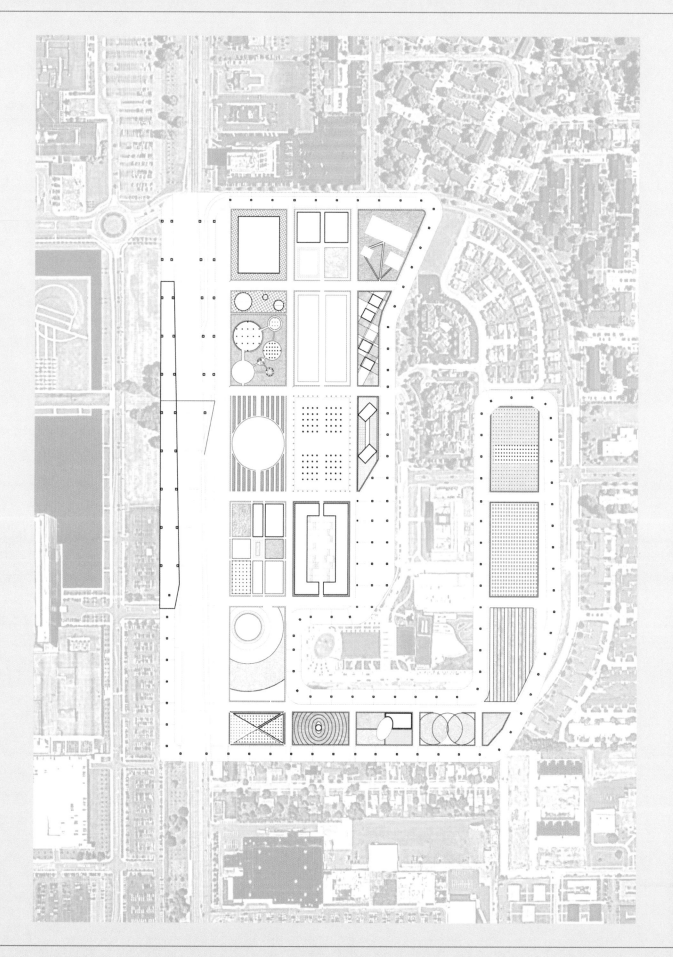

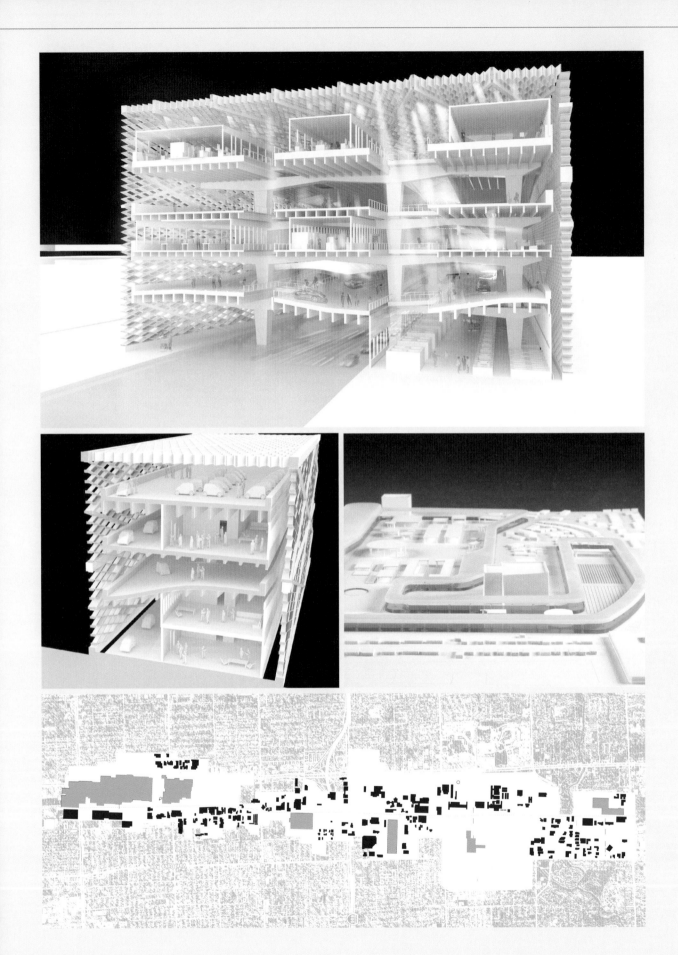

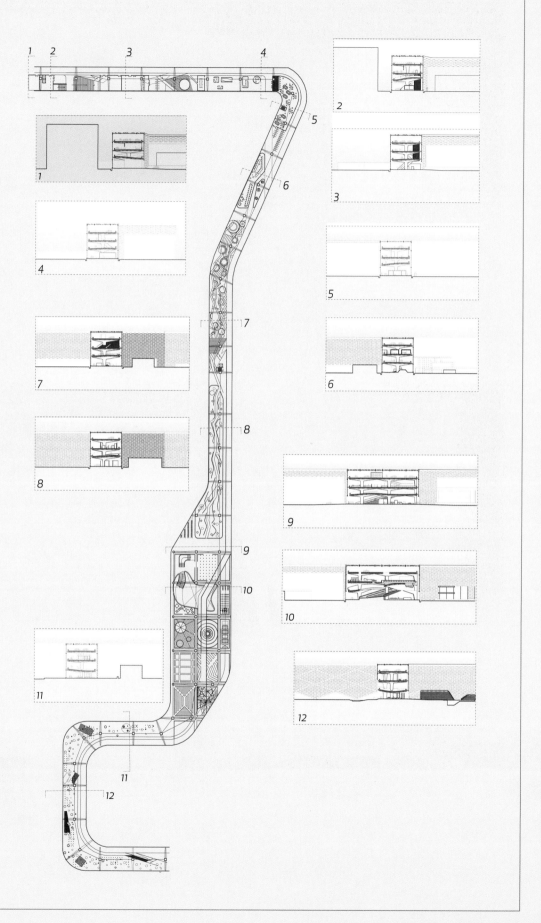

TUKTOYAKTUK: RESPONSIVE STRATEGIES FOR A NEW ARCTIC URBANISM M.ARCH. THESIS

Pamela R. Ritchot
Supervisor: **Ana Miljački**
Readers: **Nasser Rabbat, Pierre Bélanger**

The Canadian Arctic is facing a set of compounding crises that will drastically impact the future of its coastal frontier. At a time when climate change is having a detrimental impact on the Arctic landscape, Northern communities are on the frontline of resource development where industrial money promises major territorial and social change. In this way, the Inuvialuit population of Tuktoyaktuk will find opportunity in crisis as they strategically manipulate both the agendas of the petroleum industry as well as the federal government's own incentive for Northern development. These forces will facilitate the construction of a new coastal frontier–a new Arctic territory grown out of the momentum of oil urbanization and national sovereignty. This strategic growth will secure a post-oil economy for Tuktoyaktuk, while defending it from the rising sea. This form of oil urbanization provides the architectural and infrastructural imperative for this thesis, as change will occur rapidly and at a much larger scale than these communities could spark or manage on their own. The Tuktoyaktuk landscape will undoubtedly become transformed by the creation of occupiable, defensive infrastructure that secures new land from which to reimagine the Arctic territory and its temporal interface with a rising sea and a changing economy.

Mobilized by the demands and goals of the Inuvialuit population, this thesis examines Tuktoyaktuk as an exemplary model for strategic modernization and development of remote Arctic communities on the frontline of industrialization. The goal of designing this enhanced urban structure is to make use of the finite economic opportunity at hand, in order to set up the framework from which the community will thrive and grow upon the retreat of the oil operations. By maximizing the opportunities that emerge from these complexities of place, we begin to unveil a unique and timely moment for architectural and infrastructural innovation as well as a critical framework from which new discussions on the future of the Arctic territory–and remote industrialization globally, arise.

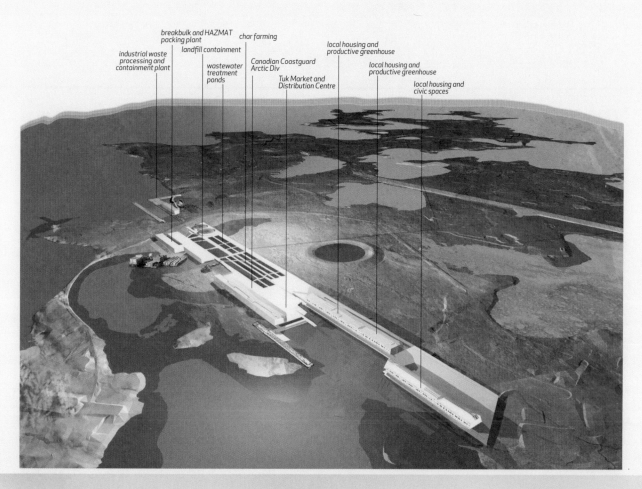

industrial waste
processing and
containment plant

breakbulk and HAZMAT
packing plant

landfill containment

wastewater
treatment
ponds

char farming

Canadian Coastguard
Arctic Div

Tuk Market and
Distribution Centre

local housing and
productive greenhouse

local housing and
productive greenhouse

local housing and
civic spaces

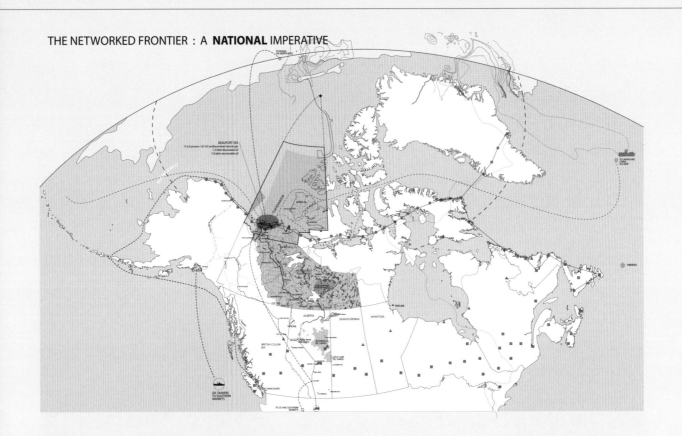

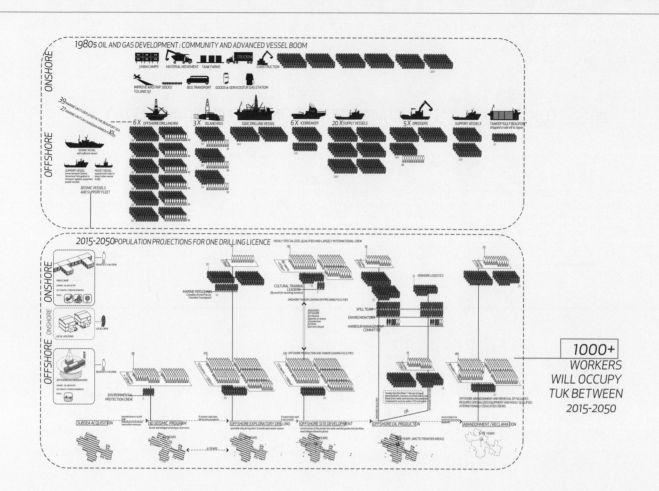

1980s OIL AND GAS DEVELOPMENT : COMMUNITY AND ADVANCED VESSEL BOOM

2015-2050 POPULATION PROJECTIONS FOR ONE DRILLING LICENCE

1000+
WORKERS
WILL OCCUPY
TUK BETWEEN
2015-2050

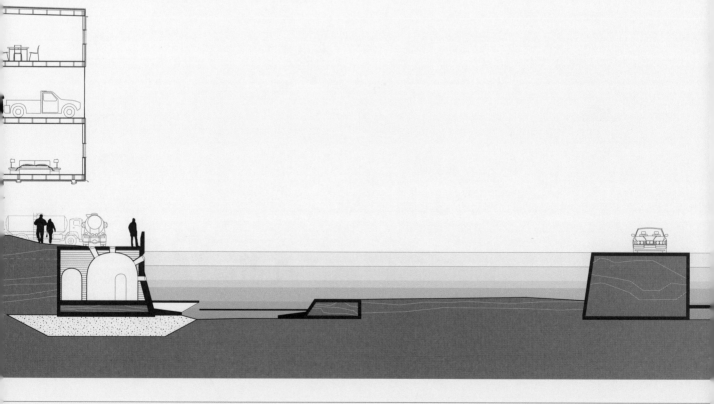

2015 : TUKTOYAKTUK'S LAND MANIPULATION BY THE OIL INDUSTRY

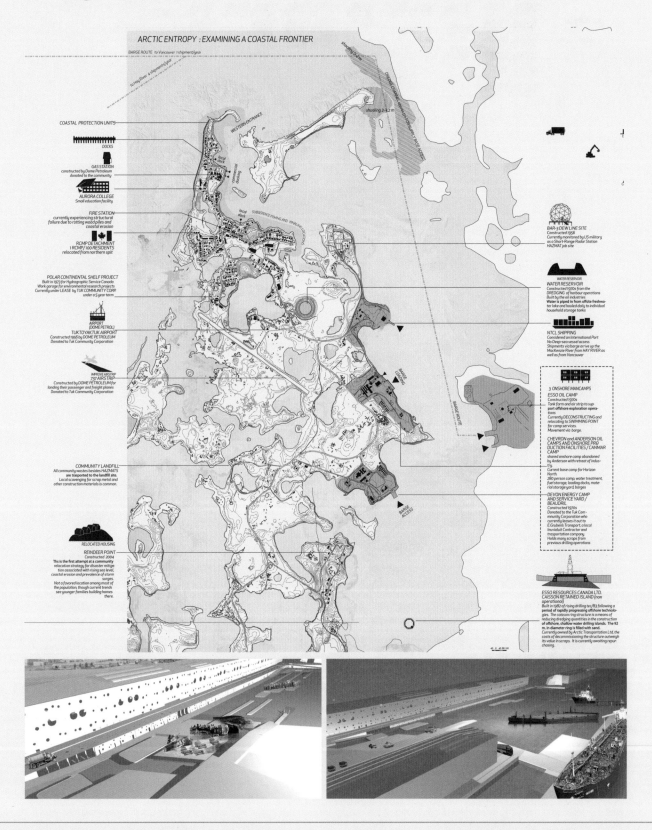

ARCTIC ENTROPY : EXAMINING A COASTAL FRONTIER

BARGE ROUTE to Vancouver 1 shipment/year

to Hay River 6 shipments/year

shooting 2-3.2 m

WESTERN ENTRANCE

COASTAL PROTECTION UNITS

DOCKS

local dock

commercial docking

GAS STATION
constructed by Dome Petroleum
donated to the community

AURORA COLLEGE
Small education facility

local dock

SUBSISTENCE FISHING AND WHALING

FIRE STATION
currently experiencing structural
failure due to rotting wood piles and
coastal erosion

RCMP DETACHMENT
1 RCMP/100 RESIDENTS
relocated from northern spit

POLAR CONTINENTAL SHELF PROJECT
Built in 1973 for Hydrographic Service Canada
Work garage for environmental research projects
Currently under LEASE by TUK COMMUNITY CORP
under a 5 year term

AIRPORT
(DOME PETROL)
TUKTOYAKTUK AIRPORT
Constructed 1956 by DOME PETROLEUM
Donated to Tuk Community Corporation

IMPROVE AIRSTRIP
737 AIRSTRIP
Constructed by DOME PETROLEUM for
landing their passenger and freight planes
Donated to Tuk Community Corporation

COMMUNITY LANDFILL
All community wastes besides HAZMATS
are transported to the landfill site.
Local scavenging for scrap metal and
other construction materials is common.

RELOCATED HOUSING

REINDEER POINT
Constructed 2004
This is the first attempt at a community
relocation strategy for disaster mitiga-
tion associated with rising sea level,
coastal erosion and prevalence of storm
surges.
Not a favored location among most of
the population, though current trends
see younger families building homes
there.

BAR-3 DEW LINE SITE
Constructed 1956
Currently monitored by US military
as a Short-Range Radar Station
HAZMAT job site

WATER RESERVOIR
Constructed 1970s from the
DREDGING of harbour operations
Built by the oil industries
Water is piped in from offsite freshwa-
ter lake and hauled daily to individual
household storage tanks

NTCL SHIPPING
Considered an International Port
No Deep-sea vessel access
Shipments via barge arrive up the
MacKenzie River from HAY RIVER as
well as from Vancouver

BARGE LOADING

BARGE ROUTE

3 ONSHORE MANCAMPS
ESSO OIL CAMP
Constructed 1970s
Tank farm and air strip to sup-
port offshore exploration opera-
tions
Currently DECONSTRUCTING and
relocating to SWIMMING POINT
for camp services.
Movement via barge.

**CHEVRON and ANDERSON OIL
CAMPS AND ONSHORE PRO-
DUCTION FACILITIES / CANMAR
CAMP**
shared onshore camp abandoned
by Anderson won retreat of industry.
Current base camp for Horizon
North.
280 person camp, water treatment,
fuel storage, loading docks, material storage yard, barges

**DEVON ENERGY CAMP
AND SERVICE YARD /
BEAUDRIL**
Constructed 1970s
Donated to the Tuk Com-
munity Corporation who
currently leases it out to
E.Grubens Transport, a local
Inuvialuit Contractor and
trasportation company.
Holds many scraps from
previous drilling operations

BARGE ACCESS

**ESSO RESOURCES CANADA LTD.
CAISSON RETAINED ISLAND** (non
operational)
Built in 1982 of rapidly progressing offshore technologies. The caisson ring structure is a means of
reducing dredging quantities in the construction
of offshore, shallow water drilling islands. The 92
m. in diameter ring is filled with sand.
Currently owned by Arctic Transportation Ltd, the
costs of decommissioning the structure outweigh
its value in scraps. It is currently awaiting repur-
chasing.

40 0 40 80 100

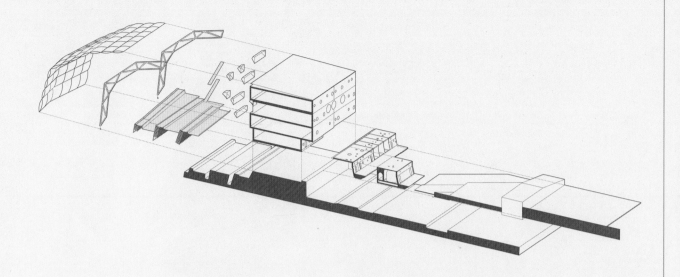

2050 : CRISIS! 60% OF LANDMASS LOST TO RISING WATERS

2050 : INUNDATION THREATENS WEAKENED HOUSING STOCK

CHANGING COASTLINE : CLIMATE CHANGE AND STORM SURGE
2040

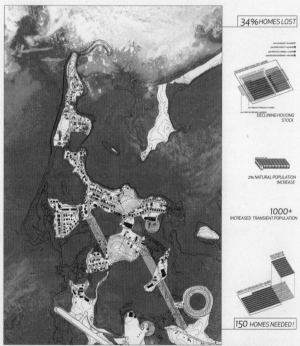

34% HOMES LOST

DECLINING HOUSING STOCK

2% NATURAL POPULATION INCREASE

1000+
INCREASED TRANSIENT POPULATION

150 HOMES NEEDED!

NUMERICS

DIGITAL RECURSIONS

Images courtesy of Mark Goulthorpe and Lawrence Sass.

"Yes, there once was a dogmatic and dogged figure called 'architect,' who collaged rectilinear industrial plates and sticks via contractual (in)tolerance! But this figure dissolved into a swirl of digits, his very definition blurring in depth with/in variant systems. And the newly malleable, hermaphrodite figure will doubtless evolve a ranging, liquid intellect, dis-focussed as to the material actuality of a work, but sentient to the manipulation of a normative range of immergence itself. Authority, now diffuse, lies in the code, no longer in the architecture."[1]

"It's getting the information out of the machine that makes all the difference."[2]

In discussion of computation in architecture, one query prevails over others: what is the difference between a designer and a programmer? What part of architectural conception–given its somewhat superhuman generative and form-finding abilities–is the computer responsible for? Computation in architecture almost threatens to breed a sort of extra-human objectivity, a threat that is not without its appeal. In its first phase, programming for design seldom carried this threat, given that its functions were generally oriented towards systematically optimizing things like ventilation, static or mechanical qualities, things that a computer could be trusted to churn out a respectably verifiable answer to; the calculative or algorithmic formulae lay outside the machine, and what the machine largely afforded was computational speed.[3] As controls and interfaces have become more subtle, more amenable to non-machinists and code-writers, appearing as if possessed of a second-order, daemonic subjectivity, vocabulary has begun to slide back almost towards nostalgia–a marked contrast from the hyper-justified programism of recent decades.

In a recent article in the New Yorker, Adam Gopnik hypothesized that as computers become more intelligent, the humans who use them begin to change

Goetz Boat Company—part of Mark Goulthorpe/ dECOi's materials review
The highly choreographed process of composite boat building offers clues to architecture about streamlining the construction process and materials use.

what they qualify as intelligence in a complicated kind of give-and-take.[4] As number-crunching and rapid-response systems are outsourced to machines, we forget that at one time, one's facility with those very same routine calculations counted as smartness itself. An operation of this order might be in play for architecture now, as computational design tools become ever more ubiquitous in the studio and we continue to debate the role of the designer. While user interfaces have developed to great lengths, there is new concern that perhaps the operator doesn't quite know enough about the workings of the programming that's going on behind the scenes. Either way, it's an uncomfortable but extremely productive alliance of human and machine, one that continues to break new ground in terms of exploration of form, fabrication, pattern generation, and efficiency.

In a recent talk in MIT's Department of Architecture Discipline Group Lecture Series, David Benjamin of The Living touched upon the important and interesting point of optimization in a world of super-optimal computationally-derived structural solutions. Looking at a curve plotted by thousands of adequate data points for his parametric derivation of a canopy structure's column placement, suddenly his subjective voice returned. Computation's mathematical power was effectively bounded, and the architect's power in evaluation returned. Paradoxically, as we asymptotically approach fully computational architectures, we are drawn back into the fray as aesthetes. As we become more agile in our manipulation of tools, power is again clearly situated with the designer. Faced with only the most robust solutions to a problem, the architect nonetheless was called upon in this instance to select *that which he found most suitable.*

Parametrics, as a conceptual concern, has received its fair share of bricks and accolades since proponents such as Greg Lynn, and subsequently others, like Ali Rahim and Zaha Hadid, first started to introduce software programs sourced from animation studios and industrial design into architectural studios. At first gasp, the effects were electric, as school after school competed to introduce these techniques into design curricula. The hypnosis, in retrospect, was easy enough to see: the sudden relieving of heuristic models into infinite formal possibilities, reducing architects' design approach to less a matter of considered stances and more an arbitrary action. And yet, if the edge of animation software works

Bankside Paramorph–Mark Goulthorpe/ dECOi
The ongoing project combines complex parametric computational design processes with composite material technologies informing the details.

only to effect mimesis, Hollywood's visual effects produce fantastic worlds that appear, paradoxically and banally, all-too familiar. And if industrial design technologies are always guided by clearly demarcated constraints of performance and economy, architecture appeared to have little such constraint, leading itself, in its conceptual blindness, to the abyssal terrain of the blob: amorphous pièces de résistance whose attributes lay more in a refusal of ontological determination than in a durable aesthetic program. This very amorphousness, however, brings out an essential question of architecture that the somewhat more timeworn attitudes in architectural pedagogy may be more apprehensive about engaging: what is precedence in architecture? If architecture is relieved of the problem and burdens of recuperating a given history of forms, by what heuristic can architectural

form-finding be arrived at? Conversely, is architecture to be perennially condemned by the tropes of familiarity, of recognition? Is what we consider good architecture simply a reflection of what we already know? If familiarity is not a constraint, what other internal modalities of critique can architecture bring to order in order to equip itself with the capability to judge (objects, arrangements, arrays, etc.)? Perhaps a Duchamp, a Beuys, or the Robert Morris of the felt pieces, could empathise.

Within the field of parametric computing, new focuses on fabrication and the relationship of computer space to real physicality are emerging. Two figures on seemingly different sides of the computational coin at MIT have found their research gaining urgency in its translation to tangible form. Architect and Professor Larry Sass, a graduate of both the S.M.Arch.S. and Ph.D. programs in computation, wants to bring the power of the parametric to consumers on a very individual scale. One of his recent projects, featured in the 2008 MoMA *Home Delivery* show in New York, proposes a type of mass customization of housing, where parts can be economically cut and assembled on site, creating a new meaning for prefab and individualized design. Architect and Professor Mark Goulthorpe, on the other hand, believes that old materials are for old design processes. The real appeal of outputting from a sophisticated software package is sophisticatedly realized results. The future for him is in composites that effectively override the traditional craft-based detailing systems on which so much of architecture

currently relies. While Goulthorpe may be thinking on a very long-term scale, setting goals for his research that are well outside of what is now possible, and while Sass is firmly rooted in the possible, the immediately realizable with tools and materials we already have, both contribute to active debates at MIT. For these two designers deeply invested in technology, the interface to the real is the most important next phase and their two proposals for it are playing out in studios and workshops throughout the School.

It might seem too pragmatic to obsess over the details of the built when ideas about complex geometries and innovative scripting techniques are on the table, but both Goulthorpe and Sass realize that the real power of parametrics and robust computational systems lies outside of the computer. As Sass reminds us, the design process has always been one of iteration and testing, and physical models carry important design revelations that are impossible to experience elsewhere. For him, rapid prototyping technologies work so that the architect can quickly see what she's designed, working back and forth between computer and model, testing ideas. It's actually working the computer back into a traditional design process where "you make something, you reflect upon it, you make something, you reflect upon it, and it develops quickly based upon how quickly you make your file. But if it takes a long time, like in the use of hand devices, it goes slower."[5] Moreover, the use of parametric components in digital models almost requires a "parametric" or a rapidly repeatable and testable physical model interface. But there are two different types of fabrication being discussed here– studio-level design tests and full-scale habitable structures.

Where Sass sees prototyping tools as accelerating a very traditional form of design dialogue, Goulthorpe uses the principles behind parametric computation to dramatically reconceive the entire design process. If parameters are limits to work within and there is a very dynamic type of

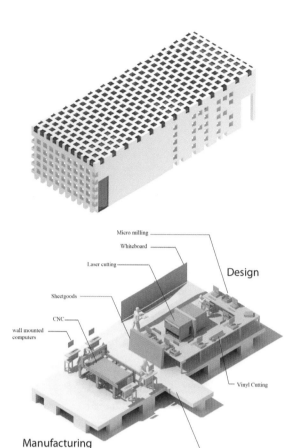

Mobile Fab Lab–Larry Sass
The next step in accessible rapid prototyping is building facilities on-site from easily constructed parts.

back-and-forth that is possible, many options all fitting the designer's criteria, he sees design itself taking on a new shape. "What is most interesting, perhaps, is that one is here not so much designing an object as designing the *possibility* of an object, a system which can give multiple digital births, which certainly demands a reconsideration of 'design' process."[6] This new configuration almost works backwards, saying that in this climate of ranges for acceptable values, perhaps the system is the product, and the outcomes are just multiple iterations that satisfy an overall system. The radical aspect of Goulthorpe's embrace of the parametric is not what complex geometries or innovative structures can be reaped, though they certainly remain exciting by-products. Rather, it is the fundamental critique of the designer's decision-making process as made plain in the logical relationships between parameters as they themselves are designed.

One Main–Mark Goulthorpe/ dECOi
The ends of finishes and furnishings in the One Main project are also treated as scriptable surfaces since the production process renders this treatment easily accessible.

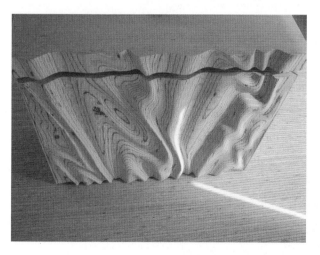

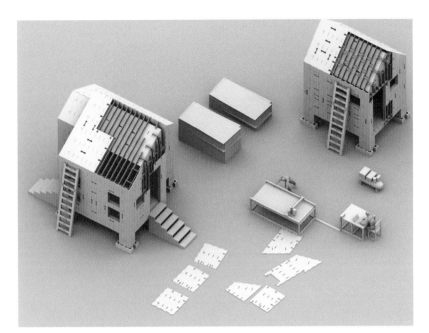

In his foreword to a collection of Goulthorpe's essays, John McMorrough summarizes this condition as a step deeper into the workings of architecture itself. "An eminently modernist vocation, architecture remains an exploration of the limits of a medium, but now this medium is the method, not the message."[7] And indeed Goulthorpe agrees, citing choreographer William Forsythe's work for opening up his eyes to a new type of creative endeavor and a new type of deliverable. "Their architectural design," he writes, "was not so much a formal proposition as it was a processural one, no longer an architecture but the possibility of an architecture."[8] If the medium is the method, Goulthorpe couples his interest in exposing the workings of the method with further critical and philosophical distance. At one remove is the very notion of parametric architecture, design based on a series of acceptable values rather than singular correct ones. At the second is an understanding of what the implications of this unraveling might be on the discipline, on the foundation of decision-based design, and what potentials this might hold. In this sense, Goulthorpe's use of the parametric is as a mode, rather than

a style, or even a tool in the primitive sense. In this way, he operates independently of specific software or interfaces.

Developments in fabrication technology don't just mean easier or more affordable construction, they permit a broader re-thinking of the way design disciplines integrate fabrication into their conception. Because details actually drive the assembly of a building, architects often design

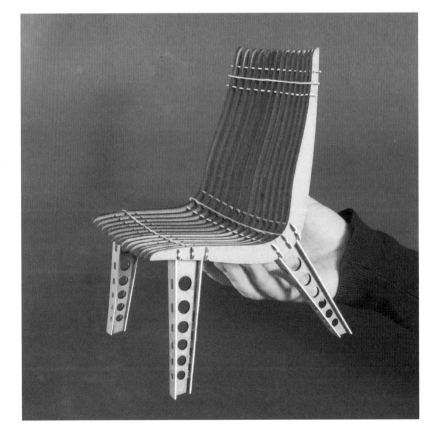

CNC Chair Design–Maggie Nelson
One of Sass's students with a mock-up of her design for a CNC-cut chair.

to them, knowing that however the overall form of a building, it will be broken down into its component parts for construction details and shop drawings for tradesmen. Their methods and practices affect the way that architects optimize, and thus design, buildings. Small-scale rapid prototyping machines allow quick prints in a variety of materials, but only up to a certain size. To harness the power of rapid prototyping machines in a large scale requires re-thinking how you design for construction, and how you design with specific tools in mind. Much as the entire early design phase has been revolutionized by computational tools, so are the later phases of construction now encountering a crossroads with still unclear implications for specialized professionals like engineers, contractors, and project managers. "What does the new organization of labor among these professionals look like? Is the news good or bad, and from whom?"[9]

CAD drafting is now commonplace, scripting and parametric form-making are curricular assumptions, and BIM products that monitor building maintenance are on the rise. But what still remains to be seen is the automation of construction and the integration of rapid prototyping technologies into full-scale fabrication. Considering the amount of computing power that goes into the design of buildings these days, it is indeed surprising that the end of that workflow is often measured construction drawings printed on rolls of paper. Larry Sass conducts research in the area of rapid prototyping and its relationship to building construction because it seems that all the ingredients are finally coming together for a revolutionary rethinking of the industry. Current research projects are focused on the design fabrication using computer modeling and prototyping to be used as representational tools in the design process versus paper drawings.

Construction is often the most expensive portion of building new, and the efforts of pre-fabrication towards rapid construction often result in cookie-cutter sameness, hardly a desirable characteristic. Sass believes that affordability and ease of construction should not preclude personalization. In his project to design housing for New Orleans in the wake of Katrina, Sass developed a kit-of-design-parts menu for housing components so that homeowners could choose the cabinetry and ornamentation that spoke to them, in essence allowing them the type of involvement in the look and workings of their house that is usually the province of high-end clients. A computer program would then work through the specifics of the design, outputting sophisticated CNC two-dimensional patterns that could then be cut on-site from standard plywood and assembled using only a rubber mallet.

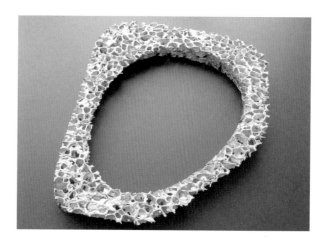

Sinthome Model—waterjet cut aluminum—Mark Goulthorpe/ dECOi
Rapid prototyping allows conceptual computation models to be tested quickly and easily.

While Sass concerns himself with the very practical aspects of getting buildings made rapidly, economically, and with a level of personalization and detail, Goulthorpe looks outside of architecture for inspiration and philosophical allegiances to other arts. He designed his atelier, dECOi, to incorporate outside disciplines and influences, as well as varied scales and platforms. The sort of flexibility that has come of this approach bridges even further into the practice, as it has come to embrace the parametric, not only as a design practice or tool, but as a radical philosophy for designing potentials. As dECOi developed in the 1990s, a key goal was for it to remain open to collaborative, and especially technological, developments. That has indeed remained true. Not loyal to any particular medium or software, the firm has conceived of projects from theoretical computational directions, urging on developments in architectural technology and critically selecting from what is available. It's important to note that Goulthorpe's interest in computational architecture predates much of the software and techniques we use now.

Goulthorpe finds himself in a unique historic position. Having started his practice before the use of computers in architecture was widespread, he nonetheless incorporated aspects of computational logic early and thoughtfully. Musing on this in an interview in *Praxis*, Goulthorpe celebrates the perspective afforded by being an old-timer in a constantly new field. "We learned to draw with one technology and then had to expand our creative capacity to appropriate another . . . whenever new technologies emerge, certain capacities are lost and others are gained, and nostalgia in this regard is really misplaced; simply a new standard is in the offing that intellect has need to explore."[10] This type of long-range appreciation is tinged with the skepticism of an expert. So embedded is Goulthorpe

One Main–Mark Goulthorpe/ dECOi
The interiors were cut and assembled in pieces off-site, allowing installation of furnishings, finishes, and surfaces to arrive all at once, eliminating many typical trades.

in the cutting edge of research and applications of design computing that he is well aware of the pitfalls and shortcomings unique to any one platform. For him, software isn't a lifeline to practice, it's another layer of constraints and possibilities that can be weighed against competitors. This is a very powerful position.

In 2012, the ACSA (Association of Collegiate Schools of Architecture) will hold its 100th Annual Meeting, titled *Digital Aptitudes*, co-chaired by Goulthorpe. The focus of this conference will be the changing nature of technology in architecture, and the theoretical constructs wrought by the tools we use. From the meeting's brief: "as history has taught us, a change in technological paradigm is rarely absorbed efficiently, or in an undisputed manner, even if its effects are profound or beneficial." This critical self-reflection within an academic discipline indicates at once an acceptance of and at the same time a curiosity about the potentials and the ramifications of computation. As advanced tools like 3D visualization and scripting exit the realm of expert technicians and become available to practitioners at large, a desire emerges to find historical analogues and to situate the present within a continuum of technological development.

The call for papers for one panel at the conference, titled *Post-Parametric Environments*, asserts a historic place for the parametric, claiming it as already part of architecture's complex arsenal. Configuring a new meta-project using knowledge gleaned from the immediate past, the prompt states that "fundamental assumptions about parametric thinking, design, and computation need to be re-assessed according to the physical realities of our actual environments and sensory thresholds."[11] There is a gap, then, as this major disciplinary consortium diagnoses it, between computational practices now, and their correspondence to and implications on the physical world. How can we begin to use this knowledge of parameters to actively change the way architecture conceives of its directive? What of this emphasis on the actual as opposed to the virtual?

More than parametrics or computation at large, an overriding strain within Goulthorpe's work and his writing is the idea of expanded notions of practice and discovery. Merging an interest in philosophy and design theory, the long-range goal is to create new ways of experiencing and communicating architecture. It is telling in this way that Goulthorpe returns again and again in his writing to an analogous, or at least symbiotic, relationship between his work in architecture and that of avant-garde choreographer William Forsythe's in dance. Both employing complex rule-based logics to direct artistic output, they begin to question their respective fields from within. In both of these projects, the very production of dance or architecture, the means by which production is conceived and notated, becomes the product itself. Writes Goulthorpe on his lessons from Forsythe: "You have to rethink your creative mode of practice, and if we're going to exploit the potential of computers it will not be through the extension of current modes of thought but by entirely reinventing the creative circuits through which we conceive these projects."[12]

What seems like a dramatic shift in architectural technology has actually been underway for a long time, and it is important to see parametric work within a trajectory. The first computational tools to be widely adopted by the discipline at large were for drafting, automation of the pen-and-ink notational system by which designers communicated with fabricators, contractors, and builders. Though it seems now to be the most rudimentary of developments, the introduction of CAD programs brought with it a radical shift in the workflow and rapid editability of architectural designs. This can be seen as a first-order integration of computation into design. A second-order technological shift might be three-dimensional digital modeling–computer visualization of spaces that allowed designers to radically alter the way they represent and interpret their designs. No longer were

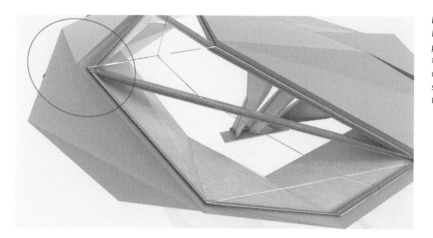

Bankside Paramorph–Mark Goulthorpe/ dECOi
Detailing of composite materials construction process–integrating all fabrication concerns into the design process, rather than designing details afterwards, promotes a new type of comprehensive design, giving the architect more control over the production of the end product.

plans and sections disconnected mute constructions from one another, but dynamically linked and mutually alterable. Parametric and scripting tools might be seen as a third order, a way to not just model architectural ideas in space as singularities, but to dynamically alter them, testing, rejecting, and tweaking results.

But the use of parameters is not an end in itself, nor is it a defined practice, but simply a tool like those that preceded it to aid in the design process. dECOi thoroughly embraces such a logic but also acknowledges its inherent insufficiency. Part of critical engagement with technology requires recognition of its obsolescence, when it is time

to move beyond the tools at hand. dECOi and Goulthorpe's academic research do not stop with the development of specific novel applications–the drive to "develop an appropriate architecture that seems relevant and somewhat adequate to the dramatic technical shift that is taking place around us," ensures a constant *reaching beyond*.[13] The beyond in which we find ourselves presently lies in fabrication, construction, and the new BIM (Building Information Modeling) tools that go with it.

One Main–Mark Goulthorpe/ dECOi
Interior as built, showing integration of furnishings as well as technical details including lighting and ductwork.

Looking at other industries, boat building in particular, Goulthorpe champions the use of new material technologies as well.[14] What use, this move asks, is a completely dynamic modeling and design process if it is eventually bound by traditional methods of construction? In order to fully express the possibilities of these new computational tools, a parallel innovation must take place in fabrication. Goulthorpe believes that to produce the most robust, rich design product, all aspects of its conception must be aware of the life it will lead beyond the computer. He is concerned with the "transition-to-construction, which . . . must develop out of the investigative process and be sustained into production" because to not develop the physical in tandem with the virtual is to root it in a perpetual conservatism and to limit its potency.[15]

These sorts of critical technologists, developing the way we use tools along different and interesting paths, are enormously important within the MIT community because their ideas don't necessarily line up with one another. There is still much to be learned about the way that rapid prototyping and parametric design processes will eventually be integrated into the practice, and it's important not to arrive at any conclusions too soon. To actively theorize on the use of technology while simultaneously using it at an Institute known for its aggressive reach for the new is important for fostering dialogue and preventing a counterproductive forestalling of development. As Goulthorpe rightly points out, "the question of technical change, which emphasizes the extent to which technology as 'extensions of man' (in Marshall McLuhan's terms) is never a simple external prosthesis, but actively infiltrates the human organism, certainly in a cognitive sense," driving the discipline into a complicated back-and-forth of self-examination at the hands of new practices.[16] That both Sass and Goulthorpe have zeroed in on the transition to physical form as an important nexus of these issues indicates trending toward a next phase of negotiation and discussion between designers and the tools they use. Whether or not "[the] expanding technology of computer software and digital fabrication techniques promises to make it possible for architects to regain their proper and responsible role," as some might optimistically foretell, it's clear that things are certainly changing for the different.[17]

1   Mark Goulthorpe, *The Possibility of (an) Architecture; Collected Essays by Mark Goulthorpe / dECOi*. New York: Routledge, 2008, 179.

2   Federico Casalegno, ed. "An Interview with Larry Sass," MIT, Cambridge, Fall 2003; web accessed at http://web.media.mit.edu/~federico/creativity/sass/sass_trans.htm on 4/12/11, 4:47 pm.

3   Nigel Cross, *The Automated Architect*. London: Pion Limited, 1977, 3.

4   Adam Gopnik, "Get Smart," in *The New Yorker*, April 4, 2011, 74.

5   Federico Casalegno, ed. "An Interview with Larry Sass," MIT, Cambridge, Fall 2003; web accessed at http://web.media.mit.edu/~federico/creativity/sass/sass_trans.htm on 4/12/11, 4:47 pm.

6   Mark Goulthorpe, "Parametric Profligacy, Radical Economy," in Peggy Deamer and Phillip G. Bernstein, eds. *Building (in) the Future; Recasting Labor in Architecture*. New York: Princeton Architectural Press, 2010, 81.

7   John McMorrough, Foreword to *The Possibility of (an) Architecture*, xvii.

8   Mark Goulthorpe, "Parametric Profligacy, Radical Economy," 46.

9   Andrew Ross, Foreword to *Building (in) the Future*, 11.

10 Mark Goulthorpe, Praxis Interview: "Precise Indeterminacy" in *The Possibility of (an) Architecture; Collected Essays by Mark Goulthorpe / dECOi*. New York: Routledge, 2008, 124.

11 Website for the ACSA Digital Aptitudes Conference Call for Papers: https://www.acsa-arch.org/conferences/100_callforpapers.aspx, accessed 17 March 2011 2:37pm.

12 Mark Goulthorpe, *The Possibility of (an) Architecture*, 129.

13 Mark Goulthorpe, *The Possibility of (an) Architecture*, 83.

14 Mark Goulthorpe, "Parametric Profligacy, Radical Economy," 54–56.

15 Mark Goulthorpe, *The Possibility of (an) Architecture*, 44.

16 Mark Goulthorpe, *The Possibility of (an) Architecture*, 38.

17 Robert A. M. Stern, Preface to *Building (in) the Future*, 15.

PLYMOUTH ROCK FILM STUDIOS OPTION DESIGN STUDIO

Instructor: **Mark Goulthorpe**
Teaching Assistant: **Kaustuv de Biswas**

The studio for Fall 2009 will design the theater hub of Plymouth Rock Film studios in Plymouth, MA. This is a real-world project that aims to bring Hollywood to the east coast by establishing a major film campus with 24 sound stages and ancillary support structures on a 1000 acre site–by far the most ambitious break-out of the film industry from its California stronghold. It is located in Plymouth, the 'first' settlement town, since it aims to be pioneering in being a showcase sustainable development and community, offering a vivid new context in which to make films, and as a model to other developments worldwide–so the 'first' of a new type of settlement. The project is currently undergoing strategic design, which involves engineers and architects from Arup in London, who are laying out an 'ecological' blueprint for what an entirely benign development might entail, involving a 30-year plan for driving towards an entirely renewable operability.

The theater hub is the centerpiece of the complex, where film premieres and events will take place, with a great diversity of use. Of necessity, it must establish a decisive image and identity for the entire studio complex, as well as being seen as a manifestation of its sustainable ideals. Plymouth Rock has reached out to MIT and other centers of research excellence with the idea of championing deci-sive game-changing technologies in pursuit of zero carbon strategies. I've estab-lished the link with Arup, and I've also brought leading boat-building technologies into play, drawing from the world-renowned industry in Rhode Island (Goetz Technologies), suggesting new CAD-CAM fabrication techniques that might offer a legitimate vernacular architecture with a distinctive new look and feel, redolent of contemporary local skill.

The studio will be immersed in the quite radical and holistic 'flows' that Arup have outlined, where waste, energy, food, etc become drivers of architectural form; but most crucially we will pursue the client's expressed interest in establishing a vital new architectural beacon through inventive use of prescient building technologies drawn from sophisticated related fields of design/fabrication. We will engage with some of the leading engineers, urbanists and architects from Ove Arup, as well as with the legendary boat builder Eric Goetz (several Americas Cup yachts), and the charismatic film producers that are the driving force of Plymouth Rock-David Kirkpatrick and Earl Lestz (Paramount/Disney).

Lisa Hedstrom | MArch
Cutaneous Theater

By using the technologies of the boat building industry, the Cutaneous Theater is able to embed ancillary programs in the hyper-performative skin, like heating, cooling and vertical circulation. To maximize the skin's performance, the theater also embeds smaller unitized programs, where the proximity of their relative conditioning will minimize the effective conditioning needed throughout. This strategy challenges the traditional approach of building multiple structures as redundant and excessive, especially in the difficult New England climate.

Embedded in the hillside to take advantage of thermal mass, the form of a unitized aggregation is defined in a parametric model where holistic 'flows' like daylighting, natural ventilation, waste and energy become drivers for the form. Each bay is defined by span, structural depth, orientation to prevailing winds and solar gain. Each element is formed out of insulated polycarbonate over a polyurethane foam mold in local nautical fabrication shops and is limited in size to accommodate transportation on a commercial truck. The elements are designed with stairs, seating, and infrastructural plugs premilled into their form, shifting labor from man to machine.

Each program has a specific relationship to the parametric model with the theater accommodating wide spans and almost entirely opaque to lighting conditions. The roof is deployed to open to the north and west, capturing light and ventilation, which can help quickly cool the space and reduce the need for artificial lighting. On the northern facade, the aperture contracts, blocking light and noise for a galley of digital editing rooms. Between the modules, space can expand locally to accommodate fire stairs, elevators, utility shafts and ventilation ducts. One bay is allocated as a loading dock, minimizing paved surfaces on site, while the central atrium provides a social anchor to take advantage of the collective creative potential of the occupants.

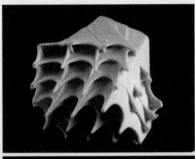

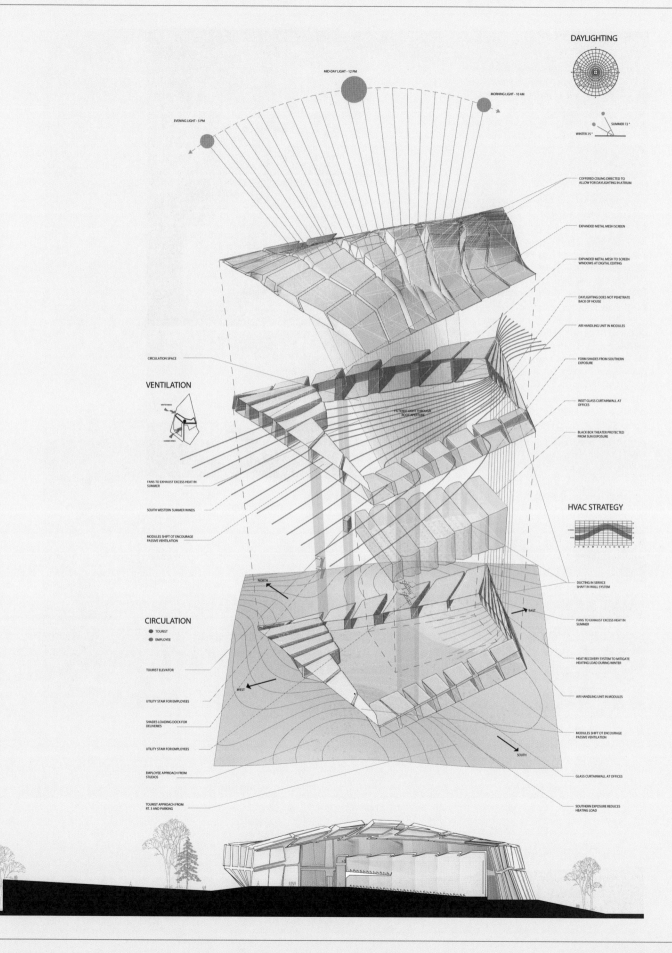

DAYLIGHTING

MORNING LIGHT - 10 AM

MID-DAY LIGHT - 12 PM

EVENING LIGHT - 5 PM

SUMMER 72°

WINTER 25°

COFFERED CEILING DIRECTED TO ALLOW FOR DAYLIGHTING IN ATRIUM

EXPANDED METAL MESH SCREEN

EXPANDED METAL MESH TO SCREEN WINDOWS AT DIGITAL EDITING

DAYLIGHTING DOES NOT PENETRATE BACK OF HOUSE

AIR HANDLING UNIT IN MODULES

FORM SHADES FROM SOUTHERN EXPOSURE

INSET GLASS CURTAINWALL AT OFFICES

BLACK BOX THEATER PROTECTED FROM SUN EXPOSURE

CIRCULATION SPACE

VENTILATION

FILTERED LIGHT THROUGH ROOF APERTURE

FANS TO EXHAUST EXCESS HEAT IN SUMMER

SOUTH WESTERN SUMMER WINDS

MODULES SHIFT OT ENCOURAGE PASSIVE VENTILATION

HVAC STRATEGY

NORTH

EAST

WEST

SOUTH

DUCTING IN SERVICE SHAFT IN WALL SYSTEM

FANS TO EXHAUST EXCESS HEAT IN SUMMER

HEAT RECOVERY SYSTEM TO MITIGATE HEATING LOAD DURING WINTER

AIR HANDLING UNIT IN MODULES

MODULES SHIFT OT ENCOURAGE PASSIVE VENTILATION

GLASS CURTAINWALL AT OFFICES

SOUTHERN EXPOSURE REDUCES HEATING LOAD

CIRCULATION

● TOURIST
● EMPLOYEE

TOURIST ELEVATOR

UTILITY STAIR FOR EMPLOYEES

SHADES LOADING DOCK FOR DELIVERIES

UTILITY STAIR FOR EMPLOYEES

EMPLOYEE APPROACH FROM STUDIOS

TOURIST APPROACH FROM RT. 3 AND PARKING

FORM FOLLOWS SUNLIGHT OPTION DESIGN STUDIO
SPRING 2010

Instructor: **Stephen Cassell**
Teaching Assistant: **Ari Kardasis**

This research-based studio will investigate the relationship between form, meaning and sunlight. Architecture has a long tradition of generating form and meaning in response to the sun, and the control of how light moves through space. The advent of digital modeling tools enables the quick simulation of light conditions, making it extremely easy to see the affects of light on a space. Paradoxically, this ease of visualization has eroded our fundamental knowledge of the sun and light in the service of design. In essence, these tools have wrested control from the architect. At the same time, there has been a field-changing explosion of work on advanced form-making through the use of digital modeling tools and especially parametric modeling. The potential to connect these variables to larger issues of performance–like sunlight–has only begun to be rigorously explored.

The goal of the studio is to gain control of daylight as the primary formal generator of space and form, through a series of iterative exercises using the parametric design tool grasshopper (a plug-in to Rhino). We will begin with the reinvention of the sundial, which will lead into a series of investigations to arrive at a 'toolkit' of honed techniques for the control of form and light. During the first half of the studio every exercise will involve testing the digital through the fabrication of a physical model using either the laser cutter or 3d printer. The studio will culminate in the design of a one room building whose goal is formal invention through the total control of natural light.

Yoonhee Cho | MArch
A System Designs Buildings

Can the parametric design techniques of solar movement generate a building? In the course of a year, and a day, the gradual change of sunlight is a great source to generate extraordinary and unexpected outcomes. The tiles, as a design instrument, are precisely calibrated by the input factors of sun angle, solar intensity, the ratio of hole, the amount of leakage, and time zone. These tiles constitute the unit of façade facing four directions; South, East, West, and Roof.

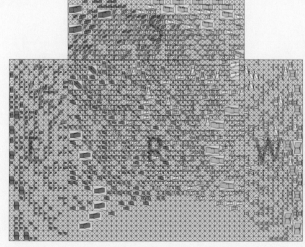

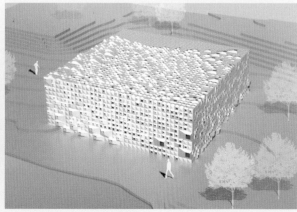

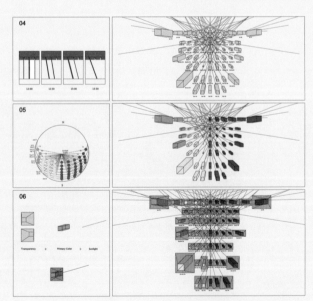

Huang Zhe | MArch
Architecture Clock

The project begins with the reinvention of the sundial, which leads into a series of investigations to arrive at a 'toolkit' of honed techniques for the control of form and light. It takes advantage of the thickness of the wall: the light patterns are shaped by a combination of outer edges and inner edges of the apertures on the wall due to the movement of the sun. By carefully designing the outer edge and inner edge of the aperture, we could tell the solar time from the light patterns. Finally, this research result applies to a church building to test its effect. The different latitude location would be a parameter to determine the shape of the church.

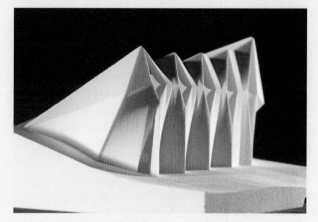

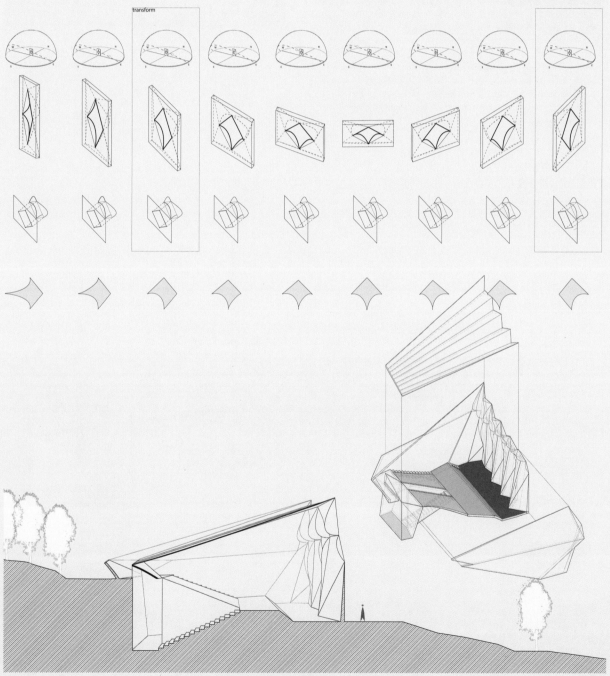

Oliver Wuttig | MArch
Form Follows Sunlight

The studio was organized as a series of small exercises that dealt with the possible relationship of natural lighting and architectural form. The final project brief demanded a building system, which could be adapted to two distinctly different locations, Cambridge, MA and Marfa, TX, best addressed through a parametric envelope strategy. The program brief was limited to a sanctuary and focused instead on the possible architectural effects produced through the control of natural lighting. The goal was to produce a visually compelling architectural facade, rooted in a rigorous, systematic application of a solar strategy. The exterior envelope is organized in a series of hourly wall panels made from stacked masonry-like polycarbonate units supported through a steel rod armature. Each unit corresponds to a specific day of the year, based on the solar azimuth. Through the rotation, a series of gaps are created, which track the movement of the sun and produce animated lighting effects on the interior surfaces of the building. The main space is lined by a series of niches, which correspond to the solstices and equinoxes of the solar calendar, with the spacing between units laid out to mark the passing of one minute. These niches are lit in return by a series of light-wells, whose geometry is depending on the specific solar azimuth and altitude. Whereas in the first proposal the wall elements strictly follow the plan logic, a second proposal reorganized the units in order to create a direct relationship between the geometry of the envelope to the solar azimuth, creating a series of hyperbolic walls.

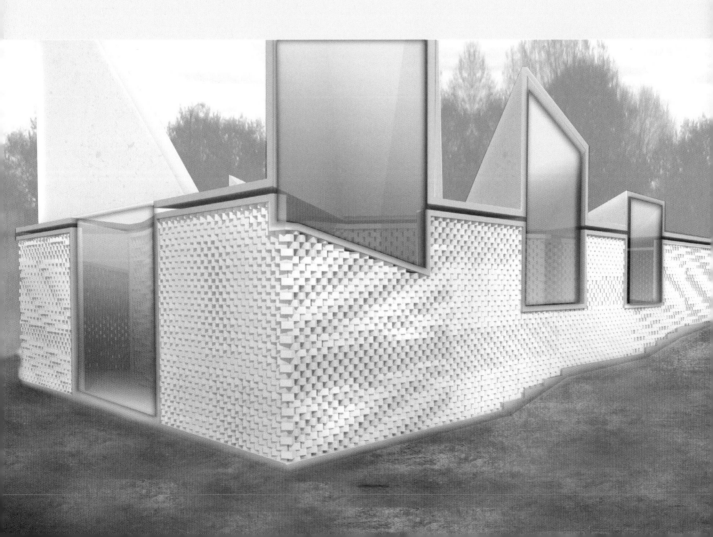

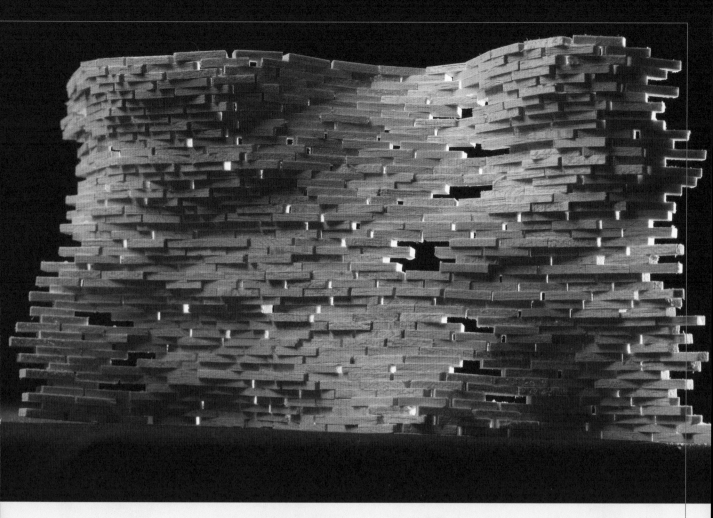

CAMBRIDGE, MA
LAT 42.375° N, LONG 71° W

EXTERIOR WALL PANEL
EXAMPLE

MARFA, TX
LAT 30.375° N, LONG 104° W

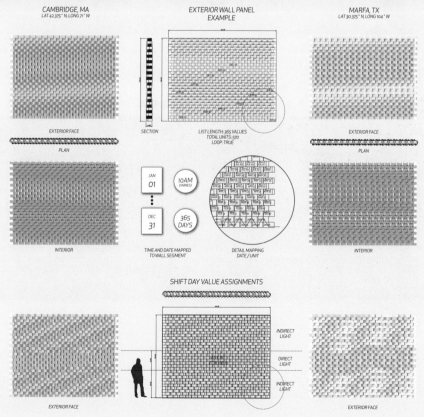

EXTERIOR FACE

PLAN

SECTION

LIST LENGTH: 365 VALUES
TOTAL UNITS: 570
LOOP: TRUE

EXTERIOR FACE

PLAN

INTERIOR

JAN 01
⋮
DEC 31

10AM
(VARIES)

365 DAYS

TIME AND DATE MAPPED
TO WALL SEGMENT

DETAIL MAPPING
DATE / UNIT

INTERIOR

SHIFT DAY VALUE ASSIGNMENTS

EXTERIOR FACE

INDIRECT LIGHT

DIRECT LIGHT

INDIRECT LIGHT

EXTERIOR FACE

VOLTADOM FAST [FESTIVAL OF ART SCIENCE AND TECHNOLOGY] PROJECT
Skylar Tibbits

Voltadom populates the corridor spanning building 56 & 66 on MIT's campus. This installation lines the concrete and glass hallway with hundreds of vaults, reminiscent of the great vaulted ceilings of historic cathedrals. The vaults provide a thickened surface articulation and a spectrum of oculi that penetrate the hallway and surrounding area with views and light. VoltaDom attempts to expand the notion of the architectural "surface panel," by intensifying the depth of a doubly-curved vaulted surface, while maintaining relative ease in assembly and fabrication. This is made possible by transforming complex curved vaults to developable strips, one that likens the assembly to that of simply rolling a strip of material.

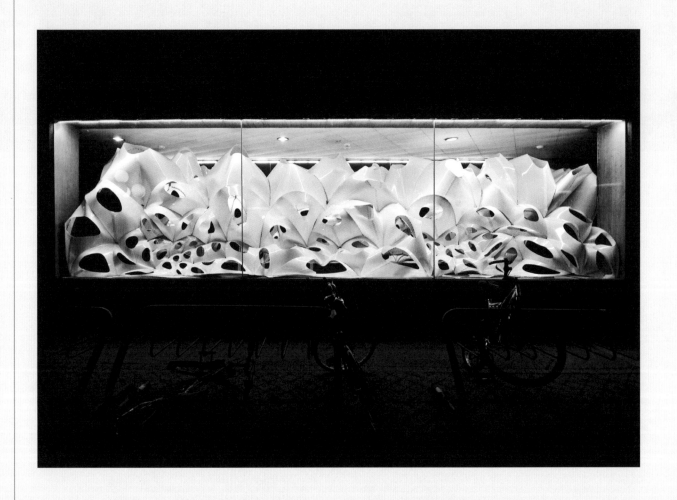

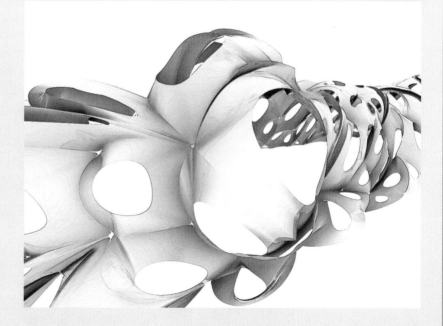

DIS[COURSE]4 FAST [FESTIVAL OF ART SCIENCE AND TECHNOLOGY] PROJECT

Craig Boney, James Coleman, Andrew Manto

The conceptual goal of Dis[Course]4 was to break down the vertical stratification of MIT. By occupying a building stairwell, one of MIT's few sectional anomalies, the project is poised to generate inter-floor/interdisciplinary discourse. The project was sited architecturally, meaning considerations were taken to ensure physical compatibility between site and project. This demonstrates the project's operative lack of specificity and suggests reconfiguration of the global system. Unlike other site-specific projects, Dis[Course]4 is flexible in its ability to adapt to physical conditions of site through a designed versatility and physical flexibility. The project embodies a rigorously investigated manufacturing process as a physical representation of the combined efforts of designers and engineers.

During the design process material data was continually collected thru the generation of prototypes and their analysis. Each material tested demonstrated unique physical qualities such as workability, fold-ability, and machinability. That data was then reinserted into a computer model to re-inform the whole. Composed of over 5,000 parts the project required a fluidity between design and manufacturing in order to appease both conceptual agendas and budgetary restrictions. We developed an intelligent component capable of approximating any number of 'wholes'. This technique with the combination of custom computer software, 'scripts', allows for the deployment of the system on any desired 'whole', outputting individual component actuation levels.

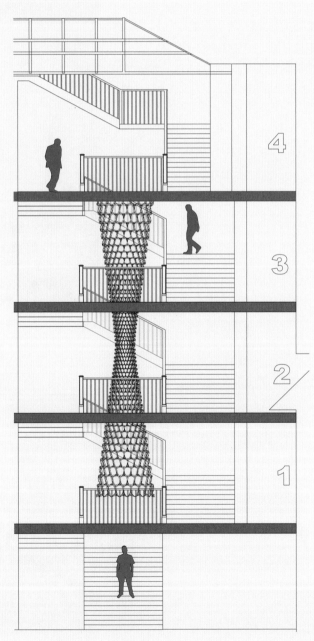

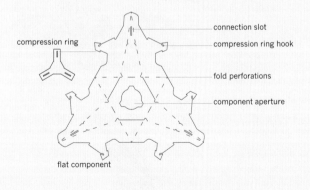

compression ring

connection slot

compression ring hook

fold perforations

component aperture

flat component

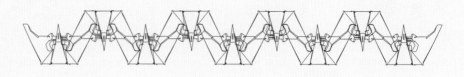

BASE SURFACE _____

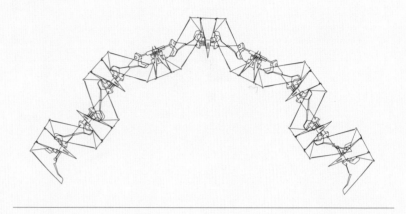

ACTUATED SURFACE _____

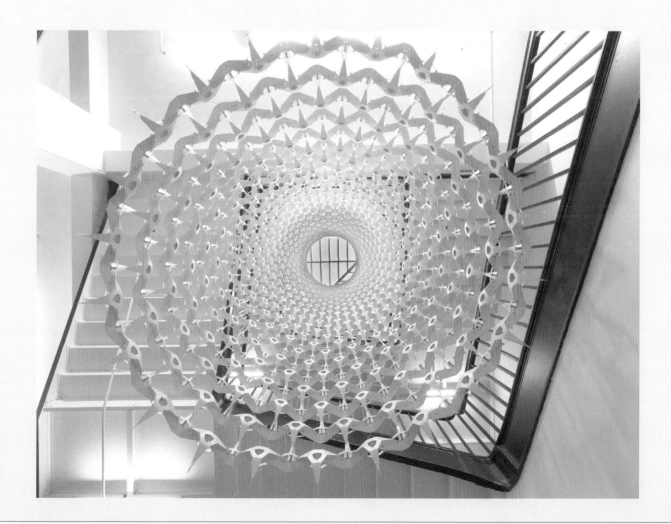

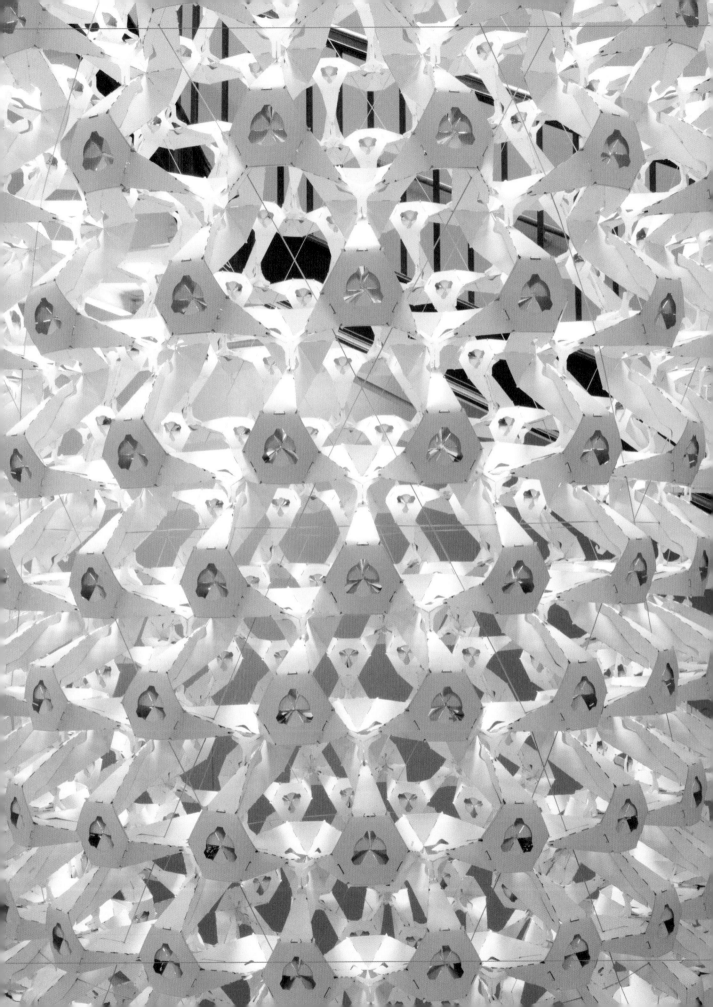

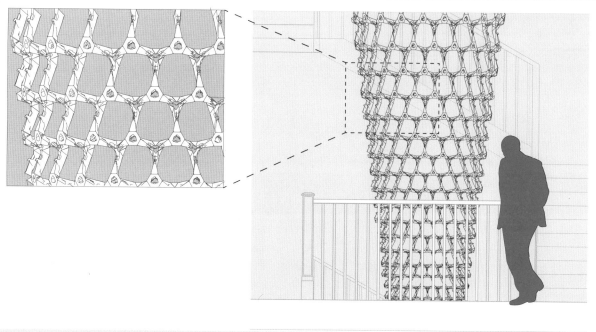

SCALED IDEAS
NOTES ON TEACHING AND RESEARCH

Lawrence Sass

Most of us have yet to notice the transformation in furniture manufacturing
from hand tooled products to digitally fabricated, mostly two-dimensional
assemblies. In the U.S., furniture that was once produced by master carpenters
in local factories is now developed and sold by product designers and people
with access to computers and wood-cutting machines controlled by computers.
This is particularly the case for furniture covered with cushions and upholstery.
Hidden from the user behind fine leather and canvas is CAD/CAM manufactured
wood framing. Also happening is sales of furniture by novice designers online
as two- and three-dimensional products manufactured from computer models.
Alternatively, large furniture chains such as Crate and Barrel and Ethan Allen
are generating new product lines for each season with the help of flexible rapid
production CAD/CAM. One of the best examples of this transformation is Ikea,
whose furniture is designed from the start to be flat-pack delivered and easily
assembled by the user, again aided by CAD/CAM manufacturing.

For the past five years, graduate students in my *Materializing Design* course at
MIT have participated in the production of many wonderful chair designs almost
ready for prime time production. They generate and manufacture these products
in less than five weeks with basic CAD software and access to three types of
CAD/CAM machines. The goal of the assignment is design and physical production
of a chair ultimately manufactured with a computer-controlled machine. Once the
final chair has been approved (the chair has to hold me) it can be authored and
uploaded to websites such as Ponoko or Cloudfab for sale and distribution as a
digital product.

Digital manufacturing is new for architects, yet not so new in product design. The
design and production process is a mixture of architectural question and product

Digitally fabricated chairs
from the Materializing Design course.

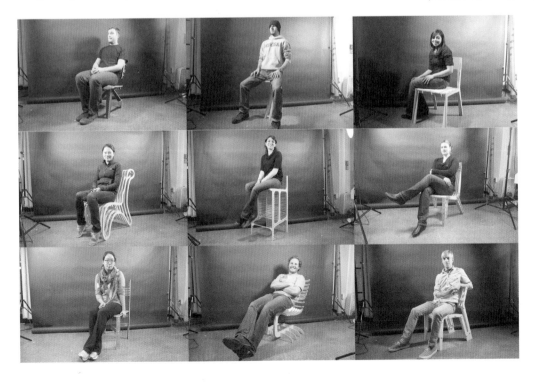

design processing virtually in CAD. Designs are questioned and problems are solved physically with many models small and large representing ideas at many scales. First, students analyze drawings, photos and physical prototyping of chairs designed by well-known architects and product designers. For example, one student in the course chose the Eames chair to begin his study. His analysis produced data on comfort, chair size, curves, lines, and some styling. This operation is best performed through reconstruction of the chair in CAD and manufacturing as a 3D print one eighth the size of the real chair. Second, the student starts designing their chair by synthesis of their ideas about chairs and the design analysis. Design at this stage is a discussion between classmates, teaching staff and most importantly themselves. 3D prints of designs are manufactured of plaster and plastic also at one-eighth full scale. The goal is to study the chairs form. Next, we leap from miniature to modeling life-size components of real materials, designing and manufacturing with the CNC machine, and testing connections for ease of assembly, appearance and strength. Design is finished off at one quarter scale, with the laser cutter and a greater understanding of real materials. Within the class, we refer to these hand size artifacts as construction models. The design is challenged by destroying the model with hand pressure, dropping, and shaking as a way to challenge structure and assembly. If successful, the models are scaled from 1:4 to 1:1 and manufactured on a larger CNC machine of plywood and in some cases aluminum.

The result of this exercise is a complete understanding of a digitally-based design process and reproducible, high quality products. Past methods to design and manufacture furniture started with ideas drawn on paper by designers and master carpenters who applied their experience and specialized techniques to production. They scaled designs from paper to physical product based on many years of experience in production. Success in chair comfort, structure, efficiency in manufacturing and design was not measured by extensive design prototyping.

The industrial age measured design quality through expertise and experience in labor. With experienced labor came greater quality. Alternatively digital production allows the inexperienced designer a chance to gain knowledge by design doing. Best of all, it opens the possibly of lowering cost and increasing quality with flexible design tools and flexible manufacturing machines. Scaling, experience, and expertise are less of a factor. For students, production knowledge is earned through application of computation, CAD/CAM and design synthesis to a real product. Students and practitioners can expect that the next revolution will also be a jump in scale from furniture to homes and

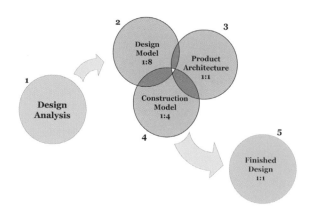

Process diagram from analysis to finished product.

Laser cut construction models.

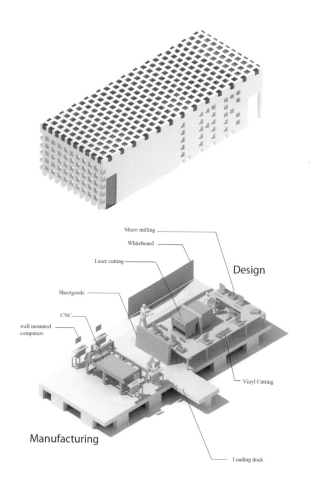

Field fab
System for a prefabricated fabrication facility.

commercial buildings whose innovation will be affordability, without the sacrifice of quality.

Field Fabs are new concepts in factory production for rural and urban environments that support CAD/CAM manufacturing. It is an emerging project in the Digital Design and Fabrication Group at MIT that will someday be deployed and equipped onsite from a kit of parts. Field Fabs will empower people in extreme environments to digitally design and deliver their products in any setting. A great example of this is Fab Labs installations by Neil Gershenfeld of the Center for Bits and Atoms at MIT. Post assembly, it can be used to instantly manufacture cafeterias, hospitals and toilet and waste facilities. The first goal of the Field Fab for buildings is to produce the frame of a rugged plywood or plastic. Infill panels, toilets, kitchens, furniture, and finishes can be designed and fabricated on-site by people in the village. New buildings created with the Field Fab will also need electrical, plumbing, energy and waste systems integrated into walls, ceilings and floors for efficient working structures. A Field Fab can also be used to design and manufacture small artifacts such as medical devices, furniture and mechanical equipment at the point of devastation. Most importantly, all products can be fabricated on the spot from design data generated in or offsite of the Field Fab. From this challenge, new questions will arise related to design production, communication, and design thinking across scales and cultures.

Fab lab in Soshengove, South Africa.

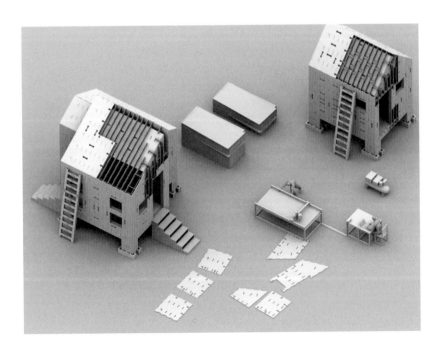

Examples of building structures produced by a Field Fab.

WHEN THINGS BUILD THEMSELVES
NOTES ON TEACHING AND RESEARCH
Skylar Tibbits

For the past four years, my research has been divided between two fronts; the large-scale installation and on the research side, programmable matter and self-assembly. The two don't necessarily appear to meet graciously in the middle; however, the one certainly has reinforced the necessity for the other. The story behind the installation starts at the end of my five-year B.Arch. from Philadelphia University with a short stay at Zaha Hadid Architects. At the time, I was excited by the new technologies at my fingertips, digital fabrication machines, new software, and all of their powerful potential. I started teaching myself code (while studying in Rome and frustrated by the lack of digital technologies) and blindly walked myself into a deep world of computer science. The two technologies, code and machines, began a family of physical structures, from one small gallery to the next, a tour that continues today.

Simultaneously, I was invited to curate an exhibition in Philadelphia. Along with my colleague Marc Fornes, I collaborated on a show we called, *ScriptedbyPurpose*. This show gathered roughly 30 designers, architects, and engineers who were leading their fields with respect to generative and computational design. We designed the show and constructed a large installation that filled the two story gallery. Unbeknownst to us, this show and installation somehow initiated a lineage of invitations to exhibit more work around the world. We first went to Berlin, and then Frankfurt and Calgary, designing large experimental structures.

Logic Matter Prototype
Made from 60 roto-molded plastic units: embedding digital logic into material parts.

We generated them through code, sent them to digital fabrication machines (lasercutters and 3-axis routers at the time), and built these exciting spatial structures. Each time, we focused on new architectural, spatial, material, or geometric problems. We tried to scale them up and learn from our mistakes. We were then invited to exhibit at various galleries in New York; Lyon, France; Paris, France; the Guggenheim, and so on. We ultimately tested materials from polyethylene, aluminum, expanding foam, roto-molding, and various others with self-built fabrication machines, laser cutters, waterjets, cnc routers, and considerable blood sweat and tears.

All of this experience led to the latest of these large-scale installations, designed as part of MIT's 150th Anniversary Celebration and FAST festival. I designed and constructed, with the help of amazing students and faculty in the Department of Architecture, an installation, *voltaDom*, that looked at complex curved vaulted surfaces and new possibilities for construction. The installation continued a line of research from the previous installations on tessellation and constructing complex surface curvature from simple materials. VoltaDom attempted to push past flat panel and triangulated surfaces, eventually approaching occupiable volumetric surfaces. I developed a method for simple design, fabrication, and assembly of these vaulted surfaces from flat sheet material, rather than the labor-intensive process of formwork and casting or masonry. The structure occupied the corridor from building 66 to 56 between February and June. Along with the previous installations, I developed a position on computational protocols and their relationship to fabrication, from standardization to mass-customization and the likes. But

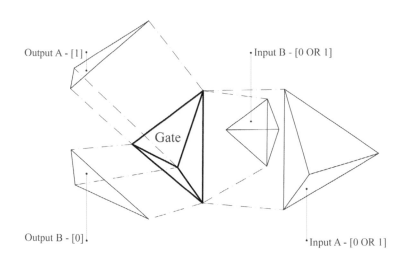

Logic Matter
Digital logic diagram describing input and output faces of each Logic Matter unit.

Decibot
a large-scale reconfigurable robot made from electromechanical devices that can translate from a line to any 3D configuration back to a line. Constructed with waterjet aluminum sheets and waterjet internal gears, this robot measured roughly twelve feet in length.

Macrobot
Similar to the Decibot, this can translate from a line to any 3D configuration back to a line. Constructed with waterjet aluminum sheets and waterjet internal gears, this robot measured roughly eight feet in length.

somehow the hours, week and months assembling these things just didn't add up.

I would sit there, rivet gun in hand, pounding away at thousands of rivets one-by-one, thinking to myself about the process of generation, the process of fabrication, and now about the process of assembly. Something wasn't there. There was all of this explicit information that we generate through code, where each piece knew its neighbor, knew its orientation, placement in the large structure, its name, how many connections, etc. This information was then translated into machine code to operate the fabrication machines with even more information: spindle speeds, feed rates, depth and step-over. However, when we pulled the pieces off the bed, they were completely devoid of information, they were dead! All of the assembly information from their generated code, all of the machine information was gone. The parts were simple bricks with fancy shapes and required us, the builder, to contain the information to put them in the right place. With all of that time slaving away at these crazy installations, I started thinking that there had to be a better way, a way to embed more information into our material parts, to make an installation assemble itself.

While all of this was happening, I was applying to graduate schools and eventually decided to study at MIT, landing in the Design + Computation group. I began studying AI with Patrick Winston and Marvin Minsky, took classes at the Media Lab, and quickly started collaborating with Neil Gershenfeld's Center for Bits and Atoms. I signed on for a second Masters in Computer Science and started studying Programmable Matter and the way that we can embed digital information into material parts. I researched the types of information available in our construction processes today and realized there are relatively few methods for construction.

Type 1: User-As-Information–This was me, or the brick layer, or the robot arm, each of us forced to contain all of the information to build the desired structure. The robot arm is no different than the brick-layer in that respect. The parts are completely dead, with no information. The builder is left to adapt to circumstances and hopefully build the correct structure!

Type 2: Environment-As-Information–This is the Roomba scenario or the site-conscious design solution. The information needed to construct is actually embedded in the

environment, rather than the builder or the materials. The Roomba knows nothing about the room it is trying to clean; it simply listens to the walls and eventually cleans the room with some level of accuracy. Or the builder simply listens to the context and adapts each step in the assembly process to update the final result based on the environment.

Type 3: Specificity-As-Information—This is the jig-saw puzzle or Ikea scenario. Mass-customization allows for completely unique parts, each part having a specific place in the overall structure. All of the information to build the structure is embedded in the parts, the user simply (or not-so-simply) needs to find all of the parts in the correct order to assemble the structure, and the parts should guarantee that the structure is built accurately. However, these parts are only useful for building one thing, never anything else, and as I mentioned this process can be extremely tedious—finding one part in thousands or millions, as in the number of elements needed to build large structures or building, is very difficult.

All of this research on the various types of construction information and my collaborations on Programmable Matter led to a discovery that we could actually try to embed more of the information that we generate during the coding and machining process directly into the material parts and utilize ideas inherent within our own bodies like self-assembly, replication, and repair as inspiration to design around forces rather than brute force assembly techniques. It became apparent that this could re-invent what we had learned since the industrial revolution and the transformation of raw materials, sending them through a machine or process, fighting time, tolerances, energy and failures, to hopefully produce a desired part. On the contrary, we could simply

BiasedChains
A toy prototype that allows the user to assemble the chain, piece-by-piece, with various orientations to "program" the fold sequence. The user then shakes the chain and rigid 3D structures emerge.

take raw materials, embed explicit information into their geometry and allow the parts to assemble themselves!

Together with my collaborators, we realized there were naturally a simple set of ingredients that allowed for self-assembly, occurring within our bodies or across a variety of natural phenomena. First, you need a simple set of instructions. This is the DNA, or instruction sequence needed to design the desired structure, whether it be proteins or buildings. Next, you need parts that are programmable; at the very least, they must contain a state (they could also contain logic or more powerful computation). Then, you need to design and embed a force (or multiple forces). This could be heat, gravity, shaking, water, pneumatics and so on, that will allow the programmable parts to enact each step of the instruction sequence. Finally, you should embed redundancy and some form of error-checking if we want to guarantee a successful construction.

This possibility has led me on my current quest—designing, prototyping and testing large-scale systems that can self-assemble. I've worked on projects from reconfigurable robotics, to bricks that embed digital logic to aid the user in construction, or self-assembly toys that shake and fold 3D rigid structures. I'm working to scale these systems up and envision new applications from a variety of industries, from earthquake structures that can dynamically react to ground conditions and change from rigid and flexible states, to quickly deployable structures or simple construction systems that literally build themselves from the ground up. The

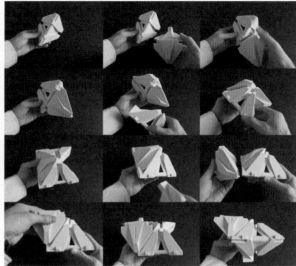

exciting opportunity with self-assembly is its limitless scale, possibilities for embedded computation, and near neighbors of self-repair and replication that are soon to come.

This spring, I taught a course along with Nick Gelpi that focused on self-assembly as a design, fabrication and spatial tool. We used self-assembly as a language to communicate design across the disciplines, from the sciences, math and any other courses the undergraduate students were taking. (Self-assembly is one of the very few topics discussed in nearly every discipline.) Self-assembly became a generative tool for them to think about geometry, the growth of space, and the connection between scales. Next, it allowed them to question our processes of making, how their notions of self-assembly can propose new machines and methods for actually building at the model scale or at 1:1. Students developed systems from self-replication masonry walls, to self-repairing arches, scaffolding and on-demand growing/ expanding structures, with a variety of others. Finally, the students explored the notion of self-assembly as a tool for creating space, with the program of a labyrinth. Self-assembly offered a mode to generate the structure and actually take on the scale of the human's interaction with the labyrinth, discovering how the inefficient and convoluted could be design parameters, rather than errors in a system. Whether it's on the pedagogical side, research, or design and architectural side, I am interested in the power of computation to open up new methods of looking at the world. This can infiltrate our processes from generation to material fabrication through to construction, but it ultimately allows for a new lens re-imagining what's possible and finding the design and science to achieve it.

Logic Matter

Sequences showing digital logic computed through spatial construction. On the left, the inputs [1,1] are given and computed to produce the output [0,0] which has a spatial result in the upward unit placement. Logic Matter only allows the correct computation and spatial result by blocking all other possibilities based on the given inputs. This construction kit can be used to describe 1D, 2D or 3D geometry, used to make arbitrary structures from patterns of binary input, or used as an intelligent material, aiding the user in construction.

HOW TO MAKE [ALMOST] ANYTHING MEDIA LAB

Instructors: **Neil Gershenfeld and J. Meejin Yoon**

Provides an introduction to the resources for designing and fabricating smart systems, including CAD/CAM/CAE; NC machining, 3-D printing and scanning, molding and casting, laser and waterjet cutting; PCB design and fabrication; sensors and actuators; analog instrumentation; embedded digital processing; wired and wireless communications. Emphasis on learning how to use and integrate these tools as well as understand how they work.

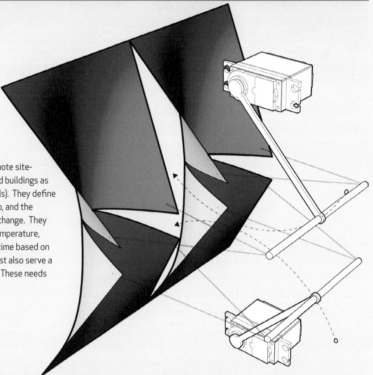

Andrew Payne | PhD, Harvard GSD
Touchwall

There is great interest in understanding how buildings can promote site-specific responsiveness to dynamic conditions. We often regard buildings as solid, durable objects (after all they are built from inert materials). They define the places we live in, the cities we visit, the universities we go to, and the organizations we work in. However, all buildings are subject to change. They must respond to environmental parameters such as sunlight, temperature, humidity, wind, rainfall, and air quality; all of which change over time based on variable geographic or meteorological conditions. Buildings must also serve a function—often aiming to meet the needs of its intended users. These needs also change as the behavioral patterns of its occupants evolve.

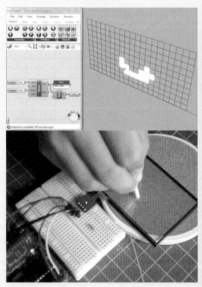

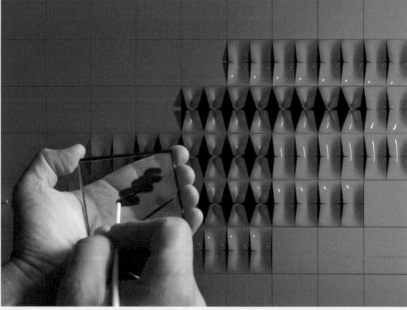

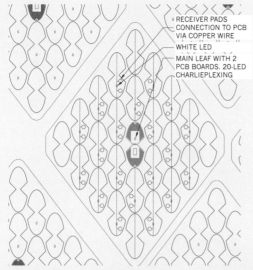

RECEIVER PADS
CONNECTION TO PCB
VIA COPPER WIRE
WHITE LED
MAIN LEAF WITH 2
PCB BOARDS. 20-LED
CHARLIEPLEXING

Yeon Wha Hong | SMArchS Urbanism
Canopy

This sound-responsive LED light canopy was conceptualized as a leaf canopy with light outputs to augment party situations. It is essentially a canopy that visualizes different dynamics going on in different parts of a large area. For the prototype, one segment of this canopy was fabricated, the most basic module in something that can potentially cover varying sizes. This module is composed of an Atmel microprocessor, a mic sensor, and 25 LED lights configured in an array. The light canopy is programmed such that it is responsive to sound levels. It is programmed so that the lights glow when it is relatively quiet, are steady on when it is medium quiet, flash randomly when loud, and flash uniformly when very loud. "White" LED lights, which are of a cooler hue, were used. Right now it is powered via battery, but it may be connected to another type of power source. It could even potentially be wirelessly programmable. The "leaves" are acrylic pieces with copper A-C pads etched on them. They could also potentially be sewn on or have vinyl-cut conductive lines applied to any surface. This canopy seeks to create an environment that augments and reinforces the changing dynamics of a space.

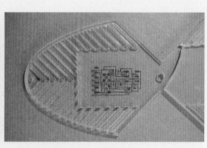

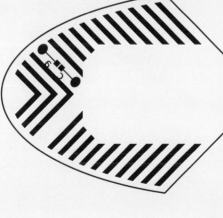

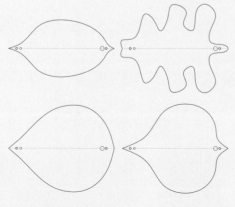

CANVAS LEAF OPTIONS

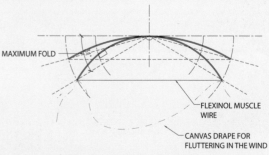

MAXIMUM FOLD

FLEXINOL MUSCLE
WIRE

CANVAS DRAPE FOR
FLUTTERING IN THE WIND

SIDE VIEW, LEAF WITH LED ONLY

Masoud Akbarzadeh | MArch, SMArchS
Robot Arm

The main aim of this exercise was to become involved in the design process of the machine itself. A frequently-used machine within architecture and fabrication contexts is the Robotic Arm. The RA is one of the most important tools for architects who are dealing with complex fabrication techniques. This tool has been a boon for students and architects dreaming of constructing the complex geometries, something that requires advanced machine capability. This capability is called Degrees of Freedom in industry. The more Degrees of Freedom a machine has, the more complicated is the engineering required to build it, and the more capability it has to build things.

In designing the connections, and literally fabricating all parts (save nuts, bolts, and wires) of this robotic arm, the architect gains a familiarity with the tools he uses that necessarily feeds back into the collaborative process between man and machine. This robotic arm is delicately controlled and carefully customized for specific uses.

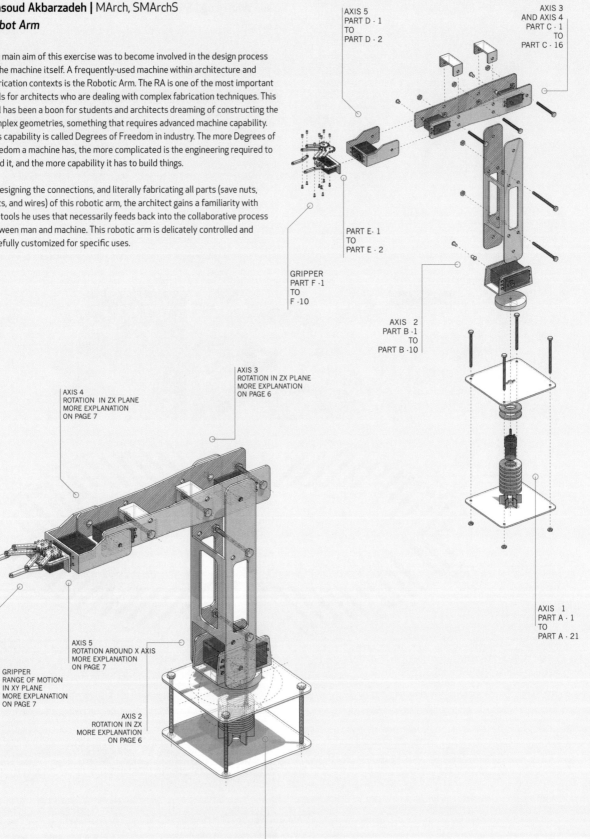

AXIS 5
PART D · 1
TO
PART D · 2

AXIS 3
AND AXIS 4
PART C · 1
TO
PART C · 16

PART E· 1
TO
PART E · 2

GRIPPER
PART F ·1
TO
F ·10

AXIS 2
PART B ·1
TO
PART B ·10

AXIS 3
ROTATION IN ZX PLANE
MORE EXPLANATION
ON PAGE 6

AXIS 4
ROTATION IN ZX PLANE
MORE EXPLANATION
ON PAGE 7

AXIS 1
PART A · 1
TO
PART A · 21

AXIS 5
ROTATION AROUND X AXIS
MORE EXPLANATION
ON PAGE 7

GRIPPER
RANGE OF MOTION
IN XY PLANE
MORE EXPLANATION
ON PAGE 7

AXIS 2
ROTATION IN ZX
MORE EXPLANATION
ON PAGE 6

AXIS 1
ROTATION IN XY PLANE
MORE EXPLANANTION ON
PAGE 5

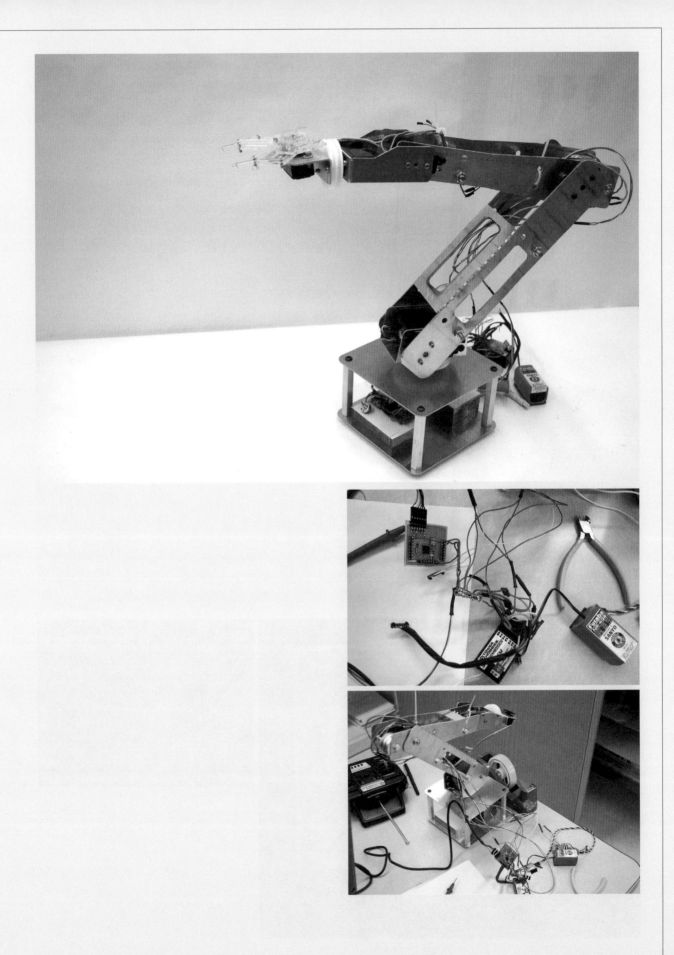

CONTESTED BOUNDARIES: DIGITAL FABRICATION + HAND CRAFT S.M.ARCH.S. COMPUTATION PROJECT

Joseph Choma

This experimentation investigates the relationship between efficiency, precision and tactile variation within architectural design and fabrication.

In order to design, one must have constraints. Within the design process, it is imperative for designers to identify constraints in order to instrumentalize them as a mechanism to generate less predictable new ideas. Often times, designers begin to work within a given medium without explicitly acknowledging how such embedded constraints will influence their design process. The experience and consequences associated with digital instrumentation will yield different results than those emerging out of physical material manipulations.

A digitally-driven design may be seamlessly precise and consistent but may also feel sterile and distant from the human body. A materially-driven design may be intimate and tactile but may lack the accuracy needed to connect elements. Digital fabrication techniques are combined with hand craft material manipulations in search of a unique hybrid tectonic that merges connection accuracies with subtle but sensual divergences between repeating modules. Prototypes have been constructed at the object and inhabitable scale. The challenges associated with translating a consistent material process over each scale have become explicit within this research.

This research does not claim to have developed a "better" fabrication process, but rather asks the question, how do we qualify fabrication processes in our current discourse? A hybrid fabrication process which combines digital fabrication with hand craft techniques suggests an alternative approach to current fabrication trends; automation and optimization. Perhaps, a slightly slower process which yields a sensibility to intimacy is something to be considered.

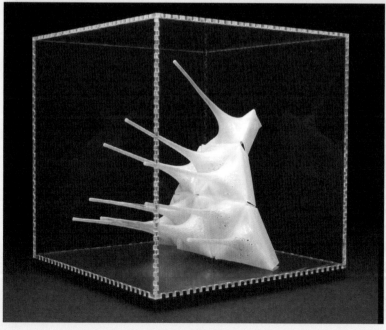

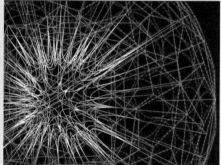

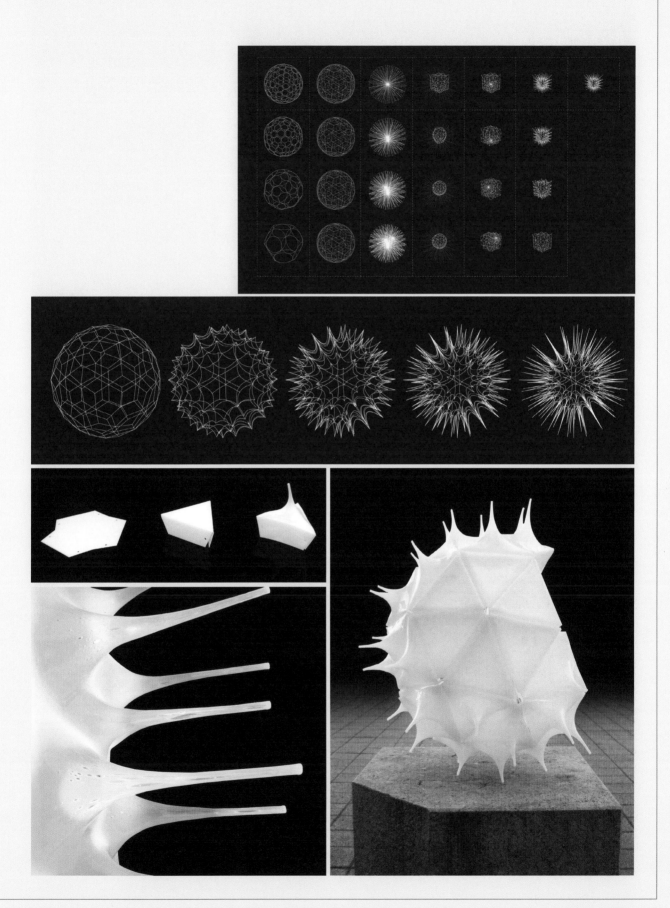

FLEXIBLE INFRA-ARCHITECTURAL SYSTEM FOR A HYBRID SHANGHAI M.ARCH. THESIS

Rafael Luna
Supervisor: **Yung Ho Chang**
Readers: **Stanford Anderson, Julian Beinart, Mark Goulthorpe**

The increasing migration from a rural to an urban setting has lead to a rapid expansion of metropolitan areas around world (50% of the world population lives in cities). The demand for living and working spaces inside the city has generated a rapid turnaround of building stock. In rapid developing cities like Shanghai, neighborhoods are replaced by higher density buildings every 30 to 40 years. Areas of extreme diversity in population and program have been replaced by high density residential towers that generate a monoculture and lose the richness of the hybrid city. Cities like Tokyo have generated self-conscious bad architecture as a result of the pressures of its high density, and increasing land value. This culture of high density has responded with new hybrid typologies that efficiently optimize real estate into a continuous flow of the city through its buildings. In order for cities to maintain a steady growth with adequate living conditions, it is important to hybridize infrastructure with building stock that generates a fluid metropolitan culture.

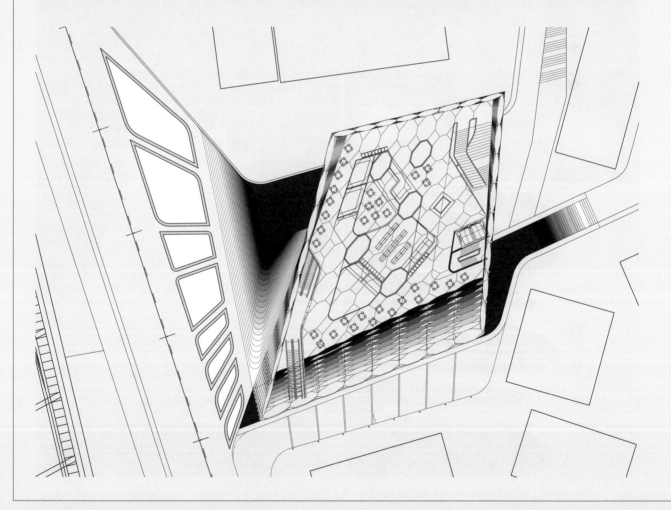

CURVED CREASE ORIGAMI PH.D. COMPUTATION RESEARCH

Duks Koschitz
Supervisor: **Erik Demaine**

Curved creases offer a wealth of new design possibilities. The challenge is to understand what 3D forms result after folding a set of curved creases. The mathematics of this special kind of geometry has been relatively underexplored and we don't have proper descriptions of these curves. Most materials in architecture come as sheet goods and this research proposes a family of curved 3D geometries that can be fabricated from 2D sheet materials, by way of curved creases.

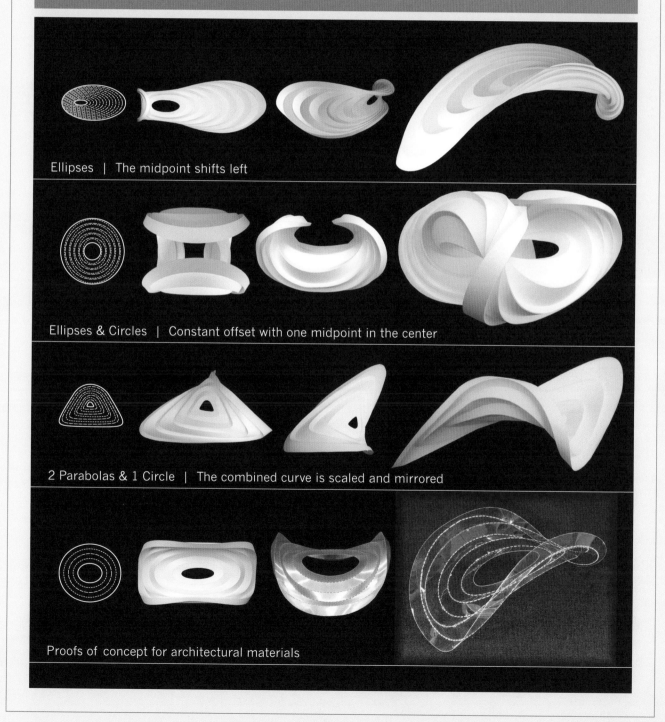

Ellipses | The midpoint shifts left

Ellipses & Circles | Constant offset with one midpoint in the center

2 Parabolas & 1 Circle | The combined curve is scaled and mirrored

Proofs of concept for architectural materials

GLOBAL

GLOBALITY / AGAINST THE GLOBAL

Historical Traditions and Global Culture
Understanding of parallel and divergent canons and traditions of architecture, landscape, and urban design in the world (including indigenous and vernacular examples) in terms of their climate, ecological, technological, socioeconomic, public health, and cultural factors[1]

Architectural Education and Students
That students enrolled in the accredited degree are prepared: to live and work in a global world where diversity, distinctiveness, self-worth, and dignity are nurtured and respected[2]

Architectural Education and the Profession
That students enrolled in the accredited degree program are prepared: to practice in a global economy, to understand the diverse and collaborative roles assumed by architects in practice[3]

As 'globalization' became more and more an evident feature of everyday lives, the ideological functions vested in the postwar concoction called 'Western Civ' was seen as increasingly insufficient for American schoolrooms whose products were now expected to transact with China and Japan. In architecture, likewise, the NAAB has–in a flash of enlightenment indistinguishable from prosaic 'business sense'–mandated that accredited programs in architecture must have generous doses of 'global history', of course with little comparable enlightenment on the matter of what that might mean. If the ideological role of 'Western Civ' was to confer a kind of historical unity–a broad trajectory of 'human development' through which 'progress' is consistently delivered through history–today's emphasis on 'world history' has something of the same expectation, in a world that otherwise seems out of joint. To say the least, this is a procrustean move, tasked with delivering a one-size-fits-all framework for disparate moments, biomes, peoples, conceptions of thought, as well as modes of production. Not to say that legions have not swarmed happily in where angels

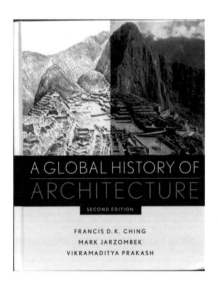

A Global History of Architecture, Second Ed.
Professor Mark Jarzombek, along with Francis D. K. Ching and Vikramaditya Prakash, literally wrote the book on Global Architecture.

fear to tread. "The Global" today convenes panels, it fills books, op-ed pages, and airwaves.

In architecture schools, students typically take two or three survey courses in architectural history, which used to span largely Western European political timetables. Of course this very narrowly constructed history informs ideas about the present and about trajectories of style, but how does it affect how they design? What does learning about the Sixteenth Century in Iraq, as one might in an expanded notion of Global History, actually do for a student, more so than learning about the Gothic, for example. The stacked deck of traditional historical education is not in question because here the issue at stake is the notion of history itself. Does one really need to brush up on Confucianism and Tang-era merchants' houses–other than to pronounce the most banal generalizations–in order to do business in China? (One could well imagine a counter-proposal for Chinese students hoping to do business in America: primers on Jefferson, Monticello, Latrobe and the Founding Fathers.) Is history in architecture–or generally for that matter–to be seen as a 'spread', a conglomeration of geographically located facts, or is it the basis for interrogating thought processes and received opinions, a kind of convenient heuristic? Does doing a studio in Cuba or Japan remarkably differ–other than the empirical narratives one gathers–in its output in terms of the skills, the range of responses, or the attitudes that are deployed? After all, so many global conversations happen today not as encounters between discrete cultural conditions but within professions: architects seem to have little trouble speaking with architects across the world,

Tongxian Gatehouse—Nader Tehrani/ Office dA
Beijing, China 2003

film-makers talk to film-makers, salespeople to salespeople. All of these conversations attest to the fact that professional preoccupations are far more efficient 'universal translators' than an overweening emphasis on cultural and anthropological 'difference' might allow. Is 'history' then simply the ice-breaker–the amuse-bouche, "Isn't it terrible what's going on with Ai Weiwei?"–to start conversations whose interests lie elsewhere? In the absence of any real grasp of global languages, what better can be offered? Certainly NAAB, and a host of the new 'Global Studies' effort in American curricula, seem to intend it that way: if anything, the 'global' is being explicitly argued as a move away from the 'critical', and yet one more lockstep in the preparation of the professional.

Shanghai Corporate Pavilion—Yung Ho Chang / Atelier FCJZ
West elevation

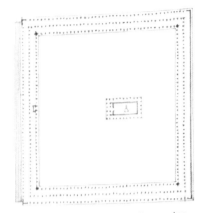

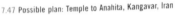

7.47 Possible plan: Temple to Anahita, Kangavar, Iran

7.48 Horse statuette of Parthian war

The Parthian Empire

The Parthians, about whom actually very little is known, took over the Hellenistic Seleucid Empire; originally they were nomads from northern Iran and Central Asia, but because of their trading skills, the Parthian Empire (247 BCE–224 CE) became the glue that held together the vast Central Asian trade networks. They brought with them, however, little in the way of architectural culture, and so for the most part adopted the Hellenism of the Sassanians before them, blending it with their own particular aesthetic. As a result, there is remarkably little architecture to show for some five hundred years of Parthian rule. Remaining consummate and feared horsemen, they governed as a military elite, leaving, by and large, the local administrations intact. There were, as a consequence, several regional capitals. Though warfare with the Romans and with nomadic invaders from the north was more or less constant, the 2nd century was a time when the caravan cities of Palmyra, Hatra, and Mesene (formerly Characene), situated at the confluence of the Tigris and Euphrates rivers, grew in wealth and influence. It was also a time in which, given the lack of centralized authority, different religious practices began to flourish simultaneously. Iranian sun, fire, and mystery cults took the place of ancient Mesopotamian practices.

Christianity, Judaism, and various baptismal sects expanded into Mesopotamia. Strong relations between the Parthians and the Chinese resulted in envoy exchanges.

When the Chinese envoy arrived at the Parthian border, he was greeted by an escort of twenty thousand horsemen. Parthian elites, on the whole, adopted Zoroastrianism (see 400 CE), an emerging religious practice based on fire worship. This they fused with certain Hellenistic practices, creating fire sanctuaries dedicated to specific divinities, saints, or angels. Parthian fire altars served as regional and national pilgrimage sites. One such site, Takht-i-Suleiman, in western Iran, around the rim of an extinct volcano with a lake at its core, was frequently visited by the royal Parthian elites. The architectural expressions, however, tended to be modest. Only later, during the Sassanian period, when Zoroastrianism became a state religion, did the large and grand architectural works such as those at Takht-i-Suleiman begin to emerge.

The most important urban Parthian founding was Ctesiphon (see "400 CE"), on the east bank of the Tigris at its confluence with the Diyala River, 32 kilometers south of Baghdad. Originally a garrison city, it developed into a regional capital, as it was situated on the so-called Royal Road, which connected Susa with Anatolia.

The road, begun by the Assyrians up with guard posts and stables t fast communication. It is not clea Ctesiphon became important, but that the spoils of a large campaig the Roman Empire in 41 BCE wer in the new capital, which had bec winter residence of the kings afte The Romans sought to take the c so in 116, 165, and 198 CE, but i Ardashir overthrew the Parthian m and established the Sassanian En Ctesiphon remaining one of its ca

Though its date is much in dis exists a temple thought to be ded the ancient deity Anahita, the div water—and hence associated wit healing, and wisdom. The buildin at Kangavar in western Iran, next spring, became prominent in the period in the 4th century CE, whe as a summer resort for Sassanid temple, however, predated the Pa who possibly did little more than interior. The outer precincts certa Hellenistic or Sassanian in tone. almost square structure, just ove on a side, with a continuous dou colonnade set on a plinth and wi one side by a continuous flight of

212 ■ West Asia

A Global History of Architecture, Second Ed.
Professor Mark Jarzombek, Francis D. K. Ching and Vikramaditya Prakash

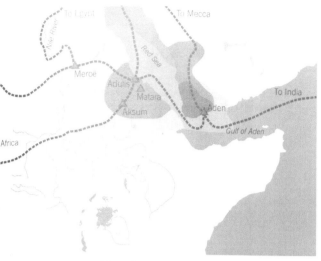

Area of Aksumite influence, 200 to 500 CE

The Aksumite religion was related to Mesopotamian and Arabic religions insofar as it was polytheistic; deities were perceived as controlling the natural forces of the universe. In the 4th century, King Ezana converted to Christianity and declared Aksum a Christian state—the first Christian state in the history of the world. The city contained several large palaces that, unlike the more rambling palaces of western Asia, tended to be highly symmetrical. They were approached by broad staircases that led to a forecourt with more stairs leading to a central throne or reception room. Construction material was stone and brick, probably covered with plaster. The roofs were wooden.

Aksum

...the 4th century BCE, the area of what ...day northern Ethiopia had come to ...y a strategic position in the developing ...trade routes between Africa and ...ts east in Arabia, India, and even ...na. With the decline of Kush, perhaps ...ause deforestation led to the loss of ...d for smelting, this area, controlled ...he Aksumites and with its own vast ...st reserves (now, of course, completely ...existent) was primed to become a ...onal powerhouse. Though Aksum was ...inland capital, its port cities, Adulis and ...ara, were cosmopolitan centers. The ...rs imported silver, gold, olive oil, and ...e while exporting luxury goods of glass ...tal, brass, and copper. Other important ...orts to the Greek and Roman world were ...kincense, used in burials, and myrrh, ...ch had important medicinal properties. ...n these highly valued products were ...ined from the resin of particular trees ...grew mainly in the mountainous regions ...ksum and southwest Arabia. The quality ...ksumite metalwork in gold, silver, bronze, ...iron attests to the skill of their craftsmen. ...he significance of Aksum in global trade ...uld not be underestimated. With the ...lans eager to seek alternative trade routes ...e East to get around the Parthians, they ...developed relationships with Petra. ...um, much like Petra, was a part of this

southern trade network, and should be understood in the context of developments in India. There is little of the original Aksum left today, apart from some impressive stelae, the largest being King Ezana's Stele, erected in the 4th century CE and named after the first monarch of Aksum to embrace Christianity. It is decorated at its base with a false door and apertures resembling windows on all sides. The city was originally impressively located in a gap between two prominent rock outcroppings. The remains of a vast palace and a smelting factory have recently been uncovered.

Across the Strait of Hormuz lay the Himyarite kingdom, or Himyar. Formerly a trader in frankincense, the decline in demand for that product led to trade in ivory exported from Africa to be sold in the Roman Empire. Ships from Himyar regularly traveled the East African coast, where Himyar exerted a considerable amount of political control over the trading cities of East Africa. Himyar was independent until taken over by the Aksumites in 525 CE. Aksum remained a strong empire and trading power until the 6th century, when deforestation led to its decline (much as it had in Kush)—a decline accelerated by the rise of Islam and the resulting shift in trade routes. The area's arid geography today gives little indication of this once lush and forested territory.

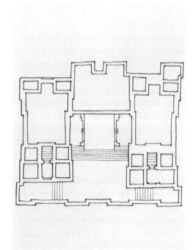

7.50 Plan of an Aksumite palace

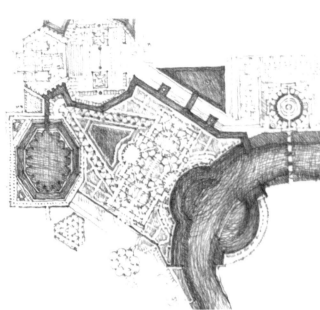

16.21 Drawing of a fragment of Piranesi's plan for Rome

16.22 Print from the *Carceri* series by Piranesi

Piranesi and Romanticism

In Europe, the 18th century was an expansionary age adjusting to the colonial project philosophically, economically, and politically. In particular, it was oriented toward accumulating wealth from far-flung global territories. Naive historicism, like that of the neo-Palladians, gave way to a search for more solid societal underpinnings that involved scholarly standards, academic affiliations, and incontrovertible historical facts based on proven archaeological discoveries. If the Adam brothers put this to work in their architectural practice, Giambattista Piranesi (1720–78) interrogated it in his engravings. Robert Adam worked for a secure elite and lived the life of an outward-looking member of an opportunistic colonial world. Piranesi lived surrounded by the faded glories of Rome in front of his eyes. But both, in different ways, confronted Europe's newfound role as the locus of the global colonial world with an as yet episodic sense of its own historical identity.

Copperplate engravings were all the rage at the time, but Piranesi elevated the art into an idiom all its own. Scouring the often malaria-infested Roman *campagna*

for pictorial possibilities, Piranesi portrayed broken stones, crumbling bricks, collapsed vaults, and overgrown facades of haunting intensity, bringing unexpected and revealing angles into view. This was a Rome far different from the one imagined in England, where it was embedded in a rhetoric of order and manliness. Piranesi envisioned a cataclysmic end of time, with nothing left to show for Rome's erstwhile grandeur. The Colosseum is an empty crater; the foundation wall of Hadrian's Tomb a vast, battered cliff. Adam and Piranesi represented the two sides of the Romantic movement: Adam through his zest for the exotic, Piranesi through his moody melancholia. Both admired the heroic, but from different political perspectives. Adam saw the Roman past as the legitimization of English civilizational supremacy and as a living model for heroic action, while Piranesi rendered it as a meditative reflection on the short-sightedness of the powers currently in charge. These distinctions define the difference between neoclassicism and Romanticism, the former reflecting a historical optimism, the latter reflecting on the principle of historical loss.

16.23 Drawing made from a Piranesi print Roman ruins

A Global History of Architecture, Second Ed.
Professor Mark Jarzombek, Francis D. K. Ching and Vikramaditya Prakash

Strawberry Hill, Twickenham, England

16.25 Interior: Strawberry Hill

erry Hill

members of the English elite thought
eoclassicism was the answer. Protesting
t its stiffness and artificial ty, a group of
ctuals and aesthetes began to see the
e Ages, not Rome, as more "authentic."
d of the whites, soft blues, and golds
by the Adam brothers, they preferred
greens, and browns, purposefully dark
loomy interiors, and asymmetrical
d plans. Horace Walpole (1717–97).
r of Strawberry Hill (1748–77), used
rm *Gothic picturesque* to define this
Walpole was in many respects a
erculturist. He was well educated; his
had been amassed by his father, the
minister Sir Robert Walpole, who also
ed his son's election to Parliament,
that he held until 1768. The elder
le also arranged lucrative sinecures for
n in the Exchequer and Custom House
nsured a very comfortable income for

t public life did not appeal to Walpole,
principal passion was writing Gothic
, such as *The Castle of Otranto*. He
rote a four-volume history of art entitled
lotes of Painting (1761–71). Upon the
of his father in 1745, Walpole settled
wberry Hill, an estate of some 40
at Twickenham, southwest of London,
hong fashionable villas overlooking the
es River and near the residence of
end, the poet and garden enthusiast
hder Pope. Expanding the existing
, he built a "star chamber" named after

the golden stars that adorn the ceiling, and
a "tribune," a square room with the ceiling
copied from the Cathedral of York. He also
built a library, an armory, a gallery, a china
closet, bedrooms in several colors, and an
oratory. There were towers, battlements,
and stained glass windows rescued from
demolished buildings. Walpole filled the
house with art, paintings, sculpture, china,
and heraldic symbols, both real and invented.
Attention to structure was minimal: the
fan vaulting in the gallery, a copy of that in
Westminster Abbey, was made of papier-
mâché.

If this was a gentleman's fantasy world,
as has been claimed, the architecture
of the Adam brothers was just as much
a gentleman's fantasy, even down to the
custom-designed chairs. Yet the contrast
between Adam and Walpole could not
have been greater. Robert Adam was the
consummate tastemaker for the metropolitan
gentry, insisting on a continuum between
design and public life. Walpole created an
aesthetic environment reflecting his personal
choices. His house was much visited by the
elite of the time: after 1763 Walpole even
began selling entrance tickets. Adam and
Walpole represent the paradoxes associated
with emerging modernism. Professionalism,
or at least the beginnings of what might be
called a professional practice, in the former,
and the deliberate and self-conscious search
for personal expression and the desire for
approbation in the latter.

New wing

Existing house

0 ___ 10 m

16.26 Plan: Strawberry Hill

Shanghai Corporate Pavilion—Yung Ho Chang / Atelier FCJZ
Retail area

MIT is fortunate to have a string of practitioners and historians whose expertise and backgrounds speak particularly to the global. Design Professors Meejin Yoon, Nader Tehrani, Sheila Kennedy, Yung Ho Chang, all have substantial projects, even offices, in the 'non-Western' parts of the globe, in addition to people like Alexander D'Hooghe who simultaneously maintains offices in Cambridge and in Europe. The Aga Khan Program in Islamic Architecture was one of the earliest dedicated research programs concentrated on the non-Western parts of the globe, and Professors Nasser Rabbat and James Wescoat have extensive research and practice experience across Asia and the Middle East. Professor of Architectural History Arindam Dutta specifically focuses on the history of globalization–seen as a particular economic phenomenon beginning in the eighteenth century–as a way of examining modern architectures and infrastructures. In the Building Technology stream, Professors John Ochsendorf, John Fernandez and others have extensive interests in Asia and Latin America, particularly with issues pertaining to

sustainability. And most importantly, MIT Professor Mark Jarzombek is the co-author, along with Vikramaditya Prakash and the legendary architectural illustrator and theorist Francis D. K. Ching, of *A Global History of Architecture*, now the standard textbook in the field already running into its second edition. In his recent, collaboratively-published article in the *Journal of Architectural Education,*excerpted here, Jarzombek decries the pedagogical tendency in architectural schools globally–including NAAB–where the thrust is to serve up, wholesale and stylized, cultural and historical 'traditions' to be defended and emulated, with little investigation or understanding of either the specificities of historical emergence and plays of power or the all-too modern catenations by which 'traditional' styles are arrived at. In a sense, Jarzombek argues, 'global' is now merely a euphemism for the defanging of the architect's–certainly the student's–critical intellect. Religion, for instance, has become almost a taboo subject in studios, as are difficult political sites (for instance Tiananmen) ; both these issues were explored substantially in Arindam Dutta and Mark Goulthorpe's *Digital Mosques* studio, offered in Spring 2007.

At MIT, despite disparate opinions and expertise on the subject, both scholars and practitioners are strongly agreed that the specificities of region, and history of culture should less be seen as prescriptive or determining conditions than a basis to test architectural production. Logistics, politics, economy, legal frameworks, infrastructure, all these become sites–in historical research or design investigation, in material specificities or conceptual ordering–of interrogation, venues to open up investigation into the ambivalences, the uncertainties, the vulnerabilities of the global. Otherwise, what does it mean when the field's professional licensing board declares that we live and work in a global world or economy? What implications are

Chengdu Sky Courts—J. Meejin Yoon / Höweler + Yoon Architecture
SKY COURTS is a 20,000 square foot corporate club house that incorporates short-term housing, office space, and entertainment facilities utilizing the logics of the courtyard and sloped roof. The project packs many courtyards into a defined perimeter and utilizes the sloped roof to accommodate program in the wedge between courtyards, allowing the project to read as 100% courtyard from above.

*Yeosu Silo Revitalization—
Sheila Kennedy / KVA*
This project creates an urban symbol for the sustainable new "blue water economy" of Yeosu City Region that function as an ocean water cleaning system. Ocean water from Yeosu City's "Big O" is raised up with solar pumps and then cleaned with gravity fed filtration tanks along Silo #1's 55 meter vertical drop.

there for education, and how exactly does this diagnose a new type of practice? And what do we mean by global? As established as these concerns may seem, a notion of the global is largely undefined. Is it the architects who practice it? The multi-national corporations that administer it? The sourcing of building materials? And if the global is a new phase in contrast to earlier modes, what exactly was local about what we were doing before? It may be that the 'global' represents here simply something like a case for persistent counterfactuality, 'other' locations that continually bring the conventions of architectural practice to crisis, by presenting to design new and unexpected conditions for practice, strategy, formal mobilization, and technological and technical demand. Perhaps the global is the necessary 'exteriority' that punctures through to architecture's inveterate conventionalizing tendency, allowing no hallowed tradition to remain unquestioned or permanently relevant, the unceasingly modernizing moment breaking open the traditionalizing thrust of architecture's twentieth century love-affair with modernism.

1   *II.1.1: Student Performance–Educational Realms and Student Performance Criteria.* From 2009 Conditions of Accreditation, Initial Comparison to 2004 Conditions for Accreditation. Available on the NAAB website, naab.org, under Public Documents \ School Resources \ 2010–2015 APR Preparation Resources.

2   *I.1.3 Response to the Five Perspectives*–"schools must show that they have responded to the following concerns." From 2009 Conditions of Accreditation (see above).

3   *I.1.3 Response to the Five Perspectives*–"schools must show that they have responded to the following concerns." From 2009 Conditions of Accreditation (see above).

1K HOUSE OPTION DESIGN STUDIO

Instructors: **Yung Ho Chang, Tony Ciochetti, Dennis Shelden**
Teaching Assistant: **Andrey Dimitrov**

The One Thousand Dollar House (1K House) is a advanced studio for the Master of Architecture students co-taught by Yung Ho Chang (architecture), Tony Ciochetti (real estate), and Dennis Shelden (design & computation).

According to the United Nation, 1.5 billion people in the world today live on less than a dollar a day and the majority of the poor live in the rural areas. The 1K House is aimed at improving the living conditions in the parts of the world where resources are scarce, infrastructure does not exist, and natural disasters often have struck. In other words, we believe design and economic intelligence can help with the solution to the global rural poverty on the housing front.

The basic qualities of the 1K House are defined as the following:

Livability: 1K House has to provide safety, sanitation, and comfort for residents.

Sustainability: Without an available infrastructure, 1K House has to harvest energy and treat waste in a self-sustained way. It can be built with a hybrid of the traditional, local and recycled building materials and latest industrial products.

Affordability: 1K House has to be designed and constructed with limited means. $1,000 price is set as a target for material and construction since it may be a tight budget for building a dwelling for certain rural regions in question but already a burdensome sum for some others.

Strategically, 1K House design is about deploying the power of design to compensate the lack of funds and furthermore to achieve what money alone cannot. 1K House is thus about creativity and innovation. 1K House is about bringing design and technology to the needed.

The first site for the 1K House will be situated in rural southern China ($1,000 converts to approximately 6,700 RBMs.). Permanent housing for the earthquake struck areas in Sichuan would be an ideal application of the 1K House designs.

Under the guidance of real estate professor Tony Ciochetti, the studio is also aimed to create a viable financial model for the 1K House, which in turn can serve as a generator for local economy development.

To integrate design and cost estimate exercises, Professor Dennis Shelden teaches BIM to the studio. The design process is reversed in this studio: In order to have an accurate idea of the budget, one has to start the project from materials and construction details. Shelden is an Associate Professor of the Practice at MIT who directs Gehry Technologies in Los Angeles.

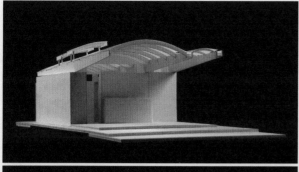

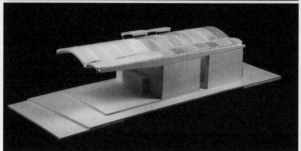

Timothy Olson | MArch
1K Roof House

The 1k Roof House design is a hybrid of inexpensive traditional building technologies and high performance mass manufactured components.

Simplicity governs the design of the 1k Roof House foundation, floor and walls. Traditional rammed earth construction employs low-cost site-obtained earthen material. Square corners, and minimal geometric complexity simplifies the required formwork. This portion of the 1k Roof House is imagined as an open source platform that foresees customization based on the preferences of the owner.

The Roof of the 1k Roof House is composed of lightweight fiberglass modules. Translucent units over the interior portion allow wintertime sunlight penetration and thermal storage within the rammed earth mass. At night, and during the summer months, a "double bubble" insulation and radiant barrier blind obscures sunlight and tempers the effects of diurnal temperature variation. Large, 1x2 meter, ventilation modules can be lifted clear of the rest of the roof to capture wind and evacuate unwanted interior heat gains. The lightweight design enables a cantilevering form that shelters a large outdoor space.

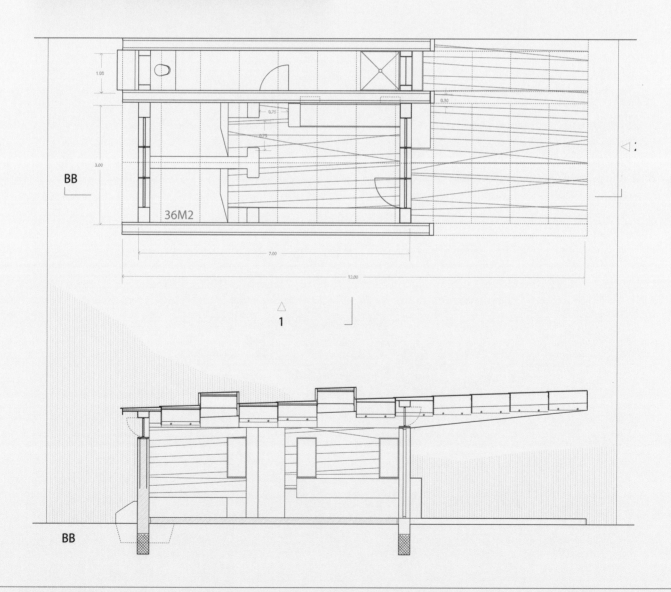

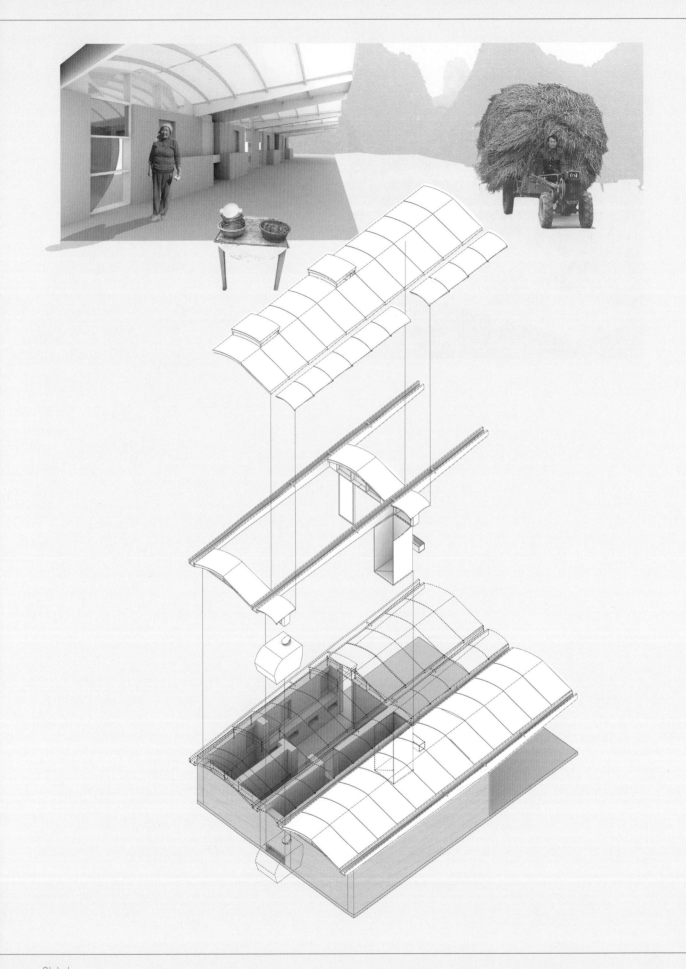

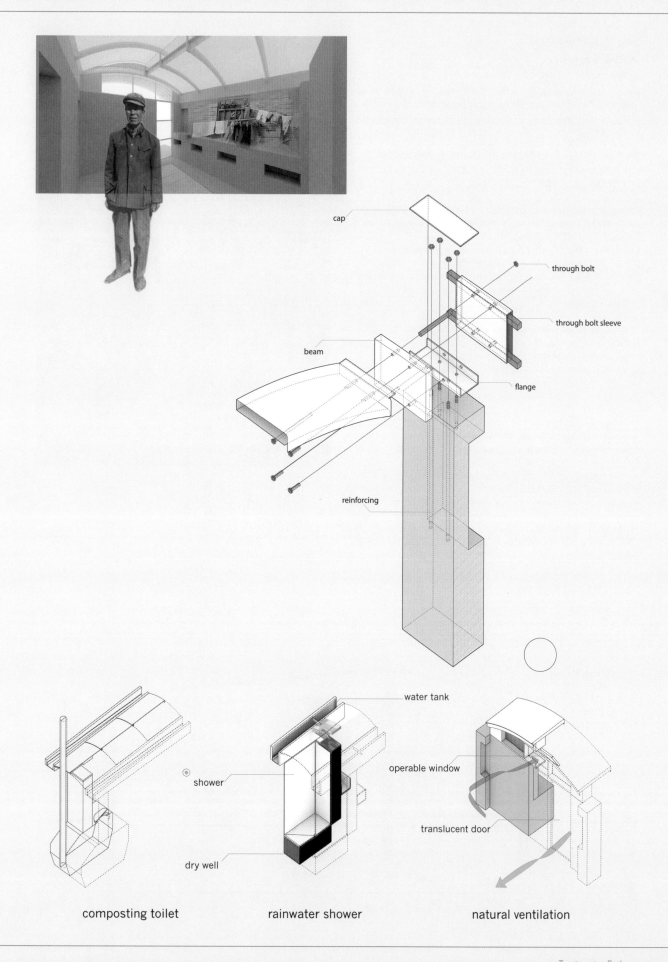

cap

through bolt

through bolt sleeve

beam

flange

reinforcing

water tank

operable window

shower

translucent door

dry well

composting toilet   rainwater shower   natural ventilation

Ying Chee Chui | MArch
1K Pinwheel House

The Pinwheel house was originally the "1K house studio" in 2009 and became a built project in 2010 summer. This is a project designed for the rural poor in the earthquake area, Sichuan, China who lost their home during the disaster in 2008.

The Pinwheel house is a housing prototype fulfilling four major design objectives: module prototyping, self-sustaining, low construction cost, and safe and easy construction.

Considering not only how the rural people live in a house but a village and a community, prototyping is the keystone of the design. The concept generates from a pinwheel unit to an urban prototype at large. It begins from a module–a house composed of 4 identical modules. One module rotates to become two and finally 4 modules complete a house with an internal courtyard. This pinwheel concept can be further expanded to housing and cluster prototype. At the cluster scale, rotation of clusters creates community and become urban prototype.

The pinwheel house adapts green design criteria through achieving a self-sustainable, high-energy efficient and low carbon emission housing prototype. It maximizes the use of natural resources by capturing natural daylight, enhancing cross ventilation, and selecting efficient materials for insulation.

Besides implementing sustainable and structural concept to the housing prototype, the prototype will serve as a proof of concept for a house affordable to the poor in rural China. The final material cost for the house is USD 6,000 including material and labor cost. The material cost for the prototype can be further lowered based on different combinations.

In view of the earthquake disaster, the pinwheel house is designed for a degree 8 robust structure for earthquake zone. Although the construction fulfils structural requirement, the building method is easy enough for the local laymen to build their own houses without the help of special technicians. The pinwheel house is not temporary housing but a permanent solution that can greatly improve the living conditions for the rural poor. The final construction takes 40 days.

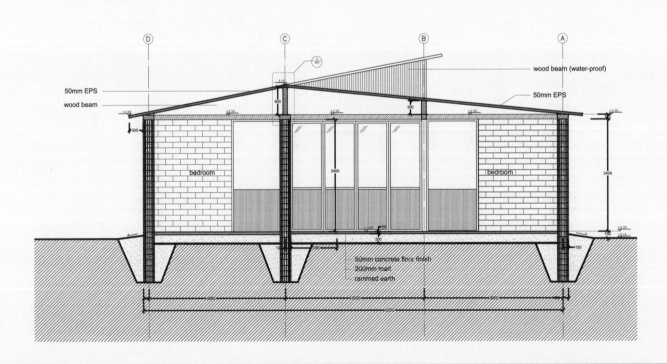

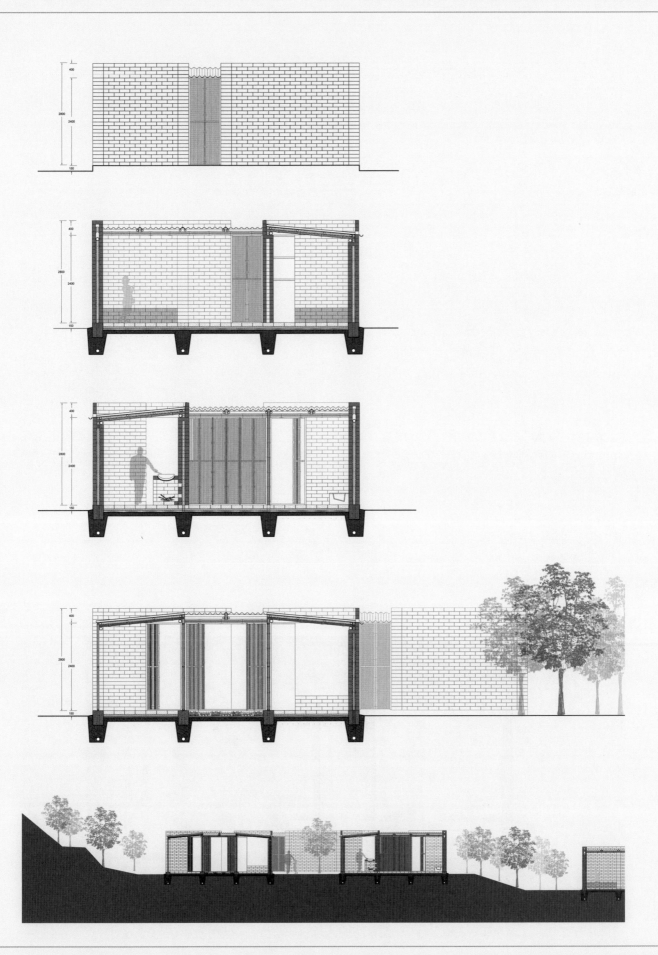

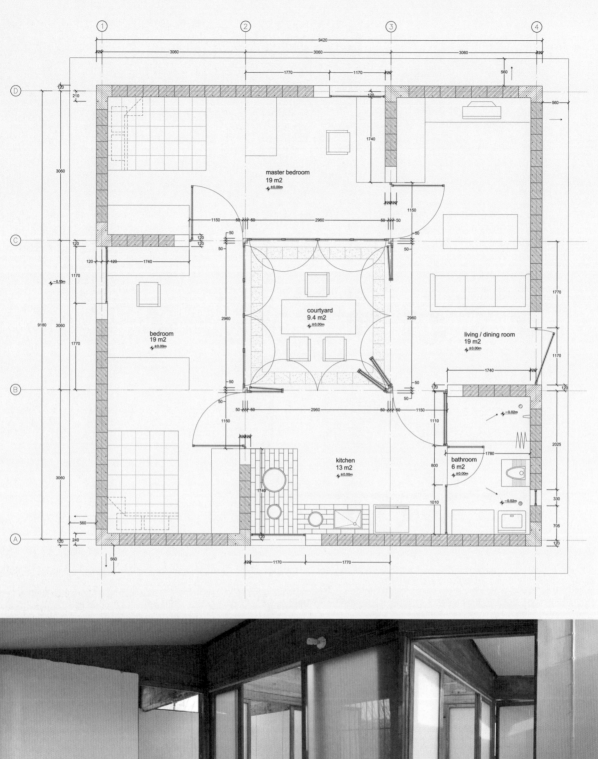

master bedroom
19 m2

courtyard
9.4 m2

living / dining room
19 m2

bedroom
19 m2

kitchen
13 m2

bathroom
6 m2

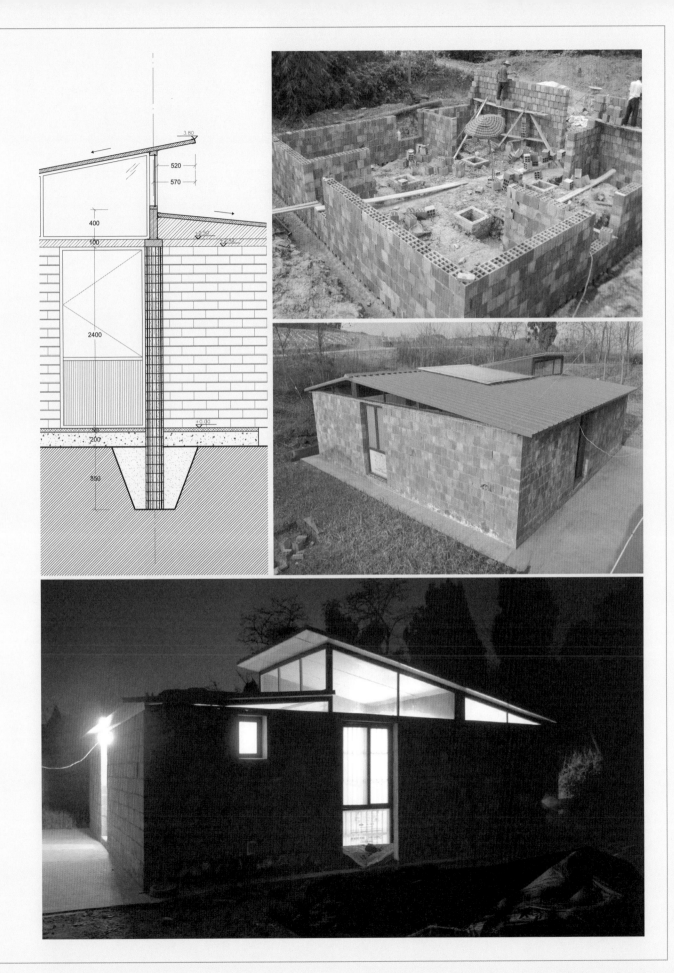

ENSAMBLE STUDIO
NOTES ON PRACTICE AND PEDAGOGY

Antón García-Abril & Débora Mesa-Molina, Ensamble Studio

"Well done is better than well said" Benjamin Franklin

"The greatest freedom is born of maximum rigor" Paul Valéry (Eupalinos ou l'architecte, 1921)

Our work as architects to develop new approaches to the architectural space is based in the equilibrium between three activities: practice, teaching and research, where practice is the ultimate and true expression of Architecture, and the ultimate goal of science, where all variables converge to enable the transition from theory to practice.

Researching and practicing

Research and practice are not only theoretically but physically connected in our daily professional routine. The office has become an intense laboratory where the limits between these two activities dilute. Each project results in a prototype for the next one and there is a constant learning from past experiences. As a premise we never stop working, and we achieve great success with the projects we develop on our own initiative, for the sake of researching about programs, technologies or architectural topics that we find problematic and relevant for our societies. We really feel the need to research, but with a very practical attitude, searching for real answers to real questions; and trying to find institutions, companies, people, to support and enrich our proposals. For us, team-work is critical. The relationship between professionals is really a key aspect in the communication and delivery of an architecture that integrates the complexity of reality, from the most technical to the most artistic aspects; from the most idealistic to the most feasible. The best buildings usually derive from a perfect symbiosis between professionals that share their knowledge. Practicing, teaching,

Balancing Act Installation, Venice
Architecture Biennale 2011 (Italy), completed in August 2011. General view of the installation inside the Arsenale building.

researching, they are all activities enriched when cross-functional teams work together to achieve the same goal. And in this sense Architecture is never the achievement of one individual.

In our work, the support of industry is very important at all levels and so we incorporate this variable from the beginning, to test the interest of the research, to test its feasibility, to learn about past experiences, etcetera. Finding a good balance between what society needs and what industry offers and demands is a constant challenge we have been facing throughout our whole research itinerary. Industry also gives us a lot of clues as to the potential of existing technologies if we manipulate the standardized processes they are usually subject to. Our position is to take advantage of industrial processes as much as possible, as they will guarantee an efficient implementation of our research projects; but we also question those processes at all times, trying to optimize them, or to substitute them for better ones. Going to the origin of industrial processes is a key aspect to learn where materials come from and how are they transformed, and this way this process can be altered in the benefit of architecture, achieving sometimes unusual applications, but very coherent with the material itself, solutions that try to explore its possibilities beyond standard convention. We believe the way materials are put together to generate Architecture is something that should be designed for each project. The development, usage and knowledge of tools, techniques, crafts, systems, or methods of organization will define the way architecture is built, the way it succeeds or not in solving a problem or serving a specific purpose. There is a lot to be explored in this domain. Materials have not evolved much in the last century, however the way these materials can be assembled, manipulated or expressed has developed considerably, enabling multiple architectural manifestations with the same material, sometimes too many. And research must not only attend to what can be done, but also what makes sense to be done, what improves the solutions offered by industry, not only aesthetically but technically, economically and environmentally. One of the more successful researches our office is developing has to do with the technology of prestressed concrete, which we have widely explored at different scales and within different architectonic typologies and programs.

And the goal in every project we undertake is the space others will inhabit, how to achieve a specific space that enables the development of certain activities, and what is the quality of that space depending on the material and the technology used to build it. Because it is the space, and in the end the user, the one that suffers or benefits from the

Hemeroscopium House,
Las Rozas de Madrid (Spain) completed in June 2008.
Exterior view.

SGAE Central Office,
Santiago de Compostela (Spain), completed in October 2007.
Stone wall façade.

decisions we take when designing a project. And it is the space that makes Architecture different from other artistic expressions, what links it directly to society and its demands.

Teaching

To learn to think as architects, and to convey our ideas to students, researchers, and society, the academic network is the perfect platform where experience and knowledge are shared and continued. Because it is in Academy where the origin of the chain of knowledge transmission can be found. And in this forum we believe it is the duty of the architect to generate new questions, share concerns develop techniques and processes, invent systems. And above all, be able to transcend the epistemological limits of the discipline enabling truths and beliefs to cohere in a true knowledge, in this case, the creation of architectural space at the service of people. And it is the role of the architect, as a professor, to enroll students in this process of architectural and technological research.

The Truffle
Costa da Morte (Spain), completed in February 2010.
Exterior view.

(top) **Cervantes Theater**
Mexico City (Mexico), under construction.
Assembly process of The Dovela (roof structure) at the factory.

(bottom) **Reader's House**
Madrid (Spain), under construction.
Restoration of Madrid's Old Slaughterhouse warehouses. Insertion of the new
structure (bridges) through the windows of the existing warehouse.

In this domain, we have found our experience as architects, as researchers, as builders of our own works, is our best value as teachers. It is our own experience that we believe we can better teach. This experience is, of course, full of references, of history of contemporary culture, of political reasons and economical situations that we address and frame; but it is the way we think and implement our ideas, and the way they become true that results in stimulation for students and other professionals. So we like to base teaching in the dialogue with the students and between students, offering them our practical and research experience to make them develop their own tools to practice architecture. We teach to make future architects understand how an idea is formed, developed and finally built. And we believe self example in any discipline to be really effective as a teaching methodology.

The concept of the studio we developed tries to achieve a good balance between creativity and technique. Working with complex situations to define programs, and at the same time guiding students to focus on a specific technology to develop their proposals, enables a deeper knowledge by both individual research and group exchange of ideas. Working with general concepts and particular applications, understanding global and local scales, prepares the students to deal effectively with the numerous variables each project involves. Students go through a whole process of design, studying complex programs of multiple scales, and giving relatively complete answers. We usually try to create a framework that is close to reality, establishing a clear schedule of work that will enable the necessary level of project development and detail. Projects' depictions try to present real situations, so that the students analyze and get to understand and respond to the context they live in. We believe students at university, besides architecture, should learn about general culture, politics, economy, geography, and a huge etcetera through dealing with actual programs; and studios enable this kind of learning throughout a reasonable period of time.

This interest in developing programs that respond to our present and close future is something that MIT has been developing at both educational and research levels, understanding that it is an effective way of connecting students with the problems and needs of their times. Being enrolled this year with our students in a joint studio MIT-HIT (Harbin Institute of Technology), we have experienced a very fruitful exchange of ideas and cultures, very positively intensified by a trip to China we did to learn about the real context in which the students were designing their proposals for a Winter Olympic Hybrid in the city of Harbin. In this sense we would like to highlight the importance

Berklee–SGAE Tower of Music,
Valencia (Spain), under development. Elevation of the model.

of the trip to stimulate, to implicate the student in the context, to understand and also to realize the importance of the physical experience in Architecture, something that is so important and at the same time so much gradually abandoned by architects.

Despite the scale and complexity of the syllabus, the studio tried to balance an initial phase of wide thinking, analyzing, studying references, conceptual speculation where students were able to explore and express their own world working with much freedom; with a second phase that focused on materializing these ideas, where technology and construction had to appear without losing the spirit of innovation and experimentation, where the work became much more rigorous and structured. The same way we do in our office, we encouraged the students to address

Link City,
Prefabricated linear city prototype, research project in development.
Image showing one possible application of the system in Madrid's landscape.

after a continuous dynamic of hard work, they found the satisfaction of arriving to a specific result, a proposal that tried to make things better, and that contained a humanistic vision that took into account society's needs. And they realized that the best way to arrive to this point is constant hard work. (And a big dose of self-criticism.)

We demand of students what we demand of ourselves as architects, to always try to give responsible answers, to open new alternatives or horizons and so perform as researchers, to learn from what has already been done, and then, to innovate not for the sake of being original but to be really active and useful as architects to our society. For us, MIT is the perfect platform to convey these ideas as we share the same concerns and the same active and productive attitude to confront the architectural scene today. It is an ideal meeting point where students, teachers, and professionals of all kinds can discuss, where the equilibrium between practice, teaching and research can really take place. And so, we feel at home.

construction strategies from the conceptual phase, so that design and constructive logic could be perfectly ingrained. And the goal, as when practicing, was the realization of ideas, and so the students went through a difficult but necessary process of controlling their proposals, of understanding what was being spoken, drawn or modeled, travelling through all the design itinerary, facing some of its problems, and trying to solve some of their doubts; and

WoHo (World Homes),
prefabricated social housing prototype, research project in development.
Image showing one possible configuration of the system.

CIRCUS MAXIMUS: OLYMPIC SPORT HYBRID IN HARBIN, CHINA
OPTION DESIGN STUDIO

Instructors: **Antón García-Abril, Débora Mesa-Molina**
Teaching Assistant: **Yashar Ghasemkhani**

Harbin, with a population of around 10 million inhabitants, is one of the largest cities in China, and a key political, economic, scientific, cultural and communications hub. Its location at the Northeast of the country and its historical itinerary, explains the inevitable Russian influence. Harbin is striving to become a main trade and shopping center of the region and boasts abundant natural resources, good transportation systems, main industrial bases and plenty of human resources. This fast developing city has built in the past 15 years what used to take a hundred; and newly built up neighborhoods extend far from the city center facing a lack of public services that are waiting to be developed. Harbin is known as the "Ice City" because of its cold winters, and it is a potential candidate to host the 2022 Winter Olympic Games. The students will work in this evolving context considering not only the architectural, but also the economic, social and urban realities of it.

Although technology and society have developed considerably over the past decades, sports facilities remain quite the same. How can this architecture better adapt to the present times? Sports facilities can host different sports activities and entertainment events, but also programs of a different nature that will increase their utilization and improve their financial viability. Departing from these premises, the students will design a key multi-purpose sport institution to be located at a strategic spot of the city, revitalizing this specific area. They will work at an intermediate scale between architecture and infrastructure. Fixed typologies will be revised and questioned; and sports programs will be integrated and complemented to improve the cultural and commercial offer of the neighborhoods.

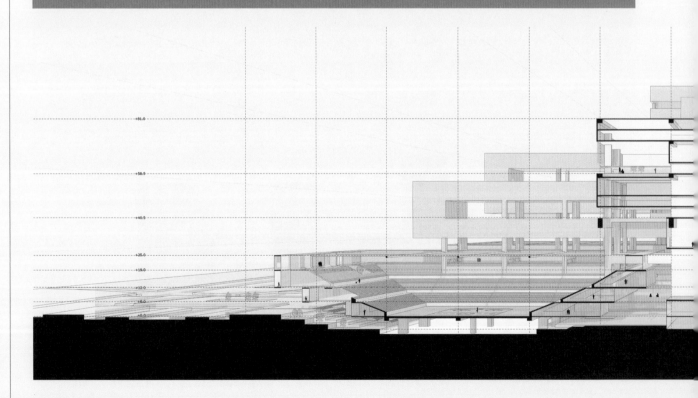

Yoonhee Cho | MArch
Athletic Archipelago

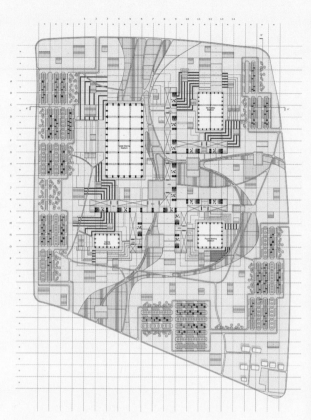

A group of islands, seemingly separate and independent, are connected to each other by being attached to the ground. The "Stadium Complex" for the Winter Olympics, located in Harbin, China, also looks operated individually, but exists as one entity. This project is an architectural exploration and outcome of constant adjustments and negotiations between various components which are sometimes conflicting with each other, or helping the design decision of other factors. The key idea of this project is to learn the back-and-forth methodology of working from small to large scale, or from the structural aspect to the architectural decision, and so on. For example, the proposed landscape is an unexpected outcome stemmed from the tension between existing nature and artificial grid system. At the same time, the landscape design mutually affects building design. Building design changes the scale of module by which the artificial elements of the landscape is determined. In the meanwhile, the landscape leaves the imprints of green areas, distributed over the site, on the building plan.

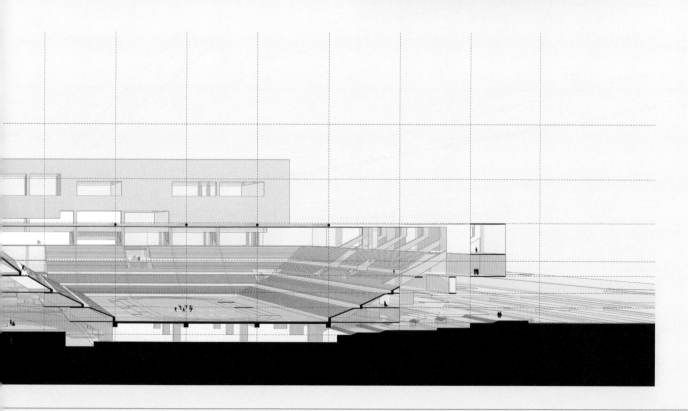

Matthew Bunza | MArch
Temporal Infrastructure

This project is a direct response to two mandated presuppositions of this speculative design studio–the first is that the program of multiple Winter Olympic sports venues be combined into one singular hybrid building; the second is that the project should utilize pre-stressed concrete as the primary building material.

Sited on an expansive as-yet unbuilt floodplain of the Songhua River located just north of the city of Harbin in Northeastern China, any proposal must at once deal with complex climatic, cultural, and civic contexts. The city of Harbin–which was once the terminus of the great Trans-Siberian railway and is now set to grow more in 10 years than it has in 100 years–bores a multicultural identity coming from the overlap of Chinese, Russian, and Western influences, but is also climatically unique in that its extreme temperatures commonly reach below -40o C in the Winter, and the city is known for its cultural ice festival as a result.

This proposal seeks to create an architectural infrastructure more on the scale of highways than of individual buildings, and recognizes that one of the unique experiences of the Winter Olympics lies within an intimate human interaction with landscape, water, temperature, and time change.

Here, a system of concrete ribs sets up a cadence of experiences (formed from modulations in the ribs where primary space is created through subtraction, while secondary space is created through infill), within which different types of program and human interactions may exist. This structural grain is oriented north/south–which combined with thermal mass and a roof system that allows south light to permeate the building–creating a large scale passive solar setup that mediates the interior spaces from Harbin's extreme temperature shifts.

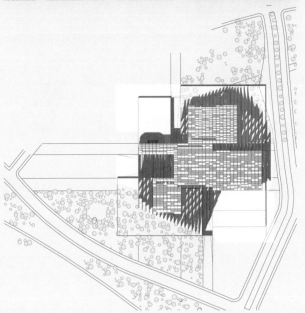

The building also harnesses the uniqueness of Harbin's climate by collecting and storing water in the rainy season, which is then released in winter to form a natural frozen, secondary enclosure–an envelope of ice. As the ambient temperature rises in summer, this natural façade melts away to create open-air spaces on the public periphery of the building, and uses the runoff to create evaporative cooling within the building and to irrigate nearby existing crops.

SECTION - EAST / WEST
1:1000

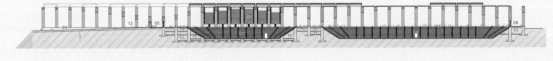

SECTION - NORTH / SOUTH
1:1000

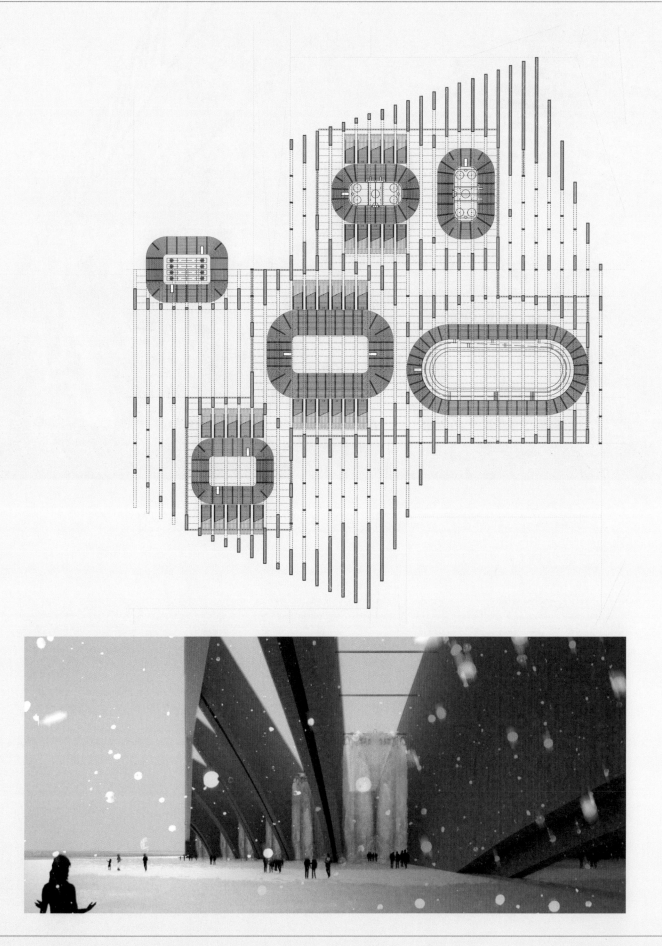

Huang Zhe | MArch
A Micro-City Supported by the Stadia

The Harbin Winter Olympic Games Stadiums project consists of five individual stadia for different sports. The main task of the project is to unify them to create a new civic urban center. In my proposal, I use these five individual stadia as "columns" to support a giant urban platform which has a series of urban programs like exhibition, retail, and cinema. The stadia with autonomous structures support the rest of the program and liberate the ground floor plan. Thus, the project produces three different spaces: a giant flat space on the top, ground space, and the space between ground and the top. The site there is a tabula rasa. It requires a monumentality to establish a town center to develop the areas around. This Olympic Games Center finally turns to be the hybrid urban public center for the daily use.

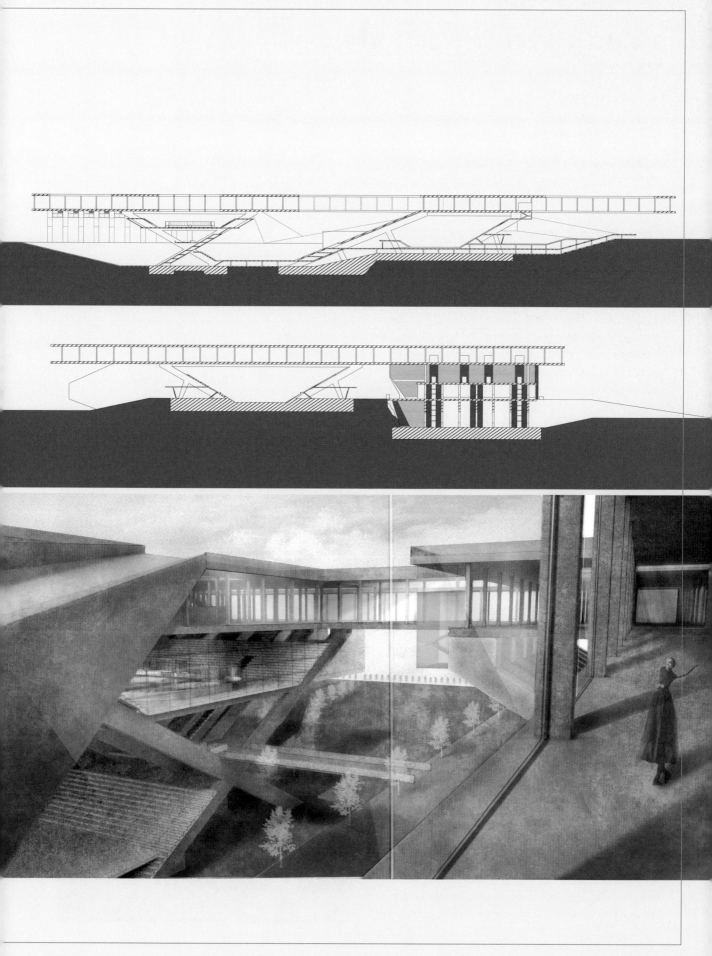

GLOBAL IN A NOT SO GLOBAL WORLD

Mark Jarzombek

This article was originally published in the Journal of Architectural Education, *March 2011: Vol. 64, Issue 2 (59-65).*

"Now there is one outstanding important fact regarding spaceship earth, and that is that no instruction book came with it." (Buckminster Fuller)

The Modern and the Traditional: a Global Dualism

It may be true, as Buckminster Fuller so aptly noted, that no instruction booklet came with spaceship earth, but that does not mean that such "booklets" are in any way lacking. The problem is that most of them are astonishingly outdated, such as for example, the one that claims to spell out the difference between tradition and modernity.[1] Used all over the world, it could be called Instruction Booklet Number One. The Leeum Samsung Museum of Art, for example, in Seoul Korea opened its doors in 2004 with one of its new buildings serving as the home of "Korean Traditional Art" and another, just a few meters away, serving for the exhibition of modern art that is tailored around what its curators call, "the flow of contemporary art."[2] The split between "the traditional" and "the contemporary" —between the fixed and the transient, and between "history" and "modernism" —is so pervasive and now so fundamental to the perspective of current self-understanding that it makes all attempts to define "the global" in more complex terms practically impossible, especially because the discourses associated with "tradition" are integral not only to international curatorial practices, but also to the national-identity projects–practically the world over–of the last twenty years.

"Tradition is Back," A shop sign in Istanbul, 2010.

The dissemination of this Instruction Booklet has been relatively rapid. In the mid-twentieth century, national identity was usually associated with modernization and engineering. Recent national-identity movements, however, have increasingly been associated with history, religion, and "culture," the latter often sanitized for internal popular consumption, touristic commercialization, and political empowerment. Furthermore, since 1975, about forty-eight new countries have joined the United Nations, each eager to define their unique identities. The result has been the internationalized spread of cultural nationalism and the ideology of tradition. Architectural restoration projects the world over have often played an important role in this. Kwanghwamun, a tower gate in Seoul, Korea, for example, was rebuilt in 2010 to invigorate national spirit. The Korean president, dressed in traditional costume, delivered the opening speech under a white banner suspended from balloons stating that the gate was restored to its "genuine form." Such projects along with hundreds of UNESCO World Heritage Sites aim to cement the relationship, reinforced by tourism, between history and national identity. Another indicator is the rise in the number of national museums in the last decades.[3]

Art history has played a role in the distribution of the Instruction Booklet since such categories as Korean Art, Chinese Art, Cambodian Art, and Indian Art seem to always

Official opening of the Kwanghwamun (tower gate) in Seoul Korea on August 15, 2010.

Image credit: Ministry of Culture, Sports, and Tourism, Republic of Korea.

"end" with the arrival of modernism in a way that reinforces museological practices.[4] The title of William Watson's magisterial book, *Arts of China to AD 1900,* says it all, as does Sheila Blair and Jonathan Bloom's book, *The Art and Architecture of Islam 1250-1800.*[5] Bianca Maria Alfieri's *Islamic Architecture of the Indian Subcontinent,* ends in 1839.[6] The last chapter of Alfieri's book is called the "The Final Phase of Mamluk Architecture," as if this "final phase" were a historical predictor of the arrival of colonial masters who ended the development of Islamic architectural history in India. These books epitomize the art historical crisis of how to address the advent of modernity in the non-West, promoting the premise that modernity represents an era that is essentially (art)history-less. It is this historiographic closure against modernity —where it is treated as a separate academic discipline—that forces modernity to be seen first as a "rupture" and then as an endless "flow" of contemporary, tradition-less realities.

Global Instruction Booklet Number One has also been institutionalized in architectural pedagogy especially in Asia, where there are not only usually two primary history offerings, "traditional architecture" and "modern architecture," but also where the first is commonly taught before the second, effectively alienating one time period from the other.[7] The split — constituting a self-traditionalization of the non-West–poses fundamental problems to the advancement of global history, which has no home in such a system. In Japan, for example, it might seem reasonable that most architecture students are asked to take a course on Traditional Japanese Architecture. It makes them into good and knowledgeable citizens. But global citizenship is sacrificed. And the problem is not just in Japan, but now practically global.

The pervasive dualism of history and modernity might have some credibility in the field of art curatorship–reinforced as it is by the globalized rise of cultural nationalism, but the history of architecture should most certainly not be written or taught in this way. Nor is it accurate. There is much more flow to history than there is to modernity. One only needs to think of the endless rise-and-fall of empires and kingdoms compared to the significantly more stable political situation of today. The Leeum Samsung Museum should improve the curatorial language of its exhibitions. One museum should be dedicated to the Flow of Traditions and the other to The Modern Art in the Era of Permanent Nations.

Billboard announcing the beginning of construction in 2007 by the Ethiopian Authority for Research and Conservation of Cultural Heritage in collaboration with UNESCO at Lalibela Ethiopia.

Argument one:

Consideration of "the global"—learning the history of others and challenging ourselves to resist the convenient and reductive taxonomies of nations — should be adopted globally, but it is not. It is undercut by a global culture of localism augmented by cultural nationalism and reinforced by art history, art curatorship and the international heritage industry.

The NAAB and the Paradox of Language

The National Architectural Accrediting Board has recently decided that it is important to educate students about what it calls "Historical Traditions and Global Culture." According to the guidelines about how to accomplish this, schools of architecture are mandated to provide students "with an understanding of parallel and divergent canons and traditions of architecture, landscape and urban design including examples of indigenous, vernacular, local, regional, national settings from the Eastern, Western, Northern, and Southern hemispheres in terms of their climatic, ecological, technosocioeconomic, public health, and cultural factors."[8]

Unlike Instruction Booklet Number One, which is brought out of hiding only as a global cumulative practice spanning the realms of art, architecture and politics, this "booklet" is spelled out in real words. But what then does "Historical Traditions and Global Culture," for example, mean? A good number of traditions are actually impositions of the ruling elites that have been naturalized over time. The Japanese tea ceremony, as it is usually performed today as a demonstration of simplicity and austerity, may now be seen as traditional, but it was created in the fifteenth century as

a protest by the aristocracy against the courtly excesses of the shogunate. In cases like this, the adjective "historical" is useful since it keeps the study of tradition anchored in historical and not in ontology vagaries. The problem, however, is that many things that we call "traditions" are not historical, but modern inventions often frozen in time for political expediency. By only teaching "historical traditions," we are not bringing into the open the circumstance that traditions are also shifting signifiers. The linkage of "global" and "culture," in the context of "indigenous," is also hardly neutral. It is a reiteration of a decade-old position that holds that "global" is to be taught and researched as a recuperation of an architecture-from-below, a premise which today is seen as patronizing. Taken together, the words "Historical Traditions and Global Culture" should have been arranged differently to read "Global History and Cultural Traditions." History is always global, and traditions are always cultural products.

Let's now study the next part of the N.A.A.B. "instruction booklet" and the catenation of words beginning with "indigenous" and ending with "national." There is no doubt that indigenous architecture is important to study, but one should not forget that in India, for example, the government has categorized many of its numerous indigenous tribes as members of the "Backward Classes."[9] This is not just a legacy of colonialism, but a conceit of civilization that can be traced back thousands of years, and not just in South Asia, but practically everywhere. In the context of our modern times, the suppression of indigenous people has increasingly important economic implications, since many of these tribes live in forested and mountainous areas rich in lumber and mineral deposits. Linking "indigenous" to "nation" creates the illusion that nations arise from their indigenous populations naturally over time, when in actuality the modern nation state, as history shows again and again, has more often than not sought to suppress the rights of the indigenous.

The !Kung (also known as the San) in Botswana are a case in point. With the creation in 1961 of the Central Kalahari Game Reserve, three quarters of their population were relocated to resettlement camps outside the Reserve. The !Kung, who had lived on this site for seventy thousand years or more, were seen as an embarrassment. Conflicts arose. Scores were murdered. In 1999, some land was returned to the !Kung, but in 2005 the government began again to remove them, leaving only about 250 permanent residents in the Reserve. In 2006, a Botswana court proclaimed the eviction illegal, allowing some of the !Kung to return to the game reserve, but many still live in resettlement camps. The difficulties the !Kung experienced did not end there. In the 1990s, the pharmaceutical giant, Pfizer, became aware of the tribe's use of a local plant, the hoodia cactus, to suppress hunger while hunting, and in 1998 the company began producing a hunger-suppressant using an extract derived from the plant. None of Pfizer's profits were earmarked for the !Kung. In 2002, a memorandum of understanding was drafted, but its implementation is doubtful.[10] To add

insult to injury, the recent construction of a fence along the Botswana-Namibia border separates the !Kung from their millennia-old hunting ranges.[11]

The story is repeated in many places, but with different emphases. When Indonesia gained independence in 1950, an aggressive government campaign was launched to modernize the Mentawaians, who lived on the island of Siberut. Traditional cultural practices, such as tattooing, tooth filing, and the wearing of loincloths, were forbidden. Individuals were forced to join either the Christian or Muslim faith. In the 1990s, cultural oppression of the Mentawai took on a more brutal form—forced relocation to resettlement sites in government-created villages. Mentawai shamanism was outlawed, and police stripped shamans of their sacred objects. International organizations like UNESCO, the World Wildlife Fund, and Friends of the Earth, have done little to help. They were often more concerned about saving the island's primates than its indigenous people.

The United States was, of course, the first modern state to enforce a top-down suppression of its indigenous populations, as opposed to having them as colonial subjects.

The Dresden Synagogue, Architects: Rena Wandel-Hoefer and Wolfgang Lorch, 2001.

National parks were about landscapes and animals and not about native populations. The approach has now more or less become state policy the world over. It has, one can say, "gone global." In other words if we want to study the premise of "global culture" as NAAB expects us to do, we should not begin with the "indigenous" and work our way up the historical ladder. Instead we need to start with the status of the indigenous in global history.

The word "vernacular," the next word in the catenation, is equally problematic. The term derives from the Latin word *vernaculum*, which referred to a shack where slaves lived at the back of a Roman villa's garden. In the eighteenth century, the word slowly came back into currency but without its architectural meaning. Instead it was used by linguists to describe European languages, particularly local dialects. This remained the case until the 1970s when "vernacular" came into architectural parlance in England in the context of research into barns and farm sheds.[12] By the 1990s it had become widely naturalized in architectural jargon. Although its etymology alone should lead to a rejection of the term's usage, it is now so well established in architectural circles that it even has come to refer to monumental buildings in the non-West. For example, on its much-used web site, the Smithsonian Institution labels the Great Mosque of Djenne Mali as "vernacular."[13] We do not know who the designer of the Great Mosque was, but by that logic, many European cathedrals could also be called vernacular. This tendency to sometimes characterize non-Western architecture—especially if it is made out of mud or timber –as "vernacular" is not only patronizing, but it is also inconsistent with the term's application in Western contexts. The NAAB guidelines, however, practically endorse this usage, by seeing vernacular as a step up, so to speak, from "indigenous."

The word "national" is obviously the most complex term in the catenation. Before the nineteenth century, India, for example, was home to numerous kingdoms, empires and states. Still today, hundreds of different languages are spoken there. Given the existence of the modern country of India, which was ultimately a colonial construct, it is, of course, convenient to think along the lines of an "Indian architecture." The problems are obvious. How, for example, does one deal with the pre-modern history of Pakistan or Afghanistan? Likewise, although Southeast Asia was significantly influenced by India through the spread of Buddhism and Hinduism, Angkor Wat is discussed today as an example of "Cambodian Architecture," even though it cannot be understood without considering the contemporary Chola Empire in India, the Srivijayan Empire to the south and the Kingdom of Dali (in modern-day China) to the north. Pre-nation-state history is significantly skewed when viewed through the lens of modern national realities. The Asian Art Museum in San Francisco has separate sections for China, India, Korea and Japan. While this might seem reasonable enough, such a structure makes it impossible to learn about the complex, intra-continental connections between these places. The museum, despite its name, makes it impossible to learn about Asia. The name of the museum should be "The Art of (Some of) the Countries of Asia as Seen Through a Non-Global World-View."

All in all, the catenation from "indigenous" to "national" not only suggests a progress toward more organized and more legitimate political structures, but also reinforces the stability of the concept "national" which returns us to Instruction Booklet Number One. The catenation tries to avoid a Euro-centric perspective by being inclusive of the architecture 'from below," but it is most definitely still a nineteenth century proposition. The catenation fails to account for histories–even ancient histories–that are transnational, trans-geographical, trans-continental and, maybe lastly, and importantly, "global;" all the more reason to shift the discussion from Global Cultures to Global History. Admittedly, "nations" are more stable and thus more convenient for the historian than what existed before, but if the goal of education is to move in the direction of "global" then we must critique the hegemony of "the nation" as a stable epistemological and disciplinary construct.

Argument Two: By "global" we do not mean the culmination of history beginning with the indigenous and ending with the modern nation state. Nor do we mean the reclamation of an architecture-from-below, but a project that can—and must —frame the contestations and ideologies embedded in architecture's historical formations.

Putting the "Global Footprint" into the Architectural Studio
The challenge of engaging the question of "the global" must occur not only in seminar rooms, but also in the architecture studio. Unfortunately, "global" is almost always made equal to "globalization." This has become an Instruction Booklet unto itself. Studios using this "instruction booklet" are often designed around pressing problems, like the growth of slums, the rapid urbanization of the countryside, and the crisis of ecology. While these issues are important, their range is much too limited, especially if the emphasis is on problem-solving. Instead, one could ask students, for example, to design a store that makes manifest its globalized contents, and by this we do not mean a store that—like Rem Koolhaas's Prada store in New York– celebrates its contents. After all, buildings of even humble proportions are today a composite of materials from probably a dozen or more different countries. In that sense,

buildings are far more foundational as a map of global realities–in the positive and negative sense–than even a shoe. And it is not just materials along with their chemistries and industries that make a building "global" but so too the economies of production and exchange, all of which can be incorporated into a building's message. Having students first research the global nature of materials and their production streams, and then having them experiment with ways to represent that in a design would be a first step to raising global consciousness. Unfortunately, we tend to focus more on the carbon footprint than on the global footprint. The point is not that the global footprint needs to be reduced. Instead it needs first to be made manifest. Then it could perhaps even be celebrated.

Religion is another common but prickly subject that is rarely discussed. Consider the following studio proposition: Design a synagogue in Dresden where there are no Jews. This might sound like an implausibly strange studio project, but it is not a hypothetical question. Such a building was designed by Rena Wandel-Hoefer and Wolfgang Lorch, and built in 2001.[14] There were almost no Jews in Dresden when the synagogue was built, since they were exterminated during WWII; furthermore, the few Jews living there had come only recently from Russia and were relatively secular in their world-view. But the site of Gottfried Semper's synagogue, which was demolished under Hitler, was still owned by the de facto Jewish community. The government decided that a synagogue should be built on the site, even without a client. Regardless of one's opinion of the building, it was an important and praiseworthy–and not uncontroversial– structure that opened a conversation about global realities.

This example inspires ideas for other projects: a neo-pagan temple in England for the so-called Druids who are clamoring for legitimacy; a mosque without a minaret, as is now legislated in Switzerland; a human rights museum in Beijing; or a mosque near the Ground Zero site. The fact that this last project is now at the center of our national debate should lead studio professors to ask why this project has not already been assigned.

Political issues present countless opportunities for studio projects. In Bahrain or Hong Kong, a teacher might propose that students design a museum devoted to the lives of Philippine workers; or in Seoul, a museum to Vietnamese wives. We can imagine a museum of journalism in Moscow;

Glacier Museum, *Fjaerland, Norway, Architects: Sverre Fehn 1991.*

an Armenian History Museum in Istanbul; a memorial in Tiananmen Square to the Tiananmen Square Massacre of 1989; or a new government complex in Afghanistan. A teacher might propose the design of a bank that anticipates a civilizational collapse and the return of a barter economy; the design of a school for our failed education system; a house where a family member suffers from Post Traumatic Stress Disorder. After all, 1.6 percent of Americans and millions of people worldwide suffer from PTSD.

How do we get students to see themselves as architectural actors IN our complex, but shared, global reality?

A student who designs a Buddhist sanctuary in Maine might be interested to learn how Buddhism left India in the 3rd century CE and how its architectural forms were transformed as it traveled across China to Korea and Japan. Students asked to design a warehouse in Ethiopia, which is experiencing a huge influx of Chinese goods, could examine the architectural, political and urban connection between India and East Africa beginning in the 12th century. Students designing a mosque in Ireland could consider how Christian architects in thirteenth-century Cordoba transformed the city's seventh-century mosque into a cathedral. Students designing projects sited within the chaos of a contemporary megalopolis should study the largest multicultural city in the pre-modern world, Chang'an (contemporary Xi'an).

Global realities are more compelling as platforms of discussion than what one finds in most studios today even when they focus on globalization. No wonder architectural education seems increasingly irrelevant. Not only should students be brought into the heart of controversies, they should be familiarized with examples that are already engaged in the great, historical questions of our time and should focus on these rather than on the latest buildings by star architects. Examples abound: a Glacier Museum in Norway; a memorial to President Reagan in California; a shrine to Jesse Helms in North Carolina; a Pol Pot Torture Museum in Cambodia. The list goes on! All of these buildings exist, but are almost never discussed as ways to get access to our contemporary position in global history.

Argument Three: Most studios, even those that claim to address globalization, have inoculated themselves against cultural relevance. This is a serious mistake. We must re-establish the global relevance of architecture through informed, critical position-taking. Furthermore, all buildings should have a Global Footprint.

Conclusion
In the above comments we have tried to paint a picture of difficulty. The "global project" as it might be called—a

project in which different people see themselves as part of a complex global history and its disciplinary and political formations—requires global participation. That is for sure. But this is unlikely given the current state of affairs where many of the current "instruction booklets" for spaceship earth are designed to work against a global-oriented epistemology. The more global–or seemingly global–we have become in the last decade, the more we realize how un-global the dominant narratives are about what "global" means. This suggests that we should not be too optimistic about a global epistemology in the near future. In the short term, however, both history-writing and the architectural studio must play a part in the critique; their future cultural relevancy depends on it.

1   See also: Mark Jarzombek, "Art History and Architecture's Aporia," in *Globalization and Art,* edited by James Elkins, Alice S. Kim and Shivka Valiavicharska, Pennsylvania State University Press, 2010.

2   http://leeum.samsungfoundation.org/eng/main.asp (Retrieved 05-07-2010).

3   Some of these are: National Art Gallery, Singapore, 2013; National Art Gallery Pakistan, 2007; National Museum of Kenya, 2006; National Museum of China, 2003; National Museum of Saudi Arabia, 2000; Uzbekistan State Museum of Applied Art, 1997; National Museum of Turkmenistan, 1998; National Museum of Bashkortostan Republic, 1992; and, the Kuwait National Museum, 1983.

4   For the critique of heritage industry see, for example: Robert Hewison, *The Heritage Industry: Britain in a Climate of Decline* (Methuen: London, 1987); Richard Sharpley, *Tourism, Tourists and Society* (St. Edmundsbury Press: Suffolk, 1994); and John Urry, *The Tourist Gaze: Leisure and Travel in Contemporary Societies* (Sage: London, 1990).

5   William Watson, *The Arts of China to AD 1900* (New Haven: Yale University Press, 1995). Sheila S. Blair and Jonathan M. Bloom, *The Art and Architecture of Islam 1250-1800 (New Haven: Yale University Press, 1994).*

6   Bianca Maria Alfieri, *Islamic Architecture of the Indian Subcontinent* (London: Laurence King, 2000).

7   In the US and Europe, the classic distinction is between Modern and the Renaissance, with far different consequences.

8   This requirement is known to school administrators as Realm A: A.9. "National Architecture Accreditation Board (NAAB) Student Performance Criteria (Approved July 10, 2009), p. 22. http://depts.washington.edu/archdept/Forms/2009_Conditions%20_FINAL%20EDITION.pdf (Retrieved 05-07-2010)

9   For a brief history of the term, see Marc Galanter, "Who are the Other Backward Classes: An Introduction to a Constitutional Puzzle," *Economic and Political Weekly,* 13, 43/44 (October 28, 1978) pp. 1812-1828. The government of India classifies some of its citizens based on their social and economic condition, using terms such as Scheduled Caste, Scheduled Tribe and Other Backward Class (OBC). These people are to be distinguished by the "untouchables." The "Scheduled Tribes," who constitute about seven percent of the population, do not accept the caste system and prefer to reside deep in the jungles, forests and mountains of India, away from the main population. The government claims that it ensures the social and educational development of OBCs, but in practice this a complicated matter. Before 1985, the affairs of Backward Classes were looked after by the Backward Classes Cell (BCC) in the Ministry of Home Affairs. With the creation of a separate Ministry of Welfare in 1985 (renamed as Ministry of Social Justice and Empowerment in 1998) the matters relating to OBCs were transferred to the new Ministry.

10   Rebirth Africa, "San Tribe and Biopiracy" *Rebirth Africa.* http://www.rebirth.co.za/hoodia/san_tribe_and_biopiracy.htm (2000,Retrieved 01-05-2010.)

11   Native Solutions to Conservation Refugees, "Seven Tribes Threatened by Ethiopian National Park" *Native Solutions to Conservation Refugees* http://www.conservationrefugees.org/threatened.html (Retrieved 01-05-2010.)

12   In the late nineteenth century, historians would have talked about Folk Architecture or Primitive Architecture. In the 1970s the focus was on "shelter." See for example, Paul Oliver, *Shelter and Society* (New York: F. A. Praeger, 1969,) and R.W. Brunskill, *A Systematic Procedure for Recording Vernacular Architecture* (London: Ancient Monument Society, 1966-1976.) One of the earliest uses is found in M. Bevan-Evans, *Farmhouses and Cottages: an Introduction to Vernacular Architecture in Flintshire* (Hawarden : Flintshire Record Office, 1964.) Bevan-Evans was an archaeologist and the county archivist of Flintshire England. The journal, *Vernacular Architecture,* published out of York began in 1970. R.W. Brunskill's book *Vernacular Architecture of the Lake Counties: a Field Handbook* (London: Faber) was published in 1974.

13   http://sirismm.si.edu/siris/top_images/eepa.top.08_2007.htm (Retrieved 05-07-2010)

14   Mark Jarzombek, "Disguised Visibilities: Dresden/"Dresden," in *Memory and Architecture,* Edited by Eleni Bastea (University of New Mexico Press, November 2004), pp. 49–78.

FUTURE OF THE PAST: AUGMENTED HISTORY, PRESERVATION AS A CATALYST FOR TRANSFORMATION M.ARCH. THESIS

Natsuki Maeda
Supervisor: **Andrew Scott**
Readers: **Gediminas Urbonas, James Wescoat**

Preservation today focuses on the historicizing of events, and the objectifying of these historic artifacts, taking away its ability for further change. It becomes a single artifact, distancing itself from contemporary discourses. This thesis is about preservation, and the role of architecture in preserving historic sites. It is a thesis where its main objective is not of the final project, or artifact, but one which provokes a discourse, where we are confronted with the core meaning of preservation. This field of preservation has existed for thousands of years, but we have not truly re-examined the role of preservation. Preserving must mean more than just to sanction off the site, killing any further transformation, but to allow it to partake in the contemporary discourse, and to give it a future. There are many questions at hand; why do we preserve? What do we preserve? How do we preserve? But in the end, how can preservation become a catalyst for further growth, is the question this thesis seeks to answer through its design. In the struggle to find answers to these questions through architecture, it was in the discourses which rose from each stand point that gave this thesis meaning.

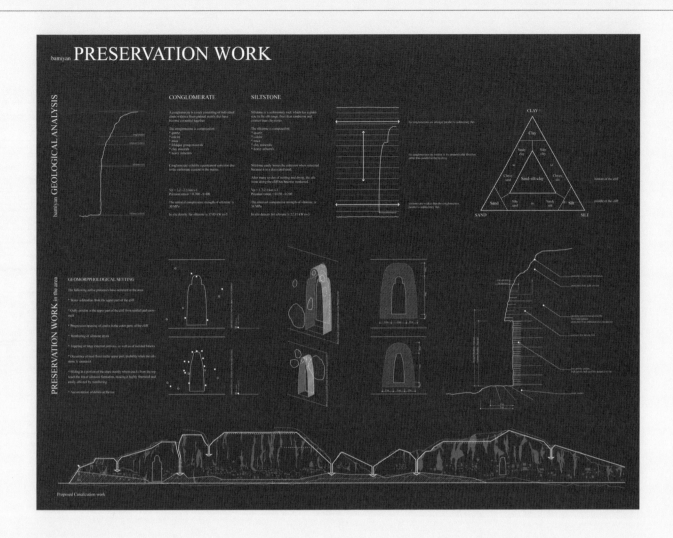

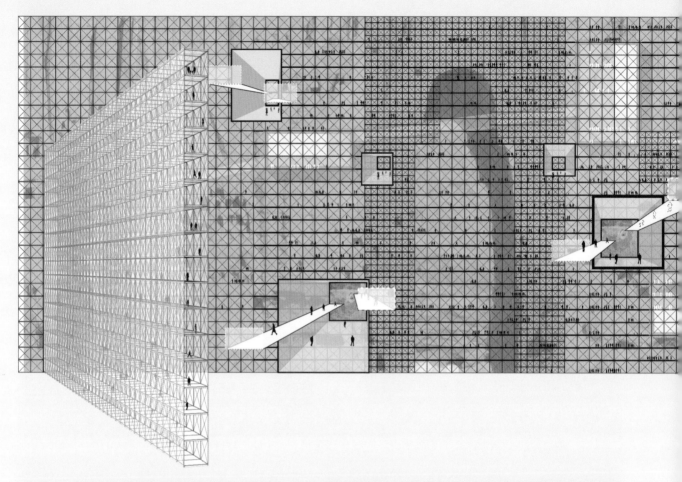

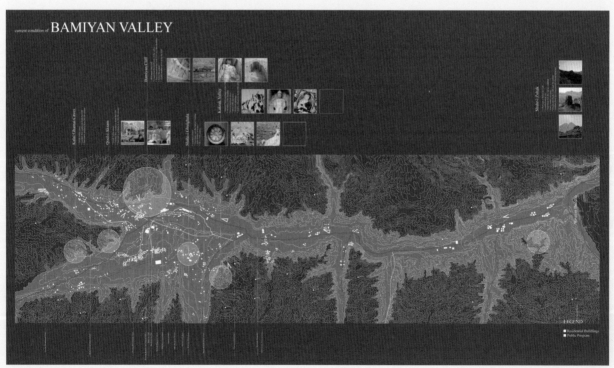

current condition of BAMIYAN VALLEY

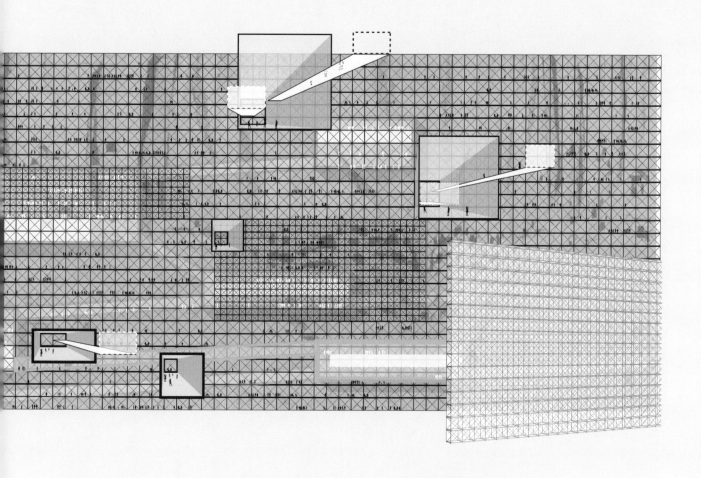

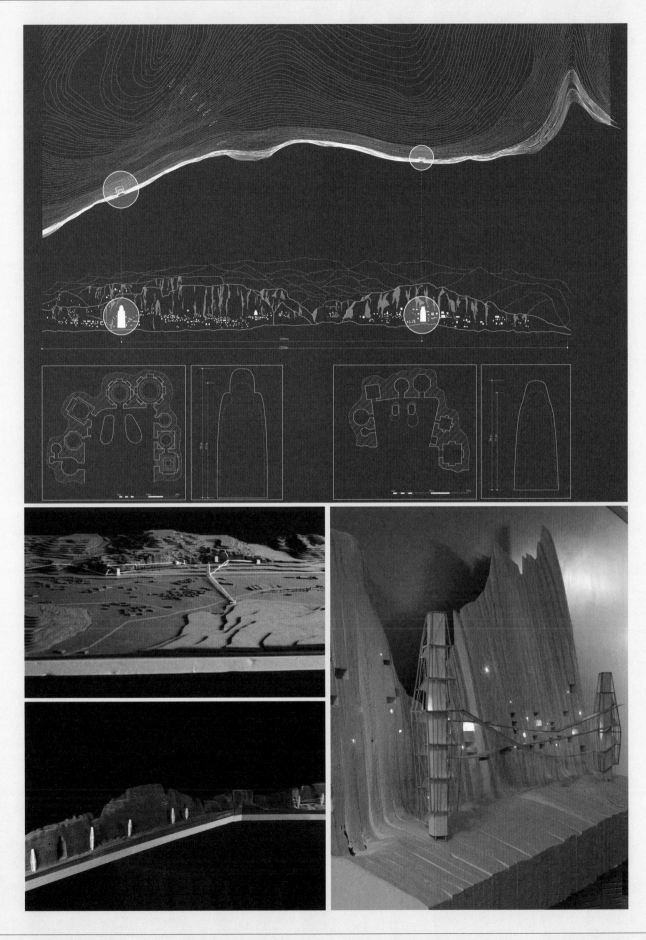

ARCHIVE

THE DEMISE OF PRECEDENT (AGAIN)

Those days are not so far from living memory that students in schools of architecture were introduced to the architectural canon in the darkened precinct of their morning history class. Alternatively, they were referred, by that occasionally so-inclined studio critic, to look up the defining ideological tome of their times–the Zevi or Tafuri or Norberg-Schulz–in the silence of the library. Sometimes, clutching sheaves of photocopied chapters and dog-eared, well-worn books that indicated what was worth seeing, they traveled, building up the harried sweat of a twentieth-century Grand Tour. These events still occur today, but with some differences. Students cross-check information, plans, pictures, about buildings, events, persons even as the professor may be setting up her Powerpoint, interjecting to correct in mid-sentence as the lecture possibly gets a fact here or there wrong. Googling and blogging has significantly transformed the context of precedence, making available counter-examples, counter-arguments, numerous distractions at the touch of the keyboard. Rather than being presented as examples and propositions borne on tangible forms of discourse, architectural images, renderings (generated for that very purpose), as well as the flagrant and specious claims of brand-name architects in glossy publications intended to advertise their work, find their way seamlessly into student projects, tantamount to either a form of bland parody or 'sampling,' a process not unlike using Guitar Hero to score the next Lollapalooza breakthrough.

What happens to the architectural understanding of precedence when images, blurbs, and formal rationalizations come de-tethered from discourse presented along some recognizable courts of dispute? As if the historian/critic came on stage and simply switched through the slide-tray with no commentary,

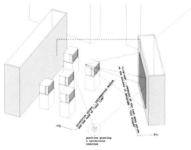

Classes, Masses, Crowds
Karlsruhe, Germany 2004-2005
Representing the Collective Body and the Myth of Direct Knowledge for the *Making Things Public* exhibit at the ZKM. On one side, a projection of 'film news' footage of the May Day parade on the streets of Belgrade–a single ideology available in a glance and powerful in its physical presence. On the other side, a field of television screens with broadcast footage of the 1996/1997 protest and of the October 5th 2000 protest. The series of television screens do not allow a simple and complete 'intake' of this material. As the protagonists of both 'stories' are ordinary people and the stage in both cases is the streets of Belgrade, the formal juxtaposition of these two types of masses strikingly outlines two limit cases of making the masses public.

The essay entitled "Classes, Masses, Crowds. Representing The Collective Body and The Myth of Direct Knowledge" was featured in the *The Problem of Composition* chapter of the *Making Things Public* catalogue published by MIT Press in 2005.

Video Production by Ana Miljački and Jeff Silva.

Images courtesy of Ana Miljački/ Project_

students left free to make their own individual or collective conclusions about what they considered important or did not like. In this sense, the 'eclipse of history' is less about history or historiography than about a more fundamental shift in the protocols, institutional forms, and disputational structures along which knowledge is broadcast and processed, a shift tantamount to what has been called the 'information revolution'. In this sense, it is not only history that appears to have lost its privileged mount in the imaginative equipmentality of the architect, a mount now more and more occupied by the technics and formulational challenges proffered by advanced building systems and technology. No longer do two or three periodicals hold the power to frame the broad disciplinary conversation, to create insiders and outsiders, to even antagonize. The time seems past when one singular or dyadic pedagogy could define a school, and when students emerging from that situation would bear distinct marks–or scars–of that experience: the Eisenman-Graves axis at Princeton, Raimund Abraham-John Hejduk at the Cooper Union, Moneo at Harvard. Studio teaching more and more entails a situation where it is the professor who seems to have to counter against various precedences or influences, brought into the classroom by the student's total immersion into media.

On the other hand, if in the old order of disputation, much bandwidth was monopolized by the outsize idiosyncrasies of a few impresarios or culture-gurus, the general dissipation of epistemic authority from the academy signaled in the new 'informational democracy' seems to have won little purchase in ease of conceptualization, or for that matter, strong variety: thesis projects at Harvard, MIT, Yale, Princeton, Columbia or SCI-Arc (and increasingly in institutional contexts as diverse as Iran or China) look more alike today than ever before. While curators have multiplied, real curation–the cultivation of the incongruous, the atypical–seems to be harder than ever. Little–in the busy traffic of informational highways–seems to have been won in the cultivation of that other leisure of the mind where architecture could contemplate its forms as pointing to a finite set of conundrums, a set we could construe as the 'discipline'. At MIT, as elsewhere, studio and history instructors alike today actively and collaboratively confront what appears to be the pedagogical conundrum of our era: the problem of passing on precedence without recourse to nostalgia or canonical imposition.

Teachers of architecture, no matter what divergence of opinion as to pedagogical belief or attitude, nonetheless hold on unanimously to one golden standard: architectural teaching does not lend itself to methodological explicitness, or even testability. Those who have tried, frustrated by that aversion to explicitness, to put pen to paper have frustrated themselves more. Rather than tethering the field as they might have hoped, like a scientist at a kitchen table their weighty weighing in tends to be simply reabsorbed into the ongoing, fervent, and fast chatting that defines architectural conversation, picked up and dropped at leisure whenever rhetoric or convenience calls for a trenchant metaphor. More often than not, weightiness proves itself a liability.

At the same time, architectural discourse, like kitchen chats, is far from a non-specialized activity. Architectural teachers also hold to the opposite premise from the above: architectural teaching is far from incoherent, or for that matter, lacking in systematicity. Indeed, it may be argued that architects of all stripes, professing incompatible points of view, across the world even, are well able to speak to each other in a shared language, one that entails in most cases a great deal of specificity. The simultaneous refusal of disciplinary unity and the exclusive vocabulary used in such refutations closes out room for productive slippage and engaged discourse. Indeed, as Mark Jarzombek points out in his indictment of architectural education's seeming turn towards pragmatism, "Practice, I would argue, is a field of cultural production; it is not about how one makes a building. The sooner we expose the practices-of-practice, the better architecture will be."[1] And so, as in many other aspects of architectural education and production, a serious self-examination is in order.

How is it that architects, while refuting any consensus as to shared problems, attitude or pedagogy, are nonetheless capable of holding conversations with their colleagues, even across continents? Why does a conversation between architects immediately sound abstruse to the outsider? Architect and Professor Ana Miljački seeks to make these structures visible, and to reveal to students, and to the discipline, just how these pockets of presumed-neutral knowledge are produced. Her agenda, in mobilizing polemics in the studio and in the seminar room, is to activate the discipline's own processes productively, to make references and allusions explicit, and to reengage the design work of architecture within a wider cultural sphere.

The entrée into architecture's own self-examination may well lie in the nexus of student/teacher dynamics the *crit*, implying all those Latin-derived names of people and their exciting activity: critic, criticism, critique. Not at all a neutral event, the crit, while ostensibly an exam of sorts for the student, becomes a soapbox for the six or so *guest-critics* sitting opposite her. A *final crit* is an enigmatic event. An animated critic might launch into extended perorations about some contemporary development in architecture, with equally animated rebuttals from his fellow guests, leaving the student whose work is presumably the focus completely at a loss as to the conversational trajectory. Little do students, focused as they are on their project, realize that they are bearing witness to that peculiar scene by which architectural teachers train each other. A public crit typically expresses the state-of-the-art of the discipline; little recuperable to either post-hoc formulation, or even properly grammatical sentences, it is the device and moving, shimmering text by which the discipline learns, exchanges notes and gossips, tests itself, forms pacts, canonizes artifacts, produces rhetoric.

The public crit also then evinces the moving front of the discipline, a tacit ordering of the discipline guised as a kitchen chat. Indeed, if words don't, both the dress and the body language of the critics give it away. The student

YouPrison Exhibition, Torino, Italy 2008
We were invited by Francesco Bonami and the Fondazione Sandretto de Rebaudengo in Torino to contribute a prison cell design to their YouPrison exhibit, together with twelve other international architects. After researching reform ideas within the U.S. prison system, prison labor laws, as well as the actual architectural implications of a cell redesign, we decided to dedicate our exhibition to explicating the dilemma that a designer finds himself in when asked to impact (through the design of a room) a system determined by agents and agencies well beyond any architect's domain.

As a direct result of recent legislation and of the general cultural embrace of "cleaning up" and normalizing American cities, the number of individuals in U.S. prisons has been steadily increasing, which has brought clear financial benefit to private prison management companies over the last decade. The interior of U.S. prisons is also one of the last sites of production in an otherwise post-industrial economy. None of this is to say that prisons do not involve architectural design—on the contrary, prison architectures often survive the governments that sponsor them—but rather, to begin to describe the intricate and vast network of agents involved in the shaping of the U.S. correctional system in order to understand what possible agency an architect might have in this situation. Not only is the contemporary architect not the same figure as the eighteenth century reformer/architect, but the cell is in fact too small a unit of carceral space to impact the deeply problematic structures and practices that extend well beyond it today.

The floor of our installation is an informational display that requires the visitor to perform our research and our dilemma spatially. Three main voices are reconstructed: the voice of the legislature and governmental agencies, the voice of all who benefit from the prison system financially, and the voice of the prisoners. Each of these agents spins the information in specific ideological directions. Above the large informational display, an illuminated polypropylene cell is presented upside down, as an invitation to contemplate architectural design. If the floor invites one to try to understand the network of agents involved in the prison industrial system or in this contemporary species of prisoner reform, the upper portion of the installation presents a limit case scenario, based on plausible future outcomes of current trends in prison management and contemporary culture. Starting with the ongoing increase in skilled and non-violent prisoner populations, our scenario involves the possible expansion of prison reform arguments to embrace ideas about the special (reform) value of creative work.

Project Team :
Ana Miljački / Project_, Lee Moreau / Project_, Dan Sakai, Ben Porto

confronts, only at the end of the semester, a bevy of quarrelsome types whose clothes nonetheless present a homogeneous array of white on black matched by comical eyewear, as if initiates of a secret, monastic order. Even their quarrel appears couched in a shared, albeit elusive, code.

A certain tension presents itself here, evidently manifested between the homogeneity of costume and the variegations of gesture; architecture comes across less a curation of influences than the acquisition of the tools to judge. Even if the role of the critic as authoritative figure may have subsided, architecture remains, in its essence, a critical activity. Rather than leave this process to the vagaries of end-semester realization, Miljački brings that dynamic to the core of the studio process—taking the problem of (unadulterated) influence as the very basis of her teaching. Her first premise is to invest into, and validate, the new ways in which students appear to be learning. Rather than simply mourn the decline of the older order of pedagogy, she brings that critical frame itself into visibility by transparently pitting it against the newer order of borrowing or imagistic osmosis.

More than anything else, Miljački implores her students to engage with that rhetoric and to see themselves as operators within it. Whether that means boning up on the arguments of the fifties or of the nineties, producing critical research works of their own, or informing their studio projects with historical narratives, the argument is everything. Ideas don't form out of thin air, and it is in fact more productive to search out the seedlings of inspiration, in all of their cultural baggage, in order to borrow, quote, reference, and dispute smartly. Ana Miljački's studios at MIT address these osmotic tendencies by which architects learn, and expect a certain degree of cultural engagement. Between the issues in contemporary theory production and consumption she introduces in her core seminar, and the highly charged cultural embeddedness of her studios, Miljački is trying to make a different kind of architect, or maybe an architect who speaks about her work differently.

Miljački stands for a continued examination of the way we produce ideas charged politically and aesthetically—based on lots of different influences. Her mashup studio isn't just a one-semester long project, it's an idea about how students learn from and build off of ideas that have been part of disciplinary discourse for years. This archival quality to understanding design production is an important aspect of what makes up architectural knowledge, but because such references are often guarded, or mentioned as asides during crits, they are often not given their due in education.

13:100 Thirteen New York Architects Design for Ordos
Architectural League of New York, NY 2008
The exhibit of the thirteen New York participants in the Ordos 100 project contends with two key issues: the participation in and the perpetuation of Ai Weiwei's work on one hand and the contemporary predicament of a young architectural practice on the other hand. We wanted to separate judgments made on the site plan—its reproduction of an overblown suburban layout—from the judgment passed on the projects and on the role of the architects in the Ordos 100 project. In order to do that we disassociated the narrative of the trip, the actual site plan, and the invitation of the one hundred architects (what we see as the narration of Ai Weiwei's master plan project) from the presentation of the work by the thirteen New York Architects. We treated the gallery as that space in which the viewer—through an intimate encounter and study of the work—becomes complicit with the architects.

The exhibit is defined by a series of formal constraints, and although that move fundamentally parallels Ai Weiwei's initial invitation, we hoped that the constraints we provided would allow for a closer look at each individual project, while laying bare the relationship between the apparatus of unifying formal constraints and the differentiation and individuation performed by the architects.

Project Team :
Ana Miljački / Project_, Lee Moreau / Project_, Dan Sakai, Ben Porto
Sound editing by Ana Miljački and Sarah Hirschman
Gallery guide by Luke Bulman / Thumb

1   Jarzombek, "Un-Messy Realism," in *Perspecta 40–Monster*, 83.

MAGAZINES AND THEIR ROLE IN ARCHITECTURE AND ARTISTIC RESEARCH PRACTICE [DISCUSSION] MIT150 TRANSCRIPT

TUESDAY, APRIL 26, 2011

Ana Miljački: Professor of Architecture, MIT
Ute Meta Bauer: Professor of Art, Culture, and Technology, MIT
Dan Graham: Conceptual Artist
Beatriz Colomina: Professor of History and Theory, Princeton University School of Architecture
This conversation has been edited for length and clarity.

Ana Miljački: On paper, this looks like an easy group of people to moderate. Dan is Beatriz's subject sometimes, Ute has curated him, and we have historian, curator, and artist all crossing paths. But once they all put something in the room, it's no longer as easy as it seems. We have seen a number of ways in which magazines figure in each of the talks, but maybe research needs to be brought back up to the center of the conversation. We saw how history and politics affected the production of little magazines. We saw how economy might be part of the reason why a magazine is a site of production. I want to now talk about this non-nostalgic, recuperative history whose impetus essentially is to challenge the contemporary architects to produce something equivalent. Even though this is historical research, first and foremost, it seems to also want to produce an effect in the contemporary. I wonder what would be the equivalent of those little magazines today? Do we really think that the medium of the magazine, in that sense of the sixties or the avant-garde, is the site of a possibly radical intervention in the discourse of architecture?

Beatriz Colomina: We are in the midst, and have been for the last ten years or so, of a transformation in the ways of communication, something that we know has been digitizing, for some time.

I was just reminded by someone that when I was working on *Privacy and Publicity*, I was in my apartment working with the fax machine. Every time I had to review something it was FedEx this, fax that. So the internet of course, and new technologies have completely

transformed the ways we communicate. So you can say that like with the little magazines of the avant-garde, there is again a technical development and another site of possible production. It doesn't mean that the magazines disappear. Of course, it's like the book or the building or something like that. No, absolutely not, what it does is transform it. So the fact that new technologies allow for information to be spontaneous is what's really the new thing. You kind of acquire your authority by your readers.

Dan Graham: I think it's interesting, because I'm not an architect, nor an art historian. Basically, I'm an architecture tourist. And also I'm very interested in astrology. So I'm doing things for two different very good magazines from Italy. One magazine is *Abitare*, and I do a column about architecture which is kind of controversial, because I dispute orthodoxy, bring in some historical things that I discover myself in my architecture tourism. And then Joseph Grima asked me to do a column, which I thought wasn't that serious, a series, about astrology and architecture every month. So columns are very important to communicate. Also, magazines are very important because we're all on airplanes. So, of course we read magazines. I know when I fly with women friends, they always have *Vogue* and *Elle*, magazines like that. But I think we read them during these long boring journeys.

Beatriz Colomina: *Abitare* and *Domus* are very into the scene as a problem of architecture. It's a lot when you open your computer in the morning and you already see the pictures of the new buildings,

Image credit: George X. Lin.

why would you want to wait a month to have a magazine? Why would a magazine think that their mission in life is to bring you the news? So they have to rethink themselves, but that's a good thing. They become their own medium. They don't have an obligation to report, and therefore that liberates them immensely. They can do art. They can ask people like Dan Graham to do a column.

Ute Meta Bauer: I would also like to note how much magazines have influenced how architecture looks. So often architectural photography and representation of architecture in magazines, or art, has changed how it looks. Because it always has to look good in a magazine. I think that architects and how they design for this is something that also should be researched.

Ana Miljački: I want to go back to one thing about the little magazines and their secondary pedagogical function of re-igniting some kind of enthusiasm among young architects, because what's interesting to me is that in the work that you look at, we see the architect becoming aware of the magazine as a site. At first, the avant-garde is more innocent, the neo-avant-garde is less innocent. And now when you produce a kind of super-energetic exhibit on the sixties to our audience, we have to think about what this does to a new generation of architects who might produce. And I think it's actually really important to remember how small these circles are, how few journals actually get made, that *Archigram* did not exist before it was seen by Japanese tourist architects as a group. Basically, starting something like this does not necessarily require a kind of institutional backing and structure that we now, when looking at them, imagine existed.

Beatriz Colomina: Exactly, it's all in perspective. In fact, there is a reason why there are no *Archigrams* anywhere. Columbia doesn't have a copy, the CCA doesn't have it, the best libraries in America don't have it, they don't have it anywhere. Why is that? Because people threw it away. Peter Cook said that he came to the States with a box, and he couldn't give them away. And talk to Peter Eisenman, they couldn't give away *Oppositions*. People who were at Cooper Union said that they would come around with big boxes, and they couldn't give them away.

Ana Miljački: Here we saw that sometimes the big magazine gets affected by the little. But what happens when a little magazine becomes big? Are there examples of that?

Ute Meta Bauer: Dan brought up *Abitare* and *Domus*. I think it's the same as exhibitions wherein you can be radical with a very small exhibition in a mainstream magazine or conversely a pamphlet can be very conservative. But I want to say why I, in general, like sometimes just magazines or periodicals more for research. It's because of the rawness. It is not yet polished often. And you find the cracks and entry points.

Dan Graham: Well, it's called the deadline. Writing for a deadline brings out the best writing, actually.

Ana Miljački: What you presented to us, the research in the Spanish gallery, but also the projects online that exist as high art and a collective voice, etc., seem to operate as invitations to an audience to do research, or to work with an archive. I wonder if we can talk about something like these exhibits that you're producing summoning a particular contemporary subject that we can call "researcher." They seem like projects in curatorial work, which summon up or recall archives. Even this sort of fake think-piece invites a kind of new subjectivity, a contemporary subjectivity that is about, and well-versed in, researching.

Beatriz Colomina: I think it would be important to make a distinction between research that is done in established archives and research that creates an archive in itself. For example, with the Little Magazines, there was no such thing as an archive. So I thought, even *Archigram*, we cannot find it in Avery [Library, Columbia], you cannot find these magazines, you have to go to Japan to unearth the architects from this group that followed the Metabolists, this architects group that everybody had forgotten. The only reason we knew anything about it was that it was written in a footnote in an article on Japan architecture. Nobody in the United States knew about these things. So a student who was Japanese went to Japan, tracked this down. He forced a reunion of these guys, and that's how they came up from there. They had a meeting for us. They don't exist anywhere. So the research sort of creates the archive, that is different from the research of Ute, which is research within the archive.

Beatriz Colomina: You don't think too much about it, you just have to come up with it.

Dan Graham: The thing I said about magazines is that they're a form of journalism. That sloppy way is important. But I have to say that that whole big pictorial spread that architecture offices feature in these magazines is bad because I think architecture has become only about façade and photographs. So I'm really distressed about some of these people who are featured in magazines. So what I've given to *Abitare* is to undercut that a little bit.

Ana Miljački: I was fascinated by your idea of fake sociology. That brings us to this topic of research that I thought we should bring up. For me, research, when it comes to a historian and PhD students, is a relatively codified notion. We can understand what you mean by research. We can even understand it when Ute is producing an exhibit that requires a certain kind of archival research. But when you produce fake research…

Ute Meta Bauer: Which is not really fake. His approach was a kind of plan of entry.

Ana Miljački: I find it as a radical intervention in the magazine.

Dan Graham: No, the research was real, but it's a fake think-piece. In other words, it's undercut seriousness. In other words, it's about what we call clichés, and I know that what I love about magazines is that they deal with clichés.

Ute Meta Bauer: I think the magazines still allow that you can be putting work out in the world. A lot of ideas and thought processes emerge, and maybe they often disappear, but I think that is why I insist that those periodicals, those small magazines, have a strong input on really executing research.

Ute Meta Bauer: I did this exhibition more as a researcher, less as an archivist, because the material I wanted simply was not available in my town. So we emptied the gallery and said "why don't we do the most brutal thing at this moment, to read just magazines in different countries and different discourses?" We put them on the table and

left them. So that was the position. The second was to show that artists are also amazing writers and they did those magazines, they inspired us to do the same. The discourse is the battle. They are not neutral, they are basically countering, so we thought to make this accessible and to discuss them, this was much more enabling others to do work and to do research.

Ana Miljački: This is what I mean, that somehow in your case, what connects the curatorial work across Documenta 11, the new narratives, the narratives online, and the projects you showed, is that in each case they're about a kind of construction of a discourse through whatever means you have–through the gallery or through the website. And in each case I think they rely on or summon a particular subject that I'm calling researcher. Somehow it requires a subject who is willing to go along with your invitation to read or research or input new information, etc. And for me that is something that makes it a very contemporary kind of thing.

Beatriz Colomina: Yes, it's an archival act. I saw pictures of the exhibits with all these open books, with all these people *reading* or the people in the gallery saying how visitors were spending so much time listening to the lectures that happened. So it becomes a kind of archival thing in itself, being used by the students of the AA and such. But returning to that earlier point that you made regarding contemporaneity. I think what is interesting is to realize that the same things happened in the little avant-gardes of the twenties. The magazines, these projects. There is not someone writing, "oh look at this great project by Mies van der Rohe," you see how he himself had to do it. These magazines are for the most part written by the people themselves, and they are very broad and the same thing is to realize they were kids. At the same time that there's *Archigram*, there are all these kids at the AA doing the projects, and they're already publicizing. So there's an energy there. And how is authority gained? Authority is gained by other students reading them. The same thing is true now with blogs. Probably the site of intensity in the print and printing generation.

Dan Graham: I would say also that a lot of these magazines and groups like Archigram or Superstudio were dealing with satire. In other words, it's not the seriousness of the big places. It was satire and a kind of aggressive humor.

Ana Miljački: Let's talk about the story that goes in the other direction. So we have the larger magazines like *Domus*, *Casabella*, becoming little in your description of what a little magazine is, or Denise Scott Brown's. But we also have the other magazines, for example, *Assemblage* is not a little magazine, nor *Oppositions*. So I was wondering how that actually encountered architecture. From another field, *Oppositions* seemed like a radical intervention in the discourse, seemed like a vehicle.

Beatriz Colomina: Well, those are no longer little magazines. This is the birth of a new kind of magazine, which is the theory magazine like *Archis*, *Oppositions*, and I don't consider those little. When you go to the little magazines, there is no staff, there are no other people involved. That is very hard for people to understand because it was just these kids. Archigram was put together on the kitchen table. And sometimes even worse. There is no such thing as a copy editor, there is no thing as a graphic designer. I was interviewing some of the people who were making these on the side, and they were telling me the same thing. It was very, very rough. "You put

this there, you put this other thing there," and that was it. Nobody was editing the text. It would just go out. But *Oppositions*, yes. Typographic designer, editor, they became professionalized.

Dan Graham: We have to talk about the future, if the internet is the magazine of the future. But I think the magazine goes into the library, and that goes everywhere to colleges and universities. But we have to get out, we have to have lunch now.

CASE IN POINT: THE CONFERENCE OF ARCHITECTS FOR THE STUDY OF THE ENVIRONMENT MIT150 TRANSCRIPT

WEDNESDAY, APRIL 27, 2011

Kenneth Frampton: Ware Professor of Architecture, Columbia University
Peter Eisenman: Charles Gwathmey Professor in Practice, Yale School of Architecture
Stanford Anderson: Professor of Architecture and History, MIT
K. Michael Hays: Eliot Noyes Professor of Architectural Theory, Harvard University Graduate School of Design
Mark Jarzombek: Professor of History, Theory and Criticism, MIT

This conversation has been edited for length and clarity.

Mark Jarzombek: I thought that the first thing we would do is to ask each of them for their opinion about CASE. There's more history and it's more complex than we can feed to you in these moments. But at least you're getting a sense of the level of discussion and discourse. So it would be nice to hear from each of them a little bit their take on what this was all about, whether it was relevant to the day, whether it was not relevant, whether it meant something to them in their more extended career or not. So let's march right down the line to get the conversation going ... Stanford?

Stanford Anderson: Back then, all the pieces that you saw, almost all of them have at the beginning Peter Eisenman. He was the one who, at least at the beginning, conceived of the idea that the group of young architects who had just been appointed at the various schools along the East Coast, should get together and have a conversation about what was the state of architecture and what was the way in which one should conduct one's teaching under those circumstances. And it was a propitious moment. In the early '60s, it was pretty clear that the Modernism wave had been introduced through the GSD, through Harvard and other schools. There were people just a half-generation older than us who were in various offices and in practices all across the country doing work that was, some said, devolved from the Modern movement, that it was losing its energy. One had a feeling that Modern architecture had to be re-thought in some way. Just re-thought, it wasn't rejected at this time.

And of course the fact that in these moments both Rossi and Venturi were preparing and publishing key critiques is an indication of that. But we didn't yet know so much about those things. We had some of the same feelings and came together to try to think about what changes should take place and how young new professors should take some positions. Let me just jump way to the end to say that there's a history that maybe we'll spell out somewhat, of people with different capacities, different interests, different ways in which they wanted to work, that at the outset somehow looked to one another and saw this as reinforcing, but as you tried to push forward, it also meant that you went into different directions, or at least different tangents. It became harder and harder to hold together as a group. Of course simultaneous with that, it turned out that these were almost all very successful young people and they began to have their opportunities along those different tangential lines, and the end of the process, yes it was an exciting run, it didn't lead to a cohesive organization with permanence, but it did spin off a number of interesting and important activities in the meantime, and helped to launch a number of careers.

Peter Eisenman: First of all, I want to recognize Mike McKinnell, who is here, who was also a member of CASE for several meetings. Mike was my roommate at Columbia when we were in graduate school.

Stanford Anderson: And then my roommate at Columbia when I was in graduate school.

Image credit: George X. Lin.

Peter Eisenman: And, Mike was responsible for introducing me to Jim Stirling in the Fall of '59 and it was Jim who said, "you and Mike, you've got to go to England." And so, the story starts for me in England and I'll be brief, but there was clearly a difference between what was happening in England–this was in '60 to '63–and what was happening in the United States. Ken [Frampton] and I had talked about coming to the United States, but we never thought we would achieve that. And then when I came back to Princeton, it was a wasteland. They hadn't hired a faculty member in seventeen years, except for Michael Graves. But you have to realize that the institutional structures were really different. Michael and I had direct access to the President of the University. Impossible today. I also want to say that Mike McKinnell's Boston City Hall would be impossible to build in this city today, or any such building. Things were opening up as we now know they would culminate in student revolts and riots in the ghettoes in '68. But a forerunner to that I think was CASE, and CASE was an ill-fated job, as I say, but did spark a controversy which I think still exists in this country.

First of all, it's the first organization modeling itself on Team 10, and the idea of architects getting together to discuss issues other than practice. It was the first time that there was something other than a professional organization operating post-war. And of course this led to at the first meeting a split where [Vincent] Scully and [Robert] Venturi left after the first meeting, saying that this was not an American meeting, that it seemed to be dominated by Colin Rowe and his people.

Stanford Anderson: [chuckles]

Peter Eisenman: No, no, this happened–come on, you were there when Scully punched Campbell, for heaven's sake. There were fisticuffs. In any case, that split between American pragmatism and European idealism I think still exists in this country, those were the battles that were fought in the late sixties and early seventies. I think that began at CASE. One of the concluding episodes of CASE, which I think is really symbolic, occurred ten years later at UCLA, where there was another teach-in called "Five Days in May," and this time I think Venturi and Scully showed up because there were the Whites, the Silvers, and the Grays. The Silvers were a west-coast group formed by Tim Vreeland, who had been involved in the

early part of CASE, but included Cesar Pelli and Greg Hodges, but interestingly enough, there was a little round man who threw a party at a garage for all of these luminaries in '74. I asked someone, "Who is that guy? Who's the host?" And they said "Oh, that's this guy Frank Gehry, he's a developer-architect." And of course we know the rest of the story. So, I think that is the conclusion to our life in the sun and Frank sort of coming out and being the host of a party that he wasn't supposedly good enough to participate in.

Kenneth Frampton: That's a good time, yes. I wasn't there, but I assume that was true.

Peter Eisenman: Did you ever see Gehry's name in *Oppositions*? Not once.

Kenneth Frampton: You know, we managed to avoid that, yes. Times have changed. I saw Frank Gehry waiting for an elevator in Columbia and I had left it too late to leave so we crossed paths and he said, "Hi, Ken Frampton," and I said, "Hi Frank." And there was a pause, he's looking at the elevator, he doesn't look at me, and says "I know you don't like my buildings, but at least you can give me a hug."

So, anyway I think what Stanford said, that of course none of this would have happened without the gentleman on my left [Peter Eisenman], who is a troublemaker, as is well known, and of course has the virtue of stimulating otherwise lethargic people who wouldn't have done anything, including myself. But Peter's hang-up, I think, was and probably still is, that there'd been a Modern movement in the United States, so in a way I think CASE was a reference to Team 10, but there were other antecedents, in a sense. The impulse to do this, to bring other people together, was very much Peter's idea. Of course, it was a big miscalculation because there were too many people. To try to get agreement and be ecumenical is a stupid idea. And so one of those kind of contradictions, you know, which also my colleague goes in for–bringing the boys together, it was mostly boys unfortunately–

Peter Eisenman: There were no girls.

Kenneth Frampton: Well, it's nothing to be proud of. In any case, I have to correct this anecdote–I didn't actually get to Princeton by helicopter–I got to Newark airport by helicopter, and then I was driven to Princeton for that meeting. And I also left the same way. And I've never recovered from that, leaving, and looking in the evening at Manhattan and the New Jersey Turnpike and this unbelievable construction of electricity and gasoline. I mean, that was such a shock to me, coming from London, the image is burned in my head. That was and still is the issue, I think the crazy consumption. Anyway, I was met by someone who drove me from Newark to Princeton. I flew in the helicopter from Kennedy to Newark. And I met this colorful bunch of people among whom was Richard Meier, and I think I can say that I had the honor of spending my first night in America in a four-poster bed with Richard Meier in another four-poster bed next to me and a few big jars, because this was in this elaborate house in Princeton, where the first CASE meeting took place. Peter's right about the divisions. What I want to say is that there really was a nexus about Michael Graves and Peter Eisenman and Richard Meier and what would become the Five Architects watched over by figures like Colin Rowe.

They were interested in radical form and space, as much as anything else. And I think that was not the occupation of Vincent Scully and Robert Venturi and not really their sort of Philadelphia circle, and not Jack Robinson and the New York thing going on. Already there were these kinds of schisms, I think, that were there on the table in the very beginning, and they simply played themselves out.

K. Michael Hayes: Let's look forward in order to go back and think about *Oppositions*, which is a direct result of the CASE group, and in some ways a kind of culmination and the success of the CASE group, I think. And I'm thinking of the first three editorials by Frampton, Eisenman, and Gandelsonas, of the original three editors, and later Vidler comes in. Kenneth makes the point of a kind of late fight for schools, makes the point of architecture's social power and social responsibility. Peter in a way counters that architecture's real social power is that it's architecture, in other words that's what its real social power is for. Then Stanford, later at MIT, pursuing a much

different model, a kind of Popperian, Lakatosian model, that of the *research programme*, starts to develop the idea that may still be present, of quasi-autonomy–that architecture has a disciplinary specificity that can nevertheless respond to changing social needs.

So my point is that all of these have some version of a mediation between form, the cognitive power of form, and the social power of form, that to me is almost still highly relevant today. But I was very surprised when we looked back at New York, at the Harlem exhibition, for example–that when you look back at that, when you read Drexler's introduction to the catalog, you know he's talking about neo-Corbusian rhetoric, there is no sense. Actually there is a sense, because the MIT project is so peculiar, it's the one that insists on a kind of social thematic, but it's so peculiar that there's no mediation, there's no dialectic, between form as having a social power versus form for society. My question is: as CASE emerged, was that more mediated notion of form and its social responsibilities, was that part of the discussion as it later was explicit in *Oppositions* and at MIT?

Peter Eisenman: Well that's how it broke apart. It was agreed after the MIT number 6, what I would call CASE 6, that the New York people were sort of agitated about the fact that we were not talking about what we would call architecture, and decided we would have a New York group, and there were two meetings set up, for the historical record, at MoMA–one CASE 7 and one CASE 8. And at both of those meetings, there were six architects that presented, not five, which is interesting. And they were all about showing work. That's when it really broke down, and it broke down into the five architects in the CASE 7 and 8, but also broke down into Jack Robertson's group. I remember at the MoMA show, he was just starting out, he was doing work with Mayor Lindsay. And I was starting the Institute, and I said "why don't you come to the institute?" And he said, "why don't you come and work in the Urban Design Movement?" And of course those poles never would come together, even though Jack and I practiced together with what we

called the Chinese Menu, for five years. I think that split was much more prevalent at the end of CASE and in Five Architects than it was, say, in *Oppositions*.

Stanford Anderson: With what's on the screen [images of the Harlem exhibition], and what's been said by Michael, it was again Peter who somehow negotiated the opportunity that there would be an exhibition at the Museum of Modern Art. It was devoted to urbanism. And it was also Peter and Arthur Drexler, the curator of architecture at the museum, who chose, of all things, to have a set of experiments run on Harlem. This is 1966.

Now, in 1966, we got really heavy reactions. But here at MIT, we did have the breaking down of the walls, and there was talk about the students in some kind of unrest. And we had a colleague, Robert Goodman, who was a young architect brought onto the faculty by the chair with the full knowledge that this was a guy with a political agenda, and he wanted to be confrontational about the state of things in this city and in this country. So that was Bob looking to advocacy planning and this was a totally new term and new concept. He did have some allies in New York city, but in totally different circles than these guys, and so he was concerned about the tent city here, which was how to develop a certain site to have the greatest social legitimacy. He was concerned about the extension of the south-west expressway right through the city, demolishing housing of people of lesser means. So this was a kind of debate that was already going on and had its own kinds of conflicts that would become larger in ensuing time. So when Peter negotiated the opportunity to have an exhibition at the Museum of Modern Art, he turned back to us, in his generosity, he's always been generous. He turned back to his CASE members and said, all right, Colin at Cornell could be a team, Robertson and White at Columbia put together a team, Eisenman and Graves would do something at Princeton. And he contacted me to put together an MIT team–Hank [Henry] Millon was my immediate colleague, and he was also in CASE, so it was obvious that he was there. But I was uncomfortable about this insertion into Harlem, and I didn't want to cause trouble. So I then enlisted Bob Goodman to become a member of our group. And he said, "how could I do that? I have these political commitments you know well, and how would I do that with a bunch of people concerned with form and looking at Harlem from that point of view?" I said, "I think that's what should be confronted, and I promise you that we will do it in such a way that we are confronting that matter, and so please be part of it." And so he joined in.

We were assigned the eastern part–Riverside, east Harlem. You can see that the Cornell team took the whole central piece of Harlem and completely reworked that in a figure/ground diagram sort of way. Really radical treatment of that area, and whereas we on the East Harlem team said that there is a great deal of tension in this part–the brownstone row-houses have great capacity, and they're occupied by people who need that housing–we're not going to touch it. On the other hand, the high-rise social housing that was built there was full of problems, and the open space was not well-used, in fact it was dangerous, so we said, we'll touch that, but also we'll jump over the East River, and use the islands–Randalls and Wards Island, and even dip into the Bronx, because the South Bronx was already bombed out. Our position was to jump to undeveloped or critically difficult territory, and say, "this is where you build. When that's done, when there's housing then, you could offer alternative housing to the overcrowded situation in East Harlem. And at that

point, you can make a decision if there is or is not to be new work in East Harlem." So this was totally in contrast to the positions that were available. But I have to say that we went through this as a long series of meetings in the summer of '66. We ended up with an exhibition that I think was in some level benefitted, at least in the newspaper criticism, from a reading of the very different positions.

Kenneth Frampton: I don't have much to say on this, really. I think it was a good thing to have that exhibition, I think it was a consciousness-raising event. It's true, I'm sure, what Stan just said in terms of the informality and the organic character of the MIT project. It opens itself very plainly to being built piecemeal and in that sense very flexible, whereas the others were all much more formal. And they were various kinds of insertions that were very extensive. They were contextual, more or less, but I think they were at the same time very categoric.

Peter Eisenman: I think the debate internally between Columbia, MIT, Cornell, and Princeton was the significant point. For me, it was that the museum was willing to turn over a huge gallery, something I haven't seen the likes of recently, an architectural exhibition as didactic, and of the moment as that exhibition was, and that Drexler turned it over to four university teams of people that had never built anything, by the way. Not only not built, some of them weren't even practicing architects. And he said, "here, take this big space" and it was I think a significant event and makes one realize how poverty-stricken our museums are of architecture and urbanism and those current problems today. I mean, you don't find that sort of thing happening in museums today.

K. Michael Hays: It's interesting to me that Drexler was doing this in '66 … less than ten years later will be the Beaux-Arts exhibition, and if you think about the Drexler shows, and I think you can argue that they're an index of the current debate, and what this represents was what the Beaux-Arts show represents–how things change so quickly, in less than ten years.

Peter Eisenman: But in fairness to Ken, who was involved in another exhibition, which we haven't mentioned–Another Chance for Housing–in which Kenneth developed a prominent type, which was built in Brownsville, Marcus Garvey housing, which still is a really interesting model today, was also sponsored by Drexler and the New York Redevelopment Corporation. When you think about the kinds of contacts and allowing things to happen. I mean, they actually built the damn thing. And MoMA had a major exhibition with a major catalog–this before the Beaux-Arts show, and before Transformations, which was the introduction of post-modernism. Drexler was somebody who was willing to take risks on the edge. And, no question that the show helped you build that project.

Kenneth Frampton: Of course it did. That show was a deal, in fact, I mean we know it was a deal. The deal was that you were to design the project and Lerup would get his exhibitions.

Peter Eisenman: But there was no deal to build, right?

Kenneth Frampton: No, no, but he carried through, he went through with the whole thing.

Peter Eisenman: I mean, how many young architects today get a chance to design public housing? Very few, and the Urban Development Corporation in New York, and the Urban Design Group. I mean, Richard Meier built housing in New York, Passanella–there were a lot of people, young architects, building housing projects at the time. And Ken had built housing in London, but had never built in the United States, I don't think, and it was quite a significant thing for young architects to be doing.

Kenneth Frampton: There was also something that happened that was kind of indicative of the ruthlessness of power in that way, because this exhibition was sponsored, and then the prototype was backed by the UDC and was backed in the design by myself and many architects in the Institute, with UDC architects. At some point, there is a conflict between the design team and the director of construction. I'll never get over this one. Because there are 650-odd units, and he rejects it because in a chain of reasoning, in half of the units people are going down to sleep and not going up to sleep–the bedrooms are below the living spaces, and not above them. He can't stand this. So he said, "well we're not going to do it like that. The way I see it, people go up to sleep." So he changed our units at the last minute so they were all going to go up.

Peter Eisenman: Did that happen? You changed it?

Kenneth Frampton: Yes, of course it happened. What happened is that then we fought that and finally said, well, this is an experiment, we'll do half of them my way and half of them your way. And there's an example of not taking responsibility for decisions, because nobody wanted to be responsible. It was ridiculous. It was just a question of a power game–who was going to win–and prejudice. And I think of course that's the micro-lesson of power in action, and what happens under certain political conditions. I think that it was a learning moment.

Mark Jarzombek: On that question, I would like to talk about the categories [*reading from a slide showing notes from a CASE meeting*]– now the categories were understandably somewhat ad hoc, and clearly given individuals belong to different types of categories, and there were some composites that I'm trying to understand here–it's not a hierarchical list in any way. Nonetheless, it might give us a good snapshot into certain types of intellectual formations. It struck me–the way we put these categories today–so we have *the city en masse phenomena*, where everybody's interested in the city as an ecological phenomenon, and I can't remember anybody being interested in mass phenomena, or at least not in a good way–then we have *industrial techniques of construction*–and this is of course still around, especially as it relates to materials and techniques, in that computer modeling has taken over, that and CAD-type things. Technological innovation is sort of embedded in that a little bit, and that to some degree survives. *Architecture and other disciplines*–today that might be biology or physics or something, certainly not what's here, which has to do with teamwork, joint research, which is sort of talked about sometimes, but which nobody really theorizes in a particularly good way. *Architecture and political structure*–so that, obviously, doesn't exist at all. *Psychology and architecture*–nobody talks about guilt– they wouldn't know what the hell you're dealing with. *Creativity*– that's sort of like talking about beauty–people go, "You're from the nineteenth century." *Form*–well, I mean, that's sort of what people do mention every now and there. But it's usually from the computer side. *History and Criticism*–we all know that's going down the tubes, because history, there's no time for it. And if you do criticism, you're told you're inhibiting the poor architect and they can't build, and they become impotent, and so you want the post-critical enthusiasm for their practice, so you can't do that. And then of course there's *architecture*–and that's what's always left over. So in looking over this list, some things have survived in this list, which are the technical side, the materials side, and so forth–but the politics, the humanistic issues, the history, and the psychological questions, these have all been sort of erased over the last twenty years, that's for sure. So is that good? Are we in a better place, perhaps?

Stanford Anderson: Or are you exaggerating? With you as a historian-critic, you feel sort of that there's just nothing anymore?

Mark Jarzombek: I feel that the less there is going on, the better the criticism can be.

Stanford Anderson: It seems to me that our own program here, *History, Theory, and Criticism*, was relatively early in that exact composition. And here again, even though this was an internal MIT achievement, because we were standing alone for seven years, we had a lot of reinforcement from people like Peter–they would spot bright young people and encourage them incredibly. They were enhanced in our pool by the connections that were developed through CASE. HTC seems to have been going on quite a while, so I hope that it is still in some places figuring into the world of architecture, and not only history. And then when you said the "other disciplines"–I don't remember just what we wrote there, but CASE 3 was organized by Hank and by me, and we had medical people who later won an extremely high international prize through MIT– Harvard Medical School. From MIT, we had a very distinguished psychologist, but the MIT psychology was very hands-on, this really neurological understanding of how the mind and the brain worked. So we tried to reach out, and we met with other disciplines, but it obviously didn't work. The group of CASE, after that meeting, felt that this was going too far, reaching into other disciplines that didn't have a real connection. They weren't ready to explore that idea.

Peter Eisenman: I don't mean to be nostalgic about the seventies, I think they were a really charged moment for both good and bad. I can remember Michael Graves and I coming to lecture at MIT, and we were booed off the stage here for talking about form. You might say that's a strange thing, but *would that could happen today,* that somebody, the student, would think enough of some issue that they were excited about. I think there's a certain laissez-faire condition that's in criticism. I mean, we, Michael and I, would write letters to the architectural critics of the *New York Times* all the time. And one did spend time in critical activity. And I think that we don't, we can't recreate it artificially. But it is not that normal today. I don't see architects or students or political leaders being involved in projects, or the kinds of projects that we were involved in in the sixties and seventies. It's just that, for whatever reason, they're not front-burner anymore.

Stanford Anderson: I'll do my very quick Pecha Kucha run-through of influences and ideas that were present at that time around here. One was the Aalto dormitory, and that way of thinking. That Aalto was taking the psychology and the physiology of people into account. Then we had the effective Dean Wurster building in this way, influenced by the style of California. When he built in the city, he developed a very strong discipline along the street front that became more open and accommodating in the back. I was feeling that Peter Eisenman and Maurice Smith were from two different worlds, but both of them in some way were exploring a very deep understanding of form, and in the one case with Peter, it may be that the form was multiplied in order to have redundancy, that moved towards his self-referentiality. Smith was multiplying form for a different reason, but in the end they were both an honorable commitment to a very deep understanding of form, and there was some way that you ended up generating a space that had a

complexity that was not generated by function alone, but instead by the ways in which you might be able to inhabit the space. But for myself, I found the capacity to appreciate both of these people.

Peter Eisenman: You're being very generous about the differences that occurred. I remember them as much more heated.

What's interesting is that the discussion between Venturi and Scully and Rowe and the Five Architects was different–the argument that Scully and Venturi were making, they were looking for an American vernacular, I think.

Stanford Anderson: I think Maurice was using something like an American vernacular to reach something 'other'.

Kenneth Frampton: I think this conversation's on the edge of not talking about the past, but about the present, because–Peter just said something about the seventies, and about how these certain kinds of projects and enthusiasms would be difficult to find in the present.

Peter Eisenman: Do you agree with that?

Kenneth Frampton: I do, and I was listening to this tone of disillusionment, at least that's how I construed it. And I think that architecture school, architecture education, is in a lot of difficulty. It's not clear what it is. I remember when I studied architecture in the fifties, you know, whether architecture was a science, whether it was an art–this kind of constant anxiety about the profession as to how it should legitimize itself in relationship to society. I think that issue is still floating around, though not very much discussed–this question of legitimation of the practice of architecture. And Stanford's slideshow of the Aalto dorm, and Smith's house provoke the thought of architecture as a craft, and not as a science, and not as an applied science, and not art in the sense of fine art either. But basically a craft, a vocation, really. And I believe that that's what it is in the end. Architecture schools have real problems in organizing their curricula–what is it that holds this discipline together, I think this is a real big problem.

Of course it's very hard to perceive what an architecture school is. I think even when you're inside one–like Columbia for example–do I really understand what this thing is? I just recently experienced going to a review yesterday where you have second semester first year students, and they're given a three hundred square foot library to design, in a very awkward and difficult site, and you really have to say, "what is the pedagogical aim of this exercise? What kind of madness is this?" And it all floats on the idea that every professor is an individual and they should all be allowed to do whatever they want–there is no curriculum, strictly speaking. What is left of the curriculum is that in the second year, first semester of this three-year M.Arch. program, they do housing. And the absolute totally insane thing is they never design a house–always multiple housing for some cramped site in a city–for what reason? There's no clear pedagogical reason. And that is a crisis, I think, for the discipline. And I think it's not unsuitable, it just means that people have to really ask questions about what is this field, and what can this field deliver, and what can't it deliver. It's very limited in a way, discourse, I think. But we don't talk about defining what's inside architecture schools. The idea is that you just saturate the subject as much as possible with as much information as possible. I don't like this pedagogical system.

Stanford Anderson: Ken, I want to pick up where you started, with architecture as a practicum, as we saw in Aalto and in Smith. On one level, that's it, but on another, these are not people who are just learning the way things are done, there's some very deep search that is going on at the same time.

Kenneth Frampton: I mean craft, not just putting things together. I like very much, and I didn't know of this concept you introduced of *groundwork*, and the ground form and the built form. I have to be honest in saying that I never knew what to make of Maurice Smith, but I think that the issue of the land and the work–it posits the presence of landscape in this field of work either directly as landscape, or as a metaphor.

K. Michael Hays: Can I sort of steer us a bit? In that we are in fact celebrating MIT, I think there are some hints of answers about this educational issue, but let's look at our subject matter. It's really interesting to me that the people who made up CASE were architects who had reflected deeply on the discipline of architecture, and knew a lot about the history of architecture. Kenneth could have gone either way almost, toward practice or toward history, Peter could have as well, as could Stan, and that one of the events was the Cranbrook Conference, where History, Theory, and Criticism, I guess for the first time, was put squarely on the table as an educational issue. Then of course MIT's HTC program is a direct legacy of that. What I'm getting at is that there's something about the figures in CASE, and I think MIT as a program inherits this a bit, of this insistence that architecture is a specific way of thinking, that it's not just about functions, it's not just about putting materials together. What happened recently, and what Mark referred to as the look or the post-critical something, is that when the problem of digital technology appeared as a technical problem, there was a bit of a hiatus in the urgency of historical and theoretical work, because we had to master the techniques first. But now that we can handle the technology, now that we've learned the techniques, I actually feel a real return to issues of discipline. Our students have really started to worry about that again. What am I doing when I do architecture that's not a problem of solving geometry or not just generated by function? What is it about the discipline of architecture that allows me to begin to do architecture? And I think a lot of that was already in the thinking of a lot of the figures around CASE. Just a quick anecdote…

When I was in the S.M.Arch.S. program here in HTC, Peter was working on the Romeo and Juliet project. And I don't know if you remember this, guys, but Peter came to a history/theory seminar that Stan was doing and presented the Romeo and Juliet project, and it was completely seamless to have done that–that was the kind of thing that we were studying. I mean, I think now for a practicing architect to come in and present the project in the history course, it would clink, right? But then, it felt completely seamless and something about that I think is important.

Mark Jarzombek: Also, one could look at it in the sense that these issues have changed, but also as you pointed out in the conflicts that mark the end of this thing, they were themselves the beginning of a type of archipelago world, in which different interest groups developed different locales. So the interest in the city went to Urban Planning. If you're interested in the city, that's where you go. And psychology went into the–I don't know where that went, today we have too much psychology, right? There's too much creativity now, I mean, everyone thinks that what they want to be is a Frank Gehry. Too much form. Everybody thinks you can press a couple buttons and out comes a building. I don't know if there's too much history and criticism, but I don't think so.

So it's almost in some sense the re-shifting of some of these categories that are being breached by their presence here, as something to work out in the context of modernism–it's seen as this sort of deadening rationalist world, and we need to provoke it into questions of psychology and creativity, form–form is the rescuer of this. In some sense, it's succeeded very well. I think the disciplinary projects that Michael has alluded to here are sort of the return to that, perhaps. So I guess that maybe there's a second round on this? Questions? So we'll have some questions from the forum–

Nader Tehrani: I feel compelled to at least break the ice a little bit. Stan, I like how you broke into the Pecha Kucha–you presented images of a certain architecture that we had associated with MIT and conceptually the way that the argument was beginning to develop, is that there are those people who are invested in form, and somehow you began to demonstrate that there was an equal skill and a polemicized understanding of form in the other camp also, even though it had a purported investment in those things around form–contingencies that deal with the social vocation of architecture, the positioning of architecture, and so forth. I'm also struck by the way in which discourse was formed in that period. But what happened, as you all pointed out, towards the end, is that in fact culture has changed radically over the last forty, fifty years, even moreso in the last ten years, with the proliferation of information on the internet, the nature of discourse has changed–horizontalized, even any utterance can be made public, and acknowledged on the same playing field as that of the authors and the canons. And I guess my question to you is where do you place architecture? It seems like there's more affinity between those forms that Stan is showing with things that I could begin to associate with the work of Eisenman, the Five Architects, and so forth. What has happened to the status of architectural discourse in this same period? Do you still see yourselves dichotomized in that kind of black and white way, or has the status of architectural discourse taken you to a point where you're unable to find the urgencies that we once had?

Peter Eisenman: Well, just looking back at history, and these people can correct me, there were two dominant axes in the sixties and early seventies–there was Cornell-Princeton / Yale-Penn. Those were the players on the board. Harvard was in shambles after Sert left, and Maurice Smith had his little compound here, as I can remember it. He didn't play with us. What's interesting is that I think these distinctions became blurred by the mid-seventies and you have Colin criticizing Venturi's Yale Math building in *Oppositions*, a really brilliant piece of work, and by the end of the two years later, doing *Collage City*, which is very similar to what Venturi was doing. The real discussion then, I think, came between Ken and Denise Scott Brown, which was articulated in *Casabella*, that after the '68 riots and what happened, I think the discourse that had survived from the fifties into the mid-sixties, I think the watershed of '68, the watershed of Venturi's *Complexity and Contradiction* and Tafuri's *Theories in History*, and then there was a shift in the Venturi game with *Learning from Las Vegas*–I think that's where another polarization occurs, when the sort of post-modern thing kicks in. Something else happens, and I think this is the argument that Denise and Ken have as one of those arguments over *Learning from Las Vegas*, which I still think is a topic on the table, whatever form you might see it in. But certainly this shift from '66, from *Complexity* to *Learning*, I think was an important shift at the time. I don't know what you guys think.

Kenneth Frampton: It was isolated, though, I mean that discourse, that was his–all the other discourse, that didn't exist as far as he was concerned, it had no relevance. But that points up this kind of–provinciality is a loaded word, but I think it works both ways, sort of. You've got to have a provinciality which has its own kind of character, without being closed off. And a provinciality that thinks it's the center of the world, isn't, really. I think that one of the American problems is that it's thought of itself, even unconsciously, that Pax Americana–

Peter Eisenman: Well why were you here if we were Pax Americana?

Kenneth Frampton: But I was just part of the colony here! What I'm getting at is that it–it's not entirely negative, but it's just a condition, and therefore it has its own kind of blindness. The blindness of Venturi and Denise Scott Brown. If Main Street is almost all right, it's all right, period, then–what does it need Robert Venturi for? Who's to take it seriously?

K. Michael Hays: For example, I think the issue of the Decorated Shed very easily became the problem of the envelope. The envelope now is absolutely fundamental both to the practice and to the …

Kenneth Frampton: A very negative state of affairs! Because the envelope is all the expression and nothing is inside. Once you take off the skin, there's nothing inside the building.

Nader Tehrani: Are you saying the Renaissance had nothing to do with the difficulties of the schism between the envelope and the internal organization of the buildings? Doesn't that have some historic resonance?

Kenneth Frampton: Well, there's always the difference between the inside and the outside, between the surface and the space, but to drive it to an extreme, probably under economic pressure, probably under media pressure, and it's only the surface and there's nothing inside, well the game's over! It's ridiculous. It's totally unethical, in fact. Using steel like this is totally unethical, but we don't say these things usually. We have to start talking about them in a sense.

Peter Eisenman: Well you keep quiet as well. The thing is, it's fine to sit here, but I would say that you are as quiet as anybody on this.

Kenneth Frampton: I don't like putting these kinds of attacks into writing, that's the truth. I prefer to write about what I think has value and ignore the other stuff.

Arindam Dutta: Well, architecture's doing just fine–we have no idea what's going on. What if what you guys are talking about, mulling over, as a sort of moment of agreement between contending factions so that you could all meet across the same table, and on the same walls of the museum, had nothing to do with your energies or your intelligence, but in fact a peculiar kind of institutional conjuncture, if I may say so, where a certain kind of expertise was vested in the university, and so claiming the university, claiming the museum, seemed like the space to occupy, and therefore produce agreement in the form of magazines and so on. It seems to me that architecture in the world seems to be doing just fine, right? There are a lot of architects who are much more well known today in the world than there have ever been in the history of architecture –that's the new shift, right? I've been to parties where lawyers are coming up to me and telling me about architects. I mean, that has

never happened before. But where authority may have shifted is from the university… which brings with it the problem of pedagogy and so on. Maybe the problem is somewhere else, I just want to suggest this.

Kenneth Frampton: I think one thing is that if one looks at the world's architecture with very wide open eyes, and without being conditioned by propaganda, there is an amazing sense of work being done all over the world. That, I think, is true, but it doesn't hit the headlines most of it.

Peter Eisenman: The real change, I would argue, is media. It's that media looks for the most stunning something new every day, and so what Ken is saying is that there may be architecture being done, but media obscures the function. I think that is a problem.

Kenneth Frampton: It's double-edged, because you know about the work because of the media –

Peter Eisenman: Yes, but the excessive media that we have–I mean, every day you can look at Archinect or whatever the sites. You can't say anything in the classroom anymore–the next thing you know, it's on YouTube and et cetera.

I lost a commission, I can remember I spoke at Columbia and I said, "I'm going to do a job in Tulsa, and Tulsa's nothing but a bombed-out city with parking lots around a series of churches." And I went there and I gave my presentation the next day, and they said, "did you say this at Columbia last night?" And I was dead–simple as that.

Kenneth Frampton: You just have to be a bit more … mediated … when you say something.

K. Michael Hays: I would say that the closeness of the profession of architecture and the university is the other part–it's exactly the distance of the university from the profession to me which makes the university again a place where … you could still actually be radical in the university by taking a distance from the profession, and that actually is a potential, I think. The problem is that we're too timid now about experimentation and innovation–invention, as distinct from innovation. And we tried to train, I'm thinking of the M.Arch. programs, we train too much, rather than educate. An education, still, could be quite radical, and go against the kind of smoothing of the two.

Stanford Anderson: You raised the question of whether the university is now sort of separate from the society. I think we have to admit that it is. If you read the *Boston Globe*–they had that fantastic thing, the *Boston Globe* gave a front page article about how marvelous MIT is and has made Cambridge what it is. Ordinarily Harvard is treated as the World's Greatest University–WGU–it's almost tongue in cheek, of course, and basically a disrespect from the city and its people towards professors. If you are a professor trying to also build, you'll have a harder time than if you are somebody who is being a professional. The professor is seen not to have a capacity. It's radically different from how it used to be–especially in Europe. If you're a professor in Europe, you have some credibility, and you get opportunities. We may have been the beneficiaries of something like the tail-end of that in the sixties.

S. Faisal Hassan: So my question is about the disciplinary boundaries, especially because we're sitting across from individuals who've talked about autonomy and quasi-autonomy, I want to pick up a moment in the history that was narrated at the beginning. In 1969, when CASE was back at MoMA, Drexler claimed that the reason why you are all architects was that this was an opportunity for political romance. And [Philip] Johnson claimed that maybe it wasn't such a great idea that there were Five Architects, maybe there should have been three or eight. Colin Rowe referred to it as "your need for a revolutionary tone as an annex in your work." So the question is: it seems to me that there's a need for the discipline to generate its discourse–is there a possibility that the discourse might actually have shifted elsewhere–in the benefit of the discipline? But the discipline just isn't aware of it?

Kenneth Frampton: What are you implying?

Peter Eisenman: Where did it go?

S. Faisal Hassan: I think because we're talking to a group that has advocated for the discipline and for its autonomy… we can find it, we don't benefit from other discourses coming in, we don't benefit from its discourse. I'm not even sure what those locations might be– could it be art? It could be something else… but it's sort of a catch 22–kind of situation, but virtue of the original stance.

Kenneth Frampton: I think one aspect of the original status is to have taken a big distance from engineering, you know, I think it's very curious that if I think of my colleagues, engineering was just not present. And we speak of engineering as doing tasks, as peculiar. I think to exclude that dimension–technique, and the place of technique and invention for the building task–is a problem.

K. Michael Hays: I think we will probably end up disagreeing on this. I think you're wrong about how enclosed architecture is. I think architecture is sending out connectors to a lot of disciplines– engineering, biology, for better and for worse. But it may, looking back at this day in fifty years or whatever, it may be that what we used to call architecture went underground sometime around 1983, and it's popping up now in very different ways, and we can't even recognize yet, and we're still going to call it architecture. That's not a sad story. I mean, architecture could radically mutate and pop up in very different kinds of place and practices, and that would be a good thing, not a bad thing, for me.

PLATFORMS FOR EXCHANGE CORE 2 DESIGN STUDIO

SPRING 2009
Instructors: **Sheila Kennedy, Elizabeth Whittaker, J. Meejin Yoon**
Teaching Assistants: **Skylar Tibbits, Mark Watabe, Murat Mutlu**
SPRING 2010
Instructors: **Ana Miljački, J. Meejin Yoon**
Teaching Assistants: **Skylar Tibbits, Joseph Choma**

This will kill that. The book will kill the building. That is to say, printing will kill architecture.
—Victor Hugo

In Victor Hugo's oblique obituary for architecture, he claims the book will replace architecture as a significant cultural producer of social and political order. Since the 'death of architecture' there have been subsequent claims to the 'death of the author', the 'death of the book' and, finally, the death of the institution which collects, stores, organizes, and makes accessible such books—the library. The library as an institution has been historically been understood as the physical repository of all human knowledge. Its charge to preserve that knowledge, control its access, and curate culture has rendered it a site of power.

As literacy and standards of living have increased, the promise of public libraries as democratic institutions accessible to, and funded by, the public have become increasingly popular. In the latter half of the 19th century, the Boston Public Library worked to create and expand both its collection and its access. Yet, in less than a century and a half, the Boston Public Library, like many public libraries has found its mission of archive and access challenged by other infrastructures of information dissemination. The Internet, Print on Demand, Google and other digital technologies have made the library's promise of universal collection and access, by comparison, insufficient. With individual hard drives able to store as much data as the complete collection of works in a medium-sized city library, a proliferation of media formats, and the increasing ubiquity of electronic information technologies, a rethinking of the role and potential of the public branch library is warranted.

The project for the semester will be Boston Public Library's 27th branch library, the Kenmore Station Media Branch Library, specializing in a unique collection of media culture from the last century. Information today exists in several different and coexisting forms of media, ranging from physical printed matter to digitalized text, from film reels to video disks, from LPs to MP3s. Information has been transferred to successive forms of less permanent, increasingly instable, yet more easily disseminated media. This shift alters the role of the library. While new forms of media may be increasingly digital, all forms of media have material and spatial realities. The Media Branch Library is a contemporary institution charged with not only the organization of this physical and digital collection but with the creation of a new institution which engages the physical and the material with the digital and distributes them to produce a new kind of civic structure within the contemporary city.

Yushiro Okamoto | MArch
J. Meejin Yoon, Instructor–2009
Anonymous Media Library

This Media Library challenges to go beyond a mere accessing of knowledge. The information you want is easily gained through your fingers, anytime, anyplace, and the meaning of a media library needs to be redefined. At a site where different flows of people and programs intersect with each individual objectives, it proposes a new relation between a "private searching" and a "public searching." The seven pods which cover the site extend the surface area of a roof, to allow many images to be projected from different directions. The thickened wall of the pods are excavated into small reading carrels to control and view the projections. The public, who walks through the interior landscapes of the ground level can look up into the sky to encounter unexpected information. Information is an experience, to be shared by yourself and the public. This Media Library becomes a public park, where anonymous reading is exhibited and to be viewed.

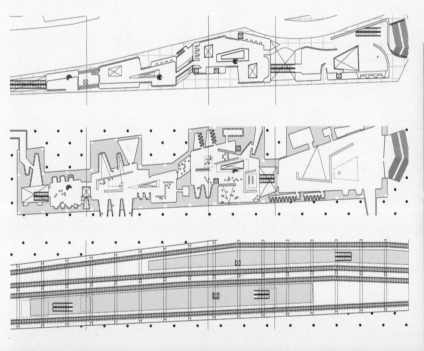

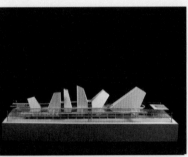

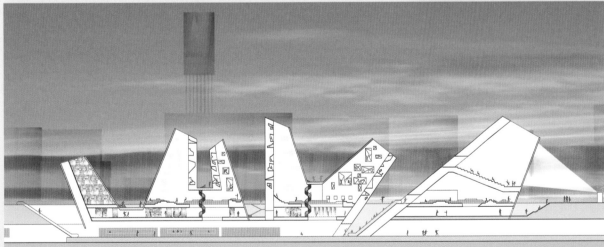

Nadya Volicer | MArch
Sheila Kennedy, Instructor–2009
Void of Media

Kenmore Station is a unique point of divergence in the city of Boston, where the gridded neighborhood of historic Back Bay gives way to the urban strip of Boston University's Commonwealth Avenue. What opportunities arise from this shift in typology, demographic, and landscape? Can the new branch library serve as mediator between these varying conditions? Through what lens can we examine both the urban situation and the transitions between old and new media?

Dappling light in Back Bay's Public Gardens under a canopy of trees contrasts with the open sky views of BU's Commonwealth Avenue. Adopting both effects into the new media library provides opportunities to accommodate both old and new media. A system of reflective and dappling surfaces is devised to transmit direct southern sunlight into areas of focused halos, for activities such as reading a book, and shadowed regions, for digital media requiring darker lighting conditions. A wide range of possibilities exists in between.

Two volumes, a half sunken plinth and a cantilevered box, collude to create an interior void. This void serves to mediate light coming into the library, transmits sky views into the subway below, and reorganizes program. The interiorized surfaces of this mediating void are scripted using RhinoScript in response to sun rays extracted from the sun course on site. Two surfaces are designated; one for reflection and one for dappling. The script run on the reflecting surface creates circular apertures in relation to the sun's rays; the closer to the ray, the smaller the aperture. Therefore, fewer holes exist on this surface that is intended for reflecting the most light. On the dappling surface, the script runs in reverse, creating larger openings closer to the where the rays hit the surface. In this way, a variety of lighting effects are achieved for the diversity of scenarios in the new media library.

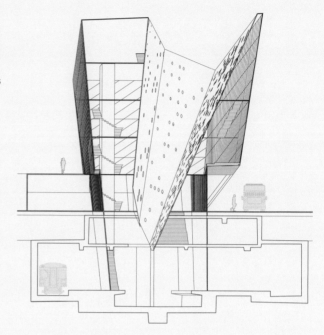

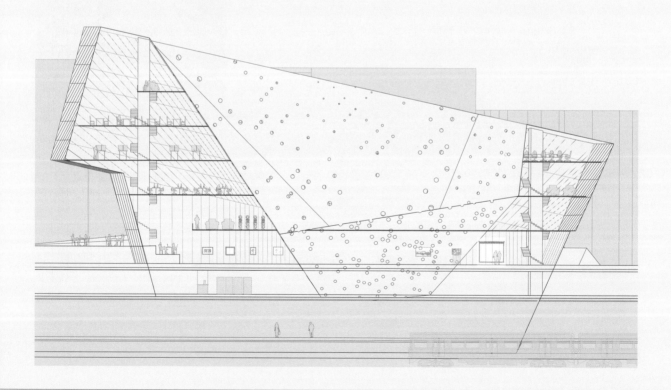

Li Huang | MArch
J. Meejin Yoon, Instructor–2010
Monument of Knowledge

Looking at the organization of knowledge by people from the 18th century, the organization of knowledge in the contemporary sense is breaking away from a branching system to one that simulates a network system, which implies that knowledge of various disciplines are related to another. In addition, the rise of digital media has a huge impact of the physical format of book. As a result, the actual stacks of books are not essential for people, however, the way to reach the knowledge is more important to individuals. In this project, all the books will be separated into 10 branches, buried deep into earth according to the Dewey decimal classification system, and exchanged by an automated storage and retrieval system. As a library built on a train station, the exchange of knowledge (books) becomes the background of the exchange of people. This system offers individuals personal kiosks to retrieve any items in this library, which mean everyone has the same accessibility to knowledge. Ten towers emerge from the ground touching each other on an upper level, which reveal the huge amount of knowledge (books) under these monuments.

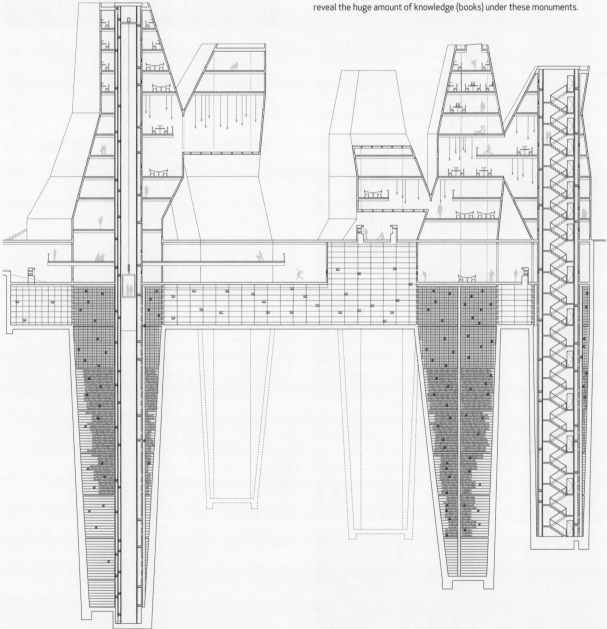

George X. Lin | MArch
Ana Miljački, Instructor–2010
The Urban Archive

Today the speed of the book seems glacial when compared to the internet which allows its users instant access to vast amounts of information. Books are digitalized and read online without any physically need to go to the library. The value of the book is lost and the architecture that houses it has become vague.

In the last 10 years, we have seen a 4.5% decrease in circulation of books in the libraries per year, however there has been a steady 12% increase in number of library visits. At the same time, access to the internet in America have increased from 44% to 72%. In the most traditional sense, the space of the library was dedicated to a collection of books, it was an interface between that organized authoritative collection of knowledge and readers who seek it out, first private and then public. But in the modern scenario, the library collection has expanded to include many additional programs such as digital media, maps, children's collection, tax help, job training and cafe. In recent years libraries are becoming social centers where one comes for specific services and information rather than for the books.

Taking on the possibility that books will become even more obsolete than they are today, that they may even reach a status of relics–my project relegates the book to the archive. The purpose of this maneuver is both to acknowledge the reality of the contemporary library (other public deliveries of knowledge and space of interaction are in fact relevant today), and to elevate the book anew as an object...through its symbolic presence in the archive...it is simultaneously presented as a towering mass of books and as a fragile object that has to be handled with special care.

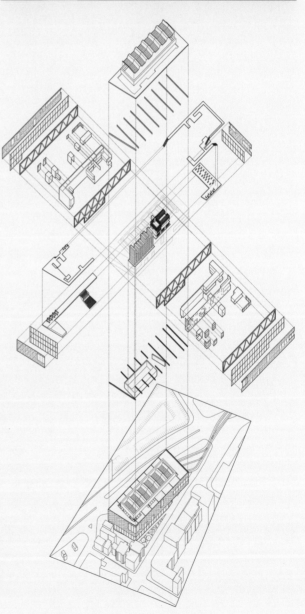

THE ARCHITECTURE SCHOOL IN AN EXPANDED FIELD
OPTION DESIGN STUDIO

Instructor: **Nader Tehrani**
Teaching Assistant: **Murat Mutlu**

Of the many programs architects have to address, maybe one of the most salient is the School of Architecture, where problems of pedagogy come face to face with a built example that is inhabited and tested daily by an audience as fierce as any–the producers and critics of the very medium. At the same time, it is maybe one the few occasions where one's audience is operating and engaging with architecture at a higher level, making it a challenge to speak to architectural questions with a greater degree of nuance, an opportunity architects don't often get.

While the school of architecture has seen some significant changes over the ages, it has also seen a good deal of typological and spatial variety, making it an open and rich kernel of speculation and research. At the same time, more recent technological advancements have changed some fundamental organizational and functional demands; namely, the computer station. So too, FAB-labs, 3d printers, plotters, laser cutters and a host of other digital paraphernalia are no longer a privilege, but an absolute necessity of the intellectual environment, if the school is to be relevant for the means and methods of current production. For this reason, most schools have incorporated aggressive capital campaigns that target new technologies as the basis of many annual acquisitions, and in turn, have sought other ways of subsidizing the programs. These research engines have also transformed the studio based programs: inserting the Fab-Lab into studio work, using conferencing platforms to conduct collaborative studios across borders, binding scholarly work and linking library work with design initiatives or multidisciplinary platforms that fuse design with engineering, interactive technologies, among other disciplines. To problematize this predicament even further, current economies cannot afford the one-student, one-desk principle, and thus the idea of the hot-desk has become a common alternative–introducing the idea that workstations that can be separated from lockers, model storage, and model making spaces. Our task will be to imagine what kind of studio spaces these would produce, and how they can produce the next generation of architect, new forms of pedagogy, and the redefinition of design thinking.

The Faculty fosters an active and collegial research environment that brings together staff and students to exchange knowledge and engage in debate on key topics. Current research centers on several key themes, including sustainable built environments; urban futures, with particular focus on housing, transport and communities; design, technologies, management and practice; and built environment history, heritage, theory and social critique in the Asia-Pacific region.

The new building will consist of educational facilities for staff and students, with a total floor area of approximately 18,000m². The areas, combined with circulation, storage and amenities (lifts, toilets, etc) as well as informal study spaces scattered throughout the building, will equate to the 18,000m2 total indicated above.

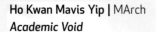

Ho Kwan Mavis Yip | MArch
Academic Void

As a testing ground for new architectural pedagogy, the school is transformed into a platform extending from the major public space–the concrete lawn. Instead of situating the school on the lawn as a figure, the design celebrates the public space as a figure itself through framing the space. The introduced huge void provides a new dimension for the public space and at the same time a new possibility for the architectural school to embrace the public space and its privileged location. The void is flexible in nature to accommodate exhibitions, ceremonies and performances. The three bridges that across the void and link the two sides are the major crit spaces which facilitates students' participation and involvement of the whole school to the heart of architectural school operation.

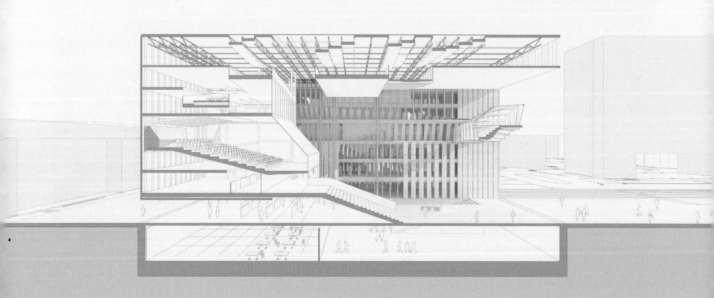

Curtis Roth | MArch
Frame

Based on the observation that the typology of the architecture school requires a roughly even distribution of both highly controlled interiors (lecture rooms, work shops, offices), and expansive programmatic fields (studios, lecture halls and exhibition spaces), the project attempts to exploit the tension within this typological characteristic through a figural frame, encapsulating a massive internal void.

The articulation of the interior as a collective void aligns itself with emerging possibilities in architectural production, where a highly calibrated relationship between the expanse of the interior and integrated infrastructural systems allow for the factory-like studio and lecture spaces to be rethought of as a site for perpetual full-scale intervention.

The frame itself allows key programmatic elements to be strategically distributed in relation to both external environmental factors and their adjacency to the interior void. Allowing for a dense strip of activities framing the continual construction of architecture within architecture. This continual spectacle of internal construction forms a new central node within the campus at large, aligning and producing a collection of public living rooms within which the activities of the architecture program are strategically located.

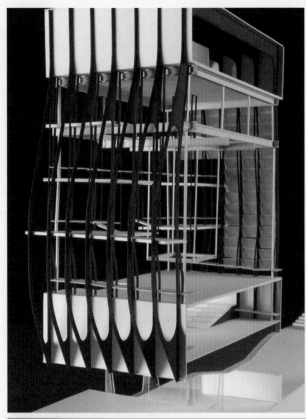

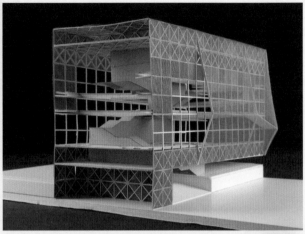

LIQUID ARCHIVE FAST [FESTIVAL OF ART SCIENCE AND TECHNOLOGY] PROJECT

Gediminas Urbonas and Nader Tehrani

Liquid Archive, a floating, interactive artwork, imaginatively extends MIT's Killian Court beyond Memorial Drive into the Charles River, to celebrate the Institute's 150th anniversary. Consisting of an inflatable screen anchored to a floating platform, it provides a backdrop for dynamic projections. Visible from the banks of the Charles, an hour-long program will feature several original artist proposals conceived in 1972 as part of the Charles River Project, a series of environmental artworks conceived by the designers, artists and scientists associated with MIT's Center for Advanced Visual Studies. Liquid Archive will bring these projects to life and demonstrate MIT's renewed commitment to creating an energy efficient environment and environmental art on a civic scale.

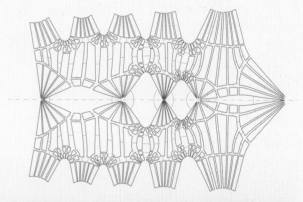

Using an array of new media and performative strategies, the Liquid Archive will showcase the transdisciplinary collaborative mode so crucial to the success of both CAVS and MIT. At a key moment in MIT's history, the pavilion will actualize the potentialities and energy of proposals, articulating the innovative and hopeful futurity that continues to be MIT's driving force.

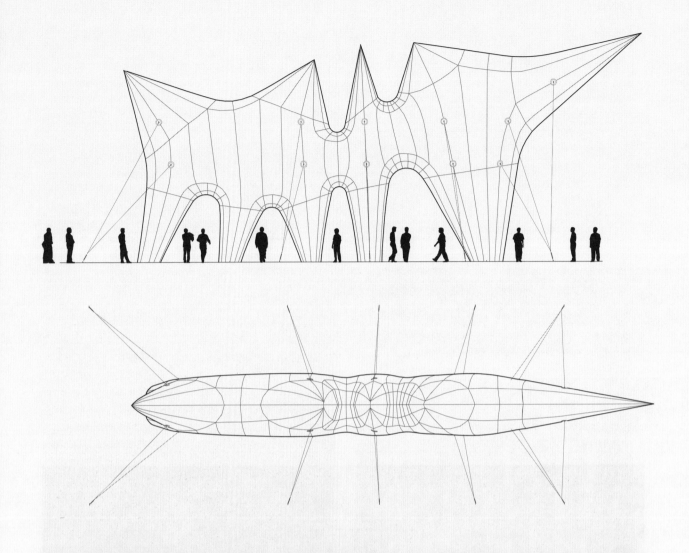

Image credit: John Horner

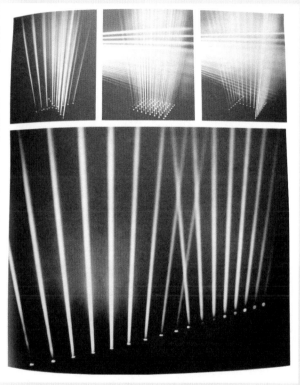

Inspirations from the CAVS archives
Top: Photographer: Nishan Bichajian "5–73"

Left: György Kepes, Programmed Light Walls for Boston Harbor, 1964
Photographer: Nishan Bichajian "8–69"

Right: Otto Piene and Fellows of CAVS, Sky Event, 1969
"Balloon Sculptures" for the Opening of New Boston City Hall, 1–69
Photographer: Nishan Bichajian

FROM MODEL TO MASHUP
A PEDAGOGICAL EXPERIMENT IN THINKING HISTORICALLY ABOUT THE FUTURE

Ana Miljački

This article was originally published in the Journal of Architectural Education, *March 2011: Vol. 64, Issue 2 (9-24).*

Critically projective

The *Ferry Slip Mashup* studio began with a hypothesis that the recent abundance of crisis narratives in general, and in architecture competitions, studios, and publications specifically, was a symptom of the end of an era in which it was difficult to imagine alternatives to the logic of advanced global capitalism. That some form of outside to global capitalism could now begin to be grasped conceptually, however different any particular image of that post- or other world might be, has in part been reigniting architects' collective will to think prospectively and therefore also historically. For, the future, we are now reminded, can be imagined only when thinking historically. If the first premise of the studio was that we needed to relearn how to think historically (with or without the help of the global financial and ecological crises), then the second premise of the studio was that we had to find an appropriately contemporary way to do that.

In 2003, French historian of science and cultural theorist Bruno Latour invited his readers to take a mental test:[1] If we thought that the time would come when we would be able to distinguish ends from means, facts from values and humans from non-humans–trusting that clarity was merely a question of progress–we could still consider ourselves modern. If we hesitated at all when presented with this idea–Latour called us postmodern. But if we believed that the world is getting ever more entangled–we might have entered another paradigm, one that Latour

Cruise ship site study
Contributed to the collective archive by Natsuki Maeda and Oliver Wuttig.

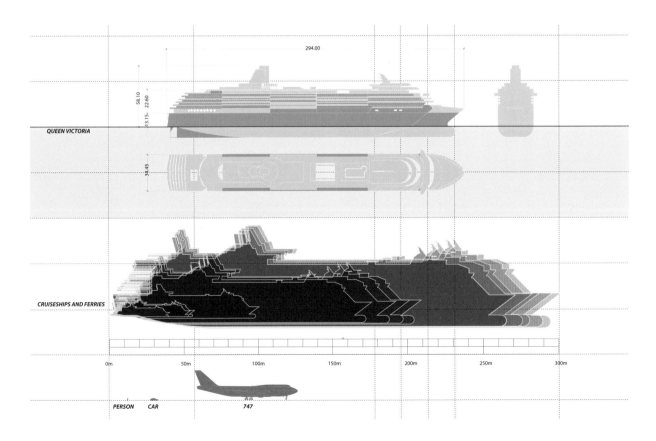

QUEEN VICTORIA

294.00

58.10   22.60

13.15

34.45

CRUISESHIPS AND FERRIES

0m   50m   100m   150m   200m   250m   300m

PERSON   CAR   747

insists on calling "non-modern." We don't need to give up the fact that modernism, as a period with a specific ethos, concept of time, and a specific idea of progress, actually occurred in order to accept the idea that we are now able to see and describe complex relationships between various agents, objects, histories and processes.

A type of periodization is important here–to supplement Latour's experiment–even if we lack a convenient name for the contemporary. Terms such as Marc Augé's *supermodernity*, Hans Ibelings's *supermodernism*, Zygmunt Baumann's *fluid modernity*, or Latour's *non-modernity*, have all resulted from descriptions of an important difference between the contemporary and the modern (understood historically).[2] If modernism can be seen (following Baumann's description of "solid modernity") as having operated with the idea that progress and the trajectory of time would eventually deliver things to perfection, or to a perfectly rationally organized world–in distinction to modernism, the general consensus is that today we can no longer tap into the authority and certainty of modernism's "project".

From Model to Mashup

For a generation of architects and critics who "grew up" with sampling, with networks as fully internalized and lived protocols, knowing about the genome, contributing to and learning from Wikipedia, donating money to and SMS-

ing with the Obama campaign–having a set of external, authoritative truths is not a precondition for action. Still, in order to intervene consciously (or even nearly consciously) in the world, as architects ultimately do, requires the production of (personal and/or collective) narratives that in some way mediate between the circumstances exterior to any given project and the design process. These narratives function as positioning devices, postulating the role of the architect and of the discipline of architecture in a complexly entangled world. Legitimating narratives have existed throughout the history of architecture, both as entire authoritative discourses (on style, on origins, on social responsibilities, on the nature of public space, on the function of cites, etc.) and as individual architects' interpretations of those discourses. But what distinguishes our most recent versions of these narratives from all earlier versions in architectural history is: that the narratives of architectural production are now fluid, multiple, and generally smaller; they are often adaptations of the best parts of a number of earlier stories, and they rely on and produce the need for research (wiki, archival, and field).

In a world in which new records are rare and remixes rule, within the music industry and everywhere else, we could decide to clear the slate and install an old type of

Study of the relationship between the cruise ship and the docking terminal
Contributed to the collective archive by Natsuki Maeda and Oliver Wuttig.

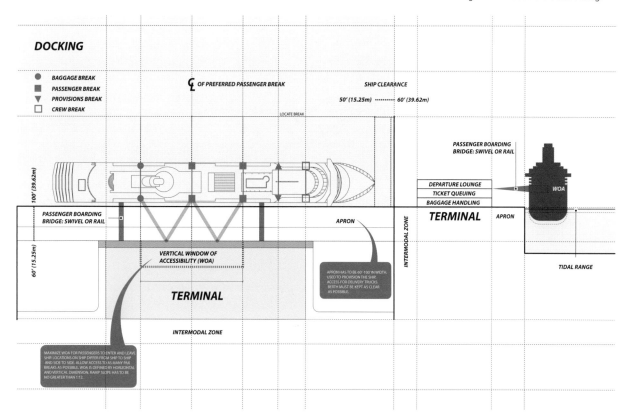

authenticity, or criticality, or even disciplinarity, or we could invest in articulating why there is no going back to an older "clearer" trajectory. Today, even clarity itself has to be seen as a type of remix. Relying on this reading of our contemporary predicament in aesthetic production in general and in architecture specifically, the main provocation of the studio was to place *the mashup* at the center of methodological investigations.

There are several definitions of mashup circulating in contemporary culture; the most important one for our studio discussions was the musical mashup, which of course entirely depends on the medium of music, but not without certain possible equivalences to architecture.[3] Musical mashup has its own history, starting with adaptations, remixes, sampling, but the most sophisticated contemporary versions of it rely on a deep musical understanding of the material used in combination to aesthetic ends that are in no way contained in the pre-existing musical material.[4] Mashup can draw material from two or many sources, and their origin is sometimes completely obliterated into a near glow of reference, while it is other times present as a deliberate signifier of an era, an atmosphere, or a tune.[5] A possibly contentious issue of whether musical mashups rely on sophisticated processing of medium specific information, or on real disciplinary knowledge–we leave to the theorists of music, but this studio's experiment with architectural mashup was premised on a critical evaluation of disciplinary knowledge.

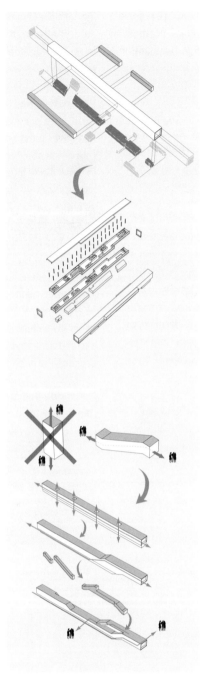

Oliver Wuttig's analysis of the 3XN ferry terminal in Copenhagen with a proposal for reworking its architecture through a single sectional shift.

aesthetic experience and outcome. What used to be Modernism's (and Harold Bloom's) "anxiety of influence" has for the contemporary generation of architects positively (i.e. in the best case scenario) turned into an "ecstasy of influence," and in the mashup studio we wanted to have that ecstasy encounter the resistance of history.[6] Thinking historically was an important precondition for ensuring that the architectural mashup would become more than a second rate copy-paste project, in which decisions to retool a piece of architectural history were based on a shallow understanding of that history (thereby avoiding types of projects that litter contemporary architectural journals and students' go-to web sites like Arch Daily). It was the ultimate hope of the studio that a willingness to operate self-consciously with disciplinary knowledge and a willingness to stake out (and update) political positions could lead to figuring new projects that are distinctly contemporary, while also grounded in long-term disciplinary issues. That is, if there were really going to be such a thing as ecstasy of influence (in opposition to mere consumption and emulation of trends) it would in large part come from a self-conscious conversation with disciplinary history and contemporary discourse.

In the long process of moving away from Modernism's "truths" and surviving Postmodernism's iconoclastic historicism, the status of a historical model in architectural pedagogy shifted as well. We rarely review a precedent these days with hopes of getting some form of an essential guideline from it, and even less often do we study precedents as blueprints of relationships or dimensions to be simply reproduced. In fact, a particular parti, a facade solution, an engagement with the developer logic, or with digital fabrication are all possible contemporary registers of architectural production and thinking and thus sources of historical material with particular lessons and lineages of questions worth building

Our studio's two main hypotheses on mashup were that working in this mode was not a question of intentions as much as it was an inevitable response to the status of knowledge in general and to the complexity of the contexts in which we operate as architects, and that mashup may be well suited to delivering an unprecedented (i.e. new) form of

upon. Since we can now access and retool any type of knowledge (technical, disciplinary, cultural), learn from an enormous database of old errors and successes, and even conduct new tests (all the while collecting information on those tests), it has become more important than ever to articulate the lineages (even if these are merely simulated) to and through the historical archives. This is to say that raw data, and vague extra-disciplinary inspiration were of no interest to us in studio, our precedents had to carry enough historical specificity with them to be understood in terms of particular circumstances and ideologies that made them possible, and ultimately comparable and connectable.

Moving from working with precedents as models to working with an archive of diverse types of architectural knowledge required a method for producing (or again, simulating) coherence, and for this we relied on one of the most archaic methods of synthesis: storytelling. Thus, through trial and error, editing and fine-tuning, students attempted to isolate stories; as if they were trajectories through the archive of the knowledge they needed (and wanted to have) in order to produce their designs. That is, the mashup brought with it pressures to consciously and intelligently store, sort, retrieve, and re-articulate architectural knowledge. Thus our studio's archives were not merely repositories of searchable data. The studio's ambition for them tended towards Foucault's famous definition of an archive as actively organizing systems of enunciations with the historian or the archeologist as the ultimate "user" of that archive. In the roles of archivists and archeologists students were asked to consider, produce and use their archives on three different levels. One, the collective archive of all relevant facts and realities described the real constraints of the project. Two, every student was responsible for a more monographic "deep dive," based around a single project. This method produced an archive that in its monographic nature most closely approached the status of the precedent. Three, the final, and most complex level of archiving involved finding historical threads around issues that students identified as particularly meaningful to explore given the constraints of the project, and given the issues coming out of their monographic deep dive and their projective ambitions for the discipline in general and their own design project in particular.

Maine State Pier: Open source archive

In order to ground our studio's highly self-conscious methodological investigations, we went to a medium-sized New England town known for its maritime tourism

and its industrial past (with no Architecture–capital A–to speak of): Portland, Maine. Studio posited Portland, ME as American architecture's frontier. It is not exotic, just self-contentedly quaint, which has historically made it even less glamorous for academia to consider than the "grey goo" of American exurbia. The city of Portland has had an RFP out for the reworking of the Maine State Pier for at least three years. Last year, the development company that won the bid lost its financial backing or, at least, lost its nerve. Consequently, the Maine State Pier planning and design conversations have continued (and have been made available in great detail for public scrutiny). The Maine State Pier is slated by the planning department and the city to take on passenger transport functions, with two other Portland piers scheduled to deal with fishing and freight separately. Once known as Canada's winter port, Portland is still an international port and point of entry, which means that on top of dealing with local islander transport, the Maine State Pier includes an international ferry terminal, along with its enlarged immigration facilities, post 9/11 security zone fences, and Homeland Security regulations. The Maine State Pier is an appropriately contemporary agglomeration of

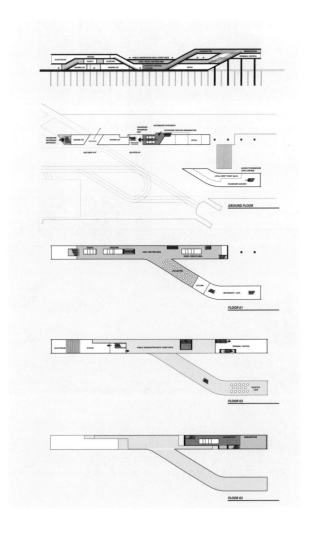

Section and plans of the 3XN terminal newly adapted to fit the program-matic and site needs of the Maine State Pier in Portland, by Oliver Wuttig.

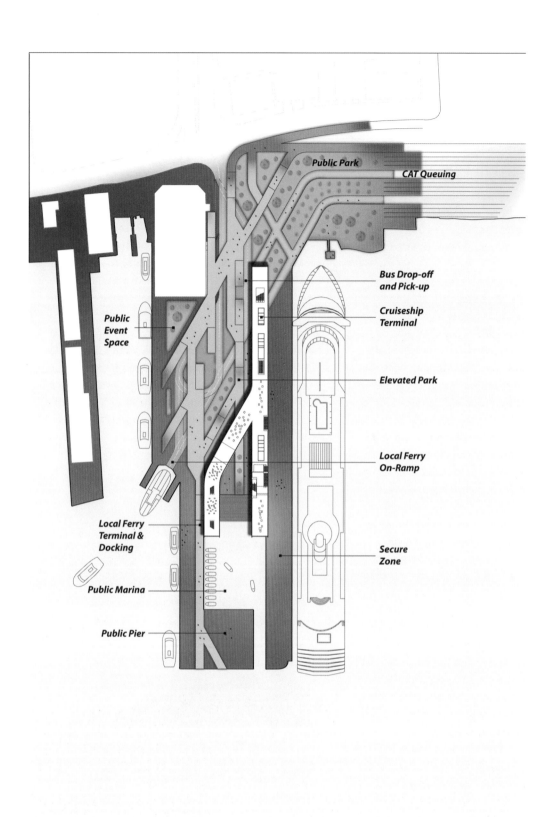

Public Park

CAT Queuing

Public Event Space

Bus Drop-off and Pick-up

Cruiseship Terminal

Elevated Park

Local Ferry On-Ramp

Local Ferry Terminal & Docking

Public Marina

Public Pier

Secure Zone

Larger site of the Maine State Pier reworked to fit the adapted 3XN project, by Oliver Wuttig

complex issues: various regulatory pressures, business plans, marine transportation logistics, structural dimensioning, infrastructural functioning, stimulus money, natural systems, seasonal cruise ship travel, public fishing needs, and symbolic dimensions of both local and, if not global, than at least international significance. Organized in teams students collectively measured, surveyed, and explained the site in an open-source mode of collaboration. This first attempt at producing an organized and highly pragmatic archive was broken down into six important issues: everything about the ships that ship in and out of Portland, a survey of Portland's tourism, the berthing and pier structures, the existing RFP (along with the hopes of the townspeople and previous gambles of the developers involved), Portland's sea levels and sea life, and homeland security regulations. The open source mode of this archive ensured that facts and constraints would inform every project without becoming the ground of a positivistic problem-solving frenzy.

Nip Tuck: Learning from adapting a monographic archive
Once everyone learned about the basic constraints and ambitions of the Maine State Pier project, we moved onto reviewing a series of more and less recent pier and transportation hub projects, adapting these specifically to the local constraints. Our Nip-Tuck exercise was the first

step in testing what it might mean to produce within a lower (historically older) order of the mashup logic: adaptation. Without yet having to completely "own" the design outcome of this exercise, but instead being responsible for taking the projects and their representational and ideological specificity to their logical conclusions ensured that no "anxiety of influence" entered the equation of architectural production. Thus it was through wearing someone else's hat that students were able to really comprehend the scale and demands of an architectural solution for the Maine State Pier, and they were able to begin to be critical of possible ideological postures they could inhabit in relationship to this project and the production of architecture in general.

Oliver Wuttig adapted a recent project for a ferry terminal in Copenhagen by 3XN architects, and Chai Pattamasattayasonthi used a recently published LOT-EK project for Pier 57 in New York. Oliver Wuttig's analysis of the 3XN ferry terminal involved deep programmatic, structural and architectural logics that governed the long bar building of his precedent. His adaptation of it responded to the specific ship sizes and programmatic requirements of the Maine State pier site. In order to make the 3XN project work on and for this new site, Oliver had to introduce a forking element into the bar building which allowed his bar

Chai Pattamasattayasonthi's rendering of the container-based ferry terminal for Maine State Pier, introducing an anti-LOT-EK emphasis on nasty weather, and thus actively beginning to change ownership of the project.

to be on two different sides of the pier, responding to both international cruse ships and the local island ferry services. He also significantly reworked the ground of the Main State Pier in a manner that had very little to do with the 3XN proposal, open up thus a line of inquiry for his own project. Chai Pattamasattayasonthi's precedent came with too little architectural articulation to really study details of connection or circulation, but since he was dealing with a LOT-EK project he was able to rely on the firm's famous and often articulated position on reusing industrial objects for the production of a type of surreal estrangement. In order to adapt the LOT-EK pier for Portland, Chai relied on the stacking of containers as did LOT-EK, which were available in the local context, but he also began to considered what materials might produce an association with the state of Maine and could be repurposed for architectural applications, thus playing into the quaint and often automatic identification and self-identification of Maine with red lobsters and fishermen's buoys. Thus LOT-EK's industrial vernacular (in Chai's analysis of their work) was made to approach the rhetoric of locality used the city, the developers, the shopkeepers in each case slightly differently in order to re-produce the citizens and the tourist expectations of this location. In Chai's case the discovery of this line of argument, through the adaptation of LOT-EK, would open a larger set of issues of "learning from" the Main street (in the Venturi and Scott-Brown sense), and the repurposing the image of the vernacular enough to estrange its image and logic without losing the reference to it and thus its rhetorical power in this context.

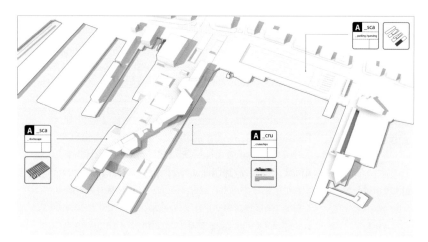

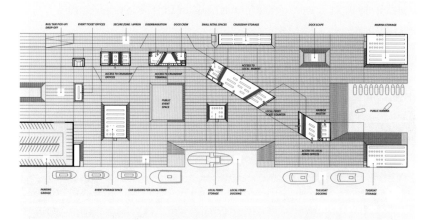

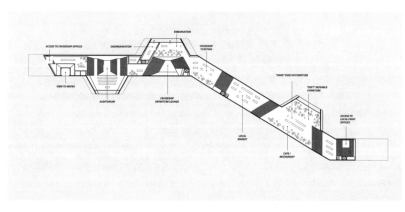

Site and plan work for Oliver Wuttig's final Ferry Terminal proposal. Influenced by his earlier "nip-tuck" exercise but now also consciously working with issues of conduit and scoop both in the architectural dimensions of the ferry terminal and the ground of the site.

Ferry Slip: Personal archives

The third version of the archive coincided with the final exercise in the design of the ferry terminal and pier for Portland. Although for many students the previous exercise based on a monographic precedent had great catalytic power for this final stage as well, students were asked to develop their own mashup archive (its content and logic of deployment) without relying on a single precedent, but instead by consciously constructing lineages and positions on specific issues they found relevant for the design of the ferry terminal and pier in Portland. They could draw from the two previous archives, and use their own tests on an equal footing with the historical and discursive material they wanted to be in conversation with.

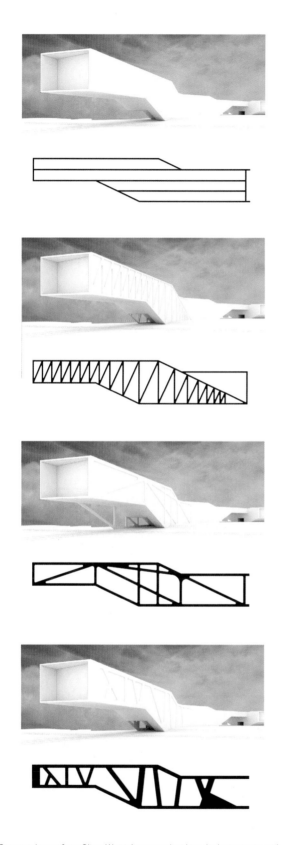

Structural tests from Oliver Wuttig's personal archive deploying more and less expressive possibilities.

Thus, everyone's archive contained highly pragmatic nuggets on the construction of the pier in Portland, precedents framed through particular lenses or lineages of concerns and tests produced within the design process itself.

Including his previous studio exercises into final–personal–archive Oliver Wuttig developed a line of argument that posited a play between nearly opposing formal tools as a way to both deal with specific programmatic needs of the ferry terminal project and to produce a contemporary hybridity of intention and reading in the project. On the scale of the architectural proposal the pair of tools included the tube and the branching view scoops, and on the scale of the site he opposed the bar to the logic of the field. He used his own design versioning process to discover possible lineages in dealing with structure and form of the project in relationship to his programmatic ambitions. It is only through trying out minimal solutions (of a kind of a modernist bar: Mies) in relationship to more expressive and stylized structural articulation (of more recent years: Jurgen Mayer) that he honed in on the tone of his own project. Discovering a kind of formal reversibility of the view or lighting scoops allowed him to produce variation and ultimately embed a type of interpretive ambiguity into the form of the project. Horizontal and vertical scoops, highly stylized formally were sometimes placed instrumentally in relationship to the embarkation and debarkation of the ships, and other times their function was less strictly scripted via that more basic notion of efficacy. Chai Pattamasattayasonthi, on the other hand, already set on a track through interpreting LOT-EK's recycling of materials in a direction that the City of Portland, the local developers and tourists seemed to embrace (given their respective rhetoric about the city and about tourist attractions) understood that he was embarking on a project that had a number of possible lineages in retooling the popular and the vernacular. Most famous of his "precedents" (now understood in this new way, as entries in his archive) were Venturi and Scott Brown examples, but more recent Herzog and de Meuron, or even the young US firm MOS, each pointed to a slightly different direction. What was common among them, at least to some extent, was their estrangement of the vernacular though a type of material or formal abstraction. But even this was not at core of each of the positions that argued for "learning from" the vernacular. Chai chose not to go all the way towards a kind of commercialized proposal that perhaps most realistically embraced the economic logic of leasing space and allowing the shopkeepers and the ultimate operators of the pier to determine the final aesthetic outcome of it as well. But instead his project embraced the Maine Tourism Association's (and colloquial) rhetoric of "absolute Maineness" while offering a type of formal

Oliver Wuttig's final Maine State Pier rendering, showing the ground and the terminal scoops.

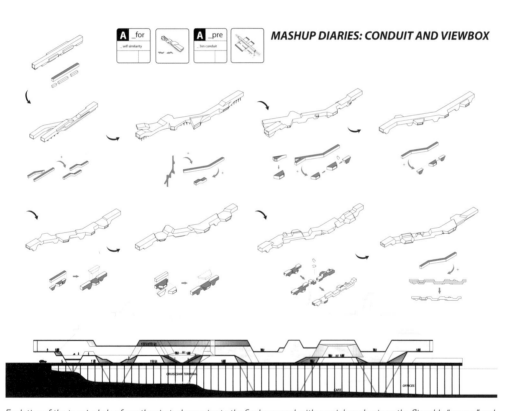

MASHUP DIARIES: CONDUIT AND VIEWBOX

A _for
_ self similarity

A _pre
_ ten conduit

Evolution of the terminal plan from the nip-tuck exercise to the final proposal, with special emphasis on the flippable "scoops" and views from those. From Oliver Wuttig's archive.

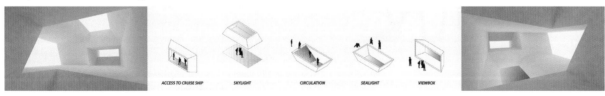

ACCESS TO CRUISE SHIP   SKYLIGHT   CIRCULATION   SEALIGHT   VIEWBOX

Formal flip of the scoop, combining spatial and programmatic use/usefulness while ensuring ambiguity
in signification. From Oliver Wuttig's archive.

coherence and even freshness that is rarely the outcome of basic economic thinking employed by developers and city officials. Once the students were allowed to borrow and steal, and define their own trajectories via their research (as long as the agenda and the linage of a certain architectural idea was clearly articulated) some of the usual anxieties about authorship (and influence) crept back into the discussion, which in part ensured that the final designs were creatively *in excess* of their controlled input material.

Storytelling: Divorcing the method of production from the final reception of the projects

The final request of the studio was to produce a linear narrative, a movie, of the production of the project, its inhabitation or its architectural agenda, such that all of the previous highly conscious and didactic methodological operations would vanish when it came to the final reception of the project. Our goal was to separate the reception of the final architectural proposals from the highly didactically clear methodology used for their production. This was as much an experiment in navigating the archive and thinking through storytelling as it was a test for the usual mindset of the critics in an academic context. Most importantly, we

Chai Pattamasattaysonthi's analysis of recent architectural transformations of the vernacular image of the house, setting up the discursive context to argue for the Maine State Pier transforming and abstracting the fishermen's shack.

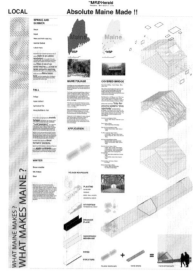

Excerpt from Chai Pattamasattayasonthi's personal archive including the programmatic analysis of the pier.

were curious to see to what extent the mashup was able to stand on its own, both aesthetically and discursively. The request to produce linear narratives separate from the archiving and retrieving of knowledge and even separate from possible positioning narratives pushed students to think through precedents in storytelling structures and genres, both in architecture and outside it. Oliver Wuttig showed his project through a standard modernist

Chai Pattamasattaysonthi's rendering of the final Maine State Pier Proposal.

Maine State Pier presented from the point of view of a local Portland traveler, who arrives by car. Excerpt from Oliver Wuttig's final movie.

Stills from Oliver Wuttig's final movie presenting the Maine State Pier from the point of view of the Cruise Ship passenger.

Stills from Oliver Wuttig's final movie presenting the Maine State Pier from the point of view of a hungry seagull.

filmmaking technique, a Dziga Vertov type of "a day in the life of" narrative, but such that the same day repeated three times from the perspective of the cruise-ship traveler, a local Maine State Pier worker and a Seagull. This narrative structure allowed him to show off the project literally from a number of different spatial perspectives while it also allowed him to humorously intertwine the protagonists across the three different "takes" of the pier. The atmospheric quality of the movie he made, in a very direct sense undermined the didactic formal reading of the project favoring the architectural effects of his form over any type of explanatory narrative. Chai Pattamasattayasonthi on the other hand extended his narrative of tourism. Structuring his presentation into a relentless series of touristy snapshots of his project including many of the affectations of tourist photography, the ultimate effect of his narrative technique was to literally project his architectural proposal into the status of an already existing tourist attraction. The final projects were critiqued in terms of their developmental logic, as well as separately from it, as proposals rich with imbedded intelligence and ideologies whose reading and misreading were both equally valuable for our studio's discussions.

In conclusion, it may be important to consider the reactions of numerous critics who participated in our studio discussions and reviews. Although the mashup studio invoked nausea for those who interpreted its contrivance as a repeat of the postmodernist narrative of *quotation*, it simultaneously managed to satisfy the latent avant-gardist hunger in others by proposing that something *new* and unrecognizable would eventually emerge from its experiments. The mashup studio proposed that, left without authoritative truths to rely on, but with greatly expanded expertise and concerns, the new generation of architects needed to relink (and even simulate links) to and rewrite the old political and cultural projects in architecture to fit their own time. That an older generation of critics thought they recognized projects (especially vastly different ones like oldness and newness) in the premise of the studio was a proof (of sorts) that at least some connections and rewriting had begun.

Plans and sections of Chai Pattamasattaysonthi's final proposal.

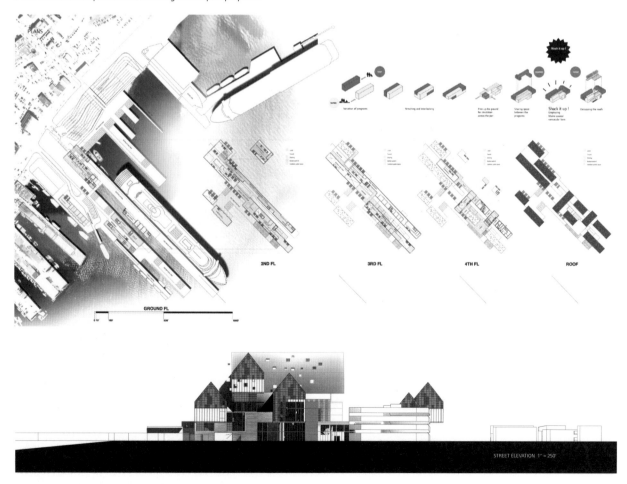

1   Bruno Latour's invitation to perform this test was published in his *Reconstituting the Social*, but the spirit of this challenge can be found at the basis of a number of Latour's works in the 1990s and 2000s, and most famously, in Bruno Latour, *We Have Never Been Modern* (Harvard University Press, 1993).

2   See Marc Augé, *Non-Places: Introduction to an Anthropology of Supermodernity* (London and New York: Verso 1995), Hans Ibelings, *Supermodernism–Architecture in the Age of Globalization* (Rotterdam: NAi, 1998) and more recent, Zygmunt Bauman, *Liquid Modernity* (Cambridge: Polity, 2000).

3   See, for example, a book of texts edited together from a variety of fields, Stefan Sonvilla-Weiss (ed.) *Mashup Cultures* (Springer, 2010).

4   A recent New York Times article goes specifically into the issues surrounding the recent history of the musical mashup, Michiko Kakutani, "A Mash-Up Culture: Ten to Watch," *New York Times*, March 17, 2010.

5   In contemporary music the most famous example of a two source mashup was DJ Danger Mouse's *Grey Album* produced through a careful combination of the Beatles' *White Album* and Jay-Z's *Black Album*, while much of the recent work by Girl Talk is a more meandering concoction of a myriad sources.

6   See Harold Bloom, *Anxiety of Influence; A theory of Poetry* (New York and Oxford: Oxford University Press, 1973), as well as a brilliant essay by Jonathan Lethem constructed out of borrowed, or plagiarized pieces from a large number of sources, "The Ecstasy of Influence: A plagiarism," *Harper's Magazine*, February, 2007.

Stills from Chai Pattamasattayasonthi's final movie in which stereotypical tourist photographs backgrounded by the sound of a clicking camera present all the important programmatic and architectural aspects of his project.

THE PARABLE OF THE GLASS HOUSE INDEPENDENT STUDY PROJECT

SPRING 2009

Christopher Guignon
Supervisor: **Yung Ho Chang**

Parable of the Glass House imagines an alternative history in which global events force Philip Johnson to rethink how he lives in his decadent modernist masterpiece. Or is it all, in fact, just a daydream that inspires Johnson to rethink the design and possible futures of his Glass House? Drawing from sources of architectural representation, from Bernard Tschumi's Manhattan Transcripts to Chris Ware's Jimmy Corrigan, Parable of the Glass House explores the comic's potential to manipulate two- and three- dimensional space with the fourth dimension of time.

Parable of the Glass House Broadsheet
Released in 2010 by little t, with considerable help from the Department of Architecture and MIT's Council for the Arts

PARABLE of the GLASS HOUSE

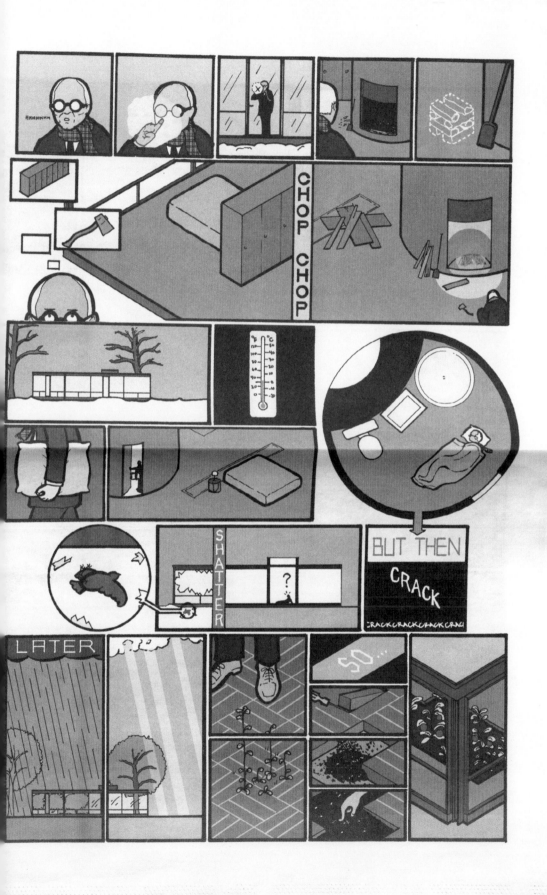

1983

1948

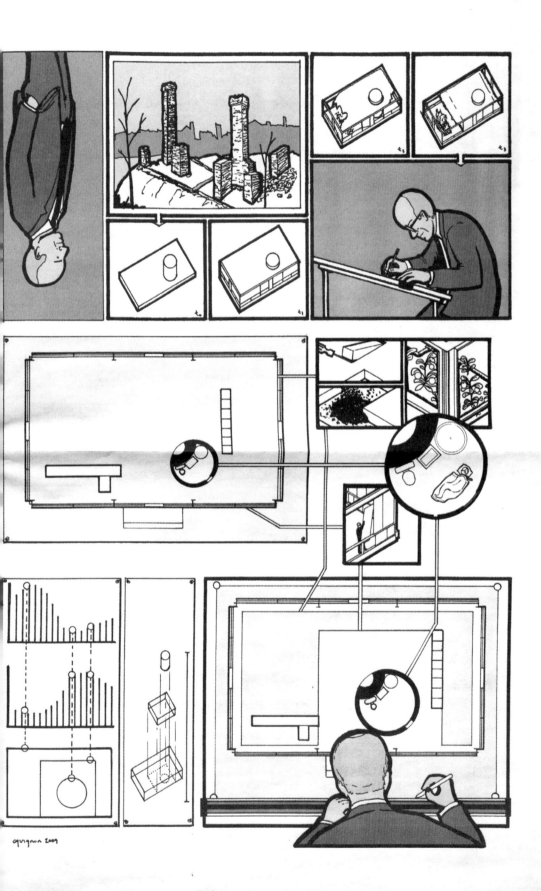

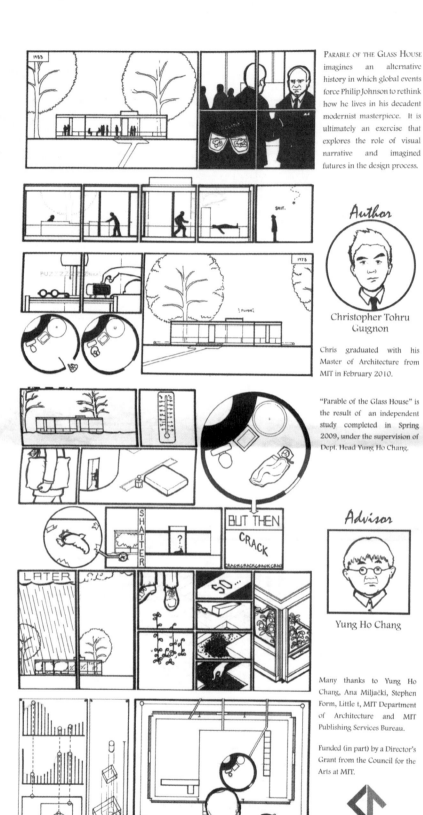

PARABLE OF THE GLASS HOUSE imagines an alternative history in which global events force Philip Johnson to rethink how he lives in his decadent modernist masterpiece. It is ultimately an exercise that explores the role of visual narrative and imagined futures in the design process.

Author

Christopher Tohru Guignon

Chris graduated with his Master of Architecture from MIT in February 2010.

"Parable of the Glass House" is the result of an independent study completed in Spring 2009, under the supervision of Dept. Head Yung Ho Chang.

Advisor

Yung Ho Chang

Many thanks to Yung Ho Chang, Ana Miljački, Stephen Form, Little t, MIT Department of Architecture and MIT Publishing Services Bureau.

Funded (in part) by a Director's Grant from the Council for the Arts at MIT.

MIT Massachusetts Institute of Technology

THE PRINT CULTURE OF ARCHITECTURE

Michael Kubo (Ph.D. History Theory and Criticism) **and Chris Grimley**

What do you primarily read
architecture books for/as?

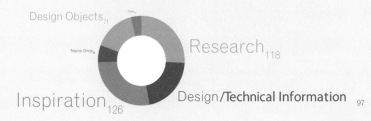

Design Objects 71
Other
Name-Drop
Research 118
Inspiration 126
Design/Technical Information 97

Where do you get architectural
information from these days?

Other
Exhibitions 60
Books 111
Blogs 100
Magazines/Journals 107
Websites 113
Newspaper

Are books a valid form
of architectural production?

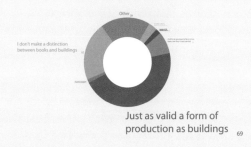

Other
I don't make a distinction
between books and buildings
Just as valid a form of
production as buildings 69

What will happen to
architectural books in the future?

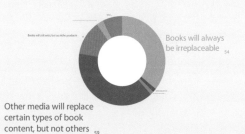

Books will still exist, but as niche products
Books will always
be irreplaceable 54
Other media will replace
certain types of book
content, but not others 59

The disciplinary definition of architecture, as a form of practice related as much to the discursive context of history and theory as to the material context of building practice, runs parallel to the history of what has come to be called print culture. Within the specific print culture of the field (which took on its first contours in the Renaissance, with the confluence of humanist discourse and a new interest in antiquity with the dissemination of moveable type and the printing press), the practice of architecture has been closely related to the practice of publishing by architects. Publishing has been a privileged as well as an obligatory means by which architects have sought to shape the context in which their work is produced, received, and interpreted.

In the modern print era, the most prominent architects in the field have often been its most prolific publishers. These architects have acted as authors (of monographs, manifestoes, histories, treatises, lectures, charters, pamphlets, transcripts, catalogues), editors (of magazines, journals, newspapers, and other serial formats), and curators (of exhibitions, events, groups, conferences, meetings, and other channels for producing and disseminating their agendas). Some have regarded the design process itself as a form of editing; others have drawn on experience in related fields like graphic design, journalism, and filmmaking in their architectural work. All of these roles have intersected with the practices of historians, theorists, and critics who have participated in the discourse of the field from their own disciplinary perspectives.

In our selection of case studies, a "canonical" publication meant one that involved a total consideration of the work as a textual and graphic object—a careful and deliberate construction of format, layout, images, and words—and which proved to have the most sustained influence on architecture's print culture.

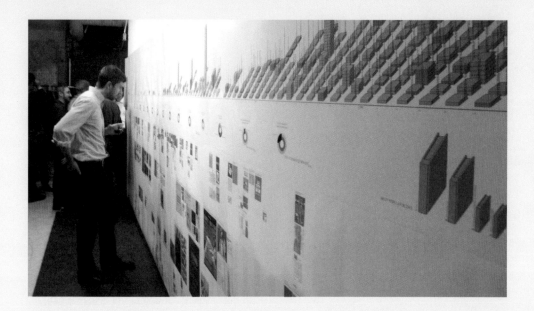

Architects have become accustomed to regarding books as tactical tools in their disciplinary arsenal, capable of instigating effects very different from those of more traditional forms of production. The relationship between publishing and building has often been exploited as a critical double form of architectural practice, as two strands of work that are typically assumed to mirror each other but which often reveal a provocative (and in many cases deliberate) misalignment. Instead of regarding publishing as subsidiary to "practice"—conventionally understood to mean the production of buildings—the most prominent architects and critics have exploited the operative differences between books and buildings, engaging with both as distinct but related forms of production. In this history publishing has acted as an alternative mode of architectural practice, one that is often more agile than other practices more typically understood as architectural.

The Publishing Practices project, exhibited at pinkcomma gallery in Boston in September 2009, traced the practice of architectural publishing through a survey of books produced by architects and authors in the last century.[1] Case studies presented the origins, composition, and after-effects of ten "canonical" architecture books, each one reflecting a particular era of architectural production and a specific attitude towards the role and effects of publishing on the part of its producers. The case studies began with Le Corbusier's *Vers une Architecture* (1923) and ended with *S,M,L,XL* (1995), at the cusp of the digital age. Beyond providing a particular picture of twentieth-century architecture as told through its publications, the case studies revealed a sustained lineage within architecture's print culture of revisions and reformulations of certain key genres

of the twentieth-century architectural book, in particular the manifesto, the monograph, and the operative history.[2]

In choosing the case studies for Publishing Practices, the decision to focus on what is in many ways the commonly accepted canon of publications from the last century was a deliberate one. By exploring what it means to talk about a "canonical" work, we sought to move beyond the conventional discussion of architecture's disciplinarity, with all the boundaries and exclusions the term implies, towards an idea of architecture as a field of cultural production (to use Pierre Bourdieu's term) in which publishing is one among many modes of practice, different from but no less important in its operation than the production of buildings.[3] Publishing and building have long had equal status as discursive modes of operation within this field. Even among newer forms of media that have circulated around architectural practice, the durability and resilience of publishing has allowed it to remain a primary means for practitioners to engage with the canon, whether of books, buildings, or architects. Indeed, some of the major proponents of the newest and supposedly most agile forms of media, such as blogs and websites, continue to rely on traditional book formats as a means of engaging with the canonical modes of architectural discourse.

In our selection of case studies, a "canonical" publication meant one that involved a total consideration of the work as a textual and graphic object—a careful and deliberate construction of format, layout, images, and words—and which proved to have the most sustained influence on architecture's print culture. Identifying them meant looking for those works that one would expect to have found consistently across the major sites of architectural

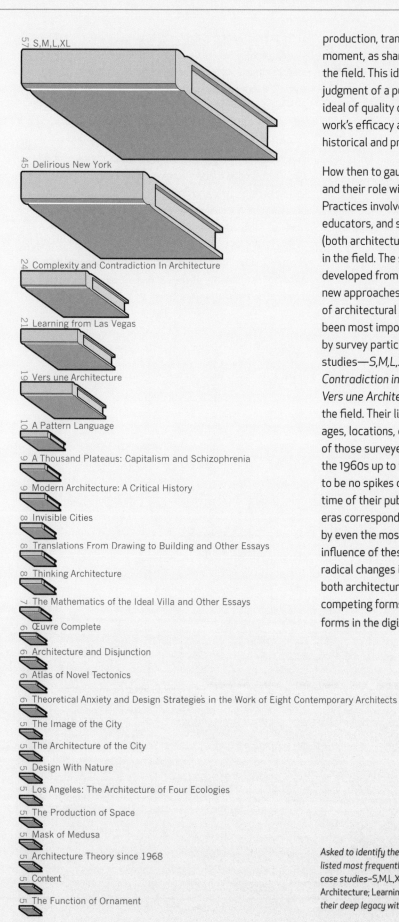

57 S,M,L,XL

45 Delirious New York

24 Complexity and Contradiction In Architecture

21 Learning from Las Vegas

19 Vers une Architecture

10 A Pattern Language

9 A Thousand Plateaus: Capitalism and Schizophrenia

9 Modern Architecture: A Critical History

8 Invisible Cities

8 Translations From Drawing to Building and Other Essays

8 Thinking Architecture

7 The Mathematics of the Ideal Villa and Other Essays

6 Œuvre Complete

6 Architecture and Disjunction

6 Atlas of Novel Tectonics

6 Theoretical Anxiety and Design Strategies in the Work of Eight Contemporary Architects

5 The Image of the City

5 The Architecture of the City

5 Design With Nature

5 Los Angeles: The Architecture of Four Ecologies

5 The Production of Space

5 Mask of Medusa

5 Architecture Theory since 1968

5 Content

5 The Function of Ornament

production, transmission, and reception at a given historical moment, as shared forms of knowledge and practice within the field. This idea of canonicity, far from being an ahistorical judgment of a publication relative to an autonomous ideal of quality or value, involved an assessment of each work's efficacy as a discursive practice within its particular historical and productive context.

How then to gauge the reception of books within the field and their role within architecture's print culture? Publishing Practices involved a survey of over 500 practitioners, educators, and students to gauge the impact of publications (both architectural and non-architectural) on those trained in the field. The survey responses and the data graphics we developed from them affirmed our criteria and suggested new approaches to studying the instrumentality and efficacy of architectural books. Asked to identify the books that had been most important to them, those listed most frequently by survey participants included five out of the ten case studies—*S,M,L,XL, Delirious New York, Complexity and Contradiction in Architecture, Learning From Las Vegas,* and *Vers une Architecture*—confirming their deep legacy within the field. Their listing was consistent across the different ages, locations, educational contexts, and current practices of those surveyed, which included architects trained from the 1960s up to the present. To our surprise there seemed to be no spikes of influence for these books around the time of their publication or among those trained in the eras corresponding to their initial appearance. Their listing by even the most recent students reveals the continued influence of these publications up to the present, amid radical changes in the production and dissemination of both architecture and books and the emergence of other, competing forms of media as print culture takes on new forms in the digital era.[4]

Asked to identify the books that had been most important to them, those listed most frequently by survey participants included five out of the ten case studies–S,M,L,XL; Delirious New York; Complexity and Contradiction in Architecture; Learning from Las Vegas; and Vers une Architecture–confirming their deep legacy within the field.

The next round of our exploration of publishing practices in architecture was Newsstand, exhibited at pinkcomma in November 2010. Co-curated with Mimi Zeiger, the author of loudpaper and curator of A Few Zines (exhibited at pinkcomma in March 2009), Newsstand took stock of a publication medium that has recently witnessed a resurgence within architecture's print culture: the newspaper. Inexpensive printing, rapid dissemination, and expanded dimensions have made the newspaper a topical platform for recent architecture and design discourse, in spite of (and according to the responses we received from the authors of many of these newspapers, often explicitly in response to) an increasingly digital world. The ephemerality and flexibility of the newspaper format provided a counterpoint to the very different temporality of the canonical architecture book we explored in Publishing Practices.

1997 1998 1999 **2000** 2001 2002 2003 2004

The survey raised the question of whether S,M,L,XL may stand as the final, definitive example of the canonical book. With its dramatic appearance at a moment of confluence between new modes of production, the rising cultural status of the architect, the first impacts of globalization on architectural and publishing practices, and the increasing influence of theory–but before the rise of digital media that would alter the traditional role of the book–its success may simply be impossible to replicate, in part the product of a historically unrepeatable set of circumstances.

"Traditionally the newspaper is where civic identity, politics, culture, etc. are projected—where the city meets information flows."

"Encountering images on a screen doesn't resonate, doesn't have the power, the poetry, or the meaning that a printed image has."

"If a thesis is about turning up the volume around a line of inquiry, what better way than to literally go for volume?"

"We thought a broadsheet was a good scale–not too small to be too easy, but not as daunting as a book."

"We wanted to revive the idea (common in nineteenth-century American cities) of the newspaper as a poster or broadside—a document that is posted in public space for a collective reading experience."

"Because it's both timely and timeless. It's quick to produce, but not too quick."

"A bit unwieldy and oversized, the broadsheet makes reading a printed publication a physical act (it takes up two subway seats at least) and asserts itself in an increasingly digital world."

"The lower the barrier to production, the more inspired, direct, and exuberant the expression."

We wanted something we could hold in our hands. Something we could touch, fold, tuck in our pocket or into a (real) file. Something that would deteriorate and age and belong to a specific place and time.

Newsstand

"Publications often reach people where websites can't; they are their own form and creative space and can move through the world in a great variety of ways."

"I wanted it to be something tangible that people could read at the conference, or on the subway or at home in the bathroom."

"Newsprint is expedient as well as being aesthetically and intellectually pleasing."

"…it was also incredibly selfish."

"We believe in things."

"Publishing is overheated. Any kid in a studio can make a book. Too many books. It implies a sense of seriousness and import that is—I'll say it—inappropriate for many applications. Ephemeral, flimsy, and even odd formats like newspapers and posters are necessary to round out the suite of publication format options. Not book vs. newsprint, but newsprint + web + book + pamphlet + email + napkin sketch + …."

"One of the great benefits of print is the extreme (and extremely extensible, since you can always add another sheet of paper) resolution. It's just not possible with current technology to read architectural drawings in a reasonable fashion. I wanted room to read, see, and compare different bits all at the same time, in the same field of vision."

"It's still nice to have an object to read. To bring it with you on the subway or on a plane, toss it when you're done, or maybe keep it forever... whatever."

"Print is a way to engage the public and gather users around a point of interaction, while at the same time allowing for easy distribution."

Newsstand PINKCOMMA GALLERY NOVEMBER 2010

In order to investigate the motivations behind the revival of the newspaper format, the exhibit presented imaginative examples of the genre from the past several years. These involved a number of publications by MIT students and faculty, including two editions of the Little t series (Little thesis, by Haruka Horiuchi and Morgan Pinney, and The Parable of the Glass House, by Christopher Guignon) and Project_insert, a foldable publication by Ana Miljački and Lee Moreau first presented as their contribution to the Young Architects Award exhibition at the Architectural League in 2008. We also produced a broadsheet of our own containing information on all of the examples included as well as comments by their producers on their interest in the newspaper format, collected once again via questionnaire. The broadsheet included a survey form by Leagues and Legions (a think tank on architectural publishing of which pinkcomma is a part) to collect classified advertisements as part of the group's participation in the New City Reader project, curated by Kazys Varnelis and Joseph Grima at the exhibition The Last Newspaper at New York's New Museum.

Inexpensive printing, rapid dissemination, and expanded dimensions have made the newspaper a topical platform for recent architecture and design discourse, in spite of (and according to the responses we received from the authors of many of these newspapers, often explicitly in response to) an increasingly digital world.

1   Publishing Practices began as a research project at SUNY Buffalo during my tenure there as the Reyner Banham Fellow for 2008-2009 and continued at MIT in conjunction with pinkcomma gallery, directed by Chris Grimley, Michael Kubo, and Mark Pasnik. The survey and data graphics were developed specifically for the pinkcomma exhibition by Chris Grimley and Kyle Jonasen of over,under.

2   The ten case studies were Le Corbusier, *Vers une Architecture* (1923) and *Œvre Complète*, published in eight volumes from 1929 to 1965; Sigfried Giedion, *Space, Time and Architecture* (1941); Alison and Peter Smithson, *The Heroic Period of Modern Architecture* (1965); Robert Venturi, *Complexity and Contradiction in Architecture* (1966); Reyner Banham's *Los Angeles: The Architecture of Four Ecologies* (1971), Robert Venturi, Denise Scott Brown and Steven Izenour, *Learning From Las Vegas* (1972); Rem Koolhaas, *Delirious New York* (1978); Peter Eisenman, *Houses of Cards* (1987); Rem Koolhaas and Bruce Mau, *S,M,L,XL* (1995). In their formats and discursive modes, these publications fell broadly into the categories of the manifesto (*Vers une Architecture, Complexity and Contradiction in Architecture, Delirious New York*), the monograph (*Œvre Complete, Houses of Cards, S,M,L,XL*), and the polemical or operative history (*Space, Time and Architecture, The Heroic Period of Modern Architecture*). There are significant overlaps between these formats, for example the specific genre of the "city as manifesto" (inaugurated in the 1970s by *Los Angeles: The Architecture of Four Ecologies, Learning From Las Vegas, and Delirious New York*) and the promiscuous mixtures of the manifesto and the monograph as mutually reinforcing genres, as in *Delirious New York*, the first edition of *Learning From Las Vegas*, and *S,M,L,XL*.

3   In the past the idea of the canon has been fundamental to architecture's disciplinary definition as well as its print culture. According to this argument, the fact of possessing and naming a shared canon—and of being able to identify certain works as "canonical"—is central to architecture's self-identification as a discipline, well defined unto itself (and not, for example, simply a subset of other practices). In this formulation, the very existence of a canon is seen to be constitutive of architecture's disciplinarity. An extreme version of this argument, for example, might be the exclusionary claim that one is not merely expected as an architect to be familiar with these books; rather, if one is not conversant with the canon, one is not properly an architect.

4   As the last member of this chronology, the survey raised the question of whether *S,M,L,XL* may stand as the final, definitive example of the canonical book. With its dramatic appearance at a moment of confluence between new modes of production, the rising cultural status of the architect, the first impacts of globalization on architectural and publishing practices, and the increasing influence of theory—but before the consolidation of history/theory and practice as increasingly separate disciplines catering to different audiences, the over-proliferation of architectural publishing, and the rise of digital media that would alter the traditional role of the book after the 1990s—its success may simply be impossible to replicate, in part the product of a historically unrepeatable set of circumstances. No publication emerged from the survey as a candidate for the 'next' canonical book; it remains to be seen whether there will be one again, or whether the idea of the canonical and the role of publishing among other practices have undergone a definitive change in the meantime.

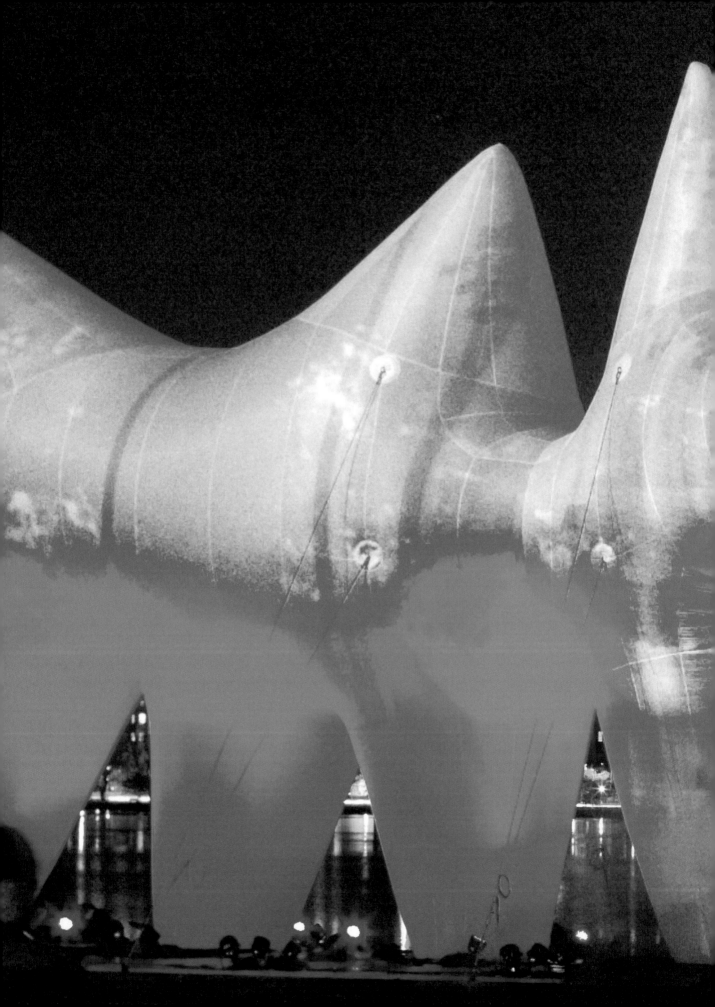

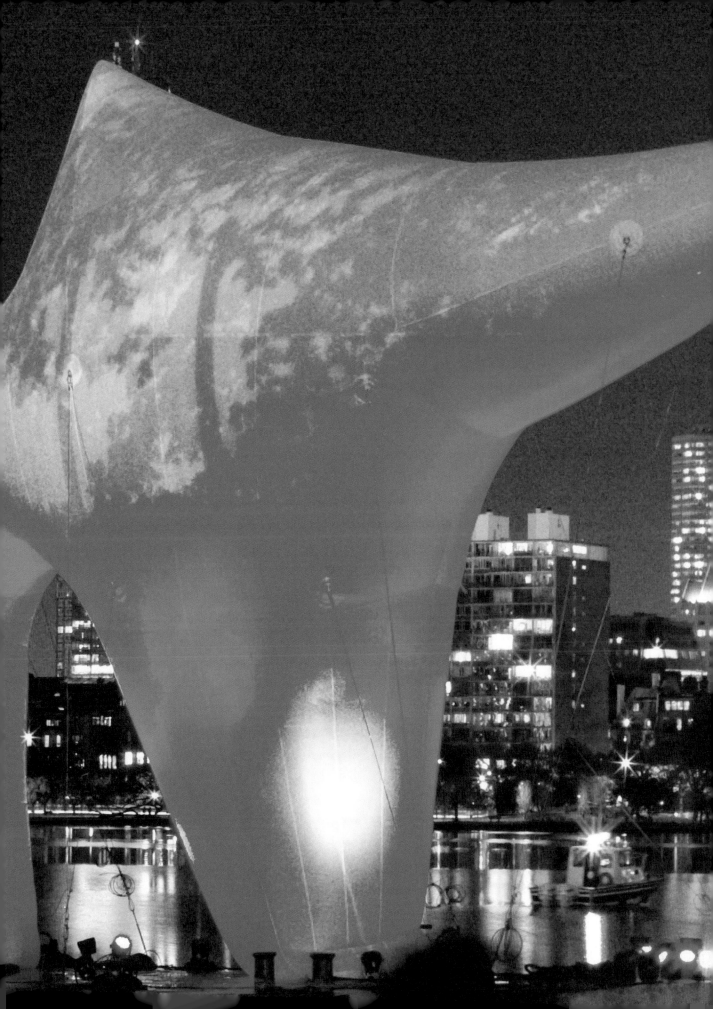

SURVIVAL

EXCURSES ONTO A DEPLETED PLANET

"It's a crisis, relax."   Ian McEwan, *Solar* (Anchor, 2010)

If sustainability is a contentious topic today, it is not for its otherwise general relevance to the discipline of architecture, or for its timely arrival on the scene of concerns. Rather, it stems from its being mired by competing concerns and the awkward allegiances forged in pursuit of a range of different objectives–it both benefits and is hindered by its status as a 'buzzword'. Sustainability seems to describe a more or less benevolent value at its heart–that we should be conscious about the consumption of resources, make sure we sustain our existence. Few people can disagree with the general premise that the earth is in danger, but the steps one must take in order to address this problem are seldom clear. A marketing tool as much as an alibi for legislative practice largely oriented towards escalating trade wars and technological exclusivity, sustainability, particularly when threaded through with energy or resource concerns, is today a charged public topic. Under such circumstances, it can be difficult to wade through sometimes-conflicting strategies for its insertion into architectural practice. Architecture is today privy to many self-appointed prophets of sustainability and the prophets appointed by hindsight (Glenn Murcutt, Sam Mockbee) as well as the green-washing witnessed amongst the worst corporate perpetrators. No wonder then that it elicits a host of reactions, sometimes avid, but more often reticence, awkwardness, tiptoeing around. And, as Mark Jarzombek shows us in his prescient 2003 article in *Blueprints*, the very basics of what we believe about sustainability are charged with complicated historic assumptions and very real implications.

For that matter, it's not just that it's awkward or uncomfortable for architects to talk about the environment, it's that the issue may have snowballed out of control–parties heretofore unheard from are suddenly weighing in on construction and engineering. Parties with little understanding of building fall prey to the name-brand recognition of environmentally-oriented certifications, as self-customizing and self-serving as feng shui. It's no wonder that this boilerplate 'expertise' appalls those equipped with some discernment on the subject of building, or conversely is cynically employed in producing otherwise atrociously expensive and lavish buildings. No wonder, sustainability today is as much a mantra by the "Drill, Baby, Drill" horde as by engineers seeking to basically devise a new genre of products for the global marketplace. Everybody wrings hands about ecology, and yet anxiously waits for the market–and consumption–to expand again, with super-liquid currency markets fuelling more energy-resource extraction than ever.

President Barack Obama's visit to MIT in October of 2009 underscored MIT's frontal position in America's efforts to devise means for clean and alternative energy sources, sources that may play a critical role whether in the politics of the Middle East or of protected biodiverse territories within the continental United States now at risk from increased drilling. Within the Department of Architecture, sustainability is treated like any other charged topic–it's unpacked, analyzed, and approached from every possible angle. It makes no sense to join a political bandwagon when there are experiments in play. Set as it is within an enormous research institute, it's not surprising that questions of energy consumption and production frequently come up in many forms within the context of architectural design as well. From student teams competing in the Energy Initiative to building technology projects inspired by Passive House technology, one learns as much about the finite qualities of materials that go into building as about pursuing formal exploration with new, synthetic-natural materials. With sustainability, technology becomes increasingly aware of its externalities, the downstream waste, pollution, and extractive usages that were traditionally handed over to a future generation or unwitting, less powerful communities.

Building has become a more totalitarian artifact, defined not only by the physical vestige of construction that stands before us, but rather the skeins of a larger system, an economy of sourcing, transportation, delivery, assembly, usage, and eventual entropy, dissipation and demolition. Professor Sheila Kennedy, whose work has been described elsewhere in this volume, best represents the experimental approach needed to explore the relationship between this economic/ecological totality of building and form. Her long-standing interest in exploring modes of production today brings within its ambit, the embodied energy within a given material, and the dynamics of its future use. The heliotropic Soft House developed by her firm, Kennedy Violich Architecture, alongside its research unit MATx for the International Building Exhibition (IBA) in Hamburg, presents us with the contours of a new, vanguardist semiosis, designed as an integrated sustainable energy concept which combines a carbon-negative wood construction system with the innovative use of flexible solar nanomaterials. A textile roof cladding harvests energy and provides a beneficial climate buffer that shades in summer, and limits heat loss in winter. Like a plant leaf that turns to follow the sun, the flexible solar cladding opens to provide views, harvest sunlight throughout the day, and create a dynamically changing façade that establishes the public identity of the architecture.

Within the Building Technology stream at the Department of Architecture, Professors John Ochsendorf and John Fernandez, in addition to their individual efforts, have led workshops with students to the developing world where alternative, less energy-intensive modes of construction are explored. Likewise, Professor Andrew Scott's Spring 2011 studio investigated the ravages of an ecotourism economy in the Galapagos, rightly reorienting focus on actual environmental impacts, rather than the perceived plenty of a resort destination.

Not everyone within the architectural faculty is persuaded of the moral dimensions posed by this 'crisis'. Professor Arindam Dutta, whose book *The Sustainability Fix(e)* is in progress, argues that rather than tying together the disparate realms of physical fact, individual or institutional initiative, and global consciousness-raising, the sustainability discourse should rather be examined as the counterpart to the ideology of neoliberalism, as a cover for what is in fact a bigger emphasis on consumption than ever. Developing a greener car, greener buildings, greener whatever, produces no imperative or compunction to sell fewer cars or fewer buildings, or even less per capita usage of square footage. Sustainability, in this view, is something of a post-modern, anti-discursive, matter of self-styling. In his article reproduced here, Mark Jarzombek makes a similar argument, viewing it as a kind of new-age 'idealism' whose import is to close off possibilities. Students in Dutta's Fall 2010 seminar investigated various implications of the sustainability fix, from the self-customizing dressage that is LEED, to the critical relationship between currency and oil markets, to the new 'closure of Third World commons' that is carbon-trading, to sustainability's complicity in turning university administrations'–including MIT's–more deeply towards corporate-funded research models. A number of their projects and findings are included here.

Beginning with what is known as the Rome Report, a 1972 publication from the Club of Rome titled *Limits to Growth*, public and political attention was focused on a particular brand of sustainability primarily the long-term implications for new ecological practices. The National Academy of Sciences first used the term *global warming* in their 1979 Charney Report, urging that continued carbon dioxide emissions would result in overall climate change and potentially dramatic warming. This early focus on emissions provides a useful industrial entrée into the topic. In 1987 came the Bruntland Report, a document produced by the United Nations Commission on Environment and Development, which broadened the terms of engagement in its introduction of an ethical imperative for forward thinking about the ability for future generations to sustain themselves. These early forays expressed concern about the trajectory of industrialization and resource consumption, but had yet to include the kind of limiting tactics of corporate interest that would begin to feature in future reports.

The history of sustainability's international agenda begins to flower around the UN's 1992 Conference on Environment and Development, which produced the Rio Declaration, a document that laid out plans and proscriptions for national environmental agendas and led to an increased interest in and legitimacy for discussions of global climate change. Agenda 21, the result of five years of research and negotiation, was unveiled at the Rio conference, promoting a plan for sustainable development worldwide. The 1997 Kyoto Protocol finally brought about measurable milestones and goals for involved countries, promoting the reduction of greenhouse gas emissions, and opening doors for new markets in products like carbon credits and offsets. The 1998 introduction of the Leadership in Energy and Environmental Design (LEED) certification system follows on the heels of these international commitments, offering menus for achieving a degree of sustainable credibility. And finally, perhaps most aggressively, sustainability means big business. A new book, *Force of Nature*, outlines the bottom-line strategy that precipitated Wal-Mart's 'going green'. Gone are the arguments about social responsibility, and in come those about profit margins with positive, easily marketable side effects.

That a major public issue has so rapidly metamorphosed from an ethical imperative to a loosely associated fiscal one is not surprising. It is the uncomfortable middle ground moment, however, where multiple arguments continue to be made and where contradictory logics are in play. LEED is a good example of this tension, since while it ostensibly offers an objective industry standard rating for sustainably-designed buildings—akin to the guidelines proposed by, say, the Bruntland Report—the certification it offers translates directly into a marketable commodity—and that's no accident. Each year, additional LEED certification levels and professional accreditations are released, always expanding the purview and reach of the organization. Moreover, unlike the Bruntland Report, the LEED qualifications offer vague, reductive guidelines that leave little incentive for true innovation beyond their check boxes.

Nevertheless, sustainability has provided an entry for many to begin to talk about architecture, and that is not to be discounted. Formerly seen as the province of educated esthetes, architecture's newly booted-up social conscience welcomes more to the table. In contrast to recent disciplinary arguments about context, form, and autonomy that can sometimes alienate outsiders, the science-esque bent of sustainability's measurable results, results that can hypothetically read in savings or profit for consumers, is eminently understandable. Architecture now falls into a sociopolitical climate where energy (with money following) rules the bottom line, a situation the discipline has largely resisted for good reason.

Outsourcing the logic of architecture, or painting it in the light of efficiency, has never quite worked for architects. Functionalist doctrine was a semi-scientific matter, with efficiency charts and ergonomic principles attached. But the fact remained that the very tenets of function were creations of the designer. What differs with sustainability is that many more voices have joined the fray, only some of them designers. Certification boards, materials suppliers, and service providers all have a hat in the ring potentially leaving little for the architect to design. Moreover, the very function of these organizations in creating a rarefied product known as sustainable architecture demands allegiance, as all other architectures, innovative though they may be, are then relegated to the heap of unsustainable, irresponsible, expensive, and bad. It's in this light that we can understand how sustainability has drawn in stalwarts of architectural autonomy like the Museum of Modern Art in New York, where one would expect to see examples of the high-design opaque variety. Architects now have a fight on their hands, to regain their 'liberal' power in an era of ever-more focused inputs from technological expertise.

BEYOND MONOCULTURE OPTION DESIGN STUDIO

Instructor: **Shun Kanda**

This studio explores the range of design alternatives and propositions responsive to the emergent transformations in [A] societal shifts and [B] environmental realities. Consider the dual factors outlined in the following scenario:

[A] reverse demographic pyramid, changing household make-up, lower fertility rate, women in the workplace; live/work choices, declining, older-age core workforce, a live/work choice, multi-generational dependence, shrinking cities, halt urban sprawl, densifying, poly-culture communities

[B] and juxtapose another layer characterized by: fossil to renewable energy transition, micro-generation, economy of scale, emergent materials & building technology, ubiquitous nature, urban agriculture & edible backyards, localized, sustainable infrastructure, alternative transportation, mobility, incremental, adaptive, recyclable development.

The scenario above describes to a large degree the extant and anticipated givens evident in our studio's PROJECT CONTEXT & SITE at Tama, outside Tokyo. These factors may be construed as the studio's Design Agenda—to weave together the myriad trajectories into architecture—within a re-configured, dynamic environment, a sustainable prototype model for the next quarter-century and beyond.

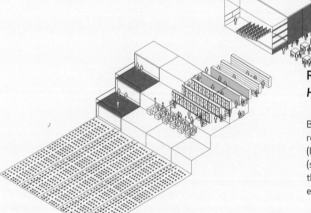

Rafael Luna | MArch
Hybrid Living for the Shrinking City

Based on the observation that the typology of the architecture school requires a roughly even distribution of both highly controlled interiors (lecture rooms, work shops, offices), and expansive programmatic fields (studios, lecture halls and exhibition spaces), the project attempts to exploit the tension within this typological characteristic through a figural frame, encapsulating a massive internal void.

The articulation of the interior as a collective void aligns itself with emerging possibilities in architectural production, where a highly calibrated relationship between the expanse of the interior and integrated infrastructural systems allow for the factory-like studio and lecture spaces to be rethought of as a site for perpetual full-scale intervention.

The frame itself allows key programmatic elements to be strategically distributed in relation to both external environmental factors and their adjacency to the interior void. Allowing for a dense strip of activities framing the continual construction of architecture within architecture. This continual spectacle of internal construction forms a new central node within the campus at large, aligning and producing a collection of public living rooms within which the activities of the architecture program are strategically located.

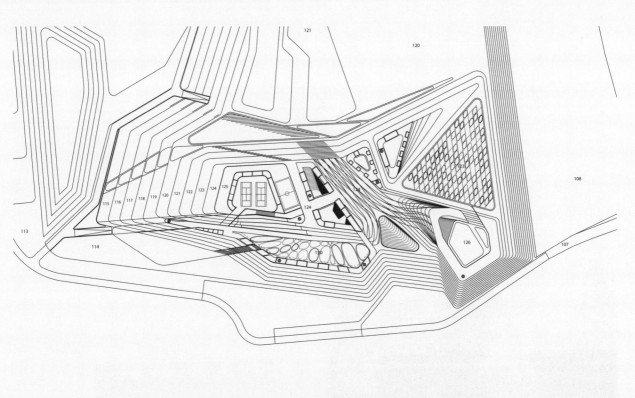

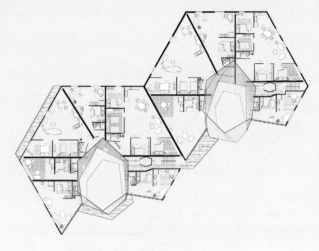

Pamela Ritchot | MArch
Field of Resuscitation in the Post-Suburban Landscape

In Japan 2020, declining suburbs equate to the declining rural population. Suburban land remains conquered, flattened, and left for overgrowth by the young urban escapees. In Tokyo, these young urban hipsters are overpopulating the city only to find their lives crowded and busy–bombarded by concrete interfaces and intricately packaged imports. They are parched, hot, and gasping for an ounce of fresh air.

Simultaneously, the rural farmer yields a tiny, inefficient crop that cannot compete with the ever-decreasing prices of global food imports. With 70% of Japan's 3 million farmers aged +60 years, food production in this region needs to reach a breaking point... As the problem progresses into 2050, global supplies of freshwater are rapidly depleting. THERE IS A THIRSTY WORLD OUT THERE! While its inhabitants experience great thirst, the Japanese landscape experiences twice the yearly rainfall and humidity of the average global region. As its inland cities remain parched, water as a scarce commodity has become a reality close to home and abroad.

The year 2050 brings a new age for Japan to start living again in the living clusters of the field of resuscitation! These clusters reconfigure the home, reconsider the suburb, and activate the built environment to initiate interdependent survival under a new set of suburban conditions:

SURFACES : Re-establishing the post-suburban ground plane involves a series of sloping planes. These sloping scapes allow for natural distribution and circulation patterns of water to rejuvenate the earth.
COVER : Sustained by a saturated, flowing ground plane, vegetation activates the PRODUCTIVE LANDSCAPE in a gradation of biodiversity within the site.
MOVEMENT : Foot and bike paths expand and contract within the field of production. In contraction they reinforce processional interactions. In their expansion, they clear the ground for a mass.
LIVING CLUSTER : The 2050 dwelling promotes an interdependent local system whose existence both sustains and is sustained by the larger site. These MICRO-COMMUNITIES promote clustered living that is embedded in the landscape breathing its life through a living lung.
FUNNELS : A stepped and staggered field on the landscape exhales water-saturated south winds into the clusters and up the harvesting vapor towers.
VAPOR TOWERS : Puncturing the home, these central channels harvest the water that is carried by the wind. Extracting the water, they bring climatic comfort to each dwelling unit and gather this critical commodity for export *and trade.*
THE HOME : the family unit of 2050 belongs to this larger, integrated cluster as they work together in the social expansion of the lung.

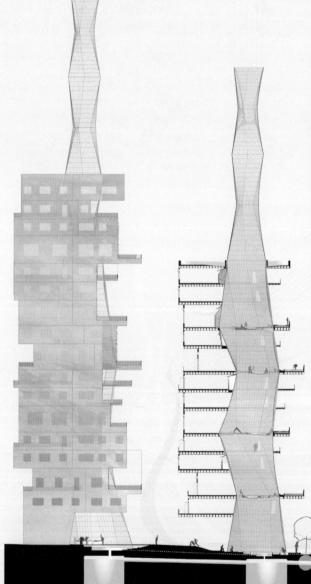

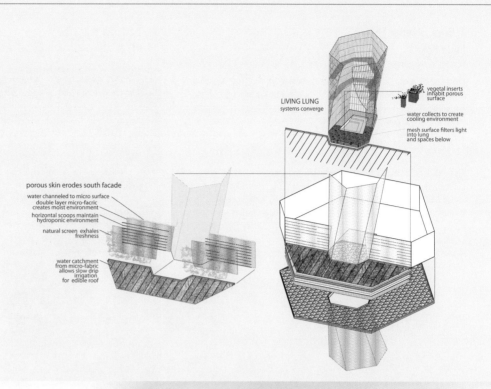

LIVING LUNG
systems converge

vegetal inserts
inhabit porous
surface

water collects to create
cooling environment

mesh surface filters light
into lung
and spaces below

porous skin erodes south facade

water channeled to micro surface
double layer micro-facric
creates moist environment

horizontal scoops maintain
hydroponic environment

natural screen exhales
freshness

water catchment
from micro-fabric
allows slow drip
irrigation
for edible roof

T. Buck Sleeper | MArch
Field Fold

Field Fold proposes a live-work-grow-eat housing typology in response to the dilapidation of the Japanese New Town. Once hailed as an affordable and plentiful alternative to urban overcrowding, the housing infrastructure of these planned communities has fallen increasingly derelict through an inability to adapt to an aging demographic, dearth of jobs, and a lack of public funding to maintain it's abundant, but generic, open space.

A proposal for a new housing typology consists of three parts: An extensive subterranean barn houses livestock, agricultural equipment, light processing, and manufacturing spaces. Cool air is drawn through these spaces up through a structural armature, within which dynamic partitions are inserted to accommodate variety and change within its users. Finally, the front porch of each unit is screened with a system of horizontal planting trays, deployed seasonally by residents to integrate vegetable gardening and shading. Greenhouses on the roof pull double duty as restaurants and classrooms.

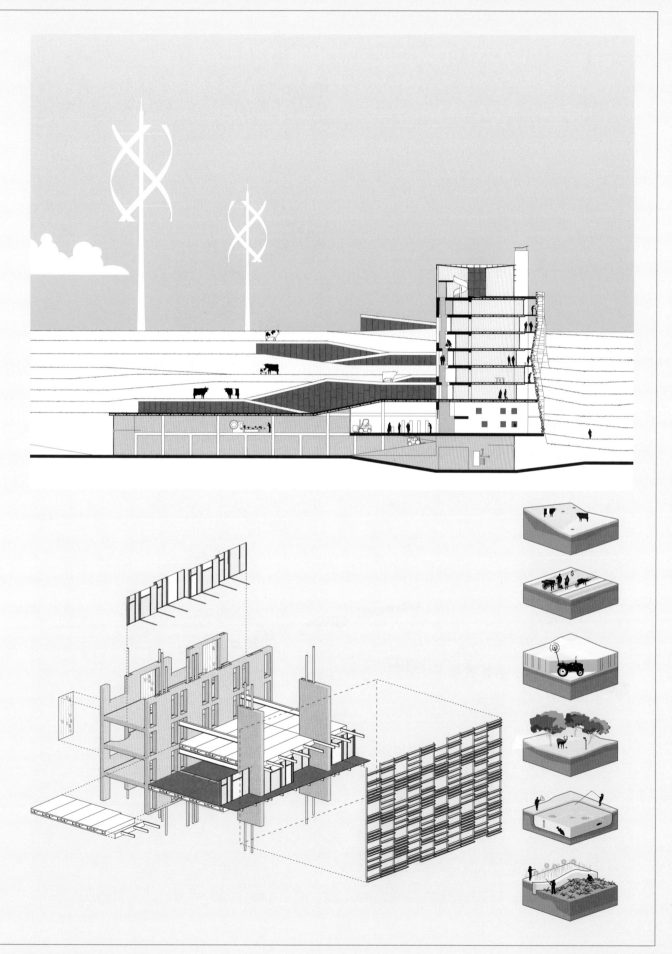

ADAPTATION + HABITATION: ARCHITECTURE AT THE INTERSECTION OF BIODIVERSITY AND ENCROACHMENT IN THE ECUADORIAN GALÁPAGOS OPTION DESIGN STUDIO

SPRING 2011

Instructor: **Andrew Scott**
Teaching Assistant: **Joseph Choma**

The context for the studio was the Galapagos Islands, situated about 550 miles off the coast of Ecuador. It was in partial collaboration with the Universidad Technologica Equinoccial in Quito, including a design workshop in Quito, Ecuador and a field trip to Santa Cruz island in the Galapagos. The islands, consisting of 6 main islands–four of which are inhabited, 12 smaller islands and 50 islets, now have a rapidly expanding population of 40,000 inhabitants that is growing at 10% annually on its three principal inhabited islands, plus a fluctuating all-year-round tourist population that pressurizes resources. At these rates, the population doubles every 7-8 years and could reach a million by 2058. The increase in eco-tourism at 14% annual growth has developed the economy but brought with it many new issues that fundamentally challenge the ability of 'nature' to co-exist with increased human encroachment, shortage of most resources, and a lack of an architectural system that sustains the scope of human inhabitation. At current rates, tourism will reach 250,000 visitors by about 2011 and half a million by about 2020, all of which place diverse pressures on the need for urbanization. While 97% of the islands' land mass is still national park, the remaining 3% that represents human activity threatens the whole. How can a balance be achieved between the man made and the natural, such that they co-exist to the detriment of neither, and the benefit of both?

The work of the studio was broad and discursive in researching and understanding the scope of issues, while also engaging 'design thinking' as an instrumental methodology to generate concepts and design strategies that pose alternate scenarios to the status quo. A key component to all of the work of the studio was speculation about the role of architecture as an adaptive element of a broader ecosystem, resulting in innovation propositions, solutions and alternative future scenarios. The studio worked in three main phases: project 1–as conceptual propositions for new alternative forms and typologies of habitation and (semi) urban aggregation; project 2 as a series of scenarios for urban expansion or interventions of the town of Puerto Ayora, based upon either ex-urban edge development, rethinking the notion of urban typologies within the grid plan, or eco-tourism development at the interface of water and land.

Currently, the focus and the research dollars are into the fields of marine, biological, and animal habitats–while the impact of the human condition on the Galapagos is almost entirely ignored. Inevitably (and ecologically) these two worlds have to go hand-in-hand, and it is not possible to put a ring around the human part and deny its emerging impact on the whole. There are many dilemmas in this island paradise, mostly relating to the importation of almost everything in the hopes of "preserving" the magnificence of the islands, versus enabling a sustainable and ecological economy to emerge–as well as the fact that eco-tourism has to be ecological in its operation and not just about looking into ecologies.

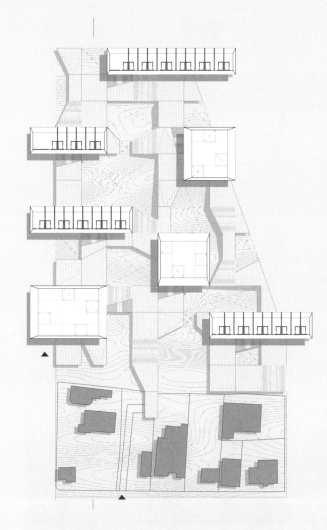

Sasa Zivkovic | MArch
Galapagos Ecological Modernism

Eradication as well as the fight for survival have a long history on the Galapagos. From pirates, tortoises and Darwin to the goat problem in the 1990s, Galapagos is a complex network of ecological and historical relationships. Architecture on the Galapagos needs to acknowledge this struggle and–within the context and history of the islands–has to raise the question if this is the right place for conservationist thinking:

At present, there is a distinct and sharp divide between man-made and natural endemic systems on inhabited islands of the Galapagos. The divide is responsible for many of the resource problems and contradictions of the archipelago: Common consensus (amongst government officials, NGOs and researchers) is that natural systems ought to be preserved and shielded off from any human influence.

However, the reality of the inhabited islands does not quite come close to a zero encroachment policy. *Galapagos Ecological Modernism* argues that the preservationist 18th century notion of the national park makes it impossible to rethink the current dilemmas of the islands. Instead of aiming for a utopian protectionist policy (which ultimately results in uncontrollable mixture of systems), encroachment should be part of a controlled design process. The acknowledgment of reality will encourage a re-conceptualization of the troubled relationship between natural and man made systems–while simultaneously addressing larger infrastructural problems outside of architecture.

The project is neither interested in protectionism nor integration: it investigates means of conceptualizing architectural encroachment upon nature (superimposition) as well as it is interested in processes of natural encroachment upon architecture (counter-camouflage). As an architectural strategy, the project intentionally embraces the (disputable) modernist agenda of elevated soffits: the eradication of natural ground vegetation within elevated modern architecture holds potential for a utilization as a design strategy for architectural encroachment tactics on the Galapagos. The layering within *Galapagos Ecological Modernism* is aiming for a coexistence of various natures as it erases (as well as it produces) hybrid ecologies.

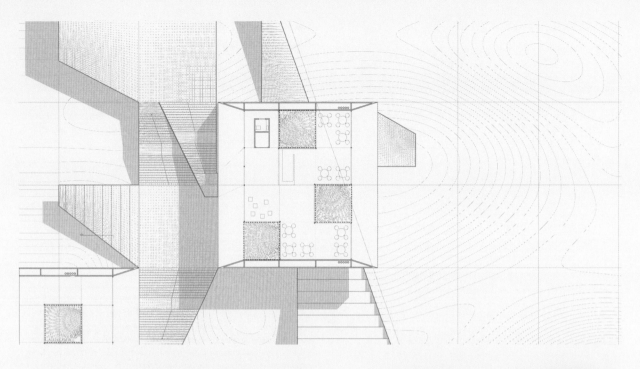

Nadya Volicer | MArch
MANgrove Agro-Resort

The city of Puerto Ayora is nestled in Academy Bay on the southern side of Santa Cruz Island, Galapagos. A coastal town, Puerto Ayora has been expanding northward in the direction opposite the sea, sandwiched between two multi-story high cliffs to the east and west. Tourism, however, has predominantly existed in the form of yachts and cruise ships docked offshore. As this lucrative industry grows, so will the number of hotels built within the city limits, thus pushing residential habitation into protected inland habitats. Expansion towards the ocean can be viewed as an interesting alternative.

One major feature of the native coastline of Santa Cruz Island are the mangrove swamps. Most interestingly, due to the natural propagation cycle of mangrove, they accrete sediment beneath their root structure, effectively producing land. In investigating a way to develop along Puerto Ayora's coastline, the productive nature of the mangrove swamp is considered as a means for the city to encroach upon nature while simultaneously cultivating its growth.

This project proposes a hybrid condition in combining a small-scale shrimp farming with an agro-tourist resort. In this way, housing could be developed for farmers who are also employed in tourism to provide the agro-tourist with a unique experience in the Galapagos Islands.

Locating itself as an extension into the ocean of Seymour Street, MANgrove Agro-Resort anchors to the shore with a restaurant and reception hut that is open to not only tourists staying at the MANgrove but also those visiting greater Puerto Ayora. A boardwalk continues into the water with a small distribution of both tourist huts and shrimp farming pens and huts. Integral to this concept is the notion of mangrove cultivation which will occur in and among the structures. Over time the integration of mangrove and the MANgrove will produce a new kind of experience for both tourist and inhabitant.

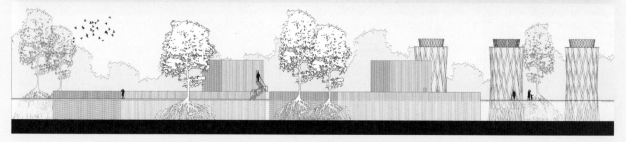

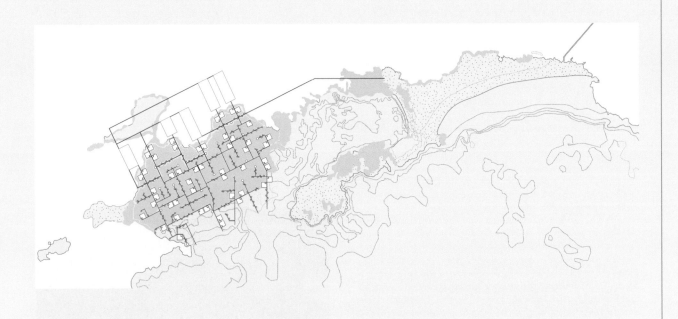

ICEWALL FAST [FESTIVAL OF ART SCIENCE AND TECHNOLOGY] PROJECT

Yushiro Okamoto and Hiu Lan Kian Yam

MIT150 celebrates past innovation and achievement, while acting as a catalyst for the next generation. In this spirit, ICEWALL plants a new future, even as its own seemingly fades away during the Festival of Art, Science and Technology. The installation is a scripted surface 50' long, 6' high consisting of blocks of ice stacked on each other. It creates one continuous surface facing the Charles River, tying MIT, the river, and the public together. Each block will have flower seeds frozen inside, visible during the Festival. The wall will be lit at night, creating a new face for MIT from across the river in Boston. As FAST concludes and ICEWALL melts away, the seeds are left behind in the ground. As the seeds germinate and bloom, the installation will continue to celebrate the sesquicentennial in the spring, parallel to MIT's own growing future.

WIND SCREEN FAST [FESTIVAL OF ART SCIENCE AND TECHNOLOGY] PROJECT

J. Meejin Yoon

Imagine a shimmering curtain of light suspended in the archway below the Green Building: an architectural-scale screen of micro-turbines that simultaneously generates and consumes energy harvested from the wind, translating wind speed into a visual register of this replenishable source of energy. Air currents sweeping across the plaza create kinetic patterns of form and light, illuminating what otherwise would be a largely invisible phenomenon. As the wind blows stronger, and the turbines spin faster, the lights shine more brightly; energy is consumed as soon as it is produced, always balancing the equation.

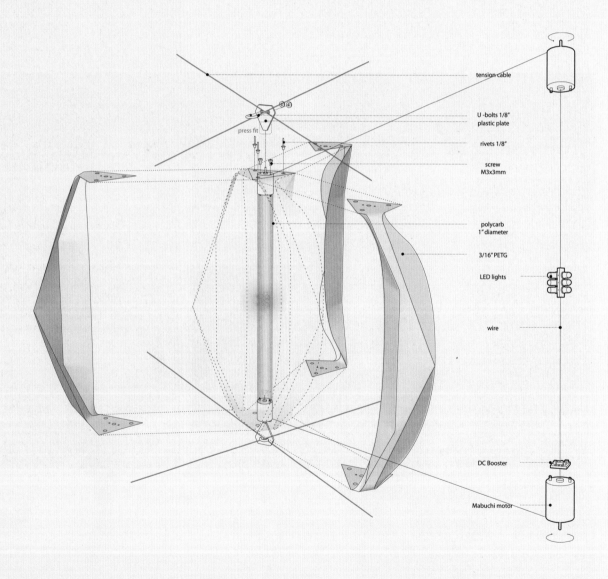

tension cable

U -bolts 1/8"
plastic plate

rivets 1/8"

screw
M3x3mm

polycarb
1" diameter

3/16" PETG

LED lights

wire

DC Booster

Mabuchi motor

press fit

Image credit: bottom left, copyright Andy Ryan; all others courtesy of MY Studio.

RENEWTOWN: ADAPTIVE URBANISM AND THE LOW CARBON COMMUNITY

Andrew Scott and Eran Ben-Joseph

RENEWTOWN is the product of a collaborative design research project between MIT's School of Architecture and Planning, and Japan's Sekisui House and puts forth an innovative vision of performative design and planning for low-carbon sustainable development, and illustrates practicable strategies for balancing environmental systems with urban infrastructure and new housing prototypes. A series of design and research phases that engaged students from architecture and planning programs resulted in a book that begins by outlining a series of principles that structure the ecological and energy goals for the community. It then develops prototypical solutions for designing, building and retrofitting neighborhoods, with a focus upon Tama, a planned 'new' town built in the 1970s outside of Tokyo. The intent is that these prototypes could be applied to similar urban conditions around the world.

The objective of the project was to propose a model of community and housing design that strives for 'zero net energy', carbon neutrality, and reduced ecological impacts. Concepts such as adaptability, flexibility, and information technology integration are also important parts of the investigations. These aspects are seen as crucial in enhancing livability and maintaining self-reliance in the context of rapid demographic change and tenuous environmental conditions. Recent high-profile efforts to address similar concerns have largely relied on the creation

Applied Prototype / *View of integrated transit spine and productive landscape.*

Images courtesy of Andrew Scott.

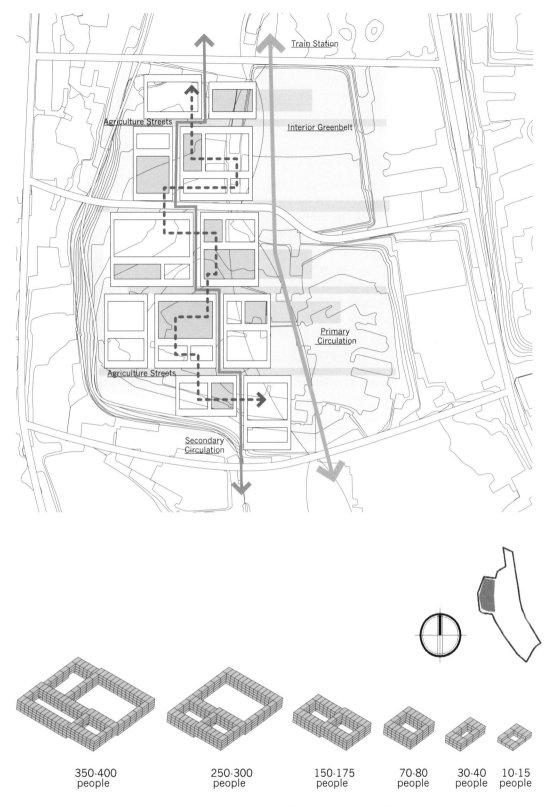

Train Station

Agriculture Streets

Interior Greenbelt

Primary
Circulation

Agriculture Streets

Secondary
Circulation

| 350-400
people | 250-300
people | 150-175
people | 70-80
people | 30-40
people | 10-15
people |

Applied Prototype / Connected Courtyards

*As a high-density building type, the Connected Courtyards are clustered near
the rail station, along the north-western edge of the site. The neighborhood is
comprised of a series of small blocks, each of which is perforated with several
courtyards. Each block is designed to be a self-sufficient community in terms
of energy production, water remediation, and, to a lesser extent, food production. As a whole, they form a multi-programmed neighborhood.*

A Continuous Landscape

**Surface Level
Vehicular Storage**

Covered areas at ground
level provide parking for
shared light electric vehicles.
It is estimated that there will
be 1 automobile for every 20
inhabitants.

Community Gardens

Residents are able to grow
flowers and vegetables in
designated plots within the
courtyards. This can be
done either as a recreational
pursuit or a supplement to the
food supply.

Aquatic Surface Courtyard

Water is collected and held
in large recreational ponds.
These can also be used for
water treatment or for the
production of fish and other
aquatic plants and animals.

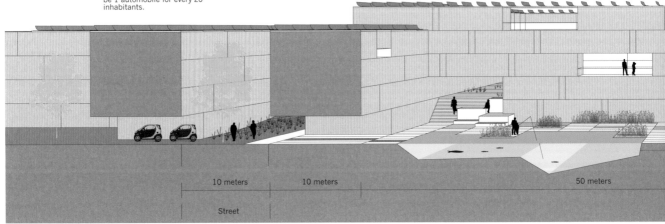

10 meters   10 meters   50 meters

Street

of new developments in open, unbuilt green-field areas. The sheer conversion of natural areas for development, however, runs counter to the notion of long-term ecological resilience and sustainability.

The project and the book propose a different way of approaching the planning and design process, by making a leap across disciplinary boundaries and scales. It begins by addressing the broader issues of urban sustainability and the challenges of retrofitting communities for a new low carbon future; it then progresses to 'applied prototypes' and their related design outcomes. Additionally, environmental issues and broader demographic and socioeconomic factors that impact the notions of sustainability in communities are identified and addressed. The applied prototypes comprise a range of integrated design solutions for housing, mobility, land use, agriculture production and energy generation. The performance levels of these solutions are made explicit through metrics associated with reductions in energy consumption and carbon reduction over time.

A key aspect of the methodology of the design research was finding the means to measure performance at an urban scale and enabling these results to influence design concepts and strategies. The major infrastructural systems of mobility, energy, water, solid waste, and green space were researched for their potential to deliver significant reductions in carbon and energy over a 40-year period and then used as integrated metrics to influence design decisions.

Living Machines

In addition to surface treatment, water is channeled through a living machine for further cleaning, and then stored in the drinking water reservoir in an adjacent courtyard

Porous Collection Courtyard

A hardscaped surface channels rainwater into an underground unitized cistern for drinking water. The courtyard could also be used as an orchard, or recreation space or market area.

Farm Streets

Streets are reconceived to accommodate belts of agriculture between buildings. These connect to the water collection systems within the courtyards as well as the green corridor at the center of the Tama master plan.

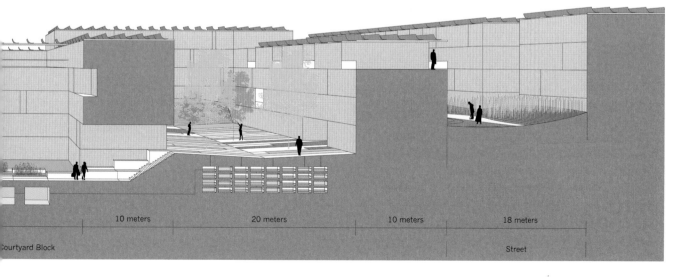

| 10 meters | 20 meters | 10 meters | 18 meters |

Courtyard Block   Street

Applied Prototype / The Loft-Block

The Loft-Block is a new typology for medium density housing that integrates walk-up linear apartments running through the width of the block with elevator access mini-towers fronting onto the street. Collectively, these form a series of south-facing wedge-like buildings, each of which can vary in width, taper and length as the through units get stretched. Each pair of buildings is then raised off the street such that the undercroft can house supporting programs–shops, industry, offices, education–and the elevated landscape garden can be used to retain or control water run-off.

The project teams developed four coordinated planning concepts to shape the transformation of the site through the future; they include various prototypes for low, medium and higher density housing. Each prototype was designed to adapt to future growth and reconfiguration; to facilitate on-site solar energy generation; to provide for water retention, storage, recycling and treatment; to support food production; to utilize ecological construction techniques; and to incorporate mobility infrastructures. Projected results from the proposals include up to 80% reduction in household energy consumption by 2050, an increase in solar power generation of 111%, and a distribution of 40 persons per car through shared mobility scheme.

Axonometric diagram from the air to show the relationship of the six Loft-Blocks to the 'mobility spine

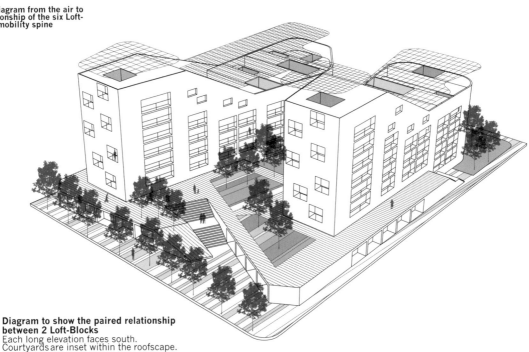

Diagram to show the paired relationship between 2 Loft-Blocks
Each long elevation faces south.
Courtyards are inset within the roofscape.

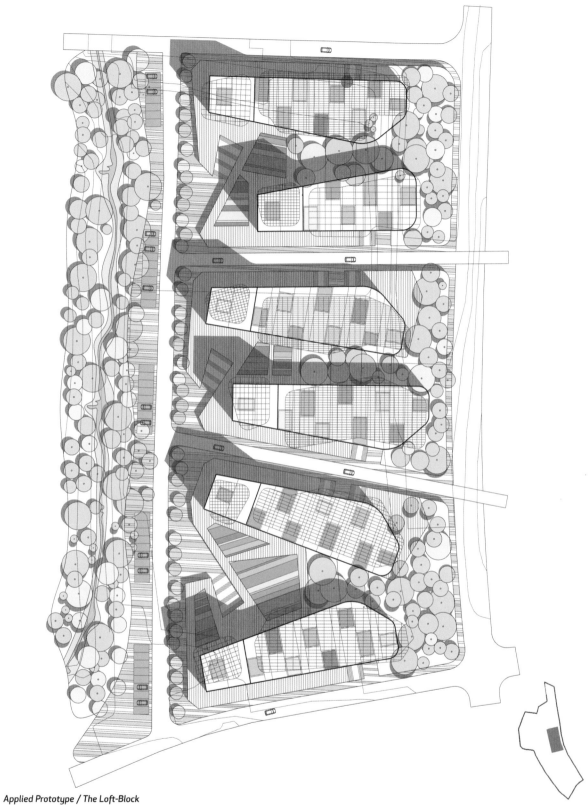

Applied Prototype / The Loft-Block

At the roof level, the units break out into a series of rooftop terraces, with a layered grid again providing solar shading and an armature for solar energy production using parabolic collectors. Windows to the south- and west-facing elevations are recessed from the wall to provide shading against excessive solar heat gains, and the simple planning of the linear through units enables effective natural cross-ventilation.

SUSTAINABILITY ARCHITECTURE
BETWEEN FUZZY SYSTEMS AND WICKED PROBLEMS

Mark Jarzombek

This article was originally published in the Blueprints, Volume xxi, no. 1 Winter 2003, 6-9.

Today there exists a range of architectural firms, both small and large, that specialize in environmentally-sensitive architecture, whether that be in the form of design-build projects, self-sufficient structures (those requiring no outside, manufactured energy), "eco-villages," or sky-scrapers with layered skins allowing natural ventilation and light. We have also seen in recent years the development of new high-tech materials, as well as the emergence of various "green" consulting companies, some advising individuals on how to place their bed based on *feng shui* principles, others advising multinational corporations on everything from waste management to product design.

In the last five years or so, the word "sustainability" has come into vogue as a way to put these disparate trends under a single rubric. The most immediate reason for the success of the term is that it has allowed advocates to avoid the stigma of environmental politics. Various definitions of sustainability have now been put forward, each with its own implications for the discipline of architecture. The debate, as a result, is not about whether one should or should not support sustainability, but rather about which version we want.

The Noble Manager Model

Take, for example, the definition of sustainability by John Dernbach, a professor of law at Widener University and a leading scholar in the area. According to him, sustainability means "freedom, opportunity, and quality of life; more efficiency; more effective and responsive governance; a desire to make a better world for those who follow us; a willingness to find and exploit opportunities; a quest for a safer world; and a sense of calling to play a constructive role in international affairs." These, he argues, not only are "basic American values," but conform to the principles of the Earth Charter, which was issued in 2000 and grew out of the 1992 Earth Summit in Rio de Janeiro, and which, according to him, "has broad resonance among the world's major religions."

This type of definition, based on the politics of universal consensus suggests that the field of environmental management might become the future Esperanto (a proposed universal language) not only of government agencies but also of religious systems. That is, various nations and cultures would subscribe to common standards of sustainable development, which would be promoted and enforced by officials with technical expertise and significant power. The implications, though somewhat frightening—given Dernbach's reliance on a broad and universally respected group of environmental leaders—are for architecture relatively prosaic, in that architecture schools would be expected simply to produce the necessarily enlightened class of experts and consultants. Schools would also be expected to shift toward the scientific edge of the discipline, given that corporate and government funding would go primarily in that direction.

The Ethical Model

A very different vision of sustainability is presented by Lisa H. Newton in her book *Ethics and Sustainability* (2002). She argues that the first task "is to outline an understanding of the individual moral life, life in accordance with a Personal

Worldview Imperative, and to show its logical relationship to environmental sustainability."

To define this Personal Worldview Imperative, Newton turns to Aristotle's definition of the *polis*—the city-state as a body of individuals working collectively to achieve the "highest good"—to emphasize the principles of virtue, happiness, and the simple life. Her point is that sustainability is not something new to be worked over by teams of bureaucrats and lawyers, but rather an essential responsibility of the individual, as foreshadowed in the writings of Aristotle, in the life of Christian monks, and even in the philosophy of Buddhism. Her purpose in constructing this relationship between sustainability and ancient philosophy is to detach the concept of a *polis* from the modern city, which for her, presumably, is the site of excess, greed, and immorality. As examples of "unsustainable" practices, she points not only to pesticide-dominated agriculture, but also to "our problems with the casinos … gambling, pornography, and the like." Her vision of sustainability ends in a technocratic utopia, which simultaneously reduces everything to a simple ethical-functional question, and ignores everything pertaining to the more complex aspects of social and urban life.

Whereas Dernbach posits sustainability as a universal movement cutting across political boundaries, Newton seeks a return to the simple life as advocated by the ancient Greek philosophers. Both, however, fail to take into account the complexities of culture, life, and technology. The first model exemplifies what sociologists describe as "a fuzzy system." It is composed of heterogeneous units that can never be—and were never meant to be—synthesized into a coherent system, and as a result, its ambition over-reaches its pragmatics. The second model is what sociologists describe as "a wicked problem," one in which conventional reality bites back, in this case, in the face of a utopian fantasy. The first perhaps puts too much faith in society, and the second, too much in the individual.

The Eco-Determinist Model
Somewhere between the extremes of a fuzzy system and a wicked problem, lies the work of William McDonough and Michael Braungart. Their book *Cradle to Cradle* (2002) is eminently readable and practical, and speaks directly to the question of architecture and design. Yet here, too, there are underlying assumptions that should be highlighted. Basically, the book makes not one but two "ecological" arguments. One is about the endangered environment and is, of course, irrefutable—it is more than obvious that environmental degradation is accelerating at an alarming rate.

The other ecological argument, however, is subtler and more difficult. It comes into view when the authors discuss "the cherry tree" as a model for design. When we think of designing a building, so the authors explain, we should state, "Here's how we imagine the cherry tree would do it." This part of the argument is adapted from the controversial, century-old theory of "social ecology," which holds that social life is much like plant life in that it is ordered by "natural" laws of growth and metabolism. The necessary correlate of this view has always been that human society in its non-natural, industrialized formations is both non-social and impersonal. McDonough and Braungart extend the argument when they contrast current industrial production with the life of the friendly leaf-cutter ants who live in an organized way and are obedient and ecological resourceful. "Like the cherry tree, they make the world a better place."

Does this mean one goes from being a good ant to being a good citizen? Seemingly so, since the authors mention in this respect the name Edward Osborn Wilson, the evolutionary theorist and Harvard University professor, whose books like the Pulitzer Prize-winning *The Ants* (1990) set off a firestorm of debate about animal and human social behavior. Unfortunately, McDonough and Braungart never refer to this controversy or, for that matter, to the older debates about bio-determinism (the theory that individual actions and reactions are largely predestined by biological factors). Instead, they simply try to convince the reader that the Nature they see and wish to emulate is no more fearsome than an ecological exhibit in a science museum. They have repackaged old-fashioned social ecology into a non-threatening vision for a green future.

Sustainability is often regarded among the lay community as something that can only be beneficial. Be that as it may, the three positions I have discussed are grounded in ideological claims that need to be better understood before one builds an architectural foundation on them. Saving the world is important, but if the choice is between a future of noble managers, conservative ethicists, or eco-determinists then "sustainability" still has some important lessons to learn.

RESEARCH INDUSTRY

Theodossios Issaias and Todd Satter

Findings from Arindam Dutta's Fall 2010 Seminar "The Sustainability 'Fix'–PostWelfare, Malthus, Phantasmagoria"

Following the Second World War, the phenomenon of the military-industrial complex in which the relationship between the defense industry and financial interests became increasingly pronounced, overtly and surreptitiously dictated economic and geo-political discourse. Similar dynamics inspired new relations between academic institutions and the military, spawning the military-academic-industrial complex. Economic incentives and the potential to turn university research into profit-making endeavors have expanded exponentially throughout the past few decades, during which time financial and other interests took an unprecedented influence over university research. A series of guidelines and laws further institutionalized these dynamics, conflating, confusing and mixing government, corporate and academic interests, increasing the potential for abuse.

Federal funding has failed to keep up with the increasing amounts of capital needed to finance scientific research. Federal research funding has been sharply curtailed even in face of the most recent global energy crisis, a development in stark contrast to that of the 1970s, when the energy crisis spawned a large increase in spending. As the government

diverts funds to other sectors or universities divert funds to other departments, laboratories have little choice but to turn to private investors. Universities are also compelled to explore and develop other money-making opportunities, such as property management and other financial ventures aimed at creating, developing and supporting research clusters or "Technopolises," which extend the physical and cultural influence of universities and their research. Technopolises and new research strategies work within, rather than outside of, geo-political and corporate structures, becoming part of a larger discourse and folding in entities outside of the traditional university. Sustainability has become as much a language game in which public discourse and laboratory research follow divergent strategies.

While funding is increasingly necessary to accommodate the advanced technology and rising costs of academic research, especially in genetics, medicine and more recently the energy sector, including alternative and "sustainable" energies, the safeguards necessary to mitigate negative or unwarranted influence from sponsors has caused many to question the integrity of some university research and made even more

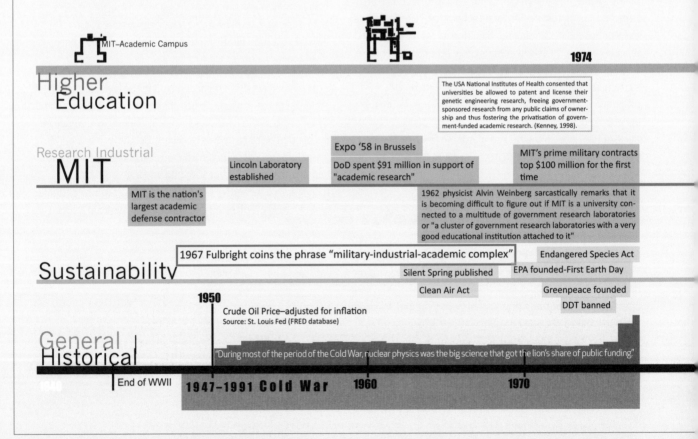

MIT–Academic Campus   1974

Higher Education

The USA National Institutes of Health consented that universities be allowed to patent and license their genetic engineering research, freeing government-sponsored research from any public claims of ownership and thus fostering the privatisation of government-funded academic research. (Kenney, 1998).

Research Industrial
MIT

Lincoln Laboratory established

Expo '58 in Brussels

DoD spent $91 million in support of "academic research"

MIT's prime military contracts top $100 million for the first time

MIT is the nation's largest academic defense contractor

1962 physicist Alvin Weinberg sarcastically remarks that it is becoming difficult to figure out if MIT is a university connected to a multitude of government research laboratories or "a cluster of government research laboratories with a very good educational institution attached to it"

1967 Fulbright coins the phrase "military-industrial-academic complex"

Endangered Species Act

Sustainability

Silent Spring published

EPA founded-First Earth Day

Clean Air Act

Greenpeace founded

DDT banned

1950

Crude Oil Price–adjusted for inflation
Source: St. Louis Fed (FRED database)

General Historical

"During most of the period of the Cold War, nuclear physics was the big science that got the lion's share of public funding."

End of WWII   **1947–1991 Cold War**   **1960**   **1970**

of it dubious. More importantly, universities, in the face of profit-potential and -motive, have found strategic means of circumventing these guidelines for best practices, and there are rarely penalties (except for the rare instance of bad press) ensuring that universities maintain some autonomy from their corporate sponsors.

The historical dynamics of the research-industrial complex, the ways in which the capacity to promote, patent, and license research, continues to influence these dynamics, the guidelines for best practices, as well as strategic ways around them. These points are exemplified through a sustained look at MIT's relation to the defense industry, especially its Lincoln Laboratory, as well as its increasing dependence and possible collusion with industries. MIT and its laboratories' relations to industry goes back to the 19th century, but the institute has been and continues to be among the most the progressive in terms of maintaining research integrity and providing safeguards against possible abuses of profit motive. However, its position among the leaders in defense funding, genetic funding, and more recently sustainable and energy-related funding, especially from Big Oil, has also spawned creative ways around these rules governing intellectual property rights.

MIT's technology licensing office, in particular, which engenders and supports start-up firms and laboratories to do research outside of the official university system, has become one such means around the prescriptions and proscriptions for best practices, affording researchers and sponsors related to the institute further control over discourse, marketing, information, as well as the substance of important research into all fields of science, especially sustainability-related projects. Energy independence and sustainable discourse therefore become ideological and epistemic, rather than neutral and objective. The codification of some relationships becomes dubious. Given recent events, programs like the BP Projects Academy and the BP Operations Academy, both in place years before the gulf oil spill, further complicate the integrity of the research-industrial complex. The MIT Energy Initiative and Energy Research Council, despite their capacity to publically market all departments at MIT as socially-conscious, are spread too thin, distributing limited (especially in relation to MIT's total budget) funds across the majority of MIT's programs in piecemeal fashion.

It also led to a massive increase in funding to universities. Between 1980 and 1998, funding for research at US universities increased annually by 8%, reaching a staggering 1.9 billion US dollars in 1997 (Press & Washburn, 2001).

The 1980 Bayh-Dole act of the US Congress empowered universities to patent and commercialise state-funded research at a time when the US economy was weakening relative to that of Japan, creating a climate in which commercial forces increasingly dictated universities' educational and academic missions and ideals.

According to a 2008 survey by The Chronicle of Higher Education, presidents from 19 of the top 40 research universities with the largest operating budgets sat on at least one company board.

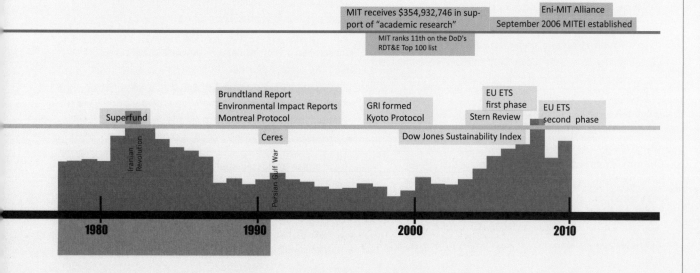

MIT receives $354,932,746 in support of "academic research"

Eni-MIT Alliance
September 2006 MITEI established

MIT ranks 11th on the DoD's RDT&E Top 100 list

Brundtland Report
Environmental Impact Reports
Montreal Protocol

GRI formed
Kyoto Protocol

EU ETS first phase
Stern Review

EU ETS second phase

Superfund

Ceres

Dow Jones Sustainability Index

Iranian Revolution

Persian Gulf War

1980   1990   2000   2010

GREENING CAMPUS

Jennifer Chuong and Niko Vicario

Findings from Arindam Dutta's Fall 2010 Seminar "The Sustainability 'Fix'–PostWelfare, Malthus, Phantasmagoria"

SUSTAINING THE UNIVERSITY

In the past decade, the discourse of sustainability has been mobilized by institutions of higher education seeking to differentiate themselves in a competitive and increasingly market-driven landscape. Particularly in the wake of the economic recession, sustainability has become a means to court funding from both private donors and the federal government with subsidies from the 2009 Stimulus Plan. Further, energy efficiency proves a long-term savings strategy and thus a prime motivation of green building on campus. The past few years have witnessed the vernissage of numerous sustainability institutes at larger state universities as well as the even more prolific spread of sustainability offices and centers at a wider range of institutions, even as academic departments have suffered budget cuts. Whereas many green ventures are student-initiated, others are vehicles of heightening bureaucratization. The curriculum has been a target of the new sustainability paradigm, with humanities departments pressurized to incorporate subject matter of "relevance" to the present and future of environmental conditions and planning. From fund-raising to campus design to curricular revision, sustainability proves a discursive apparatus legitimating the corporatization of the university as a brand for consumption.

The whole move of higher education becoming a business–students as customers, education as commodity–is one of the most dangerous things that has happened to higher education... The universities are branding themselves, and now sustainability is a way to brand your university.

—Tom Kelly, Office of Sustainability, University of New Hampshire[1]

Higher Education, Higher Costs

Modeled upon general rankings reports, the *Green Report Card* debuted in 2008 courtesy of the Sustainability Endowments Institute (SEI), grading schools based upon their infrastructure, green campus initiatives, and sustainability-directed endowments. The Green Report Card has garnered criticism from colleges' sustainability directors regarding its "cumbersome, incomplete, inaccurate, and enigmatic survey."[2] The ubiquity of rankings systems and other classification and monitoring systems such as the *Green Report Card* are manifestations of what sociologist Dorothy Smith has termed an "accountability regime" in which "coercive accountability" comes to define the institutions and protocols of contemporary society.[3]

Alongside other ranking systems, the GRC reflects the accelerating emphasis upon transparency in the world of higher education, a testament to what has been termed "the corporatization of the university."[4] This corporatization has been characterized by a move on the part of many schools towards free market values such as "transparency, efficiency, productivity, and accountability." Frank Donoghue contends that the corporatization of the university is hardly a new model; rather it is an outgrowth of a tension between "corporate" and "educational" values that reaches back more than a century. Within this market logic, increasing expenditure is deemed necessary as the university's expansion and upgrading are understood as a reflection of its qualitative value—its prestige.[5]

Costs of expansion and innovation have in turn contributed, among other factors, to a dramatic hike in tuition since 1970, a rise that has increased four times as quickly as the consumer price index.[6] The gap between family income and student tuition has been consistently and increasingly widening. This gap is frequently justified by data that demonstrates the higher lifetime earnings commanded by college graduates. Consider the paradigm shift signaled in the annual survey of 400,000 incoming freshman administered by the University of California, Los Angeles. In 1971, 37% responded that it was essential or very important to be "very well-off financially," while 73% said the same about "developing a meaningful philosophy of life." In 2009 these values were nearly reversed; 78% of students identified wealth as the goal while 48% favored "philosophy of life."[7]

This gap and the rhetoric mobilized to justify it contribute to what Donoghue, among others, characterizes as *a crisis in higher education*. If students and their families increasingly understand higher education as an investment based upon financial returns, it pressurizes the pragmatic ends they can expect on that investment. This market logic is exacerbated by ever-decreasing state funds, leading colleges to seek alternate funding. Further, these pressures are forcing schools to take a hard look at their curricula. In a recent survey, two-thirds of public institutions said that they were responding to budget cuts with extensive reviews of their academic programs with an eye to economize.[8]

The Promise of Sustainability

Sustainability is mobilized within this fiscal predicament as a means by which to gain *new clout with donors*.[9] These donations pad the institution's operating budget and/or endowment, but come with the caveat that funds be used strictly for sustainable projects. Concomitantly, the visibility and proliferation of sustainable initiatives at institutions of higher education has been staggering. In 2007, 550 college presidents signed an agreement stating that they will work to make their campuses carbon neutral as part of the *University Presidents Climate Commitment*. As of 2009, over 19% of four-year and graduate institutions had joined the Association for the Advancement of Sustainability in Higher Education. LEED certification of college campuses has proliferated; thirty-nine colleges and universities have mandated that all future construction must be LEED-accredited. Such policies have been heavily enforced at public universities that must follow the policies of their state governments (34 out of 50 states in the U.S. have required that new buildings must be LEED-approved).[10] Often such measures are imitative, based upon a survey of the "best practices" of the country's most competitive schools and developed with an eye to keeping up with, or even surpassing, the Joneses.[11]

Whereas the American public conventionally has perceived a tension between economic and environmental goals, a recent poll administered by the Harris Group suggests that a growing percentage of Americans do not perceive a conflict.[12] This shift corresponds to the role green jobs and green developments have served in President Obama's plans for the flailing economy wherein sustainable initiatives have been mobilized as a proposed means to economic recovery.

Energy-efficiency also enables colleges to save money. Carnegie Mellon in Pittsburgh is home to the first LEED-certified dormitory, New House, which opened in 2004. Estimates peg energy savings for New House at 30% (compared to the standard dormitory's usage), lifting a substantial financial burden for the college.[13] Beyond its fund-raising draw, green architecture also translates into long-term fiscal savings guaranteed by lower energy expenditures. Ecological discourse serves as the public rhetoric for projects with strong fiscal motivations.

Sustainable projects on campuses do not solely depend on private donors; they are also responding to indirect pressures from the federal government. In the wake of the economic recession, the Stimulus Plan, announced by President Barack Obama in January of 2009, placed sustainability as a core criterion for those projects that will receive funding. Of the $825 billion Stimulus package, $7 billion was apportioned for 'higher-education modernization, renovation, and repair'. A $2.5 billion subset was directed towards energy-efficient projects certified by LEED.[14]

Campus nuts and bolts

The new paradigm for sustainability on college campuses reflects the recent global tendency to focus upon carbon neutrality. The means by which institutions seek to achieve carbon neutrality, a goal shared by the 550 schools whose presidents have signed the Presidents Climate Commitment, vary; thus far, schools primarily resort to buying renewable energy credits (RECs), deriving from sources such as wind, solar power, and biomass.[15] The expense of buying carbon offsets is financially reasonable; in the case of the University of Colorado at Boulder, $50,000 siphoned off from tuition money each year would buy enough RECs to render the entire school carbon neutral. However, the purchase of carbon offsets does not reliably guarantee a neutral or negative carbon footprint and is discouraged as a means to carbon neutrality by experts.[16] In the past few years, large, land-rich schools have pursued the development of their own wind farms as a source of energy for campus use, short-circuiting the need for carbon offsets and for purchased energy.[17]

Despite the proliferation of green discourse on college campuses—in campus design, classroom discussions, and student activism, energy usage (and thus the burning of fossil fuels) on campuses continue to rise, enlarging carbon footprints. This proves to be the case on both the level of individual usage (think recharging laptops, iPods, and cellphones) and the energy usage of facilities such as new laboratory buildings. There is a marked disparity between ethical rhetoric and consumption rates, between eco-image and eco-reality.

Concomitantly, green features often serve to deflect attention from the social impact of real estate development; this is not unlike the common marketing practice known as 'green-washing', in which a rhetoric of environmental consciousness is adopted to promote a product. Campus expansion is no exception, as evidenced by the sustainable angle of Columbia's expansion into Harlem and Harvard's expansion into Allston.

Beyond campus design, curriculum reform has been a site for sustainability discourse to serve as a restructuring agent. The UN Rio Conference on Environment and Development (1992) marked a landmark call for the reorientation of curricula towards the topics and goals of sustainable development. Further, the Johannesburg Earth Summit (2002) promoted an expanded definition of sustainable development as "economic development, social development, and environmental protection—at the local, national, regional, and global levels."[18] Curricula were targeted as a means by which to spread ecoliteracy to a younger generation. Extending from platforms such as the Rio Conference and the Johannesburg Earth Summit, the first decade of the 21st century marked a trend towards the formation of sustainability institutes at large state schools such as Arizona State University and Colorado State University. Even in institutions that have not opened institutes, sustainability centers and offices oversee initiatives, operations, fund-raising, and public relations. The correlation between sustainability centers and institutes and the bureaucratization of the university is not incidental; sustainability has proven an interdisciplinary paradigm that has grown in infrastructure even in the economic downturn. Whereas many institutions have reduced budgets, staff, and faculty in light of current economic conditions, sustainability centers have grown in the same period, with *the percentage of schools with sustainability offices leaping from 22% in 2008 to 45% in 2009* (of the schools participating in one survey).[19] Sustainability offices and staff are often funded by alternate sources—by specifically designated funding at the federal, state, and private levels. In some cases, these positions are funded by money saved via energy-efficient alternatives.[20] This money is then reinvested in the sustainability office—simultaneously the public face and the invisible infrastructure of the institution's aggregating bureaucracy.

Disciplining the Disciplines

On another stratum of activity, sustainability-geared minor concentrations have spawned in a broader range of institutions. Such minor concentrations, with requirements fulfilled by courses cross-listed in several disciplines, include Environmental Policy, The Environmental Context for Business, Sustainable Land Systems, and Technology and the Environment. Unity College, a small liberal arts college in Maine, is an extreme case of this trend, requiring all graduating students to take five interdisciplinary core courses that all focus on 'ecoliteracy' as well as an Environmental Stewardship course. The *discursive flexibility and ubiquity of sustainability* is in further evidence in Goucher College's new master's program in Cultural Sustainability, a program that cultivates a broader cultural terrain for the term, geared towards an anthropology-focused degree.

Whereas the sciences and environmental studies have historically been the conventional areas for green discourse, curricular restructuring has also impacted the humanities' embrace of sustainability in the name of interdisciplinarity and "relevance." As Anna Reid and Peter Petocz have outlined, *sustainability can be translated into a range of disciplines*, for instance by connecting the topic to a study of resources (i.e., natural, economic) or justice (i.e., environmental justice as well as equity towards future generations).[21] These courses range from literature courses to anthropology courses to history courses. In the case of Philosophy departments, courses might tackle sustainability by focusing on the moral implications of our current actions as well as upon the relationship between individual and group responsibility; an anthropology course might study variation in conceptions of the environment in comparative contexts.[22]

"You need to complement the science with an ethical perspective." James C. McCusick, dean of the Davidson Honors College, University of Montana at Missoula.[23]

According to the National Wildlife Federation's publication *Campus Environment 2008: A National Report Card*, about 50% of students majoring in the natural sciences take a sustainability or environmental studies course. 36% of social science majors and 28% of humanities majors are reported to have taken one or more of such courses.[24] Reid and Petocz's study observed that teachers from outside the science and environmental studies disciplines tended to be under-informed about the eco-issues addressed in their syllabi with little more than a layperson's knowledge of the material.[25] This study does not characterize such courses favorably, revealing at the macro-scale the pressures imposed upon humanities departments from top-down mandates and at the micro-scale the pragmatic challenges of widespread, unmonitored interdisciplinarity.

How to solve the crisis of the humanities? In his *New York Times*-syndicated blog, Stanley Fish suggests one solution is to "integrate humanities instruction with the social sciences and sciences so as to highlight their relevance to real-world problems."[26] To a great extent, the pressures to integrate sustainability discourse into humanities curricula reflects a broader phenomenon —the emphasis upon "relevance" across the spectrum of the liberal arts education, conditioned by the market-driven approach to education as an investment with long-term fiscal advantages.

"I'm not one to argue for the wholesale elimination of disciplines, because they do have many meaningful purposes. But they also serve as a barrier to the reorganization of our thought. And the re-organization of our thought is that this interface between the built environment and the natural environment requires more connectivity than anything we've ever done before." Michael Crow, President of Arizona State University

Branding the university GREEN

While administrators at most institutions conceive of the greening of the campus and the greening of the curriculum as complementary projects, some educators and administrators understand the relationship between campus and curriculum as hybrid and propose that it be more fully integrated. "The facilities themselves certainly teach... We have had students tell us that the most useful parts of their entire academic experience were projects that they worked on with the grounds manager, notes Sarah Hammond Creighton, Director of Campus Sustainability at Tufts University.[27]

Holistic and far-reaching conceptions of sustainability such as Creighton's manifest the substantial transition since the early 2000s. The ubiquity of sustainability in evidence in all facets of higher education (from board meetings to student protests) may be compared with the discursive heft of diversity on campuses in the 1990s. By 2010, the Association for the Advancement of Sustainability in Higher Education listed 800 institutions as members; by contrast, the National Association of Diversity Officers in Higher Education boasted only 150 schools.[28] A topic that had previously been termed widely as *ecoliteracy* (emphasizing awareness) transitioned to sustainability —an interdisciplinary paradigm inclusive of all institutional operations, from bureaucratic infrastructure to campus planning to curricular offerings. Such a paradigm cannot be divorced from the institution's desire to retain or secure a competitive edge based upon the feedback loop of funding and prestige.

Whereas the greening of higher education claims an ethico-political premise for its sweeping restructuration of many facets of the institution, the sustainability paradigm in fact reflects another imperative—that of a market logic based upon shifting criteria for funding and a growing conception of higher education as a service industry wherein knowledge must have demonstrated pragmatic and professional applications. But with countless institutions on the sustainability bandwagon, how will they differentiate themselves as products in an overcrowded, underfunded marketplace?

1   "'Sustainability' From A to Z: A round-table discussion," *Chronicle of Higher Education*, February 23, 2007, 18.

2   Scott Carlson, "Amid Continuing Controversy, a New Green Report Card Rates Colleges Again," *Chronicle of Higher Education*, October 27, 2010.

3   Dorothy E. Smith, "Despoiling Professional Autonomy: A Woman's Perspective," in *Inside Corporate U: Women in the Academy Speak Out*, Ed. Marilee Reimer (Toronto: Sumach Press, 2004), 31–42. As cited in Gaye Tuchman, Wannabe U: Inside the Corporate University (Chicago: University of Chicago Press, 2009), 45.

4   Frank Donoghue, *The Last Professors: The Corporate University and the Fate of the Humanities* (New York: Fordham University Press, 2008), 1.

5   Ibid., 111–138.

6   See Richard K. Vedder, *Going Broke By Degree: Why College Costs Too Much* (Washington, D.C.: AEI Press, 2004).

7   As cited in Donoghue, 91.

8   "Making College Relevant," *The New York Times*, January 3, 2010.

9   Peggy F. Barlett and Geoffrey W. Chase, *Sustainability on Campus: Stories and Strategies for Change. Vol. Urban and Industrial Environments* (Cambridge, Mass.: MIT Press, 2004).

10   Shannon Massie Chance, *University Leadership in Energy and Environmental Design: How Postsecondary Institutions Use the LEED Green Building Rating System* (PhD diss: College of William and Mary, 2010), 7.

11   Tuchman, 141.

12   "Half of Americans Believe Economic and Environmental Goals Are Aligned and We Do Not Need To Choose Between Them," Harris Interactive. Accessed at http://www.harrisinteractive.com/vault/Harris-Interactive-Poll-Research-Environment-2009-02.pdf.

13   Will Potter, "The First Certified 'Green' Dormitory," *Chronicle of Higher Education*, March 26, 2004, 2.

14   Scott Carlson, "Anticipating Stimulus Money for Campus Projects, Colleges Get 'Shovel Ready,'" *Chronicle of Higher Education*, January 30, 2009, 12.

15   Scott Carlson, "Budgeting for Climate Neutrality, Colleges Consider Energy Credits," Money and Management, *Chronicle of Higher Education*, October 31, 2008, 19.

16   See Oberlin College: A Plan to be Carbon Neutral, October 30, 2009, accessed at http://acupcc.aashe.org/site_media/uploads/cap/408-cap.pdf.

17   Scott Carlson, "Land-Rich Colleges Explore Opportunities to Create Alternate-Energy Sources," *Chronicle of Higher Education*, July 25, 2008, 10.

18   United Nations (2002), Report of the World Summit on Sustainable Development as quoted in Anna Reid and Peter Petocz, "University Lecturers' Understanding of Sustainability" in *Chronicle of Higher Education*, January 2006, 119.

19   J. Kadden, "Despite Hard Times, Colleges are still Going Green," *The New York Times*, October 8, 2009, as cited in Chance, 49.

20   Scott Carlson, "Even During Hiring Freezes, Many Colleges Stick with Sustainability Plans," *Chronicle of Higher Education*, March 27, 2009, 18.

21   Reid and Petocz, 116–7.

22   Anna Rappaport and Sarah Hammond Creighton, *Degrees that Matter: Climate Change and the University* (Cambridge, Mass: MIT Press, 2007), 279.

23   As cited in Allie Grasgreen, "Humanities Professors Match 'Green' Efforts of Colleges in Class" *Chronicle of Higher Education*, September 26, 2008, 11.

24   Ibid.

25   Reid and Petocz, 120.

26   Stanley Fish, "The Crisis of the Humanities Officially Arrives," *The New York Times*, October 11, 2010.

27   "'Sustainability' From A to Z: A round-table discussion."

28   Peter Wood, "From Diversity to Sustainability: How Campus Ideology is Born," *Chronicle of Higher Education*, October 3, 2010.

USGBC AND LEED: 'LEEDING' US TOWARD SALVATION

Timothy Cooke

Findings from Arindam Dutta's Fall 2010 Seminar "The Sustainability 'Fix' –PostWelfare, Malthus, Phantasmagoria"

LEED: a la carte green building

Over the last ten years, the US Green Building Council (USGBC) and its green building certification and rating system, Leadership in Energy and Environmental Design (LEED), has grown from virtual obscurity to a dominant force within the design and construction industry in the United States. Not only has it staked its claim as *the* measuring stick for assessing sustainable and 'green buildings,' in recent years it has broadened its reach to include industry sectors outside the confines of new construction, and expanded into areas such as existing building monitoring and neighborhood development. In addition, the USGBC has grown to include markets outside the US. It now has nineteen international roundtable members currently working on complementary rating systems for countries around the globe, from Argentina to Russia (McKellar). This report will unpack this most ubiquitous of 'rating systems' in an attempt to get at some of the underlying reasons for its existence, and theorize about the future of LEED and its evolving place in the ever-changing discourse on sustainability in our contemporary world. LEED inhabits a unique space outside of the building code system, at once separate from and embedded in government, and obscures its private genealogy through emphasizing its resemblance to government regulation. By taking a brief look at the development of the USGBC and

its LEED certification system, we can begin to define its place within the regulatory and legal structures of our built environment and gain some insight into the nature of this entity of self-regulation.

In order to understand LEED–and paint a clear picture of the surprisingly sprawling, self-referential and confusing system it comprises–we need to understand the mechanisms by which it functions. As stated on its website, *usgbc.org*, and the primary point of entry for anyone interested in learning about LEED, the USGBC is a 501(c)(3) non-profit organization with the mission of making "green building available to everyone within a generation" (USGBC website). From this apparently laudable starting point we jump down a rabbit hole and enter the strange world inhabited by a raft of oft-confused and fuzzy terms–rating, certification, endorsement, accreditation. This is the uneasy realm of private market-driven self-regulation, or what has been termed "standards-based certification organizations (SBCOs)" (Lee 1247).

Broadly speaking, LEED can be characterized as a privately run, voluntary system for rating buildings and awarding certifications based on the ratings achieved. These ratings are intended to quantify a building's performance and bestow recognition on those that meet the requirements. To

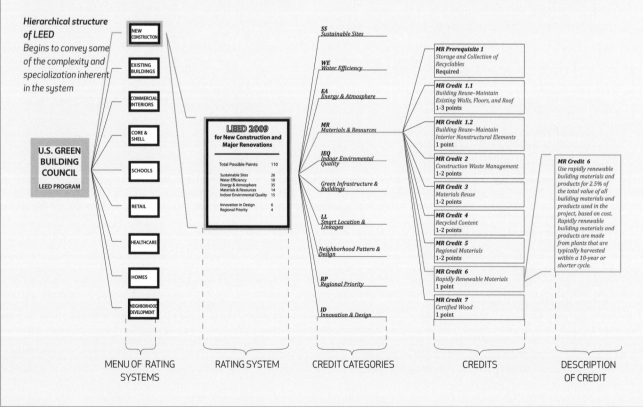

Hierarchical structure of LEED

Begins to convey some of the complexity and specialization inherent in the system

MENU OF RATING SYSTEMS — RATING SYSTEM — CREDIT CATEGORIES — CREDITS — DESCRIPTION OF CREDIT

LEED's current professional accreditation menu of options.

LEED GREEN ASSOCIATE

For professionals who support green building design, construction, and operations. The LEED Green Associate credential denotes basic knowledge of LEED and green building principles and practices.

LEED ACCREDITED PROFESSIONAL

There are currently five specialities available for LEED AP:
–Building Design & Construction
–Homes
–Interior Design & Construction
–Neighborhood Development
–Operations & Maintenance

LEED FELLOW

The nomination period for the first class of LEED Fellows will be open for approximately seven weeks beginning on November 19, 2010.
Eligibility:
–Nominees must be LEED APs with speciality who have held the LEED AP credential for eight cumulative years. (The 2011 class will consist of LEED APs who tested in 2001-2002 and have enrolled or tested to earn the LEED AP with speciality credential.)
–They must document a total of at least 10 years of experience in the 'green building field.'

classify performance, LEED uses a system of prerequisites and credits. Each credit is associated with a point, and the number of total points achieved (out of 100 possible, plus ten bonus points) determines the rating. In other words, the number of items you can satisfy on the checklist determines if a building is certified and at what level. There are four levels of certification: Certified, Silver, Gold, and Platinum.

A Brief History of the USGBC and LEED

The US Green Building Council (USGBC) was founded in April of 1993 by a small group of professionals looking to create a national green building coalition. Later that same month, on Earth Day, Bill Clinton announced his "Greening of the White House" initiative. The Operations Group Leader for the White House Greening project was Robert Watson, a National Resources Defense Council senior scientist and the USGBC's first chairman. By June, the newly formed USGBC held its first conference in conjunction with the UIA/AIA convention in Chicago. At the conference, the fledgling USGBC set as its first goal the creation of a sustainability rating system that would be developed in conjunction with the American Society of Testing and Materials (ASTM). But the ASTM's rigorous and consensus-based process proved to be too slow and frustrating for the USGBC members; they abandoned it in 1995 and instead developed their own rating system from scratch, under Watson's direction. Initially USGBC considered many existing building rating systems from around the country and the globe (among them BREEAM from the UK, Canada's BEPAC, and the Green Building Challenge), but in the end developed their own system, which they named the

Leadership in Energy and Environmental Design (LEED) green building rating system. By late 1998 they released LEED version 1.0 and launched a pilot program (Cassidy).

This first version of LEED was quite weak. Even Watson thought so; some of the credits were already standard practice within the building industry, while others were too loosely associated with the performance goals they sought (Cassidy 7). These shortcomings prompted a response. In fact, built into the USGBC organizational structure from the beginning was a process whereby technical criteria and revisions proposed by USGBC members were publicly reviewed and voted upon by the membership base. This review process formed the basis for the USGBC's evolution and growth over the following decade. By March of 2000 the LEED Green Building Rating System (a.k.a. Version 2.0) had been approved with extensive modifications and an expanded set of credits (now 69 as apposed to the 40 originally possible in the pilot program). 2002 saw the release of LEED Version 2.1 and 2005 the release of LEED Version 2.2, each containing incremental changes and expansions in response to industry and market pressures.

The rating system has grown at an astonishing rate, essentially doubling each year the number of buildings that it certified the year before. Today, the USGBC promotes LEED as "the nationally accepted benchmark for the design, construction and operation of high-performance green buildings" (USGBC website).

LEED 2009: something for everyone

The USGBC's market dominance has allowed them to claim LEED certification not only as a "nationally accepted benchmark," but also "[t]he internationally recognized distinction that a building or neighborhood development is environmentally responsible, profitable and a healthy place to live and work" (GBCI website). This expansion in recent years to include the international market has occurred at a rapid pace. During the 2010 GreenBuild Conference held in Chicago and put on by the USGBC (the gathering is promoted on the GreenBuild website as "the world's largest conference and expo dedicated to green building"), the senior vice-president of LEED, Scott Horst, proudly stated that ten percent of all LEED projects registered so far come from outside of the US; when looked at in terms of square-footage 28% of all registered projects are foreign. As we can see, foreign projects tend to be larger in size. The ten percent that Horst cites is in fact low because LEED's international expansion is a relatively recent development, and so the numbers don't yet reflect what is happening: in 2010 alone 40% of LEED projects registered were outside the US (McKellar).

What is effectively a monopoly within the US, and a rapid expansion internationally, has come about in part because of the USGBC's remarkable ability to evolve and respond to the constantly changing context in which it operates. The current and fifth incarnation of LEED (Version 3.0), launched in 2009, exhibits many of the characteristics that have made the organization so successful. As has been the case from the beginning, this current version was developed in the review process mentioned previously, described by the USGBC as consensus-based and transparent. What this means in practice is that changes can be proposed by all member organizations and draft versions are open for public comment prior to adoption. With the advent of LEED 2009, the USGBC continued to reorganize the existing commercial and institutional LEED rating systems, made several technical

changes, updated the online tool for project certification, and created "an expanded certification infrastructure based on ISO standards...for improved capacity, speed and performance" (USGBC website). This new infrastructure required the USGBC to create a new body, the Green Building Certification Institute (GBCI), with the purpose of administering the certification and accreditation portions of the LEED system. This update reflects the fact that the USGBC continues to integrate and align its system with standard-setting organizations such as the ISO.

USGBC likes to praise its own incremental evolutionary approach, but based on an interview with a consultant involved in the development of LEED 2009, this piecemeal strategy seems to stem from necessity rather than choice. In fact, the development of LEED 2009 was quite rushed due to the linear nature of the development structure (draft, public comment period, review and repeat). The result was that not enough time or resources could be devoted to this version to allow for a complete overhaul. Many desired changes were unfeasible in the time frame available, and are only being addressed in draft versions of LEED 2012, currently up for review on the USGBC website (Love).

The three main technical advancements in LEED 2009 are "harmonization, credit weightings, and regionalization"

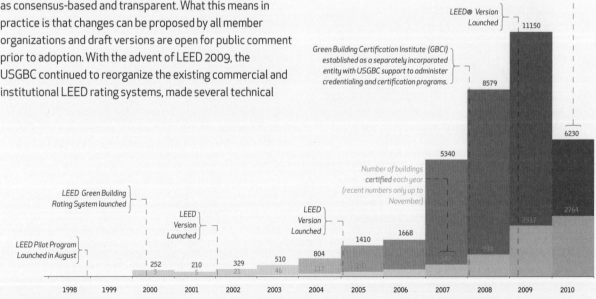

A general timeline of development and growth of LEED and the USGBC.

Eliot Tower, Portland, Oregon
LEED-ND Certified
The first LEED for Neighborhood Development project was not a neighborhood, but a single building–or according to the developer, a 'vertical neighborhood.'

(USGBC website). Harmonization refers to the fact that the credits and prerequisites from all of the LEED commercial and institutional rating systems have been consolidated and aligned so that there is consistency among them. (This consolidation, though, does not apply to their LEED for Neighborhood Development and LEED for Homes Programs due to the unique certification conditions inherent in these programs.)

Credit weightings award more points for "strategies that will have greater positive impacts on what matters most–energy efficiency and CO_2 reductions" (USGBC website). This revision caused the point system to expand to its current 100-point model. Credit weighting was implemented in response to one of the main criticisms leveled at LEED from the beginning, namely that the point system had little relation to the relative impact of each of LEED's various strategies, essentially encouraging projects to go after those LEED credits easiest to achieve relative to their associated point value ("the low-hanging fruit"). The classic example cited by the White Paper on Sustainability, published by Building Design and Construction Magazine in 2003, is the fact that of the first 38 LEED certified projects, all 38 received points

for hiring a LEED accredited professional and using locally manufactured materials, while only one project achieved a point for reducing designed energy cost by 60%.

In developing LEED 2009, the USGBC used both the impact categories developed by the EPA and weightings established by the National Institute of Standards and Technology (NIST), a strategy that evidences a shift toward greater alignment with standards organizations. But these outside standards appear to be little more than inspiration for their weightings– which in the end are modified by the USGBC to reflect their own priorities of energy efficiency and greenhouse gas emissions reductions. The weightings seem to demonstrate an inverse relationship between weight and liability. Categories that involve high-liability issues such as human health and ecotoxicity are deemphasized, while issues less easily quantified at the building scale, such as climate change, have the greatest emphasis.

Regional Priority Credits

Another change that came with LEED 2009 was an additional avenue for achieving bonus points. Contrary to what the name might imply, the Regional Priority Credit (RPC) system does not create new credits for specific regions, but merely awards up to four bonus points for existing credits that have been designated by regional chapters of the USGBC as being important based on specific geographic and climatic conditions. In its current form this system is somewhat confusing. Its essential purpose is to incentivize certain credits deemed to be more important based on the regional location of the project. The list of RPCs can be accessed via the USGBC website and are designated according to zip codes. Curiously, for projects outside the US, the RPC list is uniform for all regions–the opposite of the idea of a regionally specific credit emphasis. The USGBC claims this is an interim measure until a system of evaluating the entire globe can be devised, but regardless of its longevity, at the moment the international version of RPCs exactly contradicts the idea of regional-specific incentives. Instead, the six international RPCs currently available all pertain to energy efficiency and water conservation, categories which are, in effect, placeholders.

Pilot credits are credits that the USGBC is considering for future improvements to LEED. There are currently 41 for public use, including credits with titles such as: Acoustics, Trades Training, Quality Views, Reconcile Designed and Actual Energy Performance, Advanced Utility Tracking. It's possible to receive an Innovation and Design credit for attempting a pilot credit.

The "GreenTouchScreen®"
Produced by Quality Attributes Software (QAS) as part of a growing host of visualization tools produced for the building industry.
http://www.qualityattributes.com/

The additions and changes found in LEED 2009 might be said to be in response to two imperatives: first, to deflect criticism by incorporating new concepts and components into the system, and, second, to maintain a monopoly on the rating business. In terms of responding to criticism, the three main updates contained within LEED 2009 are the crude beginnings of a response to four main issues raised by critics: the arbitrary assignment of point values, no connection to any measurable results such as greenhouse gas emissions and/or energy efficiency, no consideration for local differences in climate and ecological concerns, and the growing complexity and proliferation of the rating schemes. LEED 2012, currently under development and available for public comment, continues to try to address these criticisms and incorporate them into its system.

Expansion Beyond The Building Scale

As mentioned previously, LEED has continued to expand its rating system beyond its initial scope of new construction and the individual building. One area of expansion is in planning and development, which has the real estate industry somewhat worried. The pilot program LEED for Neighborhood Development was launched in 2007. This was a bold step, but in many ways can be seen as a natural progression for the USGBC, as LEED persists in increasing its menu of options. The outcome of this program is still unknown. However, many of the troubling issues surrounding the concept of a private certification system being used in place of government regulation are brought to the forefront as the certification expands into unknown territory (both conceptually and literally). Because of the longer timescales of multi-building development projects, LEED ND is organized into three stages, conditional approval, pre-certification, and, upon completion of a plan, final certification. During its pilot phase, 76 projects were involved in LEED ND, but only five to date have achieved final certification–presumably because of the longer timescales. Now with LEED ND fully rolled out as of April 2010, it will be interesting to see how the system fares.

In an article published in the Midwest Real Estate News in April of 2009, Sean Suder voiced worry about the impact that such non-governmental rating systems will have on the "macrocosmic issues of community planning and the individual rights of property owners." In an ironic twist on the idea of protecting private enterprise's freedoms, he worries that this private certifying body will impinge upon industry's ability to freely do business. By ceding too much control to the USGBC on the regulation of community planning, he worries, private enterprise will be compromised: "What is known is that such influential decisions about the urban environment will be in the hands of the USGBC, a private non-profit organization. We also know that such decisions cannot be challenged through the normal channels of due process available to property owners." This raises the question of how far the LEED rating system can make inroads into the regulatory structure of the built environment before the industry becomes queasy at handing regulatory power over to a private body. Suder's article signals the possibility that a backlash toward LEED's private certification system could originate within private industry.

LEED and its relationship to architectural practice

Architecture has always had an uneasy relationship to its identity as a profession. Throughout modern history, it has reinvented itself in a constant attempt to maintain its claim on the business of designing the built environment. This history can alternatively be described as a history of the various movements within architecture. From Neoclassicism to Functionalism, and on to modernism and postmodernism, architecture remakes itself so as to sustain itself, and the narrative of this evolution is intrinsically linked to the profession's identity. Over time, architecture has also seemed to exist in a constant state of crisis, continually fretting that it is on the brink of obsolescence.

This talk of failure has never been more pronounced since the financial crisis of 2008. Architects are unemployed in ever-increasing numbers and new construction is falling. Within this context, LEED has acted as a kind of scaffolding to prop up the architectural profession. With the "LEED Accredited Professional" title, architects have a new tool at their disposal for legitimizing their practice. This tool, defensively employed, gives architects a direct claim on the sustainability movement. In fact, sustainability itself, Mark Jarzombek argues, has been adopted in order to "return meaning and purpose to architecture." If architecture is a failed discipline,

as Jarzombek asserts in his 2009 article in the Volume Project, could LEED, with its legitimizing role within the profession, help extract the practice from its current crisis of identity? Jarzombek is not convinced that the sustainability banner can ultimately "save" the practice, but it does seem to be keeping it on financial life support.

Projects involving LEED are on the rise while the rest of the building industry is in a slump. According to an article in the November 2010 edition of the GreenSource Newsletter (a publication catering to green professionals and "proudly supported" by the USGBC), despite overall drops in revenues for design firms in the last few years, with a 12 percent drop in billings for the largest 500 between 2008 and 2009, there was a 16.8 percent increase in revenue from projects utilizing a building rating system. In fact, firms that specialize in green projects actually gained market share. Will LEED, and by extension 'Sustainable Architecture,' serve as the next movement within the profession, infusing it with new life and invigorating this floundering field? Many architects bemoan this development as a move away from good design and toward an architecture of gadgetry and products. The common suspicion is that it is bad designers who do 'sustainable' architecture; good designers don't need to broadcast their building's green credentials. But this idea misses the larger point: green building, and by extension LEED, is really driven by forces outside the profession– mainly corporate interests and developers looking for new ways to promote, sell, rebrand. A classic example is the HELIOS House designed by Office dA for BP (who, in a blatant bid to rehabilitate its brand, changed BP to stand for "Beyond Petroleum" from its previous title of British Petroleum). This 2007 project to design a sustainable gas station is peppered with classic examples of LEED being used purely in the service of marketing. Office dA are considered good designers and as such have no need to use sustainability to promote themselves, but in the end they too have to buy into LEED–the market demands it.

THE LEED RATED BUILDING: tell me you are green

The classic postmodernist gesture cited in every history book on 20th century architecture is Venturi's Guild House, with its golden ornamental TV antenna. The antenna was an ironic nod to the fact that it was a retirement home for old people who watched TV all day, but more importantly, it acted as an incisive shot across the bow of modernism; from now on, the antenna demonstrated, symbol and function would be acknowledged as essentially decoupled. What was communicated would not depend on what was. It is easy to argue that a LEED plaque next to the front door gives meaning to a "green" building in much the same way that the antenna serves to indicate the Guild House's status as a retirement home. The plaque is needed to communicate that the building is "green" because without this sign its essential "greenness" is not necessarily obvious. The building must tell you what you should think about it.

It might be simplistic to make such a direct analogy between postmodernist clichés and the LEED certification plaque, but the reality is that LEED buildings are taking advantage of the tools of postmodern symbolic representation and signage all the time. Of course, a plaque next to a door is a poor substitute for the drama of a TV antenna on a roof. The parallels become more meaningful when we look more closely at some of the points available in the LEED rating system. For example, credit (2) in the Energy and Atmosphere category stipulates that up to 7 points are available for generating on-site renewable energy–for example, with wind turbines or solar panels–but given the practical constraints for most building projects a wind turbine will never be able to provide more than a slim fraction of the energy the building requires. It's possible to get as many as 7 points for generating a mere 13% renewable energy (LEED Reference Guide for Green Building Design and Construction). Very quickly, then, the turbine becomes a semantic object–the golden TV antenna of the sustainability movement. Architecture is once again what Venturi, Brown and Izenour called a discipline "with a rhetorical front and conventional behind," a "shelter with symbols on it" (Venturi, Brown and Izenour 90), and the building carrying a turbine is very much Venturi's "decorated shed." The striking resemblance to Venturi's antenna is eerie because there is nothing ironic in the wind turbines. They are not meant as a joke, but as a marketing tool. The basic difference between postmodernism and sustainability is in their respective underlying motivations. Postmodernism was irreverent in its embrace of the decorated shed and American culture; sustainability is overtly sincere in its peddling of salvation through appliqué.

Sustainability and its overlay on architectural form is reminiscent of the "mixed media" description that Venturi gives for his Guild House, which he contrasts to the purportedly "Pure Architecture" of modernism. Perhaps with the advent of sustainability as a dominant discourse in architecture, we have truly realized Venturi's postmodern agenda. For what could be more mixed media than a building tricked out with any assortment of devices and strategies to make it sustainable? In this sense, LEED could be said to be the ultimate example of postmodern techniques carried out to their fullest extents.

It's tempting to say that the LEED building is telegraphing a "greenness" that is false, but LEED buildings aren't lying: they're communicating their own moderateness, their difference from radical green building. They communicate a mainstream green building aesthetic, while the buildings that come out of the more radical green building movement communicate their radicalness through organic forms, wild designs, handprints, spirals, etc.

LEED and the mainstream green building movement appear to have become the vehicle that allows architecture to socially engage–the very thing that Scott says the discipline failed to do in the 70s, when postmodernism first arrived. But as the semantic and communicative strengths of green building demonstrate, this movement traffics in postmodernism as much as it does social engagement. And if early postmodernism diverted the attention of the design mainstream away from social problems, the mainstream green building movement, typified by LEED, is doing the same

thing for architectural practice today. In its incorporation of sustainability, this architecture, less revolutionary than conservative, is chiefly creating new avenues for growth. Architecture–the "failed discipline"–is trying once again to reinvent itself for its own survival.

Works Cited:
—Cassidy, Robert. "White Paper on Sustainability: A Report on the Green Building Movement." A supplement to Building Design & Construction Magazine Nov. 2003: 1–47. Print.

—GBCI: The Green Building Certification Institute. GBCI: The Green Building Certification Institute. Web. 8 Dec. 2010.

—"FAQs, LEED Rating System Development." U.S. Green Building Council. Web. 8 Dec. 2010.

—Jarzombek, Mark. "Architecture: A Failed Discipline." Volume Project Vol. 19 (2009): 42–45.

—McKellar, Joel. "LEED 2012 and the Greenbuild Rating System Development Update." Real Life LEED. Real Life LEED, 18 Nov. 2010. Web. 8 Dec. 2010.

—Love, Andrea. Personal interview. 22 Nov. 2010.

—Scott, Felicity D. Architecture or Techno-utopia: Politics After Modernism. Cambridge, Mass: MIT Press, 2007. Print

—Suder, Sean. "Certifying Place with the New LEED-ND Designation." Midwest Real Estate News (April 2009). Web. 8 Dec. 2010. Retrieved from <http://www.kmklaw.com/news-publications-78.html>.
USGBC: U.S. Green Building Council. USGBC: U.S. Green Building Council. Web. 8 Dec. 2010.

—U.S. Green Building Council. Green Building Design and Construction. Washington, D.C.: U.S. Green Building Council, 2009. Print.

—"USGBC White Paper–Greening the Codes." Web. 8 Dec. 2010. Retrieved from <http://www.usgbc.org/DisplayPage.aspx?CMSPageID=1780>.

—Van Hampton, Tudor. "Green Building Thrives in Shaky Economy." GreenSource: The Magazine of Sustainable Design. The McGraw-Hill Companies, Inc. 30 Nov. 2010. Web. 8 Dec. 2010.

—Venturi, Robert, Denise Scott Brown, Steven Izenour. Learning from Las Vegas: the Forgotten Symbolism of Architectural Form. Cambridge, Mass: MIT Press, 1972.

'Decorated Sheds'

(Left): ZGF's Indigo Building with rooftop wind turbines. Photograph courtesy of ZGF Architects LLP; (Right): Venturi and Scott Brown's Guild House with rooftop gold-plated TV antenna.

NATURAL LIGHT S.M.ARCH.S. BUILDING TECHNOLOGY RESEARCH

SPRING 2011

Siobhan Rockcastle
Supervisor: **Marilyne Andersen**

Natural light is a dynamic and ephemeral tool for expressing the quality of space. Whether it's used in the diffuse illumination of a museum gallery or as a dramatic and variable figure within an enclosed space, the formal and architectural intentions of daylight should be directly associated with the evaluation of its quality. As a compliment to more traditional avenues of lighting research that assess performance in terms of quantitative illuminance goals and discomfort caused by glare, my thesis aims at identifying the importance of annual light variability and contrast as finely tuned architectural effect. Under the rapidly growing context of energy conscious research, my thesis attempts to re balance our definition of "performance" to include those perceptual and aesthetic aspects of light that are often disregarded by the world of green building simulation. If it can be determined that contrast is important to the definition of space, then it becomes essential to understand how architecture is enhanced and transformed over time by the dynamic and variable source of daylight.

Through an analysis of contemporary architecture from around the world, I've developed a lighting taxonomy that categorizes architectural space in terms of contrast and light variation over time. Lighting simulation programs such as ECOTECT identify light in terms of quantity across a hypothetical section of space. Although this information is useful in analyzing whether we achieve illuminance goals, it tells us nothing about the quality of space as a product of light-driven visual effect. RADIANCE can render light over a single snapshot of time or across a window of time, but what if we want to know how space is affected by changing light levels across the course of a year. What if we want to know how 'variable' the contrast of a space is under different sky conditions and what time of day it changes from low to high contrast as a result of geometry and the incident angle of sunlight. My thesis will use a rendered set of images under sunny sky conditions across the year to create a holistic analysis of the changing effects of contrast and light variation through a series of architectural spaces. The production of this thesis relies on renderings produced through RADIANCE and analysis scripts run through MATLAB to evaluate and plot the data present within the renderings.

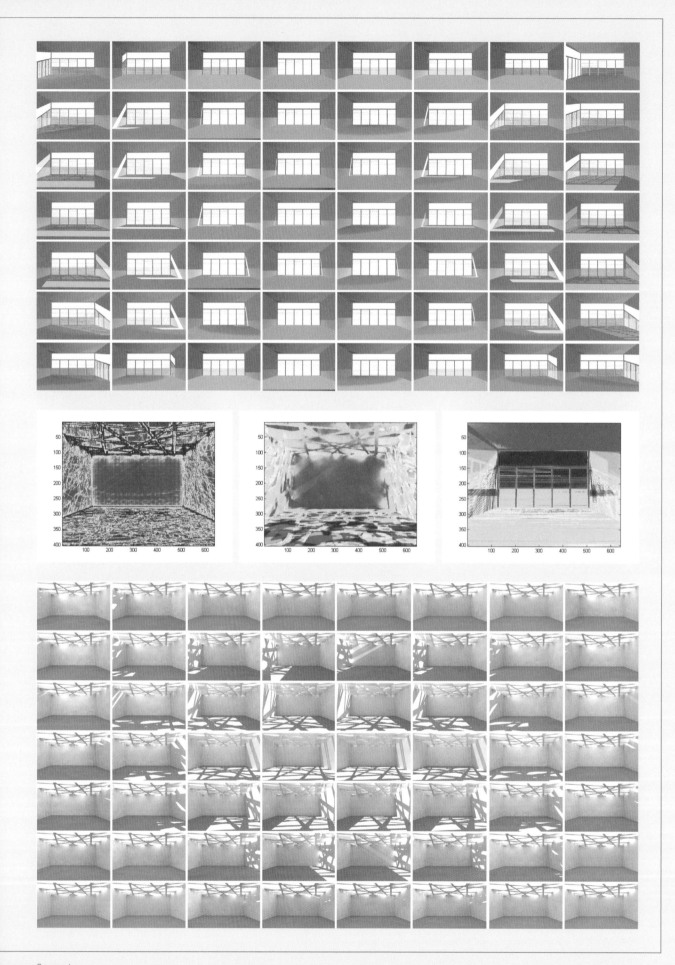

DELIGHT IN GREENER DAYLIGHT WOLK GALLERY EXHIBITION
FALL 2009

Instructor: **Marilyne Andersen**
Teaching Assistant: **Jaime Lee Gagne, Gerhard van der Linde**
Participants: **Bruno Bueno, Sam Cheng, Cristen Chinea, Shreya Dave, Justin Hipp, Kian Yam Hiu Lan, Juliet Hsu, Christelle Huberty, August Liau, Andrea Love, Alejandra Menchaca, Jie Qian, Siobhan Rockcastle, Jason Tapia, Mallory Taub, Kevin Thuot, Yang Yang, Tea Zakula**

Daylighting is inherent in architectural design and is one of the main drivers of a building's technical performance and its resulting human comfort and health.

Students in the Fall 2009 Daylighting class taught by Marilyne Andersen, Associate Professor at MIT, worked in interdisciplinary teams to analyze designated portions of the second floor extension to the swissnex Boston building in Cambridge, MA. With the aim of developing integrated solutions for facades on every side of the building, they focused on issues of glare, illumination, overheating, the ensuing energy requirements and the visual interest of the spaces.

The exhibition documented the creative solutions that the students developed to answer this multi-faceted problem using models, data analyses, and simulations. Their work illustrates how challenging and inspiring it can be to answer a seemingly simple question, "What is good daylighting?"

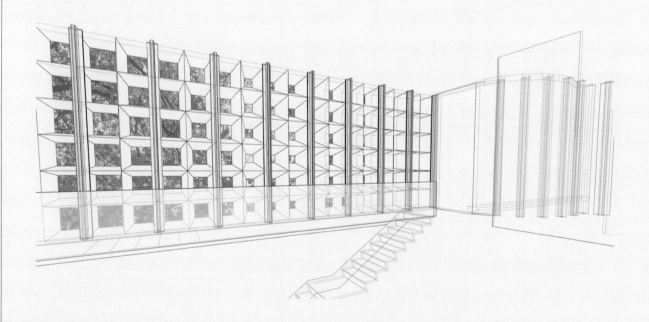

CONTAINMENT BUILDING: ARCHITECTURE BETWEEN THE CITY AND ADVANCED NUCLEAR REACTORS M.ARCH. THESIS

Lisa M. Pauli
Supervisor: **J. Meejin Yoon**
Readers: **Mark Jarzombek, Gediminas Urbonas**

Since the inception of nuclear energy research, the element thorium (Th) has been considered the superior fuel for nuclear reactions because of its potency, safety, abundance and limited waste. Cold War agendas broke from the logic of efficient energy production to establish a nationwide network of reactors designed to enrich uranium fuel for a nuclear arsenal. Contemporary dilemmas of global warming, increasing fuel prices, carbon emissions, and anti-proliferation movements have brought the discussion of clean, safe nuclear power to the forefront of American energy policy; it is no longer tolerable or sustainable to rely on a uranium (U) nuclear network. The architectural typology of nuclear energy has not been addressed in America for 35 years and is one that belies the promise of clean energy's progress through technology and public intervention. Containment Building is an architectural response to nuclear technological advancement that challenges historical separation between nuclear power and the public. It is a self-sustained, thorium-powered nuclear plant sited in and powering New York City. It is a nuclear campus that programmatically and urbanistically engages the public and contains radio isotope labs, a nuclear medicine and imaging facility, a food irradiation center, a wellness hotel and spa, an electric taxi charging station, and a plug-in park along the Hudson River waterfront.

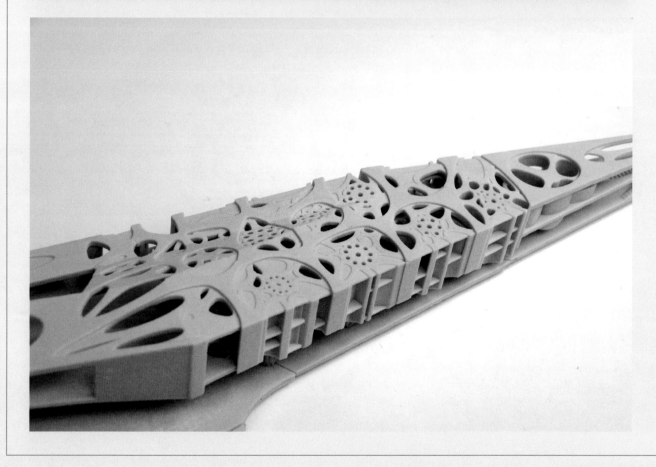

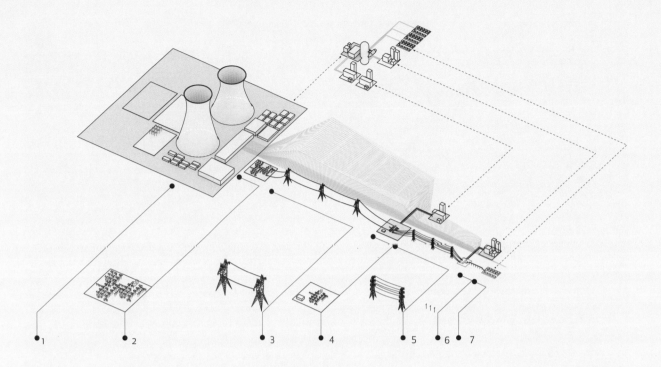

1. Electricity generated from power plant
2. Transmission to substation at power plant. Voltage increased from generator 2300-22000 volts to the amount needed to travel long distances.
3. High-Voltage transmission lines carry power to city (300mi)
4. Electricity enters NYC at 345kv, 138kv, or 69kv
5. Stepped down at area substation to about 13,000 volts to underground grid
6. Inside building: a service panel controls building's power distribution to individual apartments
7. Power leaving street transformer travels on secondary feeder, in and out of manholes and through a service box before hitting a specific building

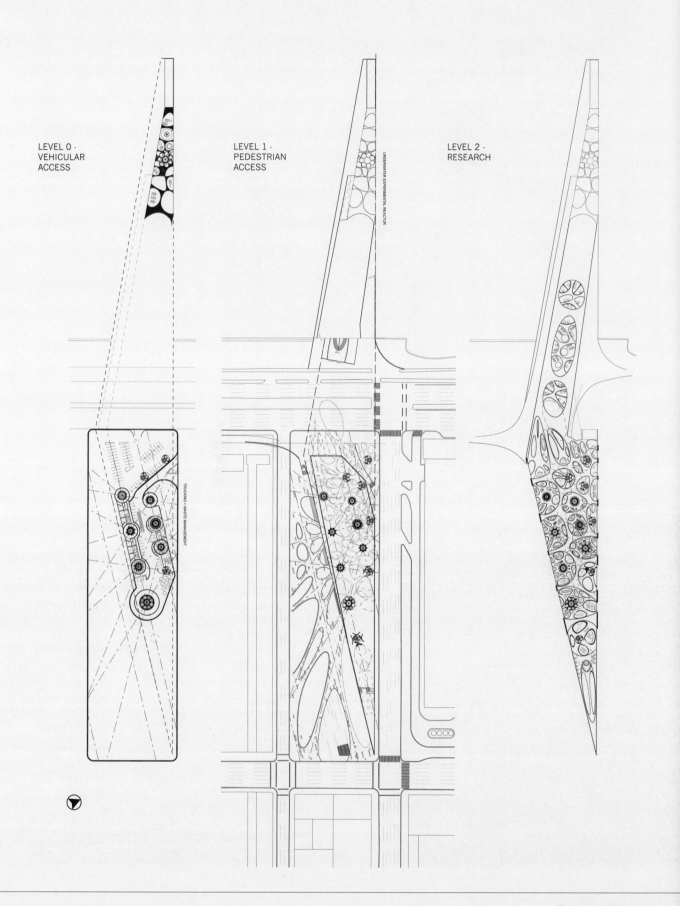

LEVEL 0 ·
VEHICULAR
ACCESS

LEVEL 1 ·
PEDESTRIAN
ACCESS

LEVEL 2 ·
RESEARCH

TRUCKING + WASTE MANAGEMENT

UNDERWATER EXPERIMENTAL REACTOR

LAST RESORTS: A TOUR GUIDE TO TERRITORIAL PROTECTION FOR THE REPUBLIC OF THE MALDIVES M.ARCH. THESIS

T. Buck Sleeper
Supervisor: **Ana Miljački**
Readers: **Mark Goulthorpe, Nasser Rabbat**

By 2100, rising sea levels will consume the Maldives in its entirety. Without land, the country cannot survive. This crisis has already begun: tsunamis, storm surges, and land scarcity already threaten the nation. In 2008, Maldivian President Mohamed Nasheed proposed using income from the country's tourism industry to purchase land in Indian, Sri Lanka, and Australia. Notwithstanding the political difficulties of inserting one sovereign nation into another, the primary Maldivian economies of tourism and fishing are inextricably linked to its immediate ecosystem. Campaigns to curb global carbon emissions are ineffective; eco-grandstanding impedes development and discourages tourist arrivals. Although the highest point on any of the country's 1,190 island is merely 2 meters, declarations that the country will disappear in the next 50 years are directly in conflict with the nation's 50-year (minimum) island lease agreements for international resort operators. Last Resorts proposes that instead of paying in cash, operators pay the government with DEFENSE, both hard infrastructure such as sea walls and jetties, and soft infrastructure such as beach building breakwaters and artificial reefs. Existing inhabited islands can be typified by a developed core and an unoccupied perimeter that acts as a buffer zone against wave action and flooding. These productive cores house schools, workshops, hospitals, and housing.

Existing resort islands are better described as a "lucrative edge" because guest rooms, dining, and other amenities are pushed to the exterior to take advantage of views to the reef and the horizon. The interior of resort islands are used for staff housing, water and electrical infrastructures, and other support features. These edge and core conditions are amenable to synthesis: resorts islands and local islands can combine to produce new hybrid types. By wrapping themselves around existing inhabited and agricultural islands, Last Resorts can defend the Maldives and create new typologies hospitality: farms become agritourism, towns become cultural tourism, fishing villages become an angler's paradise, and artificial reefs will produce the best diving in the Indian Ocean. Last Resorts will expand the nation's economy, ensure Maldivian sovereignty, and protect the archipelago's ecology. To this end, the resort typology must be redesigned to enable the activation of Hilton, Marriott, and Club Med as agents of national defense. Discarded plastics from resorts are upcycled into durable composites for sea wall construction and resilient architectures, which can be deployed to reduce erosion and flooding while permitting the accelerated growth of bioelectric reefs. Seawalls and buildings will deployed incrementally, beginning by securing critical water treatment, energy, and communications services. As resorts expand their operational capacity, the original shoreline will be obscured and a new island perimeter will emerge in the guise of an exotic defensive infrastructure.

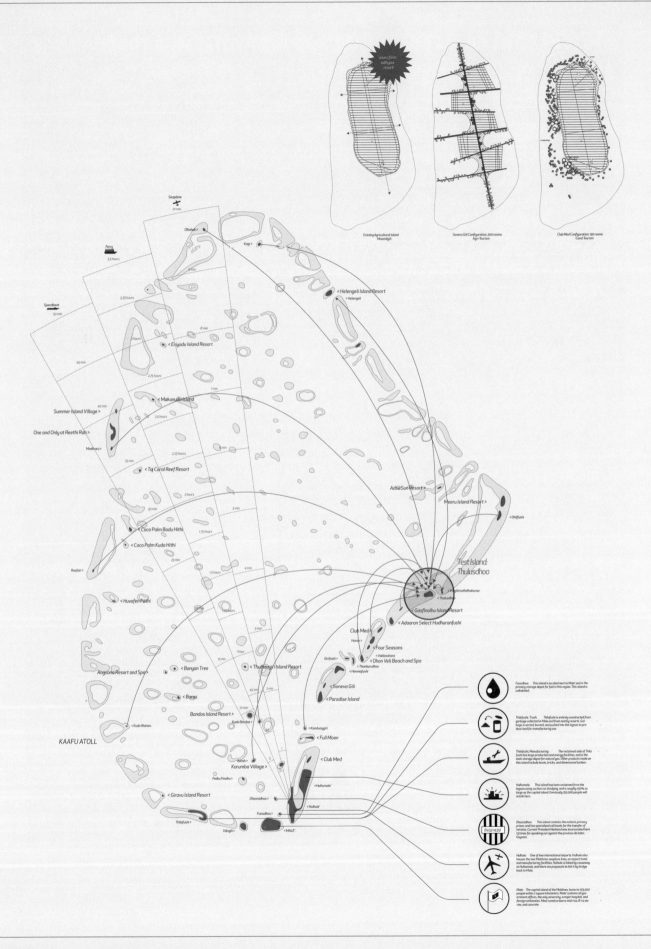

Existing Agricultural Island
Maamigili

Soneva Gili Configuration: 200 rooms
Agri-Tourism

Club Med Configuration: 150 rooms
Coral Tourism

solve a form
with your
resort

Seaplane
10 min

Ferry
3.5 hours

Speedboat
50 min

Olhahali >

Kagi >

8 min

< Helengeli Island Resort
> Helengeli

8 min

3.25 hours

< Eriyadu Island Resort

8 min

< Makunudu Island

2.75 hours

7 min

3 hours

2.5 hours

Summer Island Village >

One and Only at Reethi Rah >

40 min

Maakanu >

3 min

Asdu Sun Resort >

35 min

< Taj Coral Reef Resort

Meeru Island Resort >

2.25 hours

> Dhiffushi

2 hours

30 min

5 min

Test Island:
Thulusdhoo

< Coco Palm Bodu Hithi

1.75 hours

4 min

< Vihamanaafushi > Maldhidhufaaraa

> Thulusdhoo

< Coco Palm Kuda Hithi

25 min

Rasfari >

1.5 hours

Gasfinolhu Island Resort >

< Huvafen Fushi

> Adaaran Select Hudhuranfushi

Club Med >

3 min

Huraa >

< Four Seasons

< Vabbaohara

Girifushi >

< Dhon Veli Beach and Spa

< Angsana Resort and Spa >

< Banyan Tree

< Thulhaagiri Island Resort

15 min

1 hour

45 min

> Thanburudhoo

> Himmafushi

KAAFU ATOLL

> Baros

45 min

2 min

> Soneva Gili

Bandos Island Resort >

> Paradise Island

Kuda Bandos >

10 min

< Kudu Wataru

> Kanduoiygiri

> Full Moon

Adrah >

< Club Med

Karumba Village >

Fedhu Finolhu >

< Huhumale'

< Giravu Island Resort

Dhoonidhoo >

< Hulhule'

Funadhoo >

Thilafushi >

< MALE'

Villingli >

Funadhoo: This island is located next to Male' and is the
primary storage depot for fuel in this region. This island is
unhabited.

Thilafushi, Trash   Thilafushi is entirely constructed from
garbage collected in Male and from nearby resorts. Gar
bage is sorted, burned, and pushed into the lagoon to pro
duce land for manufacturing use.

Thilafushi, Manufacturing   The reclaimed side of Thila
fushi has large production and energy facilities, and is the
main storage depot for natural gas. Other products made on
this island include boats, bricks, and dimensional lumber.

Hulhumale   This island has been reclaimed from the
lagoon using suction out dredging, and is roughly 150% as
large as the capital island. Eventually 150,000 people will
reside here.

Dhoonidhoo   This island contains the nation's primary
prison, and has specialized cell boats for the transfer of
inmates. Current President Nasheed was incarcerated here
13 times for speaking out against the previous dictator,
Gayoom.

Hulhule: One of two international airports. Hulhule also
houses the two Maldivian seaplane lines, an airport hotel,
and manufacturing facilities. Hulhule is linked by causeway
to Hulhumale, and there are proposals to link it by bridge
back to Male.

Male: The capital island of the Maldives, home to 103,000
people within 2 square kilometers. Male' contains all gov
ernment offices, the only university, a major hospital, and
foreign embassies. Most construction is mid-rise, 8-14 sto
ries, and concrete.

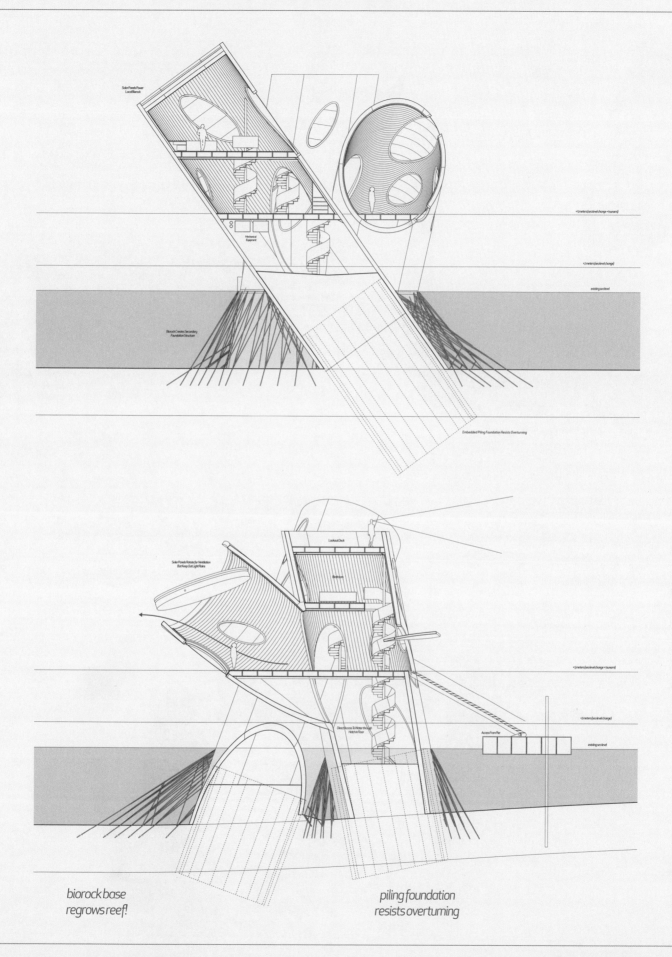

Solar Panels Power
Local Biorock

+5 meters (sea level change + tsunami)

+2 meters (sea level change)

existing sea level

Mechanical
Equipment

Biorock Creates Secondary
Foundation Structure

Embedded Piling Foundation Resists Overturning

Lookout Deck

Solar Panels Rotate for Ventilation
But Keep Out Light Rain

Bedroom

+5 meters (sea level change + tsunami)

Direct Access To Water through
Hatch in Floor

+2 meters (sea level change)

Access From Pier

existing sea level

*biorock base
regrows reef!*

*piling foundation
resists overturning*

Testing to Failure **327**

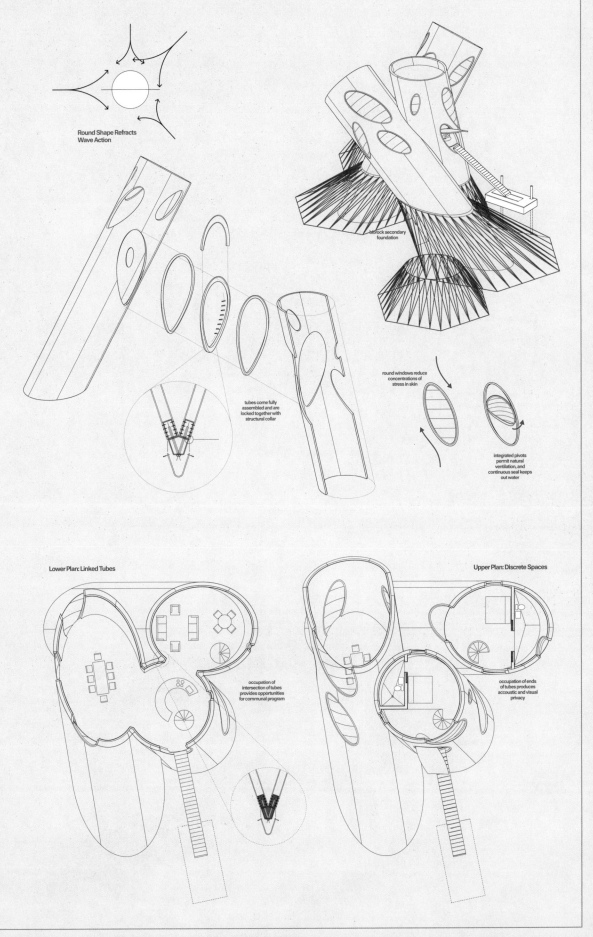

Round Shape Refracts
Wave Action

biorock secondary
foundation

tubes come fully
assembled and are
locked together with
structural collar

round windows reduce
concentrations of
stress in skin

integrated pivots
permit natural
ventilation, and
continuous seal keeps
out water

Lower Plan: Linked Tubes

Upper Plan: Discrete Spaces

occupation of
intersection of tubes
provides opportunities
for communal program

occupation of ends
of tubes produces
accoustic and visual
privacy

MISUSE

MATERIAL MISUSE

No matter what the design, no matter how innovative the forms or different the techniques, architects tend to be beholden to the 'finished' end of industrial processes. Overwrought, oversubscribed, and underpaid, architectural offices have little wherewithal or incentive to explore the capacities of the materials that they use, other than those stipulated in the advertisement brochures. Despite all appearances to the contrary, architects notoriously exploit technologies to produce what is tantamount to *visual effects*. The allusion to cinema here is not coincidental–there is more than a conceptual affinity between a Frank Gehry building and the inane, contrived lushness of James Cameron's *Avatar*. This observation must be distinguished from the kind of tendentious moralism that besets the architectural field within and without, every once in a while declaiming its superficiality and its pandering to fashion, of certain practices as divested of 'substance'. (This business of 'substance' can be a convenient instrument for the many Savonarolas that stride the world of aesthetics, indignantly arraigning unsuspecting and unwitting recipients with despoiling truth, 'honesty in materials', tectonics, social responsibility, etc. Since these characteristics are not only hard to determine but seldom within the architect's purview, entire careers, paid-up ones even, can be crafted out of these inquisitions, wherein the evils of capitalism are transposed onto architectures that one simply does not like.)

What we are talking about here, rather, is architecture's relationship to technology, to production processes. The point is that inordinate claims about technology are made in the context of architectural projects, with architects having been no wiser than merely picking out products and materials from standard catalogs, at best having approached some better-informed consultants in the process. Spec

Images courtesy of Sheila Kennedy / KVA

Fabrications, Plaster & Drywal—Sheila Kennedy / KVA
SFMoMA, California
Temporary installation for 'Fabrication'—an exhibition of the work of twelve international architects shown simultaneously at the SF Museum of Modern Art, the Museum of Modern Art (New York), and the Wexner Center for the Arts (Ohio).

books and catalogs are the tools of the trade for architects, and incorporating technology into one's practice often becomes a matter of choosing carefully among a finite number of options. Seldom do we see architects, proficient as they may be in design, trudge the more rarefied path back into the process of discovery, of investigation into molecular qualities, tolerances, the performative characteristics of materials and technologies. At a place like MIT, these pathways seem all the more available, charted out by the proximity of heavily influential disciplines such as materials science, or research frameworks such as presented by the Media Lab, and so on.

Historically, there have only been a few moments where a building material has become a headline of its own. The advent of new production techniques for rolling and casting glass in the mid-1800s meant that more consistent and thinner panes could be produced, setting off a revolution in design. The Crystal Palace at the

BCA Bathrooms—Sheila Kennedy / KVA
In his essay, "The Appeal of the Real," on the work of KVA in Material Misuse, Christoph Grunenberg credits the heightened awareness of everyday building materials in their bathroom renovation project as part of an intellectual trajectory of questioning and criticism of the present. "Exposing hidden plumbing and permanently 'exhibiting' disused fittings and appliances, the conversion not only revealed social rituals and gender conventions but also, in the process, demystified Duchamp's supposedly aesthetically neutral artefact as an object heavily loaded with cultural, corporeal and sexual associations."[5]

*Interim Bridges Project—
Sheila Kennedy / KVA*
*Pedestrian walkway, archaeological observa-
tion platform and exhibition, 'The Temporary
City,' open during the excavation for Boston's
Big Dig.*

These turning points introduced new material properties to designers who actively collaborated with engineers to develop them, and fostered a disciplinary fascination that yielded new formal potentials. When architects speak about innovating with materials, they often focus on a single technology, incorporating it into their work in novel ways that reflect industry-wide interest in something new. ETFE panels, aerogel, and transparent concrete are some such recent materials in wide circulation that provide new properties to play with. But what is often missing is a more critical industry- or discipline-wide discussion about how materials come to market and how components become standardized in composition and size. It is one thing to take what is available and experiment with it, it's quite another to question what's available in the first place, and why.

Great Exhibition of 1851 in London presented what was then an entirely new idea about the relationship of the indoors and the outdoors, lightweight structures, and the possibilities of natural lighting. Similarly, the exploration of steel-reinforced concrete in the early 1900s meant entirely new building forms and structural spans could be achieved, and enclosures could be thought of in vastly different ways. New materials brought about nothing less than a paradigm shift.

To be sure, the manner in which architects approach the performative characteristics of materials and technologies would be different from the functionalities that engineers would adduce to them. For one, they would lay less emphasis on measurable features, or perhaps weigh measurable elements in the manner that they affect sensibility. Discovery in this context may well mean mucking around, undoing the very modes of valuation that make research, so-called, viable. The Situationists would call

this *détournement*, turning things away from their conventional use to reveal other latent possibilities. Left all too often with merely the pre-specified palette of product catalogs to choose from, a more engaged version of research and design for architects would be to interject into the value chain, sifting out a kind of *misuse* of objects as opposed to use. Art appears here as a kind of surplus outcome, quite against the grain of the streamlined effects of the marketplace. At MIT, the institutional context of a premier engineering school, and the Media Lab, affords a particularly close relationship to the linkages between materials research and the processes by which new kinds of uses and things are devised.

The number of people actively involved in materials research at MIT defies enumeration, given that so many of the discrete, erstwhile engineering 'disciplines' have found their cores hollowed out in order to become, in one way or another, a kind of materials science. The proximity of researchers in materials science and the facilities for fabrication of experimental new composites and joining strategies means that the shelves of Home Depot don't define the raw materials architecture students work from. Beyond the freedom to extend the reach of architecture into materials development, this means that students begin to think about research as an active part of design and incorporate new ideas in real time into their work. New processes and properties are routinely tested and designed for in studios and workshops, bringing in expertise from other disciplines. Mark Goulthorpe's studios, in fact, often visit the boat-building firm Goetz Boats to learn from their compositing and fabrication strategies, reaching beyond what's commonly available and open to fruitful developments elsewhere.

While the architect works in representations of buildings, producing drawings and plans for others to execute, one thing that can't be put on paper is materiality. The very inability to represent how a surface feels, and how it interacts at details and joints, is an invitation to think about it in different ways, it warrants different media at the very least. Many have found it useful to experiment at a 1:1 scale

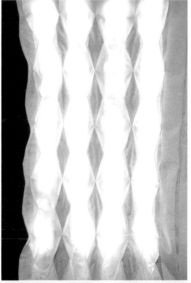

Soft House—Sheila Kennedy / KVA
The Soft House Project reconceives enclosure, shading, and power within the home. Curtains laced with photovoltaic cells hang moveable on a track surrounding the perimeter of the house. This track forms a DC ring which brings power directly to devices like computers, cell phones, and electric cars, which use DC power anyway. By avoiding the inefficient conversion from DC to AC power, a good deal of the photovoltaically-collected energy is conserved and used on-site.

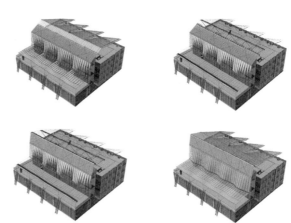

Soft House—Sheila Kennedy / KVA
(left) View from Interior at middle floor with Soft Duct above.
(above) Axonometric views of façade system in use.

with prototypes and materials. Not only does this practice allow the designer to more closely control and calibrate the final result, it permits a new platform for experimentation and discovery. It works not on expectations, but on intuition and replicable results. Materiality is, after all, the interface to the user's experience, so to test those relationships in advance is to better understand the implications of design. Reverberations, temperature, echoing, color, softness, and reflectivity are all manipulable and crucial aspects of this testing process.

It's quite uncommon in architecture education to have a literal engagement with material. Students generally deal with a conceptual idea of materiality, something that can be approximated or imagined, but not generally felt or tested in any real sense. There is no mechanism, even in building technology classes, for testing true performance of designs, only equations and models to help approximate them. But this need not be so, and in fact the introduction of full-scale prototyping can add a rich layer of knowledge that complements more standard designing practices. Professor Sheila Kennedy brings into her studios a focus on the literal, rather than figurative or metaphorical, characteristics

Yeosu Silo Revitalization—Sheila Kennedy / KVA
This project creates an urban symbol for the sustainable new "blue water economy" of the Yeosu City Region that function as an ocean water cleaning system. Ocean water from Yeosu City's "Big O" is raised up with solar pumps and then cleaned with gravity fed filtration tanks along Silo #1's 55 meter vertical drop.

of materials, in the belief that these industrial minutiae actually comprise a rich ground for radical intervention. To her, materiality is not about finishes, but rather the very stuff of what is built. To this end, she has become involved in the intellectual life of MIT on a number of levels, not the least of which is engaging the department of Electrical Engineering and Computer Science in a conversation about performance and interactivity in architecture.

The How to Make (Almost) Anything course, taught once a year by Neil Gershenfeld through the Media Lab's Center for Bits and Atoms, is a great example of MIT's dedication to a sort of DIY learning-while-doing ethos. Students take on week-long projects that explore everything from rapid prototyping to circuit bending and programming, all with little or no prerequisite knowledge. The topics covered in the class would never find themselves together in any other discipline. The stated goal is quite simple–to figure out and play with how things are made–but the projects that

come out of the class are as diverse as the students who come from all corners of the Institute to take it. Often, the most interesting projects come from those with little or no experience in fabrication or electronics, but who have a drive and curiosity to figure out what they don't know. Because MIT draws such exceptional talents in so many fields, there is an atmosphere of camaraderie and respect that is enormously productive.

While the Media Lab is a great example of institutionalized interdisciplinarity, these connections and the attitudes that accompany them are not uncommon elsewhere. It is a great benefit to the School of Architecture to be situated within an Institute largely known for engineering. Because MIT is so vast and on the cutting edge of experimentation and development, there are tremendous opportunities for students to cross-register, and more importantly to collaborate across disciplines. Many of the most exciting projects seen around campus are the result of highly specialized knowledge in different fields. Acknowledging this, and taking advantage of the many interests and talents at MIT, Professor Kennedy was able to teach the first cross-listed course between the Departments of Architecture and the Electrical Engineering and Computer Science Department in the Fall of 2010. This was not an electronics-focused architecture class, nor was it an architecture-leaning electrical engineering course; students in 4.268/6.077 *Design Innovation for Distributed Energy* worked in active collaborative research, simultaneously developing new ways to use photovoltaic cell technology and designing applications for its use. This is indicative of Kennedy's overall priorities as an architect, and as someone working with the literal applications of material technology—her students become somewhat like engineers and amass the knowledge required to make real designer-led change.

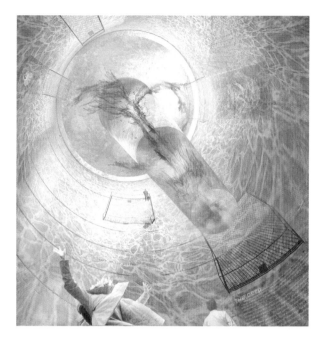

Yeosu Silo Revitalization—Sheila Kennedy / KVA
The Silo revitalization uses existing ocean monitoring buoys to bring hidden Ocean water behavior into public view. Solar powered sensors on these buoys measure current speed, water quality, and temperature and send digital data signals via satellite. The project's Ocean Water Monitoring Network receives and translates these signals from the Ocean into real time waves of light using a smart network of LEDs.

Kennedy intensely engages with materials of all kinds. Her work directly questions constructs and expectations about the way we use common techniques and components. Her interest, while sometimes very specific and specialized, operates at the scale of the industry and within the logistics of materials development and sourcing, investigating the very nature of what's available and why—not how to work with what you find at Home Depot, but how it got there in the first place. "Today, materials, building components and even programmes arrive preformed as 'products' to

the site or to the imagination. The role of the architect is not so much to form these entities as it is to deform them from their standard applications and invent for them new definitions and uses," a call to arms of sorts from within the industry.[1]

Kennedy's studios, and approaches to practice, run somewhat in a direction contrary to the usual procedure. Rather than first develop an architectonic and formal idea whose articulation is then fleshed out through a search for apposite materials, Kennedy often begins with a material or a basket of technologies and materials which are then subjected, by an intense series of investigations, from simply bending by hand to more elaborate testing of capacities, to a kind of form-finding exercise. Assumptions about the intended use for a product are thrown out, chemical and structural composition are tested and manipulated, and new properties and possibilities emerge from her research. The entire product catalog is Kennedy's platform, and no detail or use is too small to warrant repeated testing and discovery. Thus, rather than fitting materials to some pre-decided concept of social use, here socialization is explicitly perceived as an index of technology: one thinks of a transformed society through the transformed use of materials. Inhabiting the very innards of the discovery process, therefore, technology is here no more received as a given; the form-finding process moves back and forth across the chain of production and process to détourne other sets of expectations (economic, political, etc.) about what a given technology might be. Much as the architect's role extends to include experiments with materials, the materials themselves, the conventions of representation and building become fodder for further questioning. To think about materials implies a fundamental re-assessment of their existing contexts.

East 34th Street Ferry Terminal, ongoing—Sheila Kennedy / KVA
The design of the 34th Street Ferry Terminal takes a non-nostalgic attitude toward the NYC Riverfront. Pier 34 is redesigned and expanded to provide passengers with ticketing and waiting facilities and public access to three high-speed ferry berths.

These priorities are certainly clear in Kennedy's practice with partner Frano Violich, Kennedy Violich Architecture. KVA is modeled as an atelier, with high-tech prototyping facilities in-house that exist to test new design ideas. In 2000, Kennedy began a research unit within KVA called MATx, which is a stand-alone materials research concern, partnering with industry to develop new products beyond building materials. Her interest extends to the molecular and the nano, without an architectural-scale bias, with the confidence that developments of one order contribute to the collective knowledge of them all. At a forum discussing the im*material*/*ultramaterial* installations at Harvard's GSD in 2000, Kennedy used her platform to implore listeners to engage in a broader conception of architectural practice that at the same time revealed her own drives. "Could we imagine a broader palette of activities? Could we imagine architects creating new programs and applications for materials? Could we imagine architects being involved in different global platforms that influence cultural production?"[2]

Kennedy writes extensively on her firm's research and actively pursues private and non-profit, as well as academic, research and clients. She theorizes that a contemporary interest in materiality might have something to do with the advanced state of architectural representation technology. Concurrently, she feels that this drive forward from technology pushes materials to serve new purposes, to perform new tasks. She writes that as conventional means of enclosure and the 'hiding' of infrastructure are abandoned, "materials are. . . . critical starting points that open new possibilities for structuring the experience of space, for re-thinking the seemingly banal surfaces of partition, curtain wall, chase space and hung ceiling that characterize the familiar landscape of contemporary building types." It is clear that in her conception, materiality is not just skin-deep; it extends to all aspects of building, all details and jointure, as well as the coverings and hiding of infrastructural space that is commonplace.

An important aspect of MATx's charter is a multi-valent sense of utilitarian responsibility to underserved populations. Through outreach and non-profit projects, MATx brings a heightened technical knowledge to pressing social and health care issues around the world. Very much invested in bridging the 'technology gap' between technological producers–its decision-making 'elites'–and their 'passive' consumers, KVA has long sought public monies to democratize the proliferation of technologies in the public sphere, as well as asserting the firm's understated but deeply held values of forging a new New Deal of emergent, energy-saving technologies, posed against the old, energy-guzzling and resource-extractive New Deal. For the East 34th Street Ferry Terminal, for instance, the firm secured New York State agencies for off-grid sustainable energy generation including high-torque wind turbines and solar-powered solid state lighting, in addition to offering an alternate and sustainable means of transport in the heavily oversubscribed transportation system of New York City. A similar, 'remedial' sensibility can be seen to be at work in their Yeosu Silo Revitalization project in South Korea,

commissioned for the city's 2012 mini-'Expo'. The project combines the more 'scenic' consumption of the ocean with an apprehension of the ocean's function as absorbent of toxic waste, realized through a vast vertical water filter. The project emphasizes that at a certain point, the 'interface' with industrial processes confronts the face of Nature itself: artificial, man-made, extractive systems remain in the end completely reliant on the finite fecundity of natural systems. At Yeosu, this spectacle becomes something of a teaching tool for public edification in what is an increasingly poisoned and fetid planet. The 'Soft Rocker' developed for MIT's FAST Festival is a similar 'consciousness-raising' device: users (students) are made extremely aware of the energy quanta utilized by average, everyday gadgets such as the ubiquitous iPod or laptop.

The Portable Light Project is one such confluence of Kennedy's research aims and interests that MATx has been able to develop. The high-tech energy-harvesting textile used in Portable Light is so efficient at delivering important indoor artificial light for nighttime use, replacing caustic burning candles and lamps, that it appears downright low-tech. The photovoltaic cells housed on one side of the textile and the reflective metallic surface on the reverse, along with the efficient LEDs providing light from within, are integrated into familiar products like shoulder bags and weavings that can be adapted by local people. Here is an example where something that could potentially be a very expensive solar-charging station is scaled down and made accessible by virtue of cutting edge textiles research.

Indeed, as new technologies emerge for embedding electronics or for creating 'smart' materials, it falls to architects actively researching new processes to develop uses for them. The Portable Light Project is an example where productive thin-film photovoltaic cells were adapted for small-scale use powering LEDs or cell-phone chargers through advanced textile circuitry. As this type of productive material begins to enter the building market, expectations and performance grow, and architectural applications follow shortly behind. Kennedy, by virtue of being already immersed in a materials research atmosphere, is uniquely primed to investigate this brand of architectural symbiosis. She seeks to understand the electrical engineering aspects of new products, as well as developments on the nano scale, so when a new type of building skin is desired, or an advanced concrete is being developed, she can think holistically about what types of technologies might be applied where.

MATx often partners with industry to develop new products. Collaborations can take many forms, as when Kennedy's Spring 2010 Option studio worked to find ways to incorporate 3M thin film into strategies for a mixed-use complex in Rio de Janeiro in Brazil. This is one of those examples of true industry partnership, because while MIT architects were able to get their hands on a new product and test it, 3M received useful feedback and imaginative ideas early on in their development process. Students were able to work within the constraints of the new material to propose integrating it into solar shading devices and skin materials. These industrial cooperations also mean that MATx can work outside of the building industry, which places Kennedy and her research as at once embedded in and at the same time removed from the rigidly defended boundaries of architecture-as-discipline. Recent product development partners for MATx have included Dupont, Siemens, The North Face, and the US Department of Energy, extending the reach of materials experimentation throughout many

fields and networks. This also means that MATx, KVA, and Kennedy's students get to benefit from a wealth of resources that aren't generally available to architects.

Engagement in the social aspect of design is not limited to outreach and non-profit ventures, in fact the Portable Light Project seen within Kennedy's and MATx's portfolio is a drive for empowerment and the introduction of productive tools into a community. As a partnership with underserved populations and an analysis of technological applications, Portable Light is a commentary on technology and its ability to affect social behaviors, a key strand of discourse within Kennedy's work. In the way that assumptions and expectations about the built environment are reworked and revisited constantly, in Kennedy's terms a misuse or a "critical re-vision of what is already existing," is at play here that marks a significant alignment with the focuses of a research institution like MIT.[3]

It is important to see the connections between the investigation of existing building conventions and the development of new technologies in the same light, because it indicates an attitude about materiality that is quite unusual. Sheila Kennedy's interests are not limited to singular integrations of electronics into building materials, nor are they about subverting the norms of detailing and raw material usage. Together, these strains are powerfully interrelated and indicate a broader search for solutions and exploitations of the pragmatic, amounting to a radically self-conscious examination of architectural practice from within. Indeed, "this concrete approach to architecture… draws attention to the essential qualities of these basic elements," and leaves room to invent more when needed.[4]

1   Sheila Kennedy and Christoph Grunenberg, *KVA: Material Misuse.* London: AA Publications, 2001, 20.

2   Sheila Kennedy in Toshiko Mori, ed. *Immaterial/Ultramaterial: architecture, design, and materials.* Cambridge: Harvard Design School in Association with George Braziller, 2002, 17.

3   *Material Misuse*, 20.

4   Christoph Grunenberg, *Material Misuse*, 64.

5   Christoph Grunenberg, *Material Misuse*, 65.

PEDAGOGICAL PRACTICES PANEL MIT150 TRANSCRIPT

MONDAY, APRIL 25, 2011

Nader Tehrani: Professor, Head, Department of Architecture, MIT
Hernan Diaz Alonso: Chair, Graduate Programs, SCI-Arc
Distinguished Professor of Architecture, SCI-Arc
Sarah Whiting: Dean, School of Architecture, Rice University
Richard Sommer: Dean, Daniels School of Architecture, Landscape, and Design, University of Toronto
Preston Scott Cohen: Chair and Gerald M. McCue Professor of Architecture, Harvard University

This conversation has been edited for length and clarity.

Nader Tehrani: This session is dedicated to a discussion about the current predicament of architecture and architectural pedagogy. I wanted to launch this discussion first by looking back. I would like to delve into each person's intellectual trajectory and the pedagogical environment out of which they emerged.

Richard Sommer: We started to study at a moment when postmodernism had had a kind of apotheosis and was cresting. I felt where we were coming from, that we were still operating with something very new, which was essentially the translation of poststructuralism from Europe in the American context. Roland Barthes, Foucault, Derrida, all these people were just being translated a couple of years before we started, so there was this excitement around that material, around figures like Manfredo Tafuri, that architecture could be this kind of meta-discourse, it could engage with other intellectual debates in the broader humanities, yet it could be embedded in a discussion about design.

Preston Scott Cohen: I remember not wanting to believe that architecture could be constituted as a discussion around the question of type, which at that time, apparently it had to be, according to Rodolfo Machado, who was the leader of [RISD]. I just had in me this desire not to believe this was the case. So for me, the readings of Tafuri, representing the Modernists, particularly Corbusier, as having the work be embedded in those discourses very directly through the complexity of the development of the form, of the work, and that you could actually read those intellectual projects in the formal development, interested me so much more.

Nader Tehrani: What were the alibis for those complexities if they were not generated from the normative conditions of type?

Preston Scott Cohen: At my thesis review, Colin Rowe was there. And he looked at the façade of my project, a kind of Corbusian thing, and he said, "it's so deadpan." I was thrilled, because apparently he worshipped the deadpan, and I didn't think of myself as one who could ever be thought of as deadpan, so this seemed a great achievement. So I wasn't interested in the other questions, those that were unfolding in these texts.

Nader Tehrani: Hernan, you come at the tail-end of this generation. Why don't you pick up the discussion from Argentina, where in fact there are certain connections to RISD, as it turns out, because of the Argentinian axis.

Hernan Diaz Alonso: The school in Argentina was pretty dogmatic about Modernism. It was basically, either you were on Corbu's side or Mies's side, and that was pretty much it. There was a second level of professors who were under the influence of the School of Venice who were Tafurians or Rossis. None of the things appealed to me, so for me, the [1988 MoMA] DeCon show was like a moment I remember where I thought, "okay, architecture is maybe not so bad after all." So we're talking about 1989.

[My school in Argentina] was really like a combination of a technical school and a beaux-arts school. Everyone was studying Germany. So for me, before Deleuze and Guattari and all that, it was Derrida, and there was a trend that you had to start to think about that.

Image credit: George X. Lin

I remember Eisenman went to give a lecture in Argentina and then Libeskind and there was all this … intrigue. Because all our teachers despised them, so to all the young guys, they had to be interesting. For me, this kind of a discourse about camps and so on, it's something that I just learned when I came here to Columbia in '98/'99. It was much more a question of the craft of the profession than anything else.

Nader Tehrani: Sarah, of the people on the panel, you are the one that in a way slalomed back and forth between design and history and theory, and the emergence of theory as a specialization, which is a relatively new thing.

Sarah Whiting: I was a fairly naïve undergraduate at Yale when DeCon was essentially erupting there, and caught the tail end of that, where I made up my own major and was able to enjoy the idea of constructing architecture as an intellectual discourse. But I think we actually do have to step back and admit that the group of us are actually fairly anxious about the fact that there aren't clear debates right now, and we're trying to figure out why there were clear debates when we were in school, and what's wrong with this generation that's in school now. So partly this is anxiety at the fact that we're taking on the rhetoric of the old farts and trying to figure out where the blame should go. Is it the computer, is it the web …

Richard Sommer: theory…

Sarah Whiting: No, theory's not the problem. I think that part of the problem is that when we were in school, there were big figures, and there were big oppositions. There were big camps that were very clear.

I think that's the real anxiety underlying this panel, and underlying our generation, is that we feel a real need, that theory has been pushed aside, that thinking has been pushed aside, and there aren't big debates. And we want to put them back on the table, and we're trying to figure out how.

Nader Tehrani: There was a time, not so long ago, when the relationship between theory and practice was held to be the critical factor in gauging the relevance of both. But there was also a time in which the definition of practice was held to be more certain. Each of

you has invested a good deal of thinking in design, and in turn, each has redefined practice in accordance with an expanded idea of what it may constitute. All of you, we could say, are designers, but in many ways practice architecture in fundamentally different ways.

Richard Sommer: From the late 1960s up until the 1970s, there was a very important moment in architecture education, which is not distinct from crises in other professional forms of education, where there was a questioning about the agency and the instrumentality of the professions, and this was very much true in architecture, it was very much fed by a kind of post-structuralist critique of knowledge and certain forms of intellectual instrumentality. So we had this moment where it was a good thing to actually recede from normative modes of practice. There were schools of thought and of people who were very much committed to situating architecture as a form of intellectual discourse, as a form of humanities-based thinking, and this also helped us establish ourselves in a university context. I think what we're seeing now is a secession of that, generationally, and a reexamination of this question of what constitutes expertise in architecture, and what forms of agency we have.

Sarah Whiting: But I think you have to finish the story, because the retreat has been so destructive in terms of the successful opening up of architecture through interdisciplinary means, which I was a happy participant in, and still consider to be one of the most important phases in architecture. This was great, but led us further away from understanding that architecture might have any relevance. It was a sort of dilution, or a looking outside of architecture for modes of relevance. That, combined with the fear of things like Urban Renewal, led to a belief that architecture could only act on a very small scale. Ideally, the full arc should teach us that maybe we're at a point where we have the confidence to act big again, without making some of the mistakes that were made before, that you can actually return to some big problems that need big answers, and secondly, that you can't always look outside architecture for legitimacy, because you're pulling the rug out from underneath our discipline itself.

Hernan Diaz Alonso: Going back to the origin of the question, I think we need to force ourselves to think in a different way. I think for all of us, we are involved in teaching and pedagogy in academia. I think when we ask ourselves about practice, I think we produce a very different answer, a very different way of thinking than you

would have from somebody who is only committed to practice in the more traditional sense of the word.

Nader Tehrani: When we were educated, the idea of knowledge was somehow formed by the academy, and certain issues and debates were rarefied and held a kind of canonic importance. With the internet and all of the other communication media, the accessibility of that knowledge spread horizontally, if you like, to the point of the annihilation of the very Rossis and Eisenmans that you referred to earlier on, and there emerged a new generation, wherever you like, from Chile, to Iran, to Bulgaria, to whatever emerging economy, to China, to India, that was able to instrumentalize that same database. In a way, to some degree, they pulverized the very preciousness of your arguments. So how do you, as leaders of education, begin to operate in a world where you demanded a kind of resistance, the difficulty that intellectual games require in a world that is just lubricated.

Sarah Whiting: I don't think you need difficulty to move forward. I don't think that you need a model of oppositional resistance to reject. One thing that the American academy is able to do is maintain a space for discourse and for an intellectual project for architecture, and I think we can all be really thankful for that, even if the academy is a corporation, is a machine, and is often getting bigger and bigger in places.

Richard Sommer: I do think that the role of the school now is to find a way to model new modes of practice. The better schools are not thinking about reproducing the profession that they're in; they're thinking about generating new knowledge, and generating new modes of inquiry, and actually driving practice.

Preston Scott Cohen: I think the question that gets lost here is whether or not this will suggest that architecture's relationship to the university, the larger context of intellectual work, is really a very questionable relationship. If architecture is agency, and is not an intellectual project, why does it belong in the university at all? Wouldn't we all be better served to just go into the field directly? The hotter question is what use are we to the university?

Hernan Diaz Alonso: I don't think architecture can renounce its intellectual project ambitions. I think you then become something else. The question to me is not that it should stop being that or not,

to me it's about how we rethink the notion of knowledge in the way that you are talking about, the distribution, the accumulation of knowledge. It's certainly changing in front of our eyes by the week, by the day, but the intellectual project should remain alive. But I'm not so sure that the medium and the way that we operate needs to or can operate on the same level.

Sarah Whiting: I think part of the problem here is this idea that you have practice on one hand and professionalism on the other. I'm thinking the issue is, if you take it as a term like "project" instead of a term like "practice" or "professionalism," then you get to maintain control of it in the university. Part of what we have to do, and part of our anxiety is that people don't have a project. And that's partly a question of the speed, partly a question of the veneer as opposed to the depth of thinking through a problem. The other issue is our relevance in terms of a larger public discourse. I don't think that architecture was ever at the forefront of Modernism's transformation of the world. But I think that architecture was seen as relevant and had a public audience, and I think that right now we don't necessarily have that audience.

Preston Scott Cohen: My question is what should students of design become experts in, and should their primary effort be to prepare themselves to convince the world that architecture matters–is that the primary issue that they should be focused on or is there some other project?

Richard Sommer: If your work is to educate architects, and you have less and less time to do that, let's say, in graduate programs, three or three and a half years, what is it that you're immersing them in–what is the knowledge that you're transferring, or what are the problems that you want to frame? Is it how to cultivate audiences or how to make architecture relevant, or I think what you're implying is that maybe there is some expertise that you should be developing in these students, so that when and if they have the political role or social or know-how to actually take this out into the world, they're able to do so.

Preston Scott Cohen: I think it's neither one of them. I think, to really speak in clichés for a moment, it's to teach them to *think*. It's not just a cliché. It's what I thought the ambition of the more theoretical turn in the whole scheme of things was.

Hernan Diaz Alonso: I would like architecture to have a project that is not to change the world, but a project for architecture to change architecture. It is losing its power as a cultural agent. I think at least we can aim to change architecture on this path and the way that the professional model is going.

Nader Tehrani: One of the embedded predicaments that is in this discussion is the degree to which this very problem has made us obsolete. To the degree that engineers, structural engineers, mechanical engineers, project managers, and so forth, have essentially done away with those very areas in which we constructed our audiences. This is not just a question of translating what we learned in school to practice, it's the degree to which the platforms of intellectual empowerment have been chipped away to the point that some architects only need to worry about space planning, to the extent now that architecture may be able to operate at multiple scales. At the same time, there are speeds at which the world is developing which are so rapid we cannot keep up with them in the academy. And on another level, there are instruments of power that are in a way thinning out the zone in which you would ever be able to operate effectively. So when do you become irrelevant, when do you construct relevancy?

Sarah Whiting: I think it goes back to Scott's notion of "what we have to do is teach people to think." The most amazing thing about architecture is realizing it's a synthetic, generalist discipline and it's a very different approach to thinking that can engage issues at every scale. So if you see that still as a place of relevance and of possibility, and you see architectural education as a combination of courses where design is the place to do that, where history and theory is the place to do that, where technology is the foreground for a place to do that, then I still think that the academy is the place where one can fight, let's say, that irrelevance from the project manager on the ground, and still form possible projects within architecture.

Richard Sommer: I think there seems to be a lot of hand-wringing about what it is that we actually do, versus what we have to do to gain agency or audiences, and I would like to remind everyone that

many of the figures we admire from the twentieth century were able to develop a kind of architecture of great formal and cultural complexity while also maintaining often a kind of discourse about urbanization or other things that opened up much wider audiences to them, the most recent of which, of course, is Rem Koolhaas. He used, essentially, his mind and his thinking to establish himself as a kind of oracle about cities and urbanization which established his authority and his ability to get commissions as an architect.

Hernan Diaz Alonso: The main problem I see right now with the students is that there is kind of a lack of focus and ambition about what they want to do with that. What I call it is the proliferation of the consultant model as an ambition. And I think there is slowly a transformation on the students' part to go more into this idea that they are not interested in being the canonic figure, they are interested in being some sort of consultant guru for one of these micro-menus that we have. And to me, that is a fundamental problem, because some of these guys in the past, these major figures, they never apologized for architecture. And the consultant model is a kind of undisclosed apology for what architecture is not.

Sarah Whiting: That's a very important point. I think that's true all across the board. The publications coming out of schools right now are often collecting material with no editorial ambition, and no editorial statement–it's sort of passive curatorial work. And I think that that's a sort of similar thing to what you're talking about in terms of doing all the grunt work to organize, to make it possible for other voices to come to the table. I think that's a real mistake. I think if anything, when you're in school, you have the power to make statements, make mistakes, and move on. And the fact that that's not being taken advantage of is really problematic.

Nader Tehrani: Scott, you want the institution to be the platform where you teach people to think. But what are they thinking about? What is architecture? The techniques of developing policy for infrastructure are different than the techniques that involve the turning of a corner of a certain type of a building. These are vastly different media, basically, and the debates that surround them are relevant, but completely different terms. So the generalizations may not end up being productive once you sweep them all together.

Sarah Whiting: Architecture is a generalist discipline. You have to start off by exposing students to that broad horizon, and then

you have to encourage students to form their specific depth of expertise. I think you have to admit that at a school, you may not be able to actually offer the breadth of expertise, and so you have to be up front about where you have the possibility of doing that.

Nader Tehrani: Where do you see the studio model going?

Hernan Diaz Alonso: There are a couple of things that are very interesting about studio culture. One is the validity of the one-semester model. Right now, in a weird way, you can only accomplish so much so fast. So, we [at SCI-Arc] are experimenting with two-semester segments, where you have more time to work on it. But the other phenomena that I've seen recently, that has to do with visual studies and applied studies, is that seminars and workshops are becoming almost like other studios or parts of studios. It is the expansion of the studio model into the whole culture of the school that I find incredibly interesting. Also, there is a kind of re-composition about the tooling and the techniques that forces you to rethink. For example, a very simple thing like plans and sections. Plans and sections, when I was educated, were generative tools. The truth is right now you think in a much more three-dimensional way, where plans and sections become almost like cartographies or maps of something that has already been established.

Sarah Whiting: I think that there are two modes where studio is taught often. One is a catalytic mode, where you see studio as finding opportunities and forging opportunities, and the other is the constraint mode where you see problems and everything is put forth as a kind of obligation that one has to solve problems. That's the division between the project and the professionalism within the studio model.

Preston Scott Cohen: It's an interesting characterization. Because I think that is very much a way to capture the imagination, not necessarily how I like to do things right now, but in terms of environmental and economic … that seems to be one of the tools by which we are driving pedagogy right now.
How can it shift into the catalytic, potentially?

Richard Sommer: [At Toronto,] we've been struggling with this, as many schools have, with looking at the construction of pedagogy. I like Hernan's idea of the kind of notion that we need to adjust the time or the periods that we devote to certain subjects. Because there are things you can learn about in a week, or three weeks, or six weeks. And there are things that might take twelve.

Andres Sevtsuk: It seems to me that one of the key justifications, fundamentally, for the role of architecture in the university, is the presence of research, which would lead to theory. It really gets people engaged in research in quasi- or actually quite rigorous ways. And the other, which is the studio culture, that talks about design. To me, it seems like making that jump from being able to go from description to prescription is the essence of what architects do. This has been a question on the table since the sixties and people have looked into this here and elsewhere, but I wonder if you see a role for that, a more sort of research-centered engagement with a profession of what architects do, even moving forward.

Richard Sommer: To me, it's a problem of time and the kinds of educational experiences and backgrounds that people bring into the study of architecture.

Nader Tehrani: There is also a tension between the cultures that live in this institution, one of which is about quantification as the basis for action, and the other one which, loosely put, is either called artistic, or it's called critical discourse. It's an interlocutor for the very things that present facts to you which are not substantial enough on which to act. How do you navigate between these two cultures?

Hernan Diaz Alonso: One thing I would say is that one of the most current misconceptions in this conversation is that *we confuse experiments with research.* And I think sometimes what people call research are just experiments. There's a fundamental difference. Experiments, basically, they're very useful, but they're blind. You're trying to figure out things, you don't know what's going on. Research is when you start to define a much more clear agenda and you want to work on it. And I always have a certain problem with that word, the same way that I have a problem with the word "thesis" in architecture, because I think that terms that come from other disciplines quantify facts in a much more precise way than architecture words. I would try to use more the discipline of knowledge rather than research.

Sarah Whiting: I think this idea of the experiment is a really smart way of putting it, because it relates to the idea that the design studio is a different way of thinking, and that if you see it as an experiment, then you no longer see it as analysis then prescription, which I think is the worst way of posing how a studio should be set up. If you acknowledge that it's a different form of thinking, then the prescription and the analysis is happening at the same time as framing the model of the experiment, so that you don't have that separation. The minute you have that moment of separation, it means that you're importing a mode of thinking from another discipline.

SUSTAINABLE STRATEGIES FOR LIGHTWEIGHT BUILDING CONSTRUCTION OPTION DESIGN STUDIO

SPRING 2010

Instructor: **Sheila Kennedy**
Teaching Assistant: **German Aparicio**

Interdisciplinary in spirit, this vertical studio will explore the integration of flexible energy harvesting solar nano-materials with lightweight building construction as a new medium for renewable, distributed power generation in architecture. The studio will offer students at MIT the opportunity to work directly with the next generation of flexible, organic energy harvesting materials which are re-defining how and where power is produced, challenging the inherited modern conventions of centralized building services and expanding the spatial experiences and applications of the architectural surface. This architecture studio will collaborate with MIT's Course 6 Electrical Engineering and Computation Sciences, and the soft-semiconductor group at MIT. Students in the studio will create architectural design proposals for a mixed use residential/ market building with clean energy generation on the Uruguanaia Market site in the Centro district of Rio de Janeiro, Brazil.

Students' design proposals will explore design concepts of how the Active Cladding solar prototypes could be applied in the context of the politics of formal/ informal exchanges. To explore the potentials of the next generation of flexible thin film photovoltaics, students in the studio will engage key design problems in contemporary practice— the identification of spatial and programmatic opportunities presented by renewable energy, the creation of cladding designs that make use of local materials and the development of fabrication techniques that enable the designer to work fluidly between digital and physical modes of creative production. Discussion and collaboration with OPV manufacturers representatives will be encouraged throughout the design process.

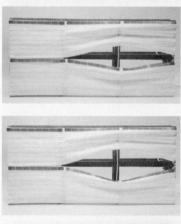

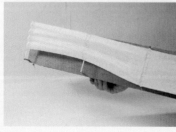

Phil Seaton | MArch
Juliet Hsu | MArch
Soft Louver, Mixing Market

The *Soft Louver* is a building envelope system designed around low-cost low-efficiency flexible solar panels and textiles. It introduces a new energy paradigm based on distributed and user-participatory "soft" energy production, an alternative to the "hard" centralized system that disconnects power production–and its side effects–from consumers.

The lightweight and soft textile system is adjustable in some places by individual users, where it serves simultaneously as a sun shade and solar-tracking photovoltaic system in Rio de Janeiro, a place in need of both; in other areas, larger scale programmatic and urban factors are given preference and allowed to determine global shaping of the building facade.

The power generated by the large PV facade is used to drive speakers in the downstairs "Mixing Market," where an essentially open plan is shaped spatially by sound instead of by walls. Different sets of speakers receive different amounts of power throughout the day as the position and strength of the sun vary, "activating" the market's spaces according to a sun schedule. As the inhabitants of the mixing market are exposed more directly to the source of their energy, it is our hope that sustainability and energy related concerns can become more culturally significant, and not merely a "technical" problem to be solved by engineers building larger and larger capacity centralized power plants.

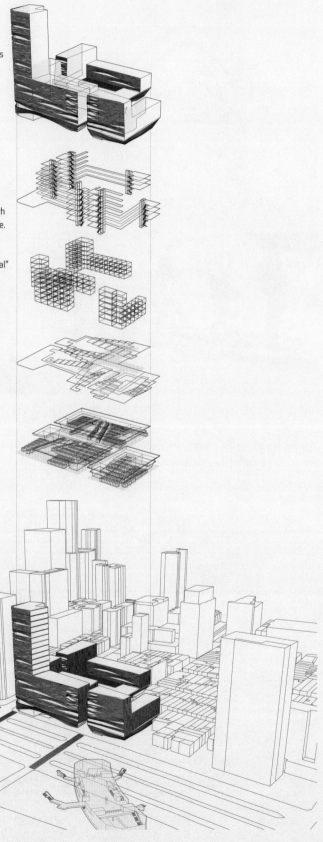

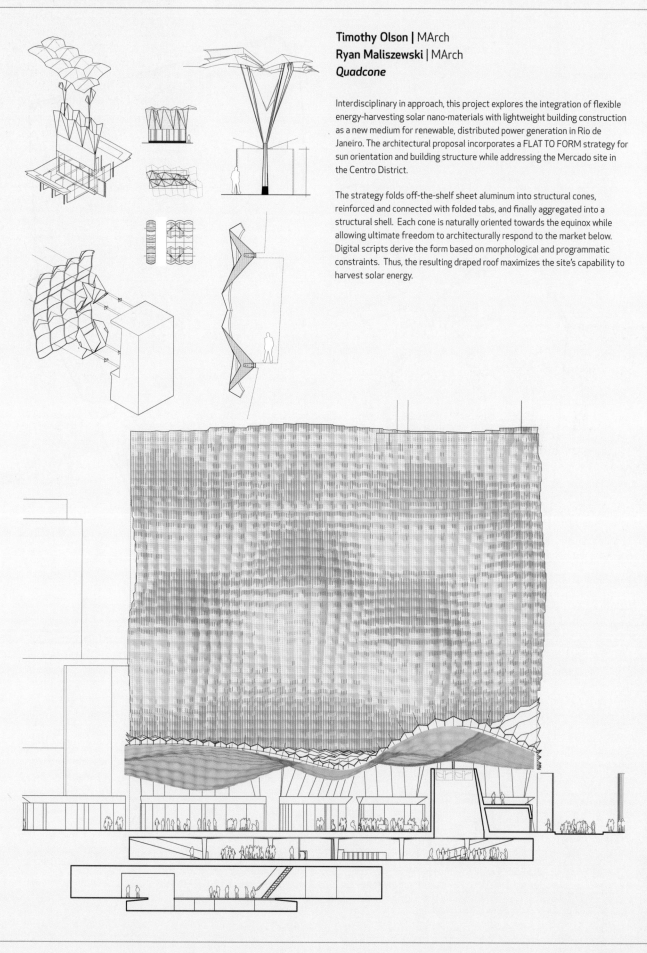

Timothy Olson | MArch
Ryan Maliszewski | MArch
Quadcone

Interdisciplinary in approach, this project explores the integration of flexible energy-harvesting solar nano-materials with lightweight building construction as a new medium for renewable, distributed power generation in Rio de Janeiro. The architectural proposal incorporates a FLAT TO FORM strategy for sun orientation and building structure while addressing the Mercado site in the Centro District.

The strategy folds off-the-shelf sheet aluminum into structural cones, reinforced and connected with folded tabs, and finally aggregated into a structural shell. Each cone is naturally oriented towards the equinox while allowing ultimate freedom to architecturally respond to the market below. Digital scripts derive the form based on morphological and programmatic constraints. Thus, the resulting draped roof maximizes the site's capability to harvest solar energy.

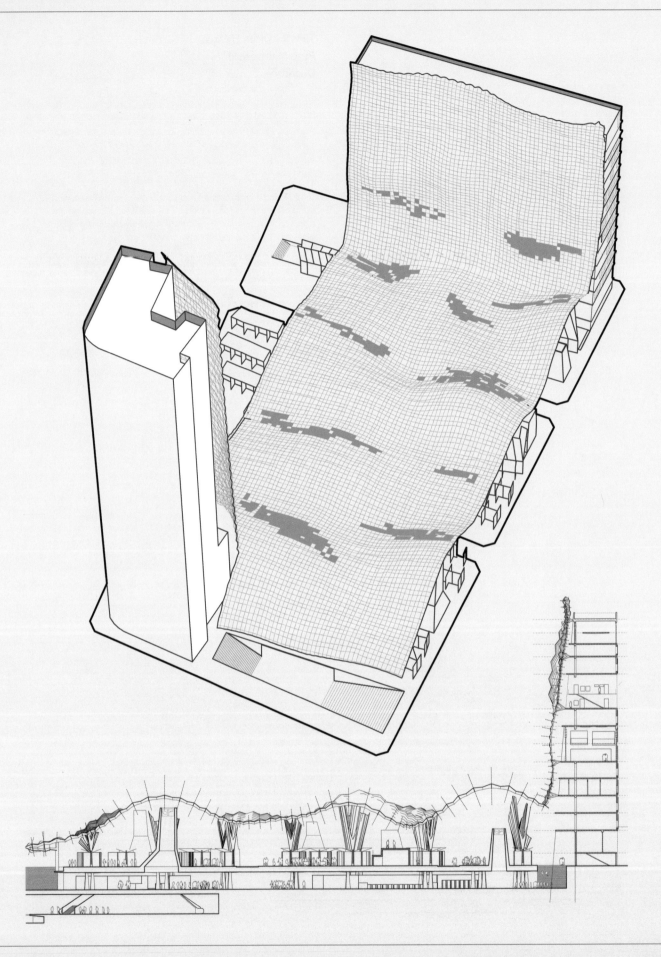

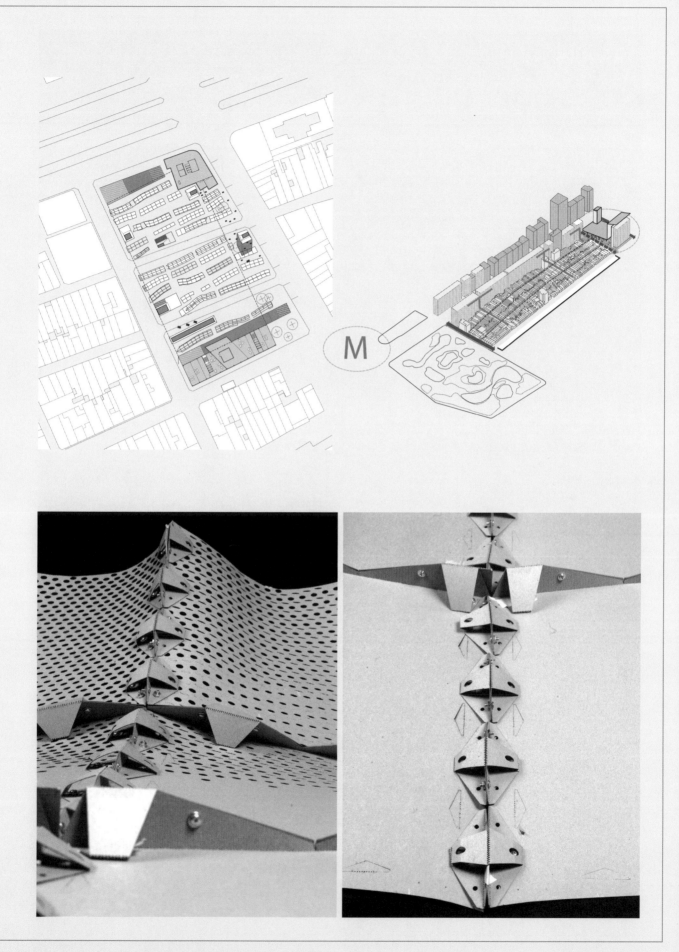

ICE HOUSE CORE 3 DESIGN STUDIO
SPRING 2010

Instructors: **Sheila Kennedy, Andrew Scott, Cristina Parreño**
Teachin Assistants: **Ari Kardasis, Siobhan Rockcastle, Timothy Olson**

The Core 3 studio offers an interdisciplinary approach to design, engaging the domains of building technology, computation and the cultural/historical geographies of energy in a semester long project for a Design Incubator located in the Newmarket area of Boston. Originally accessed in the colonial era by the South Bay Harbor and Fort Point Channel canals, the marshy ground of Newmarket was gradually filled in with land, creating a vast and ecologically fraught constructed ground for the railway and freeway transportation systems that serve Boston's refrigerated food industries. Students will work on their studio projects in close collaboration with MIT instructors from Design, History/Theory, Computation and Building Technology to create transformative adaptive re-use design strategies for the Boston Ice Company Ice Storage House, designed in 1908. The 100' tall concrete Ice Storage House poses several intriguing design challenges. The existing original structure of massive poured in place concrete is entirely without window openings of any kind and the interior of the building is a singular large void space, some eight stories in height, originally used to house stacked volumes of ice.

The design problem of the Ice House brings into focus disciplinary questions centered on the identification of relationships among 'natural' and 'artificial' landscapes of production, 'obsolete' and 'contemporary' elements of construction and technology, and the definition of the architectural character of a spatial proposition. Students will explore in detail the generative design principles and material identity of the enclosure and structural systems of their studio projects, engaging the architectural design problems of public image, façade and building skin— topics that are currently being transformed by new ecological imperatives, simulation software, digital fabrication and strategies for energy conservation. The studio design problem will be divided into three related exercises that will require analytical, synthetic and projective conceptual thinking as well as the development of technical and representational skills in architecture.

The design program for the studio is a Design Incubator for innovative design 'start ups' to be accommodated in the Ice Warehouse. It is anticipated that the program will involve a mix of about 35% new construction and 65% adaptive reuse in a mid-rise building that may extend upward and outwards form the existing concrete shell of the Ice House. The project will involve the design of a program of approximately 33,000 GSF, which includes leasable work spaces for film, architecture, graphics and industrial design start ups, shared Incubator administration and support resources, a flexible public theatre, lobby and café, a design library & green materials collection and a large fabrication facility with bicycle manufacturer Independent Fabrications www.ifbikes.com as the initial primary tenant.

Dennis Cheung | MArch
Cristina Parreño, Instructor
Cap It!

Located at 51 & 55 Norfolk Avenue, the Boston Ice Company Storage
Warehouse served as an important ice infrastructure to both Boston and
the world in the early 19th century. However, due to the invention of electric
refrigerator, the ice industry in Boston declined in the early 20th century. The
concrete 8 storey ice storage has been abandoned since then.

The project aimed to transform the existing ice house into a design incubator,
tapping into the once-significant infrastructure. By utilizing the existing
concrete wall and buttresses, a radical design that focuses on two envelope
systems will inject a new definition to the district through an insertion to the
stunning interior. These envelopes will promote interactions between the
designers and the public, thus establish a network of creativity in the area.

Alan S. Lu | MArch
Sheila Kennedy, Instructor
Theater of Production

The notion of programmatic extremism is explored in this project where a central defined figure that contains a vertically integrated manufacturing/workloft arrangement occupies the void and recoups the emptiness left by the existing ice storage facility. Such a figure inverts the typical relationship of a theater by converting the event space into a Piranesian conflation of production/manufacturing where in effect, these work processes become the spectacle themselves and the theater is one of production.

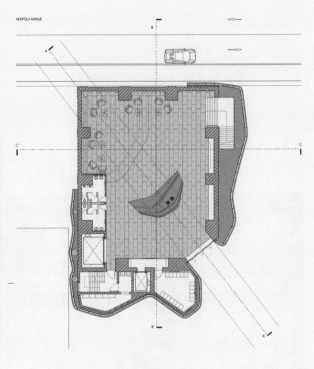

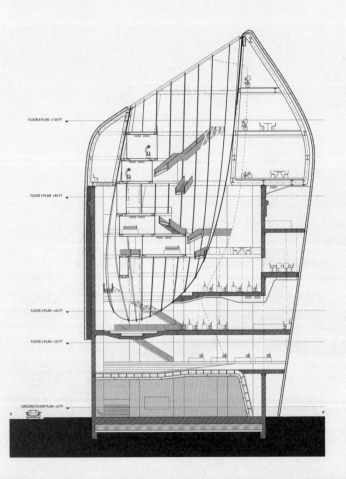

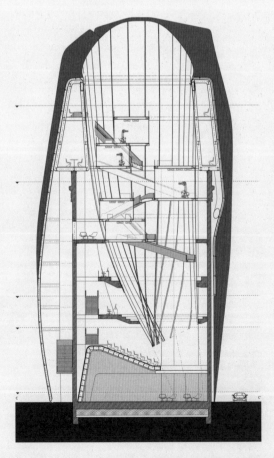

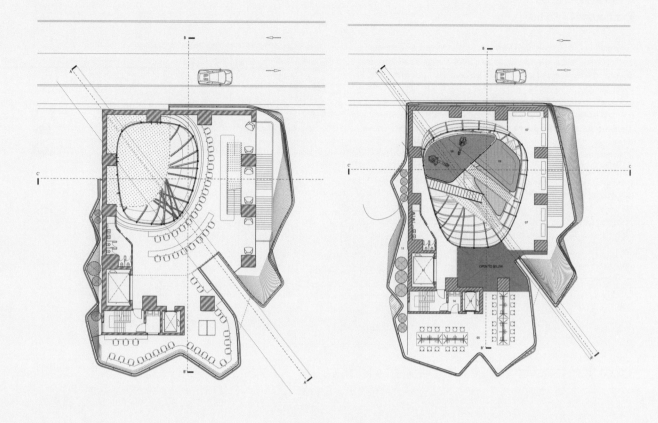

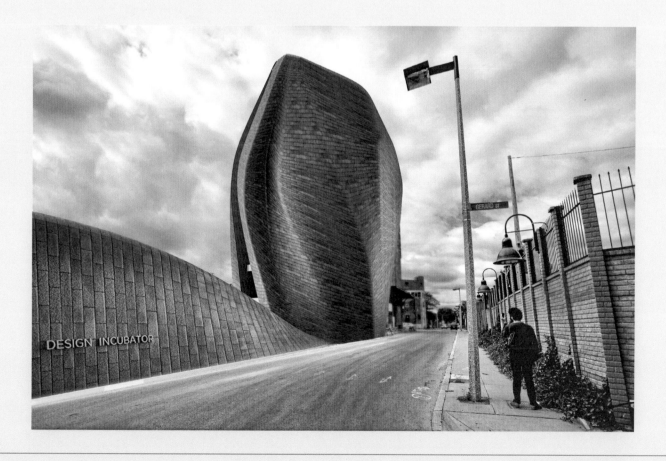

Testing to Failure 357

Alexander Marshall | MArch
Cristina Parreño, Instructor
The Cocoon

The cocoon is an envelope intended to promote a new and developing creative industry. This is a working studio environment which is intended for developing artists and designers, who desire an environment unexposed to public intrusion. The insertion into the former Boston Ice Company building, produces a multi-layered envelope which functions similar to a cocoon of an insect larvae. Star-shaped volumes are stacked in alternating succession to form collective studio spaces and critique rooms. The spaces between the new envelope and the former concrete shell are intended as fabrication platforms, which are virtually hidden from both the interior and exterior of the building. This allows for creative production obscured by the layers of the envelope. The facades are comprised of two spiraling circulation paths which connect the various "exit holes" punched through the shell of the Icehouse. These connections allow on-lookers to view the constant movement of building occupants between program spaces. The "exit holes" also offer the curious public forced views, as they frame glimpses of the interior environment.

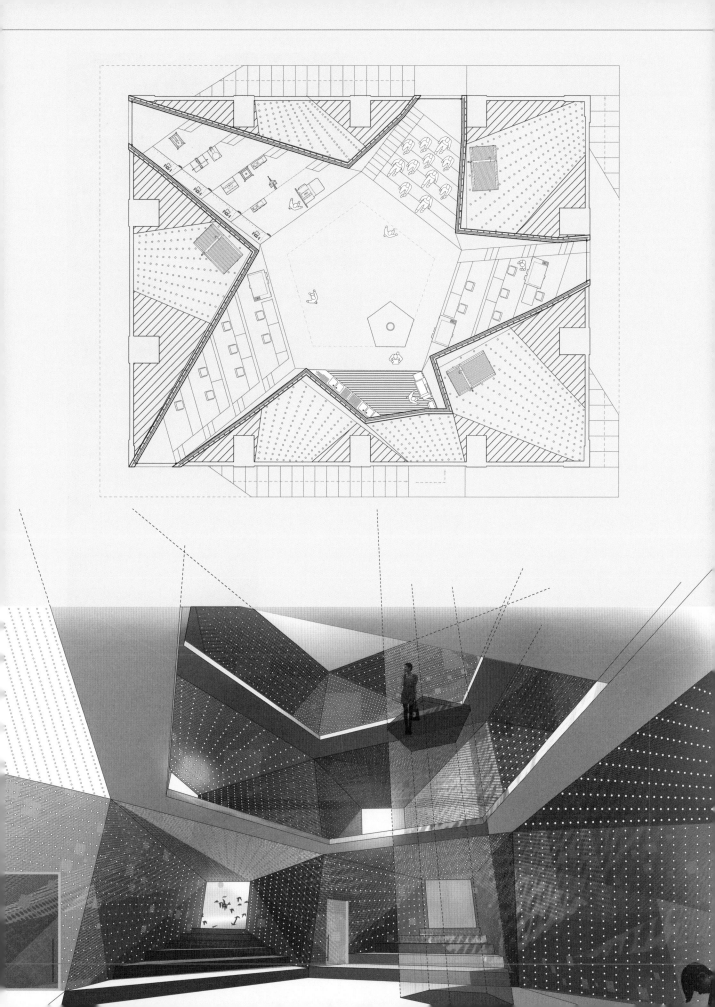

Jin Kyu Lee | MArch
Andrew Scott, Instructor

Holopticism Cube

The main idea of the project is offering various and real-time information about the design industry to the public by exposing the entire process of producing from design to shipment. The exposed processes are transformed, according to producing phases, into various kinds of images such as LCD images, ETFE facade supergraphics and real display on the vertical conveyor belt. By using the information, people can discuss the design products and give the feedback to designers and producers.

Thanks to the technologies, LCD, ETFE and vertical conveyor belt, in the project, people can have the various channels not only for knowing the design industry but also for supervising the capitalism; Holopticism. The structural languages of the project, such as the tensile force cables, the customized cantilevers and the fab labs which consist of truss tubes are integrated into the main idea of the project. Finally, in terms of aesthetics, the synthesis of the structural language, technology and the concept of the project can make the metaphor for the "Holopticism" in the existing concrete box.

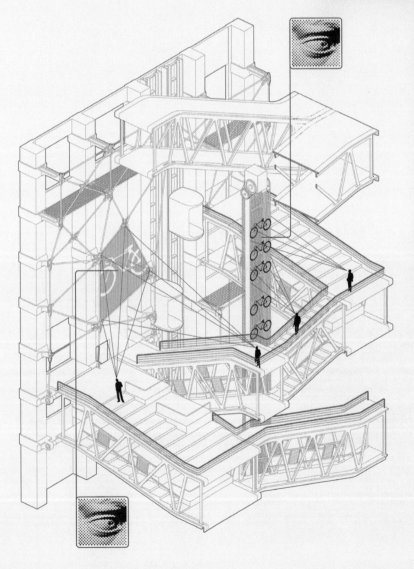

COLLAGE WORKSHOP

Instructor: **Mark Jarzombek**

Though collage as an artistic medium is close to being ninety years old, it remains a potent aesthetic. In our contemporary world where realities are complex and seamless, the principle of rupture that is inherent in collage can be used to help students get a handle on the question of 'critique' visually as well as perhaps politically. The class was designed around a series of operations around making and destroying. What the students made I destroyed—meaning I ripped apart, obscured, bent or otherwise damaged their work. I never told the students what I would do in advance. The weekly destruction of the artwork forced students to appreciate the accidental and design in concert with the accidental. Following each intervention, the students had to rebuild from the pieces. In this way nothing was produced that was a seamless whole. There was also no precise sense of ownership of the final products in the making of which many hands were involved. It was only the last person to touch and transform the collage or piece who owns it.

We moved from working with small objects, some no bigger than 1 inch square, to increasingly larger ones, on the order of 4 X 4 feet. In the process we also discussed color and color theory, a topic rarely addressed in studio culture. We worked initially solely with paper then with other materials and only toward the end of the semester did we move to paints.

The intention was to approach design completely differently from how it is done in studio, where authorship and design integrity are always respected. Both political and psychoanalytical ideas were meant to be at play. The continual attempt to demote the ego and promote aesthetic discovery in the give and take of making and destroying challenged the principle of "ownership" that is presumed to be such an important part of the conventions of design process. Everything that was made in the semester will have had by the time it was finished multiple authors.

(left) *Collage from Phase One*
(right) *Collage Interpretation from Phase Three*

AFLOAT FAST [FESTIVAL OF ART SCIENCE AND TECHNOLOGY] PROJECT

Otto Ng with Arseni Zaitsev, Ben Regnier and Dena Molnar

aFloat was an interactive installation at the MIT Chapel that produced a pool of floating lights on the marble platform. Together with the dazzles dangled on Bertoia's metal sculpture and the flicker of grace reflected on the water in the perimeter cavity, aFloat enhanced the Chapel as a place of worship for the diverse MIT community. The essence of "water without water" has inspired this work. The phenomenon of rippling water was indeed produced with a network of LEDs, piezoelectric sensors and mechanical linkages. A single touch could release an array of diminishing sparkles–a local impact on the greater whole ... a moment of chaos between points of light before serenity returns with a calm ripple.

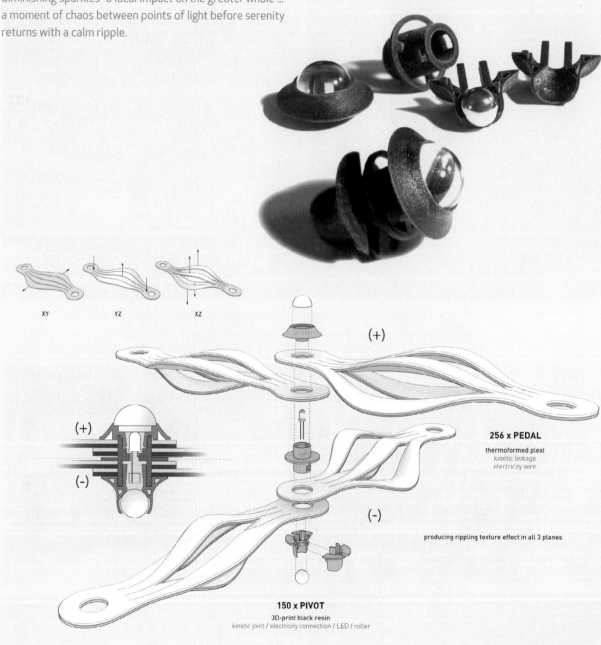

XY   YZ   XZ

(+)

(+)

(-)

(-)

256 x PEDAL
thermoformed plexi
kinetic linkage
electricity wire

producing rippling texture effect in all 3 planes

150 x PIVOT
3D-print black resin
kinetic joint / electricity connection / LED / roller

Image credit top left and right Otto Ng, bottom copyright Andy Ryan.

SOFT ROCKERS FAST [FESTIVAL OF ART SCIENCE AND TECHNOLOGY] PROJECT

Sheila Kennedy

The SOFT Rockers are smart, clean energy charging stations disguised as outdoor rocking lounge furniture. Unlike conventional 'hard' urban infrastructure, The SOFT Rocker leverages its environment in a dynamic manner by using the human power of balance to create an interactive 1.5 axis 35 watt solar tracking system. Soft power electronics designed for this project charge the 12 ampere-hour battery and store solar energy harvested during the day. Put your body weight in play with an interactive, real time energy harvesting feedback loop that senses how you orient the rocker to the sun. Charge or run any USB device from speakers to cell phones and bring your friends to enjoy cool lighting loops at night for social gatherings.

The leaf-like loop form of the SOFT rockers explores how standard softwood panels can be mass-customized to adapt their form to the latitude and sun angle of any site using parametric design software and automated fabrication with a lightweight Kuka robotic arm. The project advances digital kerfing methods developed by Christoph Schindler with wood joining techniques which enable softwood panels to be formed into a continuous undulating wood surface. The interdisciplinary SOFT Rocker project for MIT's FAST 150 event, led by Professor Sheila Kennedy and Jungmin Nam of KVA Matx in Boston, combines hi-tech and low-tech design strategies: it produces electricity but engages the body and works like furniture "by hand"; it mixes sun tracking and social dynamics; it is a site specific object and a flexible form family of 'soft' wood construction. The SOFT Rocker blurs distinctions between pleasure and work and recasts power generation as an integrated and distributed public activity rather than a centralized, singular off-site project of 'engineering'.

team:
Sheila Kennedy, James Bayless, Kaitlyn Bogenschutz, Wardah Inam, Jungmin Nam, Shevy Rockcastle, Phil Seaton, Matt Trimble, Adnon Zolij

BALLOONING (HOLLOW, THIN 3D)
NOTES ON PRACTICE
Nick Gelpi

This act of building this was like WAR. Its construction was an exercise in target practice, a process of discharging firearms, shooting all components in place with a Nail-Gun. No CNC tools were used in it's fabrication, rather old techniques of charting, mapping, reconnaissance and advancing. This construction emphasizes the independence and resilience of old technology; that of ballistic roughness and tectonic violence, as opposed to the precision of customization.

A variation of the generic POLE-BARN, this building is an EXHIBITION of LOW-TECH. A POLE-BARN is a unique building type known for expediency of construction. By embedding the POLES deep into the ground, the need for a foundation is eliminated. Instead of being weighted down by a slab, the enclosure of this building floats above the ground on POLES or piers, while every additional building component is added to the previously installed POLES. Every increasing layer of components effectively contributes to a homogenous MESH stabilizing the project like a BALLOON across its surface. This building is surface deep structurally and programmatically acting as an open container, it is an inflated hollow version of a balloon.

It remains FLAT in is collapse of parts onto a conceptual 2D structural surface. While the FRAME still supports the SURFACE, the FRAME is "of" the SURFACE, it is a felted structure stabilized through its frictions and interconnectedness.

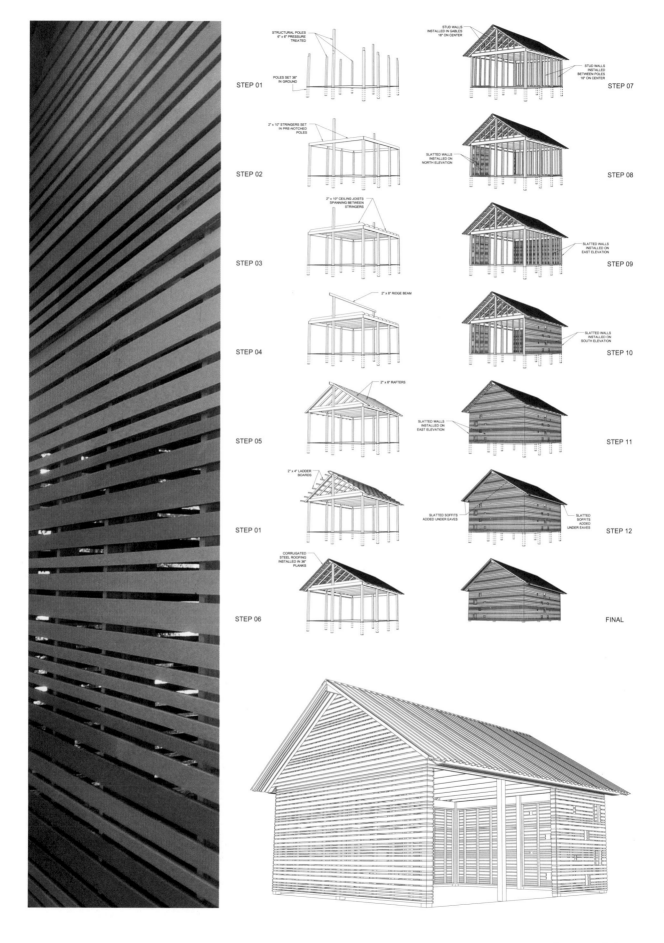

STEP 01 — STRUCTURAL POLES 6" x 6" PRESSURE TREATED / POLES SET 36" IN GROUND

STEP 02 — 2" x 10" STRINGERS SET IN PRE-NOTCHED POLES

STEP 03 — 2" x 10" CEILING JOISTS SPANNING BETWEEN STRINGERS

STEP 04 — 2" x 8" RIDGE BEAM

STEP 05 — 2" x 6" RAFTERS

STEP 01 — 2" x 4" LADDER BOARDS

STEP 06 — CORRUGATED STEEL ROOFING INSTALLED IN 36" PLANKS

STEP 07 — STUD WALLS INSTALLED IN GABLES 16" ON CENTER / STUD WALLS INSTALLED BETWEEN POLES 16" ON CENTER

STEP 08 — SLATTED WALLS INSTALLED ON NORTH ELEVATION

STEP 09 — SLATTED WALLS INSTALLED ON EAST ELEVATION

STEP 10 — SLATTED WALLS INSTALLED ON SOUTH ELEVATION

STEP 11 — SLATTED WALLS INSTALLED ON EAST ELEVATION

STEP 12 — SLATTED SOFFITS ADDED UNDER EAVES / SLATTED SOFFITS ADDED UNDER EAVES

FINAL

HOW TO MAKE [ALMOST] ANYTHING MEDIA LAB

Instructors: **Neil Gershenfeld and J. Meejin Yoon**

Provides an introduction to the resources for designing and fabricating smart systems, including CAD/CAM/CAE; NC machining, 3-D printing and scanning,molding and casting, laser and waterjet cutting; PCB design and fabrication; sensors and actuators; analog instrumentation; embedded digital processing; wired and wireless communications. Emphasis on learning how to use and integrate these tools as well as understand how they work.

ex. 1

Ella Peinovich | MArch
Wall System

The sample of compiled exercises share the goal of exploring how fabrication methods reinterpret a design during materialization, due to pixilation and machine limitations.

Seeking a double-wall screen inspired by continuous surfaces systems seen in works by Erwin Hauer and Norman Carlberg, and informed by structures found in nature like bone marrow and diatoms, each exercise sought to explore how fabrication methods may reinter,pret a design during materialization. Each of the three selected exercises seeks to re-imagine the details and craft of the connections that go into a double-wall screen. Exploring three different material and structural forms coupled with a unique fabrication method the works range from laser cut bristol board to plaster-cast, CNC surface-sculpted molds.

Exercise 01: The tension-fit laser cut kit demonstrates the use of surface folds to create a sculptural result from a flat surface. The resolution, or integrals, of the surface scores are directly related to the ratio of the severity of the curvature and the stiffness of the material. Because the modules are based in simple logic the unit can also be used to create other tensile surfaces structures, like a sphere.

Exercise 02: The 3D print exercise tests the autonomous structural integrity, yet interlocking functionality, of the double wall assembly. The interlocking assembly was developed from two offset walls, each of the walls made from an array of a stacked wall module that spans the full wall section. The function of the wall is to diffuse direct rays from the source to create an ambient light effect by scooping light and casting it onto the interior surface facing into the low-light space. The scoop could also serve as a place for an imbedded light source, and the continuous structure as a conduit for circuitry.

Exercise 03: A thin-shell, complex surface cast of a wall module utilizes of the CNC milling machine to route a laminated, double-sided mold with a non-linear intersection. The final component was first modeled in CAD software so that the surface construction could be unfolded to extract the surfaces to be milled for the mold. Complex curved surfaces are then cast as two identical halves from the same mold, which can be rotated onto the next to create a hollow composite with a 1/4" wall.

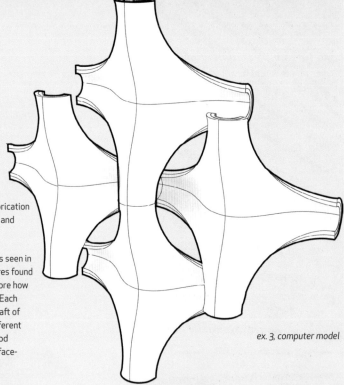

ex. 3, computer model

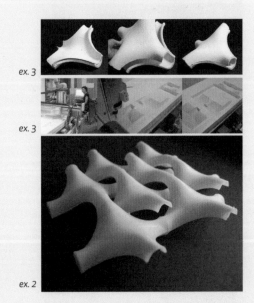

ex. 3

ex. 3

ex. 2

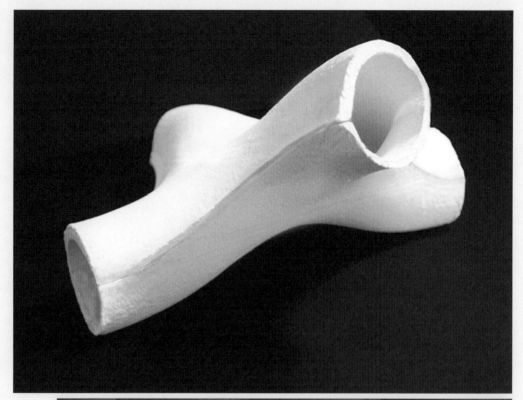

ex. 3, final prototype,
cast in hydrostone

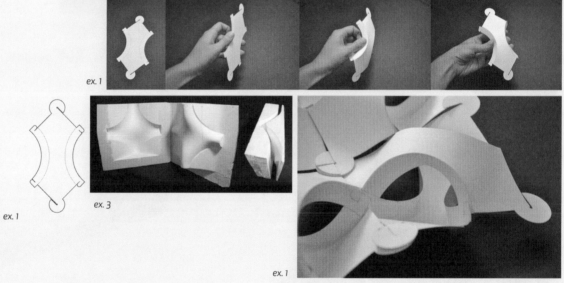

ex. 1

ex. 1

ex. 3

ex. 1

DESIGN INNOVATION FOR DISTRIBUTED ENERGY WORKSHOP

SPRING 2010

Instructors: **Sheila Kennedy and Mark Baldo**
Teaching Assistant: **Sasa Zivkovic**

The course will focus on next generation dye-based flexible semi-conductor materials (energy generation, concentration, lighting, and sensing) that are being studied by Prof. Baldo's research group. The course will consider how design research can be leveraged to create value propositions for early stage technology through approaches that consider the existing limits of new technologies, their unique physical and formal properties as well as the scale and context of their use.

The course provides a unique interdisciplinary design approach that explores technical challenges and design opportunities in the vertical integration of flexible energy exchanging materials in the fabric of the built environment. The course will enable students to understand the basic performance attributes and manufacturing and/or production processes of flexible solar materials and to explore emergent spatial, social and architectural impacts of de-centralized energy distribution in short design exercises at three scales of implementation: body, building and city. Working in interdisciplinary teams with a 'hands-on' design and prototyping process, students will develop selected design proposals and fabricate full scale proof-of-concept application prototypes capable of providing measurable results. Guests in science, design, business, and innovation will be invited to participate in class reviews.

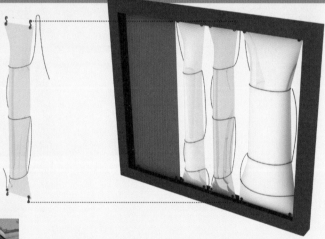

Tim Greitak, Sophie Ni, Siobhan Rockcastle | SMArchS
Solar Memory Curtains

Value Proposition
Solar powered curtain assembly for automatic sun shading

1) A low power alternative to motorized sun-shading devices

2) A "soft" and perceptually organic shading skin that can be adapted to interior or exterior curtain wall retrofits

3) Shape memory wire provides a uniquely customizable range of formal possibilities while taking advantage of the lightweight tectonics of fabric curtains.

DRAWN ANIMATIONS S.M.ARCH.S. COMPUTATION PROJECT

2011

Carl Lostritto

Architectural representation is almost always static. The productive pause of drawing invites operation, translation, deconstruction, and discourse. Drawing by hand with tactile tools is for many architects the ripest territory for thinking. A printed, plotted or otherwise digitally "output" drawing can't engender the same creative behavior. For hundreds of years it has been possible (if not trivially convenient) to mass-re-produce drawings. Only in relatively recent times, however, has digital output become so fast, ubiquitous and complex that the act of committing a design to paper has become a thoughtless and meaningless task. Producing such drawings requires little craft. With this project I explore the notion of the durational present—that the moment of perception, our concept of "now" is a period of time rather than a point in time.[1]

I produced what I call "drawn animations," artifacts of a computational process that take place over time. Instead of using a generic and externally authored process for digitally controlling print images, I have programmed a pen plotter directly with the python programming language. Because this plotter uses pens, not ink cartridges, it receives simple commands that direct it, for example, to "grab pen x; lift it up off the page; move it to this coordinate; lower the pen onto the page; move the pen with a particular speed to point y." With this infrastructure I control the drawing directly—no image exists in an intermediate state on the screen.

Resolution is both coarse and infinite. Coarse in that the width of even the finest pens exceeds that of a pixel at high resolution. But layering of lines and the imperfect behavior of the bleeding ink enable high degrees of controlled complexity. Drawings can be built up. Hundreds of lines overlapping with slight variation create tone and the degradation of the media (the pens become soft and the paper can rip) can be controlled and harnessed as a craft.

Algorithms with traceable temporal component—gaseous diffusion and a proximity web builder are used in these examples—have been adapted for direct plotter output.

Marco Fascari writes that a "facture," a term usually reserved for painting, can exist in drawings.[2] Facture is a quality or nature of a certain technique manifest in the product. The "fact" of its creation by a particular artistic process is interconnected with the subject or reference in the work. In this way, digitally produced drawings can re-engage with a cyclical design culture as tools for thinking.

1   Steven Pinker, Harvard College Professor and Johnstone Family Professor, Department of Psychology, Harvard University, describes the extent to which certain linguistic constructs, such as the "three second present" are prevalent across cultures. "Language and Thought" Panel discussion. Moderator: Irene R. Heim. MIT150 Symposium *Brains, Minds and Machines*. Wednesday, May 4, 2011.

2   Marco Frascari. *Eleven Exercises in the art of Architectural Drawing, slow food for the architect's imagination*. New York: Routledge, 2011; 10, 30.

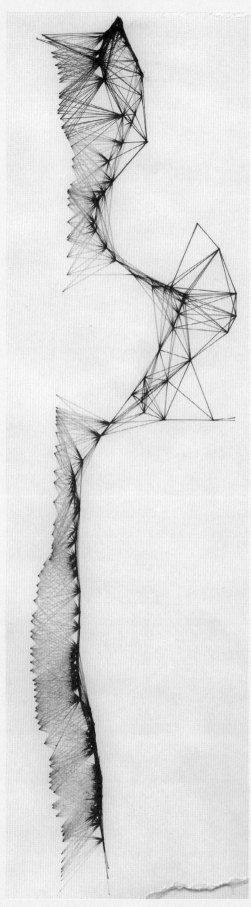

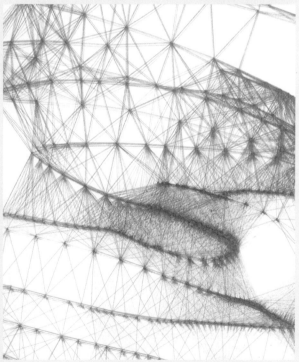

(left) **layered lines**
(top) **diffusion1**
(bottom) **web2**
(reverse) **web3**

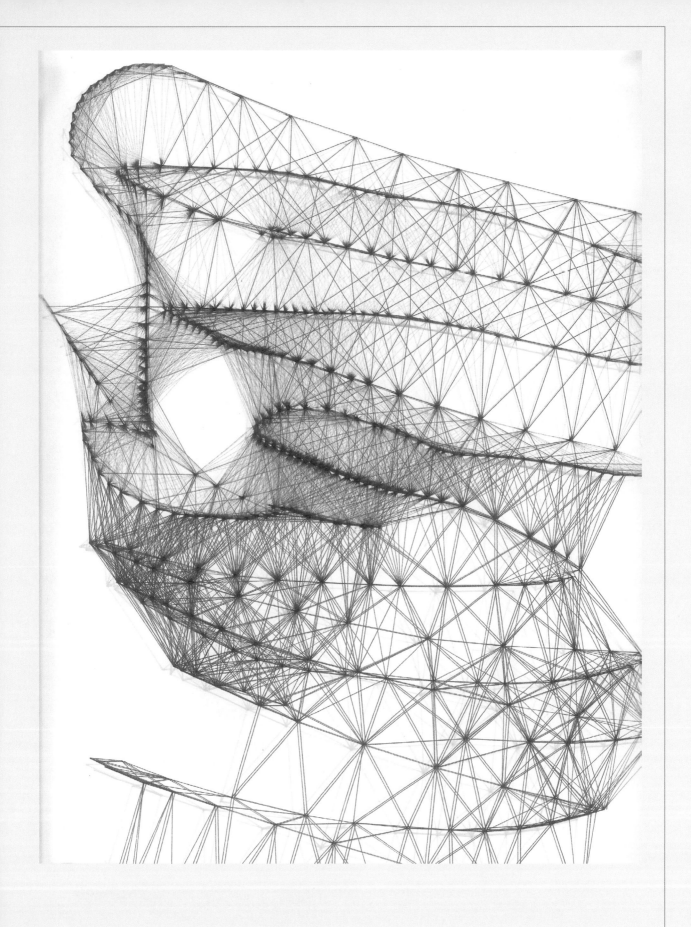

THE OPEN AGENCY PROJECT: OPERATIONS IN THE CREATIVE UNCOMMONS M.ARCH. THESIS

Haruka Horiuchi
Supervisor: **Ana Miljački**
Instructors: **Adèle Naudé Santos, Gediminas Urbonas, Antoni Muntadas**

The Open Agency Project proposes an experimental architecture office as an agency for ideas and inventions. By actively seeking unconventional design opportunities, taking advantage of loopholes in restrictive codes, and hacking/tinkering rather than master planning, this office aims to insert architectural ideas into unexpected places and spur the imaginative rethinking of familiar problems. The open-source sharing of research, process and design is embraced and DIY attitudes are encouraged in order to make good design accessible and intelligible to everyone. The Open Agency Project aspires to harness bottom-up action to transform ideas into realities, and ultimately to transform reality.

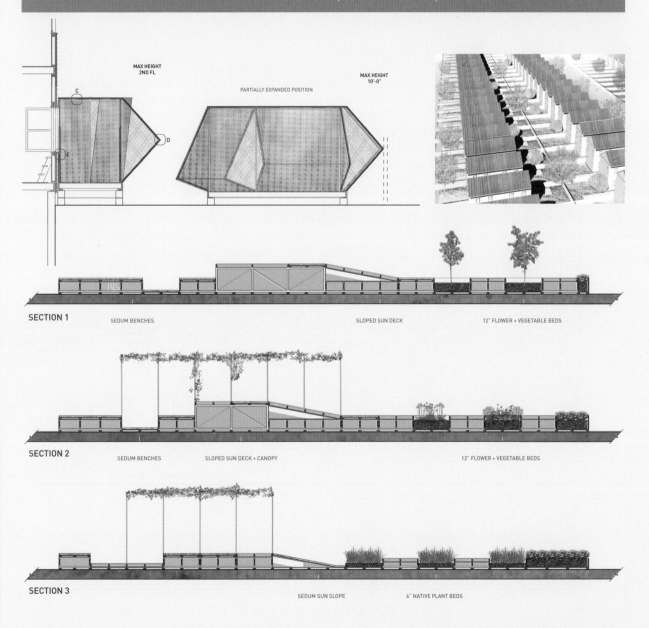

MAX HEIGHT 2ND FL

PARTIALLY EXPANDED POSITION

MAX HEIGHT 10'-0"

SECTION 1 SEDUM BENCHES   SLOPED SUN DECK   12" FLOWER + VEGETABLE BEDS

SECTION 2 SEDUM BENCHES   SLOPED SUN DECK + CANOPY   12" FLOWER + VEGETABLE BEDS

SECTION 3 SEDUM SUN SLOPE   6" NATIVE PLANT BEDS

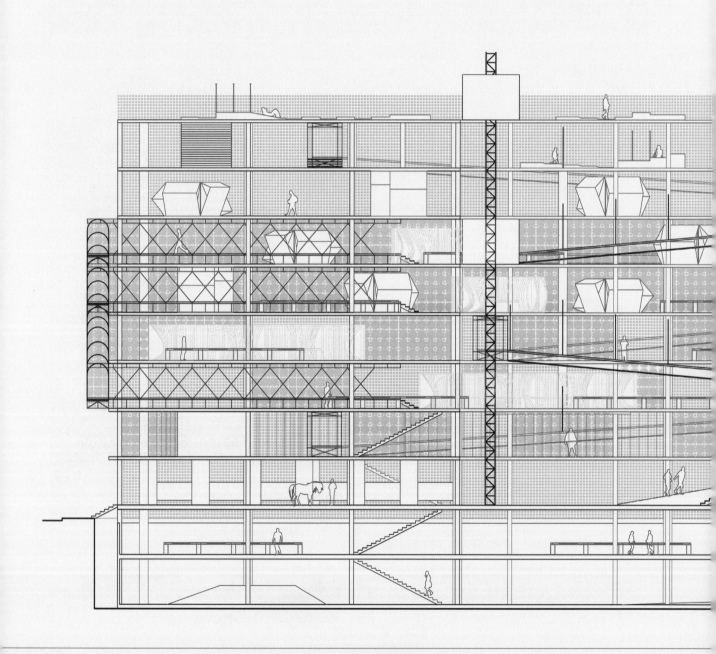

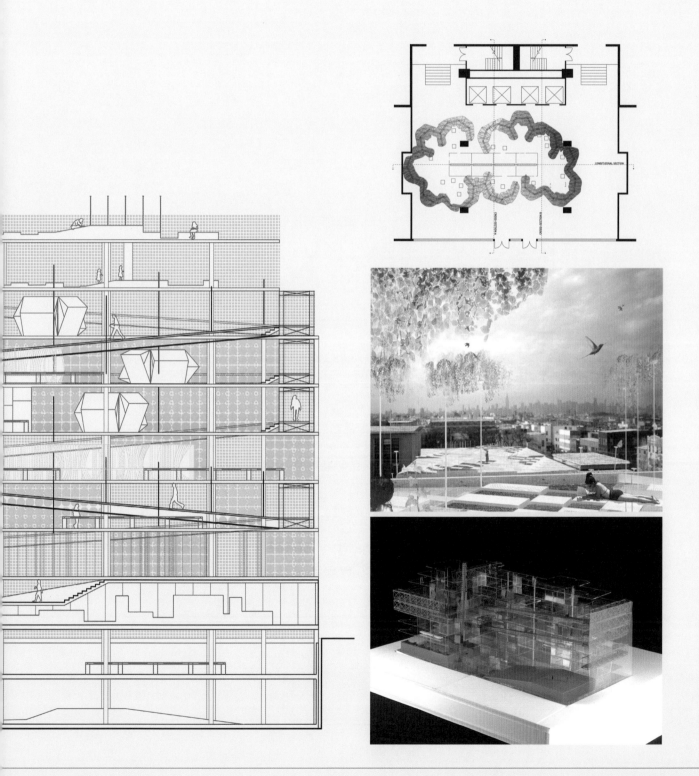

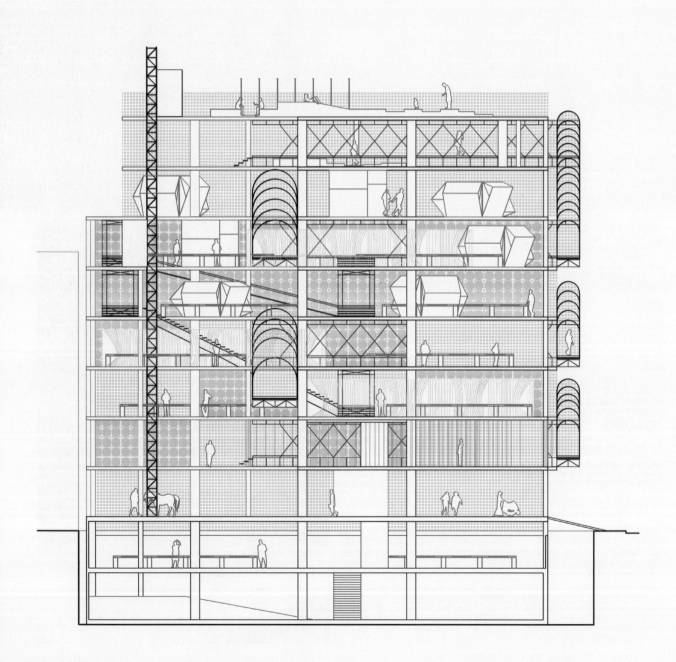

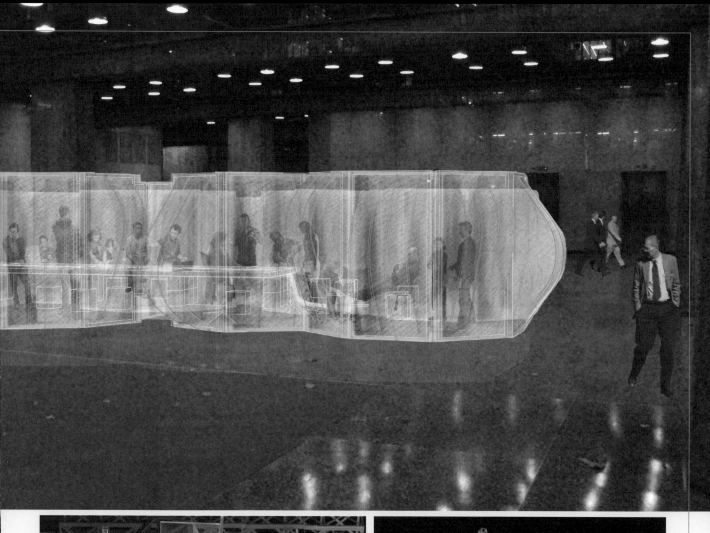

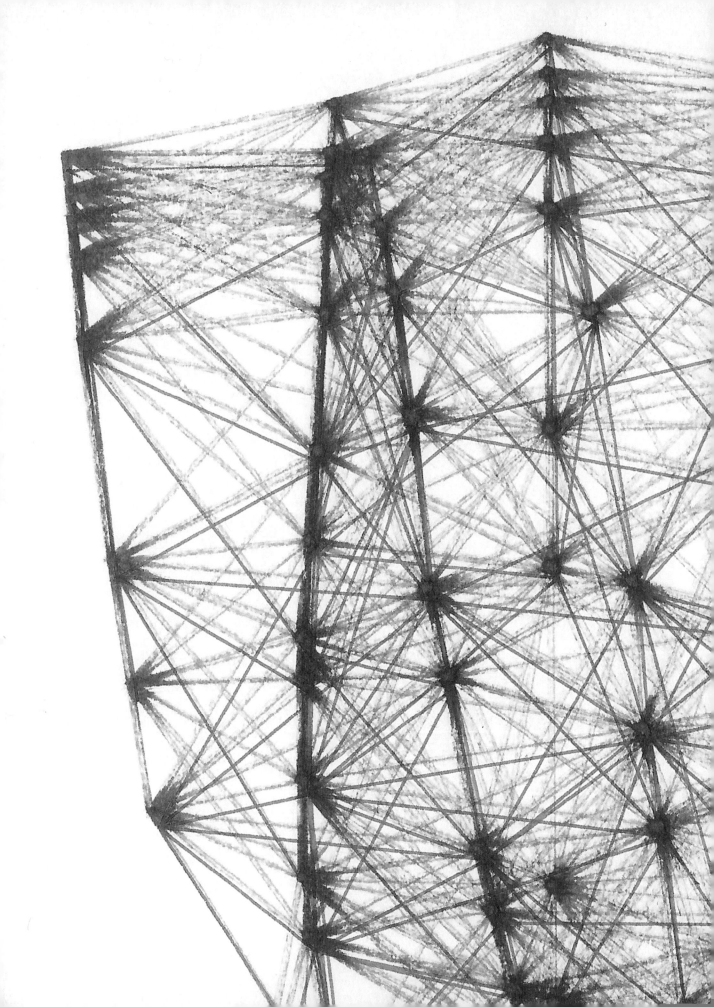

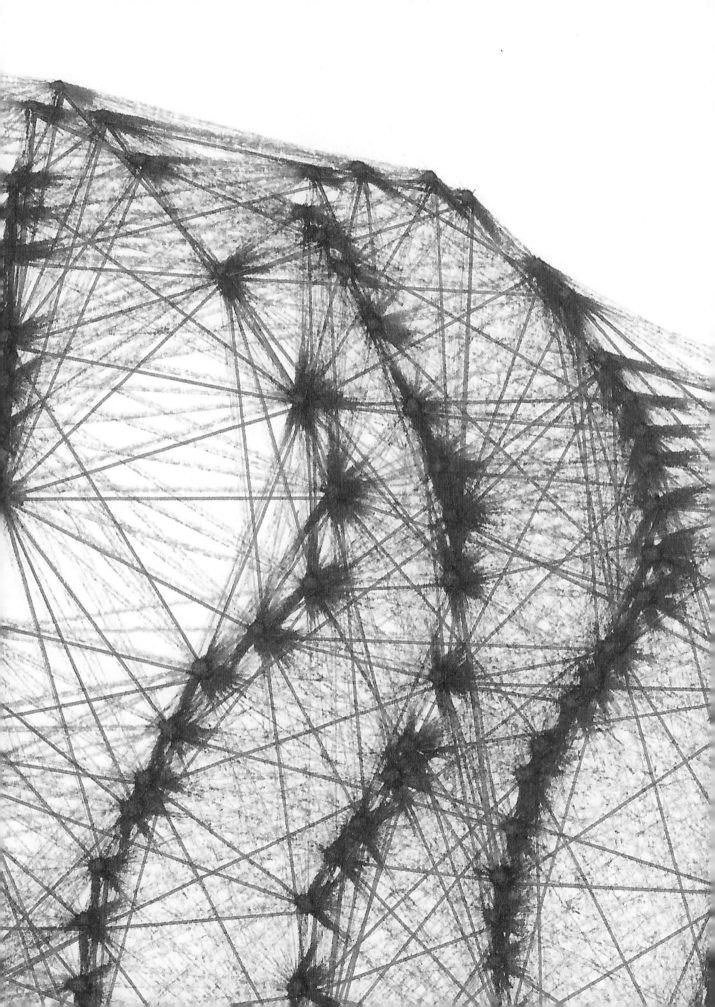

SUPPORT

TECTONICS
(DEFINITELY NOT 'CRITICAL REGIONALISM')

How can you expect an engineering solution . . . to be anything other than dumb if we impose external influences on form that are completely abstracted from any technology? Let's not forget where Modernism and the machine age came from, it came from technology . . . I don't mind coming up with a dumb solution that goes between two skins of sculpture designed by a screwed-up piece of paper, but it is not really where I get my kicks.[1]

The tectonic, on the surface (if one can encounter it there), seems like an obvious infatuation for architects. It's what we've got that's our own—we make buildings look the way they do by making constructional and expressional features meld into each other. The modernist imperative to celebrate the structural and static laws had the appearance of allowing to celebrate the very fact of architecture. But to see the opportunities inherent in thinking tectonics, it's important to realize how strong the wake of Modernism has been, and how divided the worlds of structure and form may have become. Far from imposing a unity of conception and realization forged, as Siegfried Giedion argued, within the 'truth' of chemical processes, advances in materials like reinforced concrete allowed a separation between structural logics and formal intent, and promoted a conspiracy of camouflage that continues today in the sameness imposed upon heterogeneous building elements with paint and suspended ceilings. "[C]oncrete gives the impression of homogeneity because the reinforcement remains largely unseen, extending beyond the casting only at moments of concealed connection. The relationship between structure and surface is both a visual denial and a physical correspondence."[2]

Concealment is as much an acknowledgment of the detail as is its thoughtful display, but only one of these allows for a building to speak to its users about its

Images courtesy Nader Tehrani / NADAAA.

Banq—Office dA
Boston, MA 2008

own creation. The separation of these thoughts, however, detracts from a formal and spatial consistency that can contribute materially and aesthetically to the discipline–just because you can hide how you made a building doesn't mean that the very details of it don't provide opportunities to create unique spaces within. Kenneth Frampton has written famously on tectonics, locating his interest in the reintegration of once-traditional building knowledge into the process of form-making, ultimately linking architecture's autonomy to its unique pragmatism.[3] By using structural experiments to influence formal decisions, in essence linking the two, visually and conceptually rich architecture as architecture can be developed. Rather than coming off as a structure fetishist, however, he insists: "my primary concern is with a poetics of construction rather than engineering as such, although one can flow into the other," and therein lies the potential for tectonics to extend architecture's reach–poetry.[4]

And yet, both in Frampton's conception of tectonics and that of his acknowledged predecessor in this regard, MIT's Stanford Anderson, if a certain truth or facticity of construction continues to hold forth, in present day explorations both in computationally-arrived form and experiments in new materials, this facticity may well have transposed itself from an older conception of expressive structure and material honesty to an investigation into the very mechanics–as it were–of appearance. In this new sense of tectonics, structure–what the engineer does–

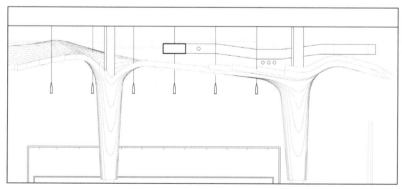

may well have been relegated to a mise en abyme, the prop in what appears to be the much more interesting theater, the play of perception triggered by building, the surfaces and formal dynamics of building; conversely, the prop is itself part of the play, to the extent that it becomes impossible to distinguish between different actors or objects in the ongoing choreography of form.

While Frampton promotes a particular reading of the architectural avant-garde as variously expressing or denying the potentials of rigorous tectonic expressionism, his is not the only mode of integrating ideas of structure into the aesthetic or ornamentational aspects of building design. In the core sequence of the M.Arch. program at MIT, students encounter an emphasis on tectonics early and often. Structures are seen as dynamic drivers of design, exciting formal problems in themselves, not just a secondary armature working away in the background. To truly experiment with structure requires a relationship to real scale, and this is where a focus on prototyping and testing is most important. From the hard-and-fast figures spun out during the annual column-crushing contest in John Ochsendorf's Structures class, to the guess-and-check-and-guess-again methods of installation design in core studio, students are actively engaged in designing and refining the detail at 1:1. Tectonics as a field of interest at MIT doesn't necessarily reflect a coherent aesthetic or style so much as an assurance of rigor, of the conceptual consistency of a design throughout its many scales. It is a mode of conversation between building components that otherwise might appear to operate independently, but it is importantly not a dogma—rule-based systems are meant to be broken, albeit consciously and with reason.

With his office NADAAA, and formerly as founder and head of Office dA, Professor and Head of MIT's Department of Architecture Nader Tehrani displays an insistent attention towards building practices and materials in terms of the perceptual effects that they might generate. In installations, furniture design, pedagogy, and practice, Tehrani's focus on the integration of construction technology is evident. Tectonics is here explored as a sort of fractal-like zooming in and out from the detail. Unlike in Frampton's reading, however, where tectonics reveal texture, the 'sensience' of the material, Tehrani's tectonics push the physical capacities of the material itself while allowing for certain patterns to emerge that are often in fact parametric or computational. His is an intellectual project as much as one of structural efficiency or honesty, so his use of tectonics is an excavatory practice, a way to mine the combination and consonance of architectural parts for clues in form, space, and surface.

In the introduction to their 2005 ARQ series monograph, *Office dA*, Tehrani and Monica Ponce de Leon identified three scales on which the conceptual priorities of the practice are based, all three orbiting around the notion of the detail.[5] Considering detail-as-joint, detail-as-seme, and detail-as-DNA creates a rich idea of what a conceptually consistent architectural project might be. On the one hand, details are necessary and ubiquitous; they form the

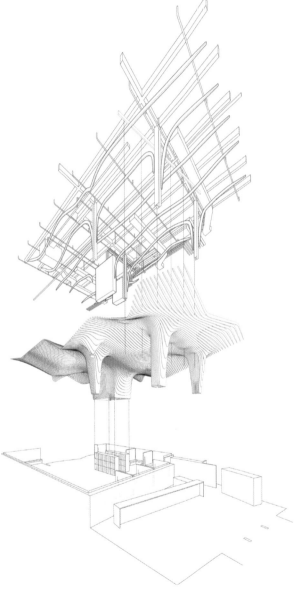

Banq—Office dA
Boston, MA 2008

Hinman Research Building—Office dA in Collaboration with Lord, Aeck and Sargent.
Georgia Institute of Technology, 2011

basis of all architecture. But in their proliferation, these opportunities are often overlooked as sites for intervention or innovation. On the other hand, a radical stance might understand the detail as the very medium through which an architect communicates his particular perspective, his ambitions with material, and his departure from the standard practice. Finally, once this appreciation of the import of the detail has been achieved, and a certain tectonic potential is revealed–if a detail can be at once so commonplace and communicative, it can also be mobilized proactively as an agent in design, as a participant in discourse. As Tehrani and Ponce de Leon explain, "our Litmus Test for this arena is the degree to which craft is transformed, to what end, and in what way it is made relevant to current debates," clarifying that the ultimate goal in every investigation is to produce new knowledge and feed it back into the discipline.[6] The tectonic here is not simply a structural concern or gravity's gift-horse, but part of a network of obsessions that contribute to a fundamentally consistent and continually relevant exploration within architecture's own language.

Unlike Frampton's regional contextualism, however, when seen in the aggregate, at the scale of the building, the effects of this very intense investigation into assembly can produce–as with the case of a Hans Poelzig or the adherents of the Neue Sachlichkeit–what Manfredo Tafuri called a kind of 'anti-grace.' Rather than produce an architecture that fits (Frampton) or fits anywhere (Foster, Pei, Gensler, SOM), this process often manifests itself in artifacts that may in fact fit nowhere, reflexively leading the mind to reflect to the elusive processes of architectural thinking and making.

One of the secret weapons in a focus on tectonics is the ability to generate and find operative patterning, dormant systems which allow one aspect of a building to bleed into another in some kind of continuum. Revealing a motif of details is more than ornamentation, though it can often serve the same purpose. Professor John Ochsendorf's research into the techniques of Guastavino tiling shows at once how simple techniques can reap enormous structural rewards, and at the same time, how beautiful these can be when exposed. Ochsendorf's book *Guastavino Vaulting: The Art of Structural Tile* (Princeton Architectural Press, 2010) is a structural history of the famous tiling family who used an innovative

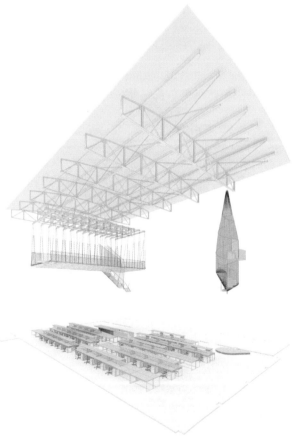

Hinman Research Building—Office dA in collaboration with Lord, Aeck and Sargent.
Georgia Institute of Technology, 2011

Photo credit: Jonathan Hillyer.

herringbone pattern to produce domed structures out of flat brick members. The scale of each brick tile, working in compression only with those few tiles around it, tells us precious little about the massiveness of the overall composition. The elements involved and their relation to one another are simple, but the effect and the structural properties are quite complex.

Extending research into practice, and furthering an intra-disciplinary notion of feeding discourse back to designers, Ochsendorf led a team of students who sought to build a version of the thin-brick dome themselves. Rather than replicating structures they already had seen work, the team used advanced structural modeling software to push the limits of what was known about these techniques. After an initial prototyping phase in the courtyard beside the Department's wood and metals shop, the team constructed a working illustration of a three-point dynamic spanning dome in New York at the Smithsonian Cooper-Hewitt, National Design Museum's "Design Now" exhibition. The implications of these findings, and the novel integration of very sophisticated technology with a historic building technique well illustrates the opportunistic nature of thinking tectonically and drawing from all possible resources.

Newton House—Office dA

It is not uncommon for Tehrani to bring his own research focuses into the studio and critiques. One exercise he developed for beginning architecture students engages directly with his tectonic project, asking students to use a single material to *turn three corners*. The difficulty comes in engaging tensile and compressive qualities, jointure and support, and complex geometry. His intent to "demonstrate the flexibility of a single medium when confronted with unconventional problems," also exposes some of the assumptions architects begin to make when using off-the-shelf techniques and materials, and that's exactly the point.[7] If one of the primary goals of architectural research in this form is to increase knowledge across the discipline, experimentation like this, where constraints are put into place to drive design, does double duty in materials and tectonics. In Tehrani's practice, the detail, while an important driver of overall design, is not wedded to a purist's notion of tectonics. It's not always structural, and that can be okay– the lightness and flexibility of associations surrounding elements in this architecture are not rigidly guarded, and a deviation from the purity of alliance between detail and skin and structure does not discount the entire endeavor.

Rather, because an exception lies in contrast to a careful consistency, cheating–exulting in exceptions–is all the more potently packed with intent.

In his introduction to Reiser + Umemoto's *Atlas of Novel Tectonics*, Sanford Kwinter writes about a new understanding of tectonics as a connection between the designer and the experiences he creates within his buildings.[8] He proposes that "the new materialism may well be a new expressionism," and it is in this light that Tehrani's projects are multivalent as expressive forms consciously enhanced by the specificity of their relationship to material and to structural logics. His most radical experimental forays have taken place in the realm of the installation. At both Harvard's Graduate School of Design, and at the Georgia Institute of Technology, he has led teams of students into experimentations with sheet materials, starting from something ubiquitous and ending with complex, unexpected results.

Projects of different scales and different uses often lead to multiple experiments on the same theme. The play with brickwork and effect in the 2003 Tongxian Gatehouse project is similar in concept to the expressive effects in Tehrani's installation work. A crossover brickwork technique is used here, which has bricks aligned at 90 degrees from their normal orientation, sticking out beyond the surface of the wall they form. This design along an otherwise planar facade served to highlight and illustrate an otherwise conventional bricking pattern. The crossing-over of two bricks at the corner of a building serves to increase its structural properties, and to perceptually zip two planes together. Bringing this detail to light and then expanding it to speak across the prominent façade activates it ornamentally, but as in similar projects, these details are never mere ornamentation. As in the Immaterial|Ultramaterial installation at Harvard's GSD, a single material becomes the focus, turning and shifting within the project to fulfill a number of different roles: tectonic and form are reciprocal: the overall form demands the precise relationships of the units, while the units determine the overall shape.

Tectonics at MIT is more a matter of pedagogy than any one practice or assignment or look. The idea of using structure and ornament indifferently not only in concert with form-making, but as an inspiration and participant in generating form itself leads to a consistent and conceptually rich project. Rigor, sometimes a buzzword for the clarity of a designer's intent across scales, is pushed as an agenda because it opens up assumptions about building assembly and requires all aspects of a building to be considered as equally integral to the final product. Professors Tehrani and Ochsendorf show in their own work and research how form-finding can root itself in eminently practical concerns and yet still push the limits of disciplinary knowledge.

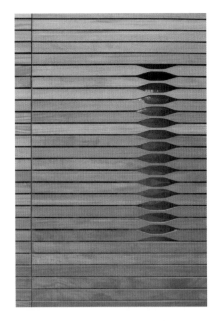

*Newton House—
Office dA*

Paul Westbury, "The Buro Happold Tapes," *Architectural Design* 72, no. 5 (September–October 2002), 77.

2   Nader Tehrani, Kristen Giannattasio, Heather Walls, John May, and Richard Lee, "Edge" in *Immaterial|Ultramaterial*. New York: George Braziller, Inc., 2002, 5.

3   Frampton, Kenneth. *Studies in Tectonic Culture; the Poetics of Construction in Nineteenth and Twentieth Century Architecture*. Cambridge, MA: MIT Press, 1995.

4   Frampton.

5   *Office dA: Monica Ponce de Leon and Nader Tehrani*. Santiago de Chile: Ediciones ARQ, 2005.

6   *Office dA*, 6.

7   "Edge" in *Immaterial|Ultramaterial*, 1.

8   Sanford Kwinter, Introduction in Jesse Reiser, *Atlas of Novel Tectonics / Reiser + Umemoto*. New York: Princeton Architectural Press, 2006.

(opposite, left to right from top)
A Change of State *Georgia Institute of Technology, 2006 (Nader Tehrani, Thomas W. Ventulett III Distinguished Chair in Architectural Design);* ***Banq*** *Boston, MA 2008 (Office dA); Helios House Los Angeles, CA 2007 (Office dA/Johnston Marklee);* ***Immaterial/Ultramaterial*** *Harvard Graduate School of Design, 2001 (Nader Tehrani);* ***Tongxian Gatehouse*** *Beijing, China 2003 (Office dA);* ***Macallen Building*** *Boston, MA 2007 (Office dA/Burt Hill);* ***Hinman Research Building*** *Georgia Institute of Technology, 2011 (Lord, Aeck and Sargent in collaboration with Office dA);* ***Mantra*** *Boston, MA 2001 (Office dA); Fabrications MoMA, New York 1998 (Office dA);* ***Boolean Valley*** *MOCA Los Angeles, 2009 (Nader Tehrani and Adam Silverman);* ***Voroduo*** *Pekin Fine Arts, Beijing 2008 (Office dA);* ***Fleet Library*** *Rhode Island School of Design, 2006 (Office dA).*

Photo credit: John Horner.

RESEARCH AS PRACTICE: MIT IN THE 70S AND 80S
MIT150 TRANSCRIPT

TUESDAY, APRIL 26, 2011

Arindam Dutta: Professor of History, Theory and Criticism, MIT
Bill Porter: Dean Emeritus, School of Architecture and Planning, MIT
John Habraken: Emeritus Professor and former Head, Department of Architecture, MIT
Alexander D'Hooghe: Professor of Architecture, MIT

This conversation has been edited for length and clarity.

Arindam Dutta: Bill, you had a very successful practice, how would you frame the relevance of research within an architecture school?

Bill Porter: I think in the seventies, we were really trying to define what research was relevant to architecture. In my own experience, for example, it started with enquiries into what urban designers did, trying to understand the logic of design, or trying to understand if there was a logic to design. And the direct benefits to me of being at MIT were that there was research going on around how to tame this machine, how to harness some of its power with a person named Arnold Ross who wrote a language called AED that allowed you to formulate logical statements in ways that were expressible directly and obviously in the language that you design. It's just that nobody had developed that until he did. That language, a level or two up from machine language, could be understood by mortals like me, and it allowed you to formulate logical statements, first-order logic. It was very simple to express in that language because of its structure. And looking back at our experience in design of the city, we tried to revisit how locational positions could be made. This is a long way from aesthetics, but you argue that urban is very good because looking at the urban edge of architectural problems gives you a lot of space because it in a sense is an expression of the edge of architecture. So there's an example where the environment in which we were in enabled us to do things that would have been impossible in other places where there was not that kind of research infrastructure. But just to conclude on my remark, we could take these large models, break them down, and look at them step by step, and we could examine the assumptions upon which each step was taken, because we were looking at industrial locations, residential locations; you could break that down into as small parts as you please. So rather than having to rely on seeing the results and making your next move based on that, that interactive component, the interactive quality of the activities made it possible to bring the designer into conversation with the materials of his or her design.

Arindam Dutta: Would you say that the computer worked for your interests in logical statements, where several designers involved a kind of inverse of themselves, such that there could be more of a leaving the terms of design? It seems like there is a desire for agreement as the basis of research which is very prevalent in both of your work.

Bill Porter: In that decade of the seventies you saw the protests and the hand-wringing around who should be making decisions politically and so on. I think there was a broadly shared impulse within our school to question the basis upon which design was performed. Whose values should dominate, and how do you discover those values? One way to bring design out in the open, to make a memorable public discourse, is to make as explicit as you can every aspect of design decision making. And if you made an assumption about a fact or an issue that should be considered or used as a basis for a decision, its challenge will be present or evident in what you're doing. That's the most obvious impulse of trying to discover what the logic of design was. It was partly an interest in how the mind worked, on my part anyway, but partly an interest in bringing into the open the processes of design so that they could become publicly debatable.

Image credit: George X. Lin.

Alexander D'Hooghe: That's incredibly interesting to hear you recount the precise terms, the reason for what you were doing. All of a sudden I can understand very well given what came before and how there was a critical need to demystify or de-mythify the architect-hero, and basically because of the enormous numbers of mistakes and errors that were made by the late modernists. What I'm struck by from a distance, and with your generation, I would say, is the following. I wanted to ask if you could correct my characterization or my reading of that moment. It's that if you look at these pictures, it becomes very apparent that it was a labor of liberation and emancipation of your generation against the dogma of beaux-arts coming back to some figures from early theory, a destruction of a bourgeois value system of architectural design, in order to replace it in a more objective viable process by which design can gain a kind of a democratic legitimacy. However the relentless use, particularly at MIT, of science and the computer and software as a stand-in for a broader scientific crisis, quickly, I'll argue, that the destruction of one church only led to the alternative replacement by another. *The destruction of a bourgeois value system and the design hero ultimately led to another orthodoxy– the scientification of the design process.* And the effective objectification of the design itself became a very prohibitive mental prison after a while. I would actually invite you to talk me down and to correct that observation. It seems from a distance, and after a while, that the orthodoxy of science, the drive of science to reproduce authority and to give legitimacy to the design process didn't really contribute ultimately to the personal emancipation and liberation, and to the personal experience of the people who went through that period. So was not one thing de-emphasized and quite simply another prison put in place?

John Habraken: I think that we should not forget that in those days, the idea of research was not so very much accepted among people teaching in architecture. And certainly not among architects. And of course the Department, the School was very rich and that was one of the things that struck me when I came–there were so many different areas of people and that one of the ways of operating in MIT was that you encouraged faculty to do their own thing, their own research, or their own inquiries. And there was very little desire to come to something that everybody shared that was apart from the intention for excellence. I remember the first time as a department head, we had to do a meeting and the review of the ACSA, when the school was evaluated, and this committee at a certain point asked, "John, what is the policy of the school–why do you teach certain things and not other things?" And my answer was that we teach the things that the faculty want to teach, and we are trying to find good faculty, so we do not define swaths and then find people, we try to find good people and let them do what they do. And we accept the fact that there are omissions and there are other things that we do. And it seems to me in retrospect that in those days, you couldn't maybe now say that a good deal of inquiry was going on, people trying to sort of push the boundaries of the field. But then the basic idea of research in a more formal sense was not yet very active and strong.

I think one of the things that I decided to do something about was that one of the central parts of teaching was the studio. And the studio teachers felt very possessive of the department, they were the center. And they saw the other faculty teaching building technology or acoustics or whatever you needed to be an architect as some kind of appendix to the thing that was necessary but had

to be taught. And one of the reasons that we decided to do the S.M.Arch.S. program for students who already had a professional degree and wanted to do research with particular faculty, was to strengthen the position of the normal architecture faculty, because they got their own students who wanted to work with them and could therefore get a Masters degree and it was a motivation to get good people in those positions. So that was pushing those areas where research could be done. And I remember that there was certainly a resistance on the architects' part because they were afraid that I would funnel money that was their money to other areas. And it was suspect because I had been doing research myself. And I tried to be fair, but the tensions were there.

Bill Porter: To add to that, the S.M.Arch.S replaced a degree called M.Arch.A.S., advanced studies. So that was a body blow to the designers; it took away the opportunity, or it could be seen this way, to teach design at an advanced level and substituted this murky, dark research thing populated by people other than, but including some of, the design faculty.

Arindam Dutta: Bill, the PLAN issue of 1980 which you edited, has a very fascinating document called "In Search of a School." So even as you were portraying the designers as possessive, on the other hand basically it was hard to find a drawing course within the school. So I'm trying to figure out about this dark thing called research and on the other hand there seems to be this absent thing based on that account called "design." It's a fascinating stand-off between an ambiguous, polymorphous cloud and something else not quite there. What was it in the context of MIT or in the contemporary situation that in the broader context interested you?

John Habraken: I also should add that among the architectural design faculty, there was something going on that you could label inquiry, experimenting. That was something that attracted me very much to MIT. I found colleagues that were attached to the interests of the urban fabric, small-scale stuff, and in their studios and in their discussions were pushing these kinds of subjects. But outside MIT was Modernism. A completely different trajectory. So the defensiveness of the architecture faculty maybe begins from all areas, but that doesn't say that they themselves were not in a kind of attitude of inquiry and interest and experiment in form. And we were all into complex forms, alternatives types of buildings, the boundary between urban design and architecture. The environmental design group was of course a very important part, although again it was a central group of people who took on the role of necessary communicators, who did the studio teaching. So in spite of the different islands of activities, everybody could find people who were doing inquiry and trying to push boundaries. And you may or may not want to call that research.

Bill Porter: We saw a shift of value or orientation after the sixties. There was a move toward more inclusiveness of people in the shaping of their own worlds, there was a reaching out to what research in other fields could bring to urban form, architectural design–there certainly was a questioning of authority as evidenced in the protests. At MIT, as many of you know, during that decade, it was difficult to whip up a great revolutionary storm because the faculty were sympathetic with this questioning that was going on in society, compared to the scenes that were happening at Columbia or at Harvard. There were protests here, I don't want to minimize that, but it was difficult to create an opposition. Probably there was a seeking for how to value the architectural effort, whatever that was, whatever your domain of action was. How do you establish a basis for it, how do you firm that basis for it, and so by these shifts came a quest for how to work in a participatory way, how to work provisionally so that you could see results immediately and then check them, change them, given your own views and impressions. And putting others, who you had brought sufficiently into the process, so that they could become a part of the shaping of their own world.

Alexander D'Hooghe: In both of your answers, my understanding is that research, yes, is an alternative to the object design of the design hero, author, whatever. But that research is not necessarily a rigorous scientific endeavor as a system of inquiry, as you called it, either through design faculty or through the S.M.Arch.S program, borrowing from other people, getting inspired from other fields. Actually, are you saying that contrary to that vulgar view of MIT from a distance, it was not attempting to legitimize itself by having the cloth of science over the top of it, the mantle of science, claiming to be legitimate in that way?

John Habraken: No, I think we could say that those who were very involved in architectural design and urban design had inquisitive minds and were trying to push boundaries and the whole thing that Bill described here. But there was also resistance, a belief that you could not formalize these things. You could not institutionalize that kind of thing. It was an experimenting with new forms, new approaches, the idea of the role of the user, and so on.

Arindam Dutta: That's certainly true of the architects, but I wouldn't say it's true of the school in general. I'm thinking of the NSF grants, and I'm thinking both your grant or Bill's grant. The legitimacy is not all a rhetorical thing. You operate within an institutional context, what kind of work you do is defined by the broader challenges, but it's mediated by the kind of strategies you adopt that you can actually get supported in order to address those issues, right? And so, I was thinking about the data idea and how it can be initiated. So, the city is the city, but when one addresses the city, what constitutes research for architecture when it is defined by what we can pursue given what there is funding for? But what does seem very clear is that the architect's voice is sort of muted, if not absent, so in a way the production of the urban scientific, it manifests itself in these particular kinds of documents that tell you how the school is trying to negotiate with the broader world. There you see a certain kind of debt–it's sort of fascinating.

Bill Porter: One of the examples of the heritage of architectural thought being brought to bear on this more experimental culture was [Stanford Anderson's] work on public spaces and how the public territory is defined, he studied Savannah. These I think were all instances where we were pitching between the culture of inquiry, gathering evidence, and reassessment of initial position, which broadly speaking one could define as the scientific method, without failing to be mindful of the architectural heritage, condition, from which we came. But the seventies I think was an era in which perhaps those were relatively new and rare, those kinds of projects, that tried to merge what we traditionally valued, and understood to be the sources of excellence in architecture, with this new experimental or participatory, more technologically-based world that we were all entering. It was a kind of wild moment in many ways. One other thing–we undertook in the mid-seventies a

study of architectural education and with several other schools as sponsors. I think it was a very important thing for a lot of people in understanding what it is they're teaching when people are learning to be architects.

Now, one can hope that this tradition would repeat, and new studies could be undertaken and the teaching of design would be subject to the kind of reflective inquiry that would help improve all the time, but I'm not aware that any other studies have been done.

Arindam Dutta: It's a good question. Where do teachers of architecture learn their teaching from? One answer could be that the existing structure is the final crit where the instructor gets critted on as much as the students do. There's a sort of on-going surface of discourse that moves every year, and that's where you might catch up on what's going on in the rest of the field.

Alexander D'Hooghe: The way you ended your argument just before, I would hopefully say that this condition of inquiry based on social sciences, inquiry about studio culture would even be continued. I think one of the reasons that it's very interesting to return to it and to bring it back is that not just at MIT, in the wider field of architectural production, we've had over the last fifteen to twenty years, an exhaustive generation of iconographies and signature architects in our field. Now there is a certain exhaustion of the individual objective hero author as architect, once more. And once more we're questioning : is there a way to de-subjectify the design process and produce a building culture that can be granted a kind of inter-subjectivity? So I do think that there is a current urgency for this line of inquiry to be picked up again. Not just at MIT, but in fact more broadly.

Bill Porter: Many people who are teaching design studios internalize what their professors told them, their exposure to this research now. The issues that were refined of the need to incorporate a much wider range of values to simply get people into the act, to question overall the traditional architectural aesthetics and the prerogative of the architect in the process, they are much more open and parallel, meaning that people who are involved in the design process start with the same problems initially and work in parallel, rather than waiting for the result of the sketch from the architect's hand. This notion of design I think should be taught somehow in the design studio, the idea of the individual quest is terribly important, and there's nothing more important in the end. Learning how to function in situations where other people have a great deal of authorship. The point is that design is much more than the expression of a particular individual, but that the individual is finding some deep aesthetic satisfaction in what they happened to have done.

Julian Beinart: MIT has historically been rather reluctant in pursuing itself publicly, as advertising. When I came to MIT I was told by Maurice Smith that we are the best underground story in the world, saying that we relished the fact that we do not extend ourselves, we do not have a public relations department, which is odd for a modern enterprise. So with the education study Bill described, like many of the other things which followed research, there was no strategy for putting it forward as a major event in modern history.

John Habraken: I would like to second that, because I think it is a very important issue Julian is raising. And I remember that I tried very hard to get this inquisitive design faculty that we had, doing these very interesting things that nobody saw, to convince them to go out and publish and write and show things. And I remember that we had a separate evening sometime in Boston in which we called everybody together and said, "You've got to come out, and if you believe in something, let people know!" It didn't happen because in that day, they still felt so vulnerable in their own inquiry, there was resistance to having a dialogue with the outside world. It was almost impossible to bring in a post-modernist to talk to the students, to have a discussion, and I think we did the students a disservice in not doing these things because of this insularity, this lack of ability to come out and say what we really believed in.

Andres Sevtsuk: I'd like to go back a second to that topic of relevance or research in architecture: I think the main challenge remains as viable today as it was in 1970–we're still struggling, figuring that out. One of the key culprits in this story that I hear a lot is that the scientific method is unfit to the types of problems that mount and the speed of decision making in design is just way beyond anything that natural science methods can handle, et cetera. But what I found really compelling, was that there's another

way of looking at it, and that one has more to do with asking the right questions with the methods we have, and actually focusing on the questions themselves and trying to understand. I'd like to hear you comment on where we stand from the two-part problem of one, are we asking the right questions in today's world of research in architecture, and two, do you think this problem of methods and the relevance to the types of questions we're dealing with is the central one?

Bill Porter: This session was titled, "Research as Practice". One of my beefs is that in practice, the fee structure is just so miserably constructed, that it does not allow for methods other than a very expedient dealing with a problem already defined and with methods already known. If you depart from that, you lose money. So as a profession, it's very difficult to enter with these new methods. And if you look at projects where there's been innovative work, the resources available to the design team exceeded those that would be available to an ordinary design project. It was an already-existing research institute that somebody was participating in, hooked up to a research lab at some place, there was extra money poured in by some manufacturer who wanted to make sure that the process was exemplary, it needed supplementation in order to achieve any level of innovation. *So research as practice I think doesn't fit very well into the structure of contemporary practice.* On the other hand, if you were to imagine methods that grew upon additional disciplines to architecture, that allowed for learning as an integral part in the process of design, that allowed for the shifting of the initially stated agenda as the design evidence accumulated, you would have a new paradigm.

Unidentified Audience Member: The thing that occurs to me in the subject of a discourse about research and practice, the word that comes to my mind is specialization, and it's one of the most difficult things that our profession, and our education, deals with. I think it's difficult to talk about research and practice unless we come to grips with specialization. And I think our profession and our educational institutions don't know how to do that very well. We still see ourselves as generalists. But yet the profession, in its most robust fashion, is increasingly specializing.

Arindam Dutta: It's not just the architects. The engineers are now taking over planning. Arup now does vast city stretches that they put in, because they can fund the research.

Bill Porter: I think the key question is specialization as research, and we just don't know how to deal with it very well.

John Habraken: One point, because if we're talking about the seventies, I think it should be mentioned that it's also the time that the PhD programs were introduced. And Stan Anderson and Julian Beinart and Bill were very much involved in that. And that, of course, was one of the most important issues to boost research and bring research into the forefront.

Bill Porter: And just an afterword on that, I think that's terribly important. In contrast with Berkeley, which had produced a PhD shortly before ours, ours was focused on History, Theory, and Criticism, whereas theirs was generally across all the fields. And I think that difference is a mark of importance, showing that at MIT we respected specialization very, very much.

EDGE INCUBATOR
NOTES ON PRACTICE AND PEDAGOGY
Marc Tsurumaki, Lewis Tsurumaki Lewis Architects

I.

The project for the Fall 2010 Studio negotiated between optimism and paranoia, the utopic and the catastrophic. Examining the potential to rethink received architectural formats based on emergent technologies and new environmental criteria. The studio engaged specific programmatic and performative imperatives to catalyze the architectural imagination. The impetus for these investigations was the impending rise in sea level due to global warming predicted for Boston Harbor and its environs over the course of the next 50 to 75 years, and it's implications for the city. Current models incorporating rapid ice melt scenarios project up to 5 feet of water level rise by 2080–a condition that, in combination with more frequent and severe storms, would have a potentially devastating impact on the metropolitan area (estimates of financial loss run as high as $460 billion). A change in sea level of this magnitude would result in a dramatic transformation of the geography of the region, inexorably redrawing the coastline across currently populated areas. Such scenarios invoke dystopian images of a drowned world out of apocalyptic science fiction, giving rise to corresponding architectural fantasies of adaptation, resistance and transformation.

Envisioning Hudson Square, Friends of Hudson Square Design Charrette, NYC, LTL Architects, 2007
The design of this commissioned study for a developing area on Manhattan's West Side exploits the collision between two conflicting urban paradigms: the 1811 Commissioner's Grid of Manhattan and the early Twentieth Century superblock. Engaging two existing, multi-block structures–the St. Johns Center and the UPS distribution facility–the design extends the interrupted east-west street grid of nearby Greenwich Village over the roofs of these architectural monoliths in the form of a series of elevated housing bridges. Literally piggybacking onto the existing fabric, the proposal activates these outmoded structures, producing a new form of three-dimensional urbanism.

Notwithstanding the relative accuracy of these predictions, they generate a fertile territory for experimentation regarding architecture's role in urban, infrastructural and ecological systems. Projects like *On the Water*, for example, and the attendant *Rising Currents* exhibition at MoMA in the Spring / Fall of 2010 (which included work by LTL Architects and four other teams), leveraged these impending conditions to advocate for new forms of soft infrastructure–as opposed to the conventional 'hard' systems of sea walls, levees and the like–that assume a greater degree of integration with natural systems and a more benign relation to wildlife habitats. Relative to architecture, questions of sea level rise open up the possibility of new configurations based on the function of water as a performative element in the design process, rather than a purely visual or picturesque feature. While critically addressing the issues provoked by these narratives of catastrophic change, the studio sought to exploit the impetus they provide for accelerating the architectural imagination.

Arthouse at the Jones Center, *opened 2010*
Contemporary Art Space, *Austin, TX; LTL Architects*
Located in downtown Austin, Arthouse is a renovation and expansion project of an existing contemporary art space, currently a rich hybrid between a turn-of-the-century theater and a 1950s department store. LTL seeks to amplify this accumulation of history through a series of integrated tactical additions. In conjunction with the programmatic expansion of the gallery and office spaces, our design amplifies the visual dialogue between the art and the surrounding environment.

Acknowledging the seriousness of the larger ecological, political and social issues entailed, the focus of the studio was on engaging these emergent conditions opportunistically to challenge received assumptions regarding architecture and its relation to natural systems. Analogous to the often bizarre-seeming adaptations of biological organisms to extreme environmental factors, inhabitation of such an insecure milieu requires invention, agility, and a radical rethinking of commonplace notions of stability, permanence, structure, ground and enclosure.

Rising Currents: Water Proving Ground, *MoMA and PS1 Contemporary Art Center, LTL Architects, 2010 (www.moma.org/risingcurrents)*
LTL Architects was approached by MoMA and PS1 Contemporary Art Center to participate in an unprecedented project, "Rising Currents," which was exhibited at MoMA, New York from March 24–October 11, 2010. Five teams of architects, landscape architects, and urban designers addressed one of the most urgent challenges facing the nation's largest city: sea-level rise result- ing from global climate change.

LTL's site at the northwest corner of the New York Harbor that includes Liberty State Park is a highly constructed landscape–a result of landfill for ship to rail transfer–that faces complete inundation by 2080. By tactically adjusting the site's historic fill, Water Proving Ground preserves this area for public use, proposing a vibrant new amphibious landscape continually activated by rising tides.

Moreover, the project questioned the dominant tendency in recent waterfront planning to repurpose the industrial edges of coastal cities primarily as recreational zones. As cities have transformed from shipping and manufacturing as sources of capital toward experience and entertainment- based economies, the maritime zones that fringe these metropolises are frequently converted to parks, shopping complexes and leisure activities. While providing increased and vital public access to waterfront resources, this tendency towards a monoculture of the edge belies a

potentially richer mix of activities and uses, and often fails to engage the dynamic history of these sites. To this end, the studio reconsidered what the notion of a productive waterfront might mean in the context of the 21st century–suggesting new confluences between emergent economies and coastal ecologies. The program of a 'green tech' incubator (derived from an actual city-issued RFP for the site) on the edge of Boston Harbor provided a jumping off point for these speculations, necessitating a direct relationship between the building proposal, the site and larger urban and natural systems.

II.

The projects in the studio exploited these conditions in a variety of ways. The inherent dynamism of water and the fluctuating conditions of the harbor provided the basis for morphologies whose geometry deliberately amplified the impact of tidal flux. Rather than reinforcing a rigid divide between land and water, these projects deployed multiple 'grounds', diagonal surfaces and shifting edges to generate unexpected experiential, spatial and programmatic effects. In these cases water becomes an architectural medium –albeit one whose characteristics are in opposition to conventional architectural principals of stability, permanence, and stasis.

One variant of this approach involved the production of a synthetic 'ground' that would provide a stable architectural counterpoint to the instability of the given site and its potential inundation. The dialogue between an artificially constructed datum and the fluid terrain below set in motion a series of sectional interactions that inverted the expected relationship between building and site. Instead of being built from the 'ground up', this project was conceived from the top down. In this way, roof became ground and the underside of the building became its primary façade, literally turning the conventions of the building upside down in response to the absence of any reliably stable reference point.

In other cases, questions of production and productivity provided the primary driving force for the design. For example, the spatial and logistical protocols of aquaculture became the catalyst for an interlaced network of fish farms, offices, and public spaces. A close investigation of the technologies and practices associated with the cultivation of various marine species generated a taxonomy of spatial types that formed the basis for the project. These conditions were combined with corresponding human activities based (for instance) on similarities in the movement patterns of fish and the circulation logics of various programs.

III.

In these cases and in others in the studio–the approach paralleled the design methodology we utilize in our own practice, not only in the context of *Rising Currents*–where we were explicitly interested in the performative potential and productivity of water as an architectural medium–but in our work in general. In all of our projects, regardless of scale, typology, or context, constraints are seen as an opportunity to be exploited for their capacity to destabilize received ideas and generate unforeseen possibilities. Paradoxes, idiosyncrasies and contradictions arising from the often competing requirements of the project are looked for–not to be elided but to be taken advantage of and amplified as a generator for the architectural strategy.

The extreme case of global sea level rise is only the most obvious example of such a constraint–in that it generates a demanding set of performative criteria that in turn open up new trajectories for architectural speculation. For our project in the *Rising Currents* exhibition at MoMA–*Water Proving Ground*–maximizing the coastline of the existing site through the manipulation of landfill provided not only the defensive strategy, but a means of optimizing

the intertidal zone for new uses and effects based on the dynamics of water. Outside of such a dramatic example, however, there are specific parameters in each project which can be harnessed to drive a response.. At Arthouse at the Jones Center, the rich history of the existing building, revealed in its structure and form, suggested an approach that would preserve and intensify the extant qualities of the architecture while integrating a series of tactical insertions. At Hudson Square–an urban proposal for downtown Manhattan–the negotiation between the grid and two existing megablock structures provided the impetus for a multi-level urban hybrid that literally piggybacked onto the extant buildings, producing an elevated public landscape and reconnecting the city with the water's edge. In each case, the design approach arises not from a predetermined set of formal techniques, but rather through a close examination of the parameters of the project. In this way, the seeming limits, prosaic requirements and unique idiosyncrasies of the project are transformed into a source of invention, play and productive opportunity.

EDGE INCUBATOR OPTION DESIGN STUDIO

Instructor: **Marc Tsurumaki**
Teaching Assistant: **T. Buck Sleeper**

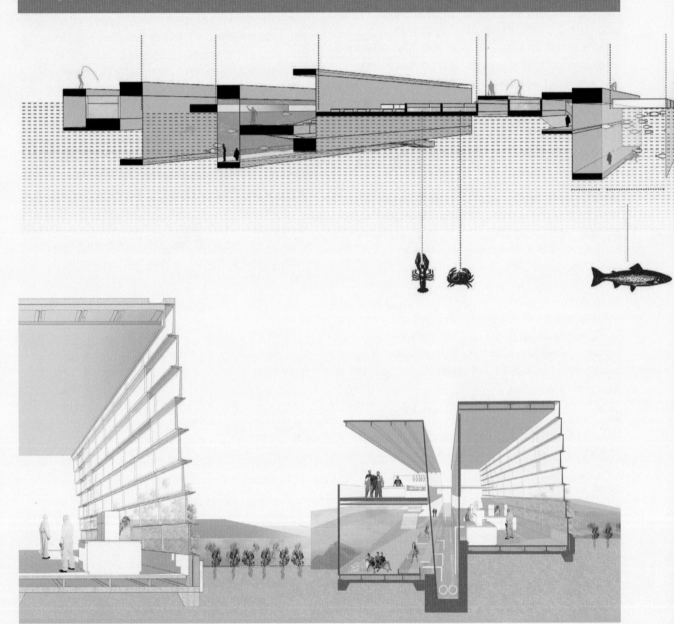

Kian Yam Hiu Lan | MArch
Fish Forms

This studio is an exploration of South Boston Waterfront as "Innovation District", which comprises a new "state of the art" incubator for emerging entrepreneurial businesses involved in sustainable technologies. This project focuses on aqua farming research, suggesting that these industrial practices could suggest new typology in waterfront industrial buildings. While fish farming is an industrial process involving high specificity related to dimension, flow and sequences. After all, such specificity suggested that fish-farming have an inherited architectonic properties related to proportion, form and organization.

Yushiro Okamoto | MArch
Edge Condition

This project questions the typical water's edge condition characterized by a
fringed or fingered edge that typifies many post-industrial urban waterfronts.
While this strategy, most commonly occurring as piers extending out over the
water, provided an effective maritime typology, it also potentially isolates the
public from the water's edge. My proposal inverts this relationship producing
an internalized artificial channel that extends from the city to the harbor and
directing a fingered edge inward to allow for public engagement with this
new urban estuary and the various marine industries it supports. A series of
fingers—part building, part landscape access the dynamics of water from both
above and below, maximizing human interface with the water.

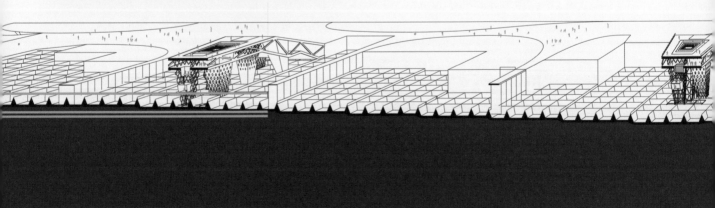

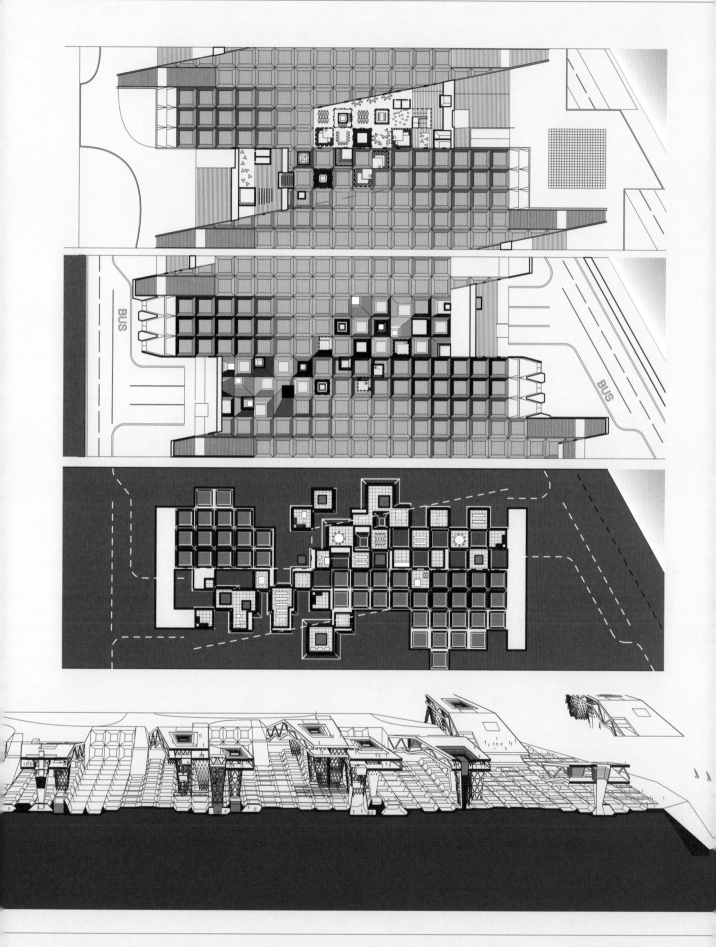

Sasa Zivkovic | MArch
Archi Punk

Fun Palace vs. *Biblical Flood*: The utopian bio-tech edge incubator at
the Boston waterfront is doomed by dystopian scenarios such as global
warming and sea level rise. The studio faces a complex web of local and
global interactions, most of which form conflicting, opposite agendas. Some
dichotomies were translated into architecture: the urge to protect the city
from the water (bunker) vs. the wish to connect to the waterfront (field), the
anarchy of the post-industrial wasteland (urban hair) vs. the new corporate
program (incubator), the cleanness of the waterfront (wooden decks) vs. the
dirtiness of the hairy marshlands (urban hair), the *corporateness* of business
(incubator) vs. the anarchy of innovation (incubator)...

This building is an inherently cynical proposal but at the same time, beyond its
surface, and contained within it's cynicism, lie spatial opportunities for a new
type of waterfront architecture.

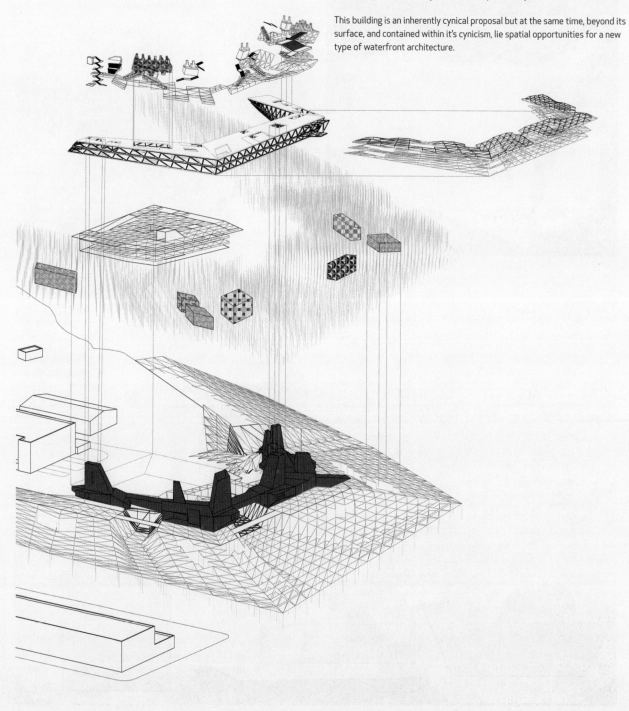

PERFORMANCE THEATER COMPLEX CORE 1 DESIGN STUDIO

Instructors: **William O'Brien Jr., Nick Gelpi**
Teaching Assistants: **Skylar Tibbits, Adela Kalenja**

Instructors: **William O'Brien Jr., Ashley Schafer, Skylar Tibbits**
Teaching Assistants: **Masoud Akbarzadeh, Theodora Vardouli, Joshua Cotten**

The program for this exercise is an annex theater building with three individual performance theaters for the Institute of Contemporary Art in Fort Point Channel, to be located at the intersection of Summer Street and West Service Road. The site has a 'double ground' condition with a ground level on Summer Street which is sectionally-contiguous with South Station, and a ground level at West Service Road which is sectionally-contiguous with the Institute of Contemporary Art. In addition to accommodating the specified theater programs, the project must provide a public means of access between both levels through the building that acts as a public thoroughfare. The figuration of the theaters in plan and section should act as catalysts for rethinking relationships between inside/outside, public/private, and their possible intersections.

Rules & Constraints of Note:
1. The project must be conceptually understood as filling the whole volume of the site—as defined by the boundaries on Summer Street, West Service Road, and the two adjacent buildings—at a maximum of 30' above the height of the building fronting Summer Street.

2. Designs must provide a public means of circulation open at all times from Summer Street to West Service Road through the building. Public circulation must also be provided to a public viewing platform that is located in the top 1/3rd volume of the site.

3. In addition to theaters, other program includes a multi-purpose hall, ticket booths, projection booths, changing rooms, other back of house spaces, restrooms, and storage as needed.

Cecilia Ho | MArch
William O'Brien Jr., Instructor–2009
Continuous Hinge

This project aims to revive the liveliness in the area by introducing a series of theatres with public access. The theaters are hinged together, spanning across A Street and cantilevering over Summer Street, to create framed space as display to pedestrians coming from different directions. The typical theatre unit will aggregate to form a continuous path that holds circulation, support program and auxiliary together with the theatre. The gesture of hinging leads to a double helix circulation path so that programs can be separated, linked and crossed with each other making possible interactions between public and private space.

The geometric configuration of theatres is based on views looking out from the theatres and looking into the theatre on both A Street and Summer Street. The intersected central space, the public cafe, will allow theatre users to see downtown and Southeast Boston. Pedestrians will also be able to look into the theatre through the exterior atrium without entering. Misaligned materials highlight the edges of the system. Applying such misalignment to floor slab creates structural mediation, controls view and lighting orientations, and introduces programmatic controls.

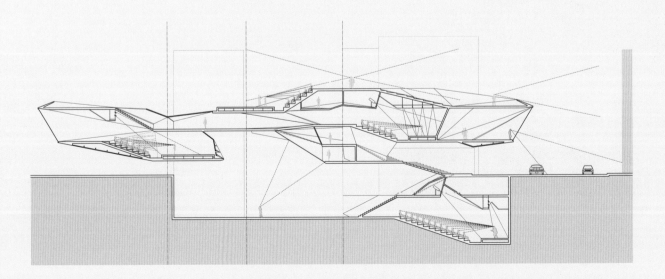

Kyle Coburn | MArch
Ashley Schafer, Instructor–2010
The New Edge: Seating Envy

Due to the importance of public space within the theater typology as identified in multiple precedents, the existing offering was investigated for the site of the theater complex in South Boston. What this revealed was a severe lack of true public space in the surrounding area; the public areas that did exist were generally uninspiring and had little prominence within the urban context.

As a reaction, the project slates the public and theater spaces (semi-public) with equal weight, interlocking the two volumes in order to generate a friction or tension between the them, providing an opportunity to question the traditional relationship between paid theater seating and the unpaid public programmatic necessitates.

In order to distinguish the public and semi-public, the public volume is articulated as a "transparent poché". Opposing the conventional soaring glass atrium the public areas are congested with a mesh of structure, circulation, seating, etc. The grain of this mesh becomes extremely fine as it meets the theater volumes and opens as it moves towards the street. What this facilitates is lack of need for a strong boundary between the theater and public spaces, a gradient occurs where the public space (unpaid) has views directly down into the theater below. These views become increasingly obstructed as one moves away from the theater spaces. To extend this notion, as the grain of the public space meets the theaters, it breaks down into varying-scale "box seating" thus establishing a complete subversion of the role of box seating within the traditional theater complex.

The unpaid public areas / box seating becomes a backbone for the design, lining the 900 seat theater on the uppermost portion of the complex and then moves down lining the 400 and 250 seat theaters below. The box seating, as defined within the grain of the public volumes serves to accommodate the central circulation, casual seating and gala areas for the project.

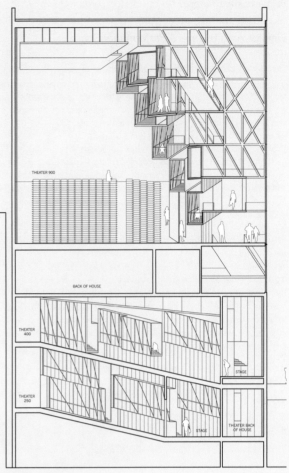

SECTION - VIEWING SOUTH

Erioseto Hendranata | MArch
Skylar Tibbits, Instructor–2010
Linkage Architecture: A Performance Space

DYNAMIC RELATIONSHIP The project is an attempt to explore the possibility of a theatre where dynamic relationships between the performing and the non-performing elements are expressed tangibly. Using a system based on the idea of linkage, the theatre is divided into smaller reconfigurable spaces that in turns create interconnected performance spaces.

NEW TYPE OF PERFORMANCE The system challenges both the notions of performance and architecture. Spatially, each of the six possible configurations opens up opportunities for dramatic experience—governed by gravity and eyesight. Consequentially, the kinetic performance requires specific types of instant, succinct, and abrupt shows as opposed to more classical notions of performance.

RHYTHM & SEQUENCE Each linkage moves and re-configures itself throughout different scenes of the shows. Three rigid blocks operate as foyer spaces while the other five loose blocks are constantly re-adjusted. The outermost linkages are the dance theatres while the two combined in the middle are those of drama, which require more space. Externally the ground becomes an open-air theatre where impromptu performance can occur. While not in use for either performance or practice, the block goes onto vertical position notifying the abeyance of the theatre. Altogether, the global shape of the theatre is constantly re-configured through local changes on each linkage.

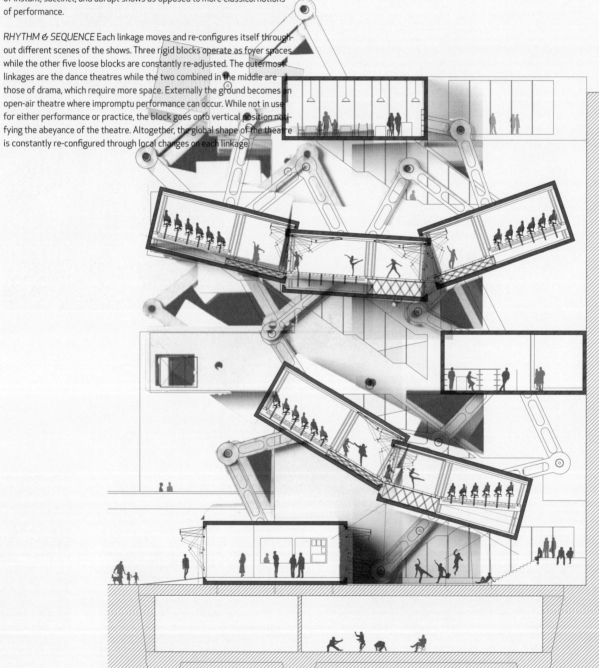

UNFLAT PAVILION FAST [FESTIVAL OF ART SCIENCE AND TECHNOLOGY] PROJECT

Nick Gelpi

A freestanding pavilion, created by flexing two dimensions into three, this house deploys a fabrication system used to create a membrane, which is simultaneously structural, functional and representational in a single act. Entirely constructed of laminated plywood, a strain relief pattern is cut into flat plywood stock which transforms into three-dimensional architectural features. Flat sheets are bent and unfurl into skylights, columns, buttresses, windows and vents, in the act of becoming UNFLAT. This building is the analogue of a "Hologram," embedding three dimensional information into a two-dimensional flat surface. In the act of UNFLATTENING, more complex information emerges from its surface.

This project demonstrates an architectural role reversal across its surface. On one elevation, a soft skin is hung on a structural frame. On the other elevation, the skin becomes structural, lifting the frame from the ground, inverting the normative structural hierarchy in an act of tectonic confusion. The project uses a promising method of fabrication with flexures, as many hundreds of parts become discreet, yet remain continuously attached to the sheet, eliminating the need for fasteners. This structure isn't hard, heavy, bulletproof, or monumental. It is modest, soft, cheap, low-tech, and full of holes.

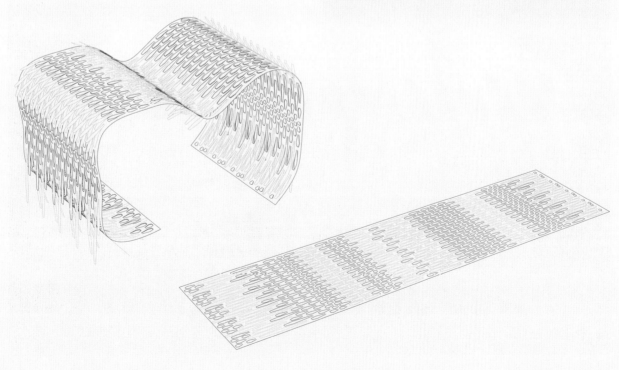

Photo credit: Anita Kan.

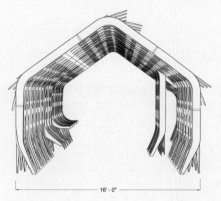

① ELEV SIDE RIGHT
1/4" = 1'

16' - 0"

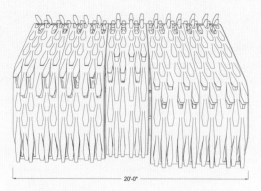

② SKIN ELEV REAR
1/8" – 1'

20'-0"

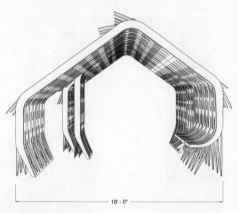

③ ELEV SIDE LEFT
1/4" = 1'

18' - 0"

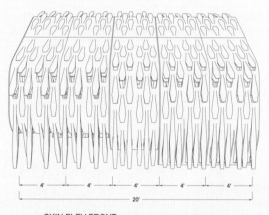

④ SKIN ELEV FRONT
1/4" = 1'

4'   4'   4'   4'   4'

20'

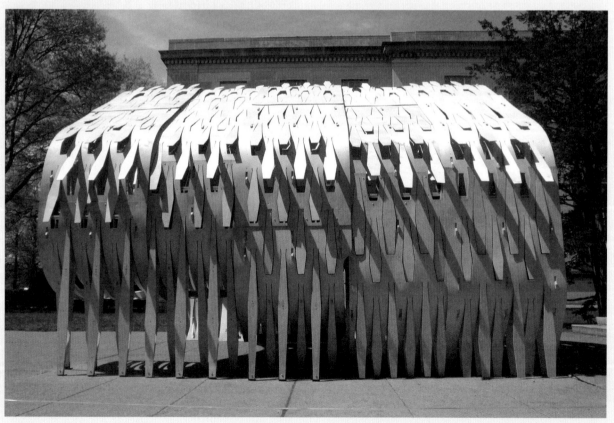

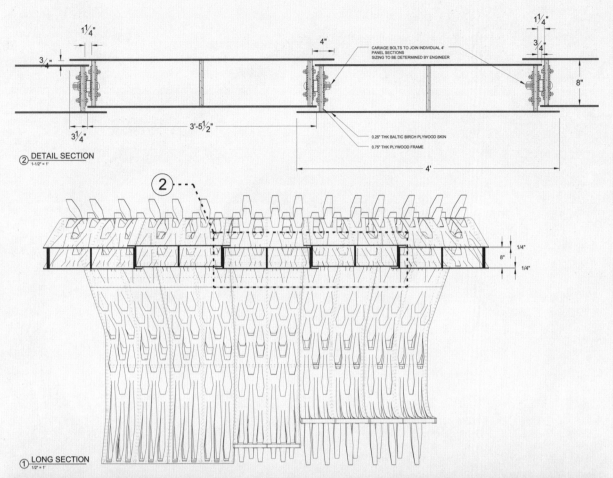

1¼"

3/4"

1¼"

4"

3/4"

CARIAGE BOLTS TO JOIN INDIVIDUAL 4'
PANEL SECTIONS
SIZING TO BE DETERMINED BY ENGINEER

8"

3¼"

3'-5½"

0.25" THK BALTIC BIRCH PLYWOOD SKIN

0.75" THK PLYWOOD FRAME

4'

② DETAIL SECTION
1-1/2" = 1'

②

1/4"

8"

1/4"

① LONG SECTION
1/2" = 1'

Photo credit NRG

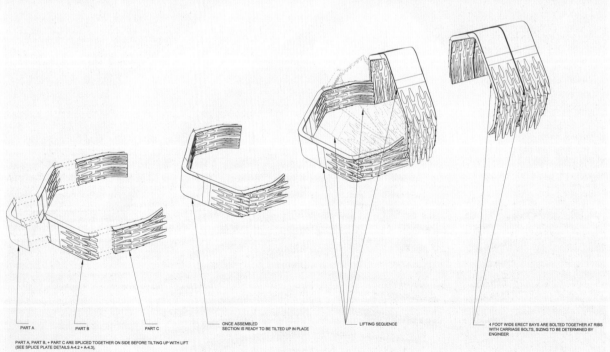

Photo credit: Anita Kan.

PART A   PART B   PART C   ONCE ASSEMBLED   LIFTING SEQUENCE   4 FOOT WIDE ERECT BAYS ARE BOLTED TOGETHER AT RIBS
                                                       SECTION IS READY TO BE TILTED UP IN PLACE   WITH CARRIAGE BOLTS, SIZING TO BE DETERMINED BY
                                                                                                                   ENGINEER

PART A, PART B, + PART C ARE SPLICED TOGETHER ON SIDE BEFORE TILTING UP WITH LIFT
(SEE SPLICE PLATE DETAILS A-4.2 + A-4.3).

OBJECTS IDENTICALLY CONCEIVED, INDEPENDENTLY FIGURED
NOTES ON RESEARCH AND PRACTICE

Joel Lamere

Designers are not always in the position to position; there are projects narrower than god or the internet, and less subject to crisis than capital, where the broader conception of 'project' as 'projective' cannot come to bear. Here still, the task of figuration remains; designers are obligated also to form. The discursive promise of form demands an engagement with its possibilities beyond the sad (and common) conflation of figure with diagram, pattern, parameter, inherited form, material mandate, or worse still, the demands of performance. The particularities of figure retain mandates of their own, and remain the province of designers.

In part through my research, explicitly preoccupied with questions of form and material geometry, I have been fortunate enough as a collaborator to imprint figure on several prominent regional projects. The dogged commitment to the particularities of figure, as manifest in these projects, is not merely a matter of process; it is an invested ethos, engendered too in pedagogy. In this sense, the reach of this ethos transcends individual figures, which are inherently limited by their coupling to static artifacts, extending also into the character of students' future imprints.

The captions and images below are organized to illustrate the distinction between 'facts', as the unassailable circumstances of a project, and 'figures' as the simultaneously accessible and disciplinary agendas teased out in each. In most cases, the larger narrative is intentionally obscured in favor of the vignette, which serves (rhetorically) to underscore my contribution of particularities. In bracketing the conceptual framework, the artifact comes into sharper relief. The narrowed attention toward context-independent investments reveals that objects identically conceived are yet independently figured.

Community Rowing Boathouse
by Anmahian Winton Architects
Completed 2008, Brighton MA

CRI Exterior Surface Detail

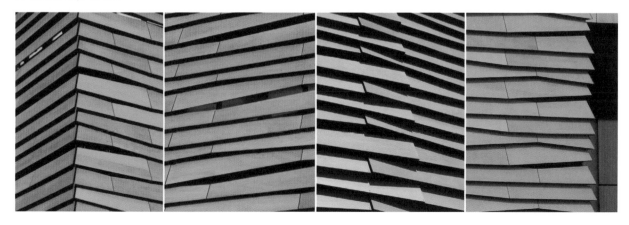

Facts:
This boathouse along the Charles River in Boston serves more rowers than all
of the private boathouses combined, and provides a strong new identity to
an organization once relegated to leasing unused buildings from the Department of Conservation and Recreation. The project consists of two buildings
with distinct design strategies. In each case, the quiet volumes are encased
in highly articulated and patterned assemblies that serve to mediate the
building's scale and respond to the changing relationship of the observer to
the object and the object to its environment.

Figures:
Patterned louvers, arguably included to mask locker room windows and
mechanical vents on the most visible face of the building, are calibrated to
respond to varied scales of encounter: smooth continuity from afar; discrete
figures from a middle ground; tectonic assembly from nearby. My investment
in disciplinary concerns also manifests in how the pattern ranges, terminates,
and bends. At corners the pattern is truncated and the trimmed edges
project orthogonally, producing an extruded pattern along the volume's short
edges. Dissimilarly, where the building bends subtly near the center of this
facade pressing outward against the louver pattern, the panels express a
stitch along two lines of panel joints.

CRI Elevation

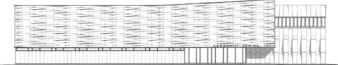

BJI Detail

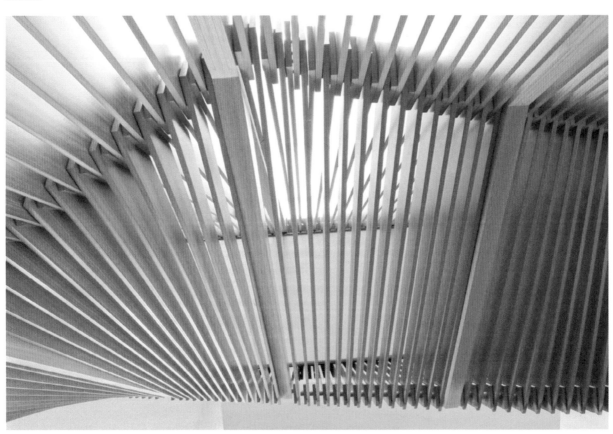

Facts:

Built in the mid 1800s, Rhode Island Hall sat in relative disrepair on Brown University's main green for much of the latter part of the 20th century. The Joukowsky Institute for Archaeology and the Ancient World, a markedly contemporary institution despite its Old World pedagogy, recognized in this an opportunity. This project takes as its genesis the conflict between the Joukowsky Institute's desire for a unique and significant new home, and the strict Brown Planning guidelines for historical buildings. Prevented from making any alterations to the original building shell, the architectural intervention turns inward.

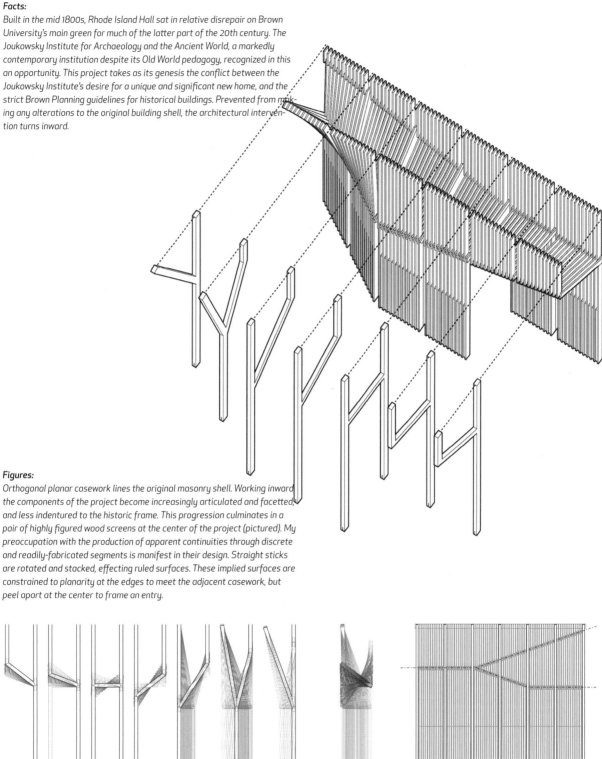

Figures:

Orthogonal planar casework lines the original masonry shell. Working inward the components of the project become increasingly articulated and facetted, and less indentured to the historic frame. This progression culminates in a pair of highly figured wood screens at the center of the project (pictured). My preoccupation with the production of apparent continuities through discrete and readily-fabricated segments is manifest in their design. Straight sticks are rotated and stacked, effecting ruled surfaces. These implied surfaces are constrained to planarity at the edges to meet the adjacent casework, but peel apart at the center to frame an entry.

Boston Harbor Islands Pavilion
by Utile, Inc. Architecture + Planning
Completed 2011, Boston MA

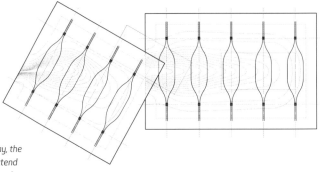

Facts:

The first architectural object built atop Boston's Rose Kennedy Greenway, the Boston Harbor Islands Pavilion is designed to house ticket kiosks and extend the presence of the nearby Boston Harbor Islands. The project is composed of two prominent concrete canopies that define the site, hovering above the kiosks and producing a sheltered public space. Benches, permanent exhibits, and a large-scale stone map of the islands articulate this space, which acts as an important threshold into Boston's evolving waterfront.

Figures:

Conceived as symmetrical and generic translation surfaces, I pressed the two canopies into a highly specific relationship, distorting the central axis of the lower canopy to acquiesce to that of the upper canopy. Three edges of each canopy are perfect straight lines, with only the fourth figured in any way. This concentration gives each canopy a clear direction and holds the canopy's complex curvature in subtle tension with its own orthogonal plan, the surrounding context, and convention in general. Pairs of plate steel ribs traverse the complex topography of the canopy's underside between columns. The equal spacing at the center contributes to their structural efficiency, while eliciting an ambiguous reading between the rib's ornamental and structural purpose.

25-Arch Folium
by GLD (Gunadi Lamere Design)
Completed 2010, Baltimore, MD

Facts:

Produced for Evergreen Museum's biennial sculpture exhibition of 2010, 25-Arch Folium is inserted in a forlorn grotto at the north end of the secondary axis of the museum's classical garden. The folium transforms the experience of the grotto at a local level, acting as a translucent light well to draw sunlight down, returning the site to its former status as a destination within the grounds. A bench, terminating the form at its base, offers respite; visitors are engulfed by the light sleeve, in stark contrast to the dark weight of the stone walls.

Figures:

Each the shape and structure of the folium are tied to the figure of the classical arch that frames other iconic thresholds at Evergreen, including the grotto entrance. Visitors encounter the oculus only once seated, revealing this generative figure of the arch as it frames the sky beyond. The arch, originally a means for the distribution of compression forces in solid construction, is rotated into the horizontal and materially transformed into closed tension rings that bind the object. It is no accident here, in a project solely produced by my firm, that the figural enterprise and conceptual apparatus coalesce.

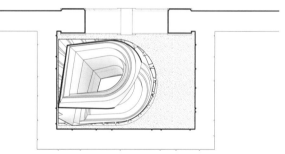

Reflected Ceiling Plan

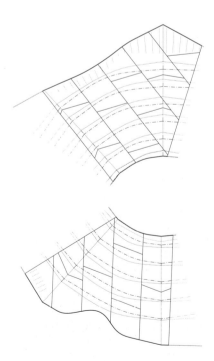

Panels

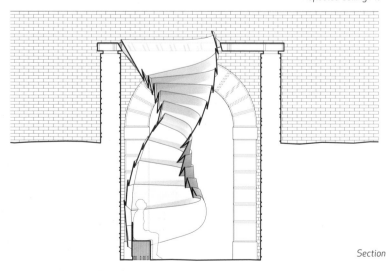

Section

COLUMN CRUSHING COMPETITION STRUCTURES

Instructor: **John Ochsendorf**
Teaching Assistant: **Philip Seaton**

The Column Crushing competition is a favorite annual part of structures class, pitting teams of students and their balsa-wood constructions against each other, with a calibrated crush-test machine as the judge. From the lab brief:
Design a minimum weight structure which can support the maximum possible axial force. As a measure of performance, the failure load will be divided by the weight of the structure. For each column, we will also determine the maximum force times the length squared as a weighted measure of performance to reward taller columns.

This is a real example of testing to failure–in order to measure the true strength of a column, it must be destroyed.

THRUST NETWORK ANALYSIS [TNA] PH.D. BUILDING TECHNOLOGY

Philippe Block
Supervisor: **John Ochsendorf**

Conserving the past / Designing the future: New studies in structural equilibrium.
Thrust Network Analysis (TNA) is a revolutionary computational method for
assessing the safety of historic vaulted structures with complex geometries
in unreinforced masonry and for designing funicular (compression-only) three-
dimensional structures.

In the powerful form-finding approach, the designer gains control over the
exploration of equilibrium form through intuitive graphical diagrams, blurring the
boundaries between funicular and free-form design. This innovative research
has applications in practice in the study and structural assessment of historic
monuments, and in the design and engineering of compression structures pushing
innovation in unreinforced masonry, from unique signature vaults in cut stone to
sustainable construction solutions for developing countries.

*A radical free-form unreinforced masonry shell
designed with TNA*

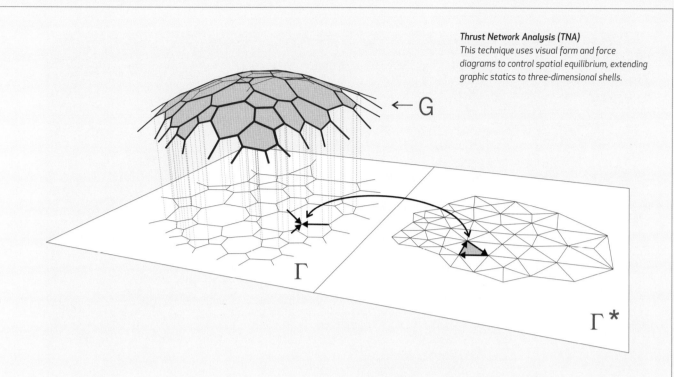

Thrust Network Analysis (TNA)
This technique uses visual form and force diagrams to control spatial equilibrium, extending graphic statics to three-dimensional shells.

$\leftarrow$ G

Γ

Γ^*

3D-printed structural scale models of a free-form stone-cut masonry shell. Collaboration with Escobedo Construction, Buda, TX.

VAULT 201 INDEPENDENT GROUP RESEARCH

Supervisor: **John Ochsendorf**
Participants: **Philippe Block, Lara Davis, Florence G. Doughty, Scott Ferebee, Emily Lo, Mallory Taub, Sze Ngai Ting, Robin Willis**

The Vault201 project emerged from the initiative of an autonomous group of design students who first came together to develop and build Vault N51 for an MIT Museum exhibition under the advisory of Prof. Ochsendorf (form finding by Philippe Block). This first prototype by the group was re-worked and redesigned for the Cooper Hewitt Museum context over the period of one semester as an independent study. The parameters which dictated the form finding methods were (1) to minimize custom-cutting required by the form and masonry patterning, thus to reduce construction time, so that it would be achievable within this extremely tight time period, and (2) to develop a form which would ensure that horizontal thrust would be taken by friction–that no horizontal thrust would be exerted upon the terra cotta walls of the museum (of unknown load-bearing capacity). The Smithsonian Museum context demanded that the design solution be fully developed with specifications, details, material research and structural load testing, to ensure that this 9' high, 17' span structure could be built and demolished within the museum without risk to museum goers or the museum itself. Silman Engineers, the engineers of record, visited MIT to supervise the load-testing of a full-scale prototype, constructed in the MIT wood shop. Tests included subjecting the one-brick-thick surface to asymmetrical loading, foundation uplift, impact tests of mallets, hammers and then sledgehammers, crown loading by John Ochsendorf and Lara Davis, and a final footing displacement of 7 inches before collapse (to insure that the structure would not load laterally against the museum walls). The bricks used for the museum construction were Green Leaf bricks, composed of 100% post-consumer or post-industrial recycled products (30% of which is processed sewage waste).

PERSPECTIVE

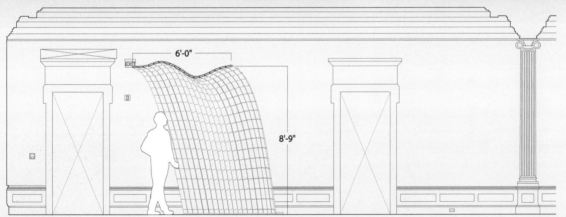

6'-0"

8'-9"

CROSS SECTION

FIELD CONDITIONS: THE STADIUM, THE CITY, AND THE MASSES M.ARCH. THESIS

Joseph Michael
Supervisor: **Nader Tehrani**
Readers: **Michael Dennis, Sheila Kennedy**

The past 30 years has seen the emergence of two seemingly unrelated problems: The first problem is the underperformance and looming demolition of Boston City Hall and the unavoidable commercial development of its plaza. The problems of City Hall and its plaza, however, are part of a larger misguided notion of public space for the masses–how, when, and by whom it is occupied. The masses, however, have always and will continue to gather regularly for the ritual of sport. This raises the second problem–the continued suburbanization of the stadium has taken the most dynamic urban spectacle out of the city. To compound this problem, sports franchises use competing cities' desire to host one of a limited set of professional teams as leverage for stadium building. If a city refuses to finance new facilities, a franchise will find another more desperate city willing to put up the funding. Stadia, costly and iconic structures, have an extremely brief shelf life, and though heavily publicly funded are almost entirely private. Boston is a self-proclaimed "Titletown." In celebration of sports is the only time that citizens gather en masse in Boston City Hall's public plaza. The iconic Boston City Hall, unlike stadiums, is stubbornly permanent and universally despised. The convergence of these two problems results in a proposal for a new kind of urban form and public space in the heart of Boston. This thesis proposes a new kind of stadium for the City Hall site, one that is not hermetically sealed for only sporting events, but one that engages the city with a high degree of porosity.

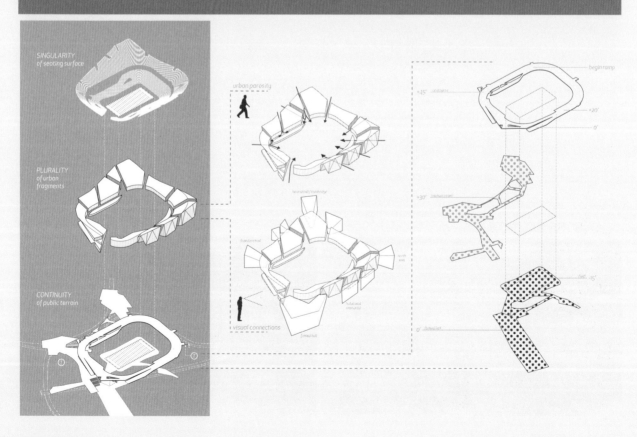

SINGULARITY of seating surface

PLURALITY of urban fragments

CONTINUITY of public terrain

urban porosity

visual connections

begin ramp

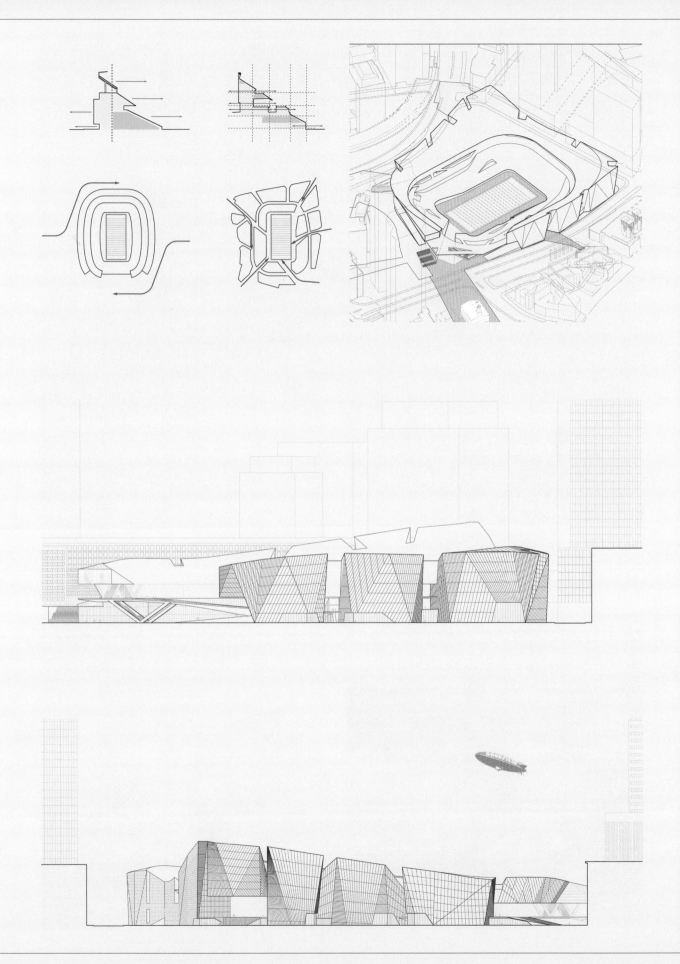

FUTURE.PERFECT: REINTEGRATING HOUSING AND PRODUCTION IN THE BERLIN BLOCK M.ARCH. THESIS

FALL 2010

Oliver Wuttig

Supervisor: **Ana Miljački**
Readers: **Alexander D'Hooghe, Joel Lamere**

The beginning of the 21st century has been marked by an apparently ubiquitous state of crisis, which transcends national boundaries and is reshaping global relationships. Financial meltdowns, the lack of affordable housing, the decline of manufacturing, resource scarcity and global warming—we seem to be immersed in a state of constant emergency, which offers opportunity for design. Architecture has the ability to play a critical role in the re-imagination of an alternate future explored through the discourse of Utopia. Investigating mixed-use strategies of both, the past and present, this thesis proposes a new block typology that intrinsically links the production of goods with issues of resource scarcity and the need for affordable housing as a counter-proposition to the planned Media-Spree Development in Berlin. Reconsidering the history of the urban block in relation to the rise and fall of industrial manufacturing in Kreuzberg, Berlin the project excavates parts of its archaic typologies as a possible way to move forward in the future.

The site is located in Kreuzberg, Berlin along the Spree river, which was designated during the boom phase of the 1990's as one of the main areas for future development for media-oriented production companies, proposing a series of office towers and high end apartments, ultimately privatizing the river front, which is currently owned by the city. Although some of the projects have been realized, the arrival of the financial crisis and continuing public opposition have slowed the transformation, allowing for the utopian speculation of an alternate future.

Kreuzberg had traditionally been the center of industry and in its wake produced a block typology which closely linked spaces of production and living. Given the shift from mass production to mass customization, the core of the project is comprised of shared manufacturing spaces, occupied by micro-factories, which support the surrounding private and collective housing blocks. Based on the renewed interest in the construction of mixed-use developments, changing demographics, and the availability of cleaner production processes, the thesis attempts to revive aspects of the archaic block typology of Kreuzberg and address the theoretical framework surrounding collectivity, housing and production within architecture.

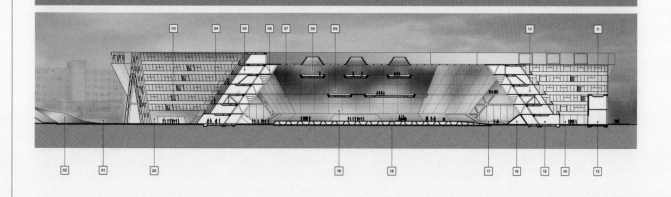

(Reverse)
01 Public Park, 02 Public Green Space, 03 Circulation Space, 04 Collective Balcony / Circulation , 05 Collective Housing Units, 06 Circulation / Storage 07 Interior Public Circulation / Production Space, 08 Micro Factory / Dirty Production, 09 Live / Work Production Spaces, 10 Collective Housing Units, 11 Plastics Manufacturing Facility, 12 Manufacturing Office Spaces, 13 Interior Court, 14 Interior Court, 15 Public Circulation / Materials Shop, 16 Circulation / Storage, 17 Public Circulation, 18 Raised Logistics Corridor / Assembly Area for Production, 19 Raised Logistics Corridor / Assembly Area for Production, 20 Interior Court open to Public Park

(Below)
01 Shared Loading Dock, 02 Ground Floor Private Housing Unit, 03 Public Park, 04 Ground Floor Collective Housing Unit, 05 Green Space, 06 Open Public space / Temporary Use Space, 07 Public Beach, 08 Spree River, 09 Plastics Manufacturing Loading Dock, 10 Viktoria Speicher / Existing Building, 11 Storage / Existing Building, 12 Recycling Facility Loading Dock, 13 Recycling Facility Parking Spaces

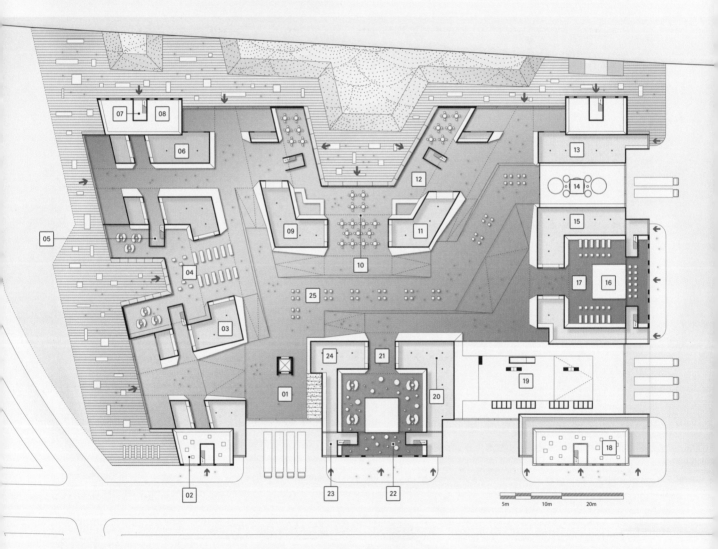

5m 10m 20m

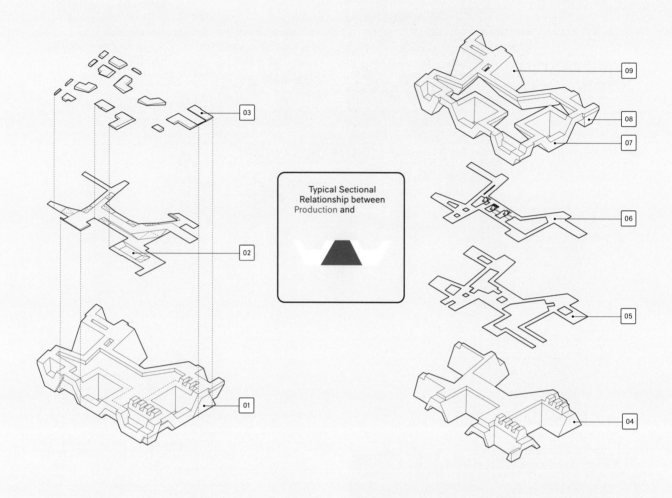

Typical Sectional
Relationship between
Production and

(Above)
01 Massing of proposed Block, 02 Continuous Ground Floor Circulation /
Raised Logistics Corridor /Shared Loading Dock / Assembly Area for
Production Spaces, 03 Service Spaces / Storage, 04 Massing of Production
Spaces, 05 Micro-Factory Floor Slab, 06 Live / Work Floor Slab, 07 Typical
Collective Housing Block, located on interior of the block, and supported by
the Production Spaces, 08 Typical Private / Family Housing Block, located on
interior of the block and supported by the Production Spaces, 09 Collective
Housing Block, Massing opens up to Public Park and Waterfront

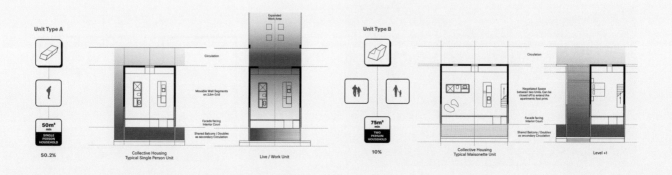

Unit Type A

50m² min
SINGLE PERSON HOUSEHOLD

50.2%

Circulation

Expanded Work Area

Movable Wall Segments on 2.5m Grid

Facade facing Interior Court

Shared Balcony / Doubles as secondary Circulation

Collective Housing
Typical Single Person Unit

Live / Work Unit

Unit Type B

75m² min
TWO PERSON HOUSEHOLD

10%

Circulation

Negotiated Space between two Units. Can be closed off to extend the apartments foot print.

Facade facing Interior Court

Shared Balcony / Doubles as secondary Circulation

Collective Housing
Typical Maisonette Unit

Level +1

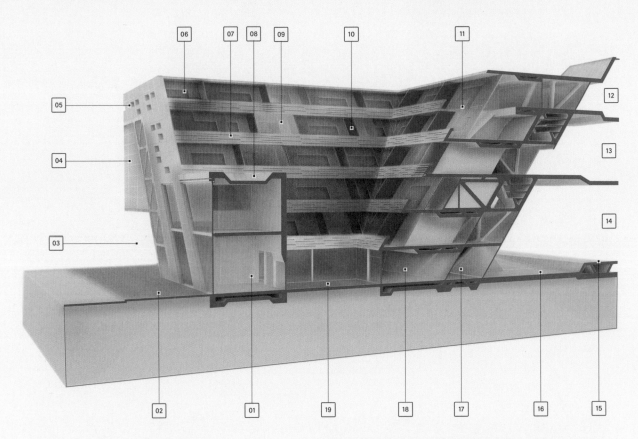

01 Showroom for Products designed and manufactured within the Block, 02 Sidewalk, 03 Access to shared Loading Dock, 04 Recycled Plastics Facade enclosing Micro-Factory Production Spaces, 05 Precast Concrete Facade Panels for Collective Housing Units, 06 Recycled Plastics Facade enclosing Collective Housing Units, 07 Collective Balcony Spaces and secondary circulation. Closed off by movable wall panels, 08 Collective Roof Terrace, 09 Interior Vertical Circulation, 10 Movable Wall Panels to create private Balcony Space, 11 Collective Maisonette Unit, 12 Production Space for dirty Processes with direct ventilation, 13 Live / Work Micro-Factory Production, Area, 14 Assembly Area for Production, 15 Raised Logistics Corridor, 16 Public Circulation, 17 Structure/ Circulation / Storage, 18 Public Circulation / Access to interior of the block from the Showroom, 19 Interior Courtyard

Holger Falter

Amanda Reeser Lawrence

Michael Meredith

Lisa Iwamoto

David Benjamin

Ryue Nishizawa

Philippe Rahm

Antón García-Abril

Régine Leibinger

Rients Dijkstra

Gilles Saucier

Georgeen Theodore

Sharon Johnston

Walter Hood

Jürgen Mayer H.

Guy Nordenson

Hashim Sarkis

Débora Mesa-Molina

Andrea Frank

Marc Tsurumaki

Elizabeth Whittaker

Hansy Better

Caroline Jones

Shih-Fu Peng

ARCHITECTURE DEPARTMENT SERIES

Spring 2009
"Working in Mumbai"
Panel discussion with Rahul Mehrotra (Rahul
Mehrotra Associates; MIT), Mary Woods (Cornell)
and Nasser Rabbat (MIT)

"Constructing the Ephemeral"
GOLDSTEIN LECTURE IN ARCHITECTURE,
ENGINEERING, AND SCIENCE
James Carpenter (James Carpenter Design
Associates, New York City)

"Contingency as Ally of the Architect"
THE 15TH PIETRO BELLUSCHI LECTURE
Rafael Moneo (Architect, Madrid; Professor of
Architecture, Harvard)

"The Architecture of Unholy Unions"
Marlon Blackwell (Marlon Blackwell Architect,
Fayetteville)

"Frameworks"
Stanley Saitowitz (Stanley Saitowitz/ Natoma
Architects, San Francisco)

"Digital Materiality in Architecture"
Fabio Gramazio and Matthias Kohler (Gramazio &
Kohler, Zurich)

"Tony Fretton: Across Europe"
Tony Fretton (Tony Fretton Architects, London)

"Recent Work "
Riken Yamamoto (Architect, Tokyo)

"Chile-scapes: Irarrazaval Recent Works"
Sebastian Irarrazaval (Sebastian Irarrazaval
Architect, Santiago de Chile)

"The New Craft of Urban Design"
Vittorio Lampugnani (ETH Zurich)

Fall 2009
"Territorial Abstraction"
Alexander D'Hooghe (Associate Professor, MIT)

"Propositions"
Charles Correa (Architect, Mumbai) with Kenneth
Frampton, Respondent

"Roots & Bridges," Symposium
Charles Correa with Martin Filler, Phyllis Lambert,
and Robert Campbell; Yung Ho Chang, Moderator

"Designing the Social and Environmental
Infrastructure of the Global City"
Ricky Burdett (Chief Advisor on Architecture and
Urbanism, ODA London; Professor, London School
of Economics)

"Megaform"
Kenneth Frampton (Ware Professor of
Architecture, Columbia University)

"Energy and Form"
Albert Pope (Wortham Professor of Architecture,
Rice University)

"Freedom of Form Finding"
Laurent Ney (Architect, Brussels)

"Constructing the voyager's view. The design of
contemporary infrastructure"
Marcel Smets (Professor, Catholic University of
Leuven)

Spring 2010
"Housing/Urbanus"
Xiaodu Liu (Architect, Urbanus, Shenzhen and
Beijing)

"Living Spaces"
Stephen Bates (Architect, Sergison Bates
Architects, London)

"What's next? About curiosity..."
The 16th Pietro Belluschi Lecture
Winy Maas (Architect, MVRDV, Rotterdam)

"Architecture Research Office: Work"
Stephen Cassell (Architect, Architecture Research
Office, New York)

"Housing: Theory and Projects"
The 22nd Schein Memorial Lecture
Adèle Naudé Santos (Dean, MIT School of
Architecture and Planning; Architect and Planner,
Santos Prescott & Associates, San Francisco and
Somerville)

"Sustainable Energy–without the hot air"
The 4th Goldstein Architecture, Engineering, and
Science Lecture
David MacKay (Physicist and Chief Scientific
Advisor, Department of Energy and Climate
Change, London)

"Housing at Different Scales"
Dietmar Eberle (Chair, Faculty of Architecture,
ETHZ, Zurich)

"Developing and Redeveloping Public Housing: The
Design Politics of Twice-Cleared Communities"
Lawrence Vale (Ford Professor of Urban Design
and Planning, MIT, Cambridge)

Boston Housing Symposium: Yung Ho Chang,
Moderator
Timothy Love (Utile Design), Nader Tehrani (Office
dA), William Rawn (Rawn Architects), Elizabeth
Whittaker (Merge Architects), Kyu Sung Woo (Kyu
Sung Woo Architects)

ARCHITECTURAL DESIGN

Fall 2010

"Catalyzing Constraints: Recent Work of Lewis. Tsurumaki.Lewis."
Marc Tsurumaki (Architect, LTL Architects, New York City)

"pre.text/vor.wand–patterns of speculation"
Jürgen Mayer H. (Architect, J. Mayer H., Berlin)

"Curriculum for a Crowded City"
Alfredo Brillembourg and Hubert Klumpner (Architects, Urban Think Tank, Caracas and Zurich)

"Envelopes"
Alejandro Zaera-Polo (Architect, Foreign Office Architects, London)

"Designing with Scent"
Rodolphe el-Khoury (Architect, Khoury Levit Fong, Toronto)

"3.0 Bridges: Engineering/Architecture"
Shih-Fu Peng (Architect, Heneghan Peng, Dublin) with Holger Falter (Engineer, Arup)

"Meteorological Architecture"
Philippe Rahm (Architect, Philippe Rahm Architectes, Paris)

"Too Young to Reason, Too Grown Up to Dream"
Sharon Johnston (Architect, Johnston Marklee, Los Angeles)

"Synthetics"
Lisa Iwamoto (Architect, Iwamoto Scott, San Francisco)

"Buildings/Architecture versus Community"
Co-sponsored with The MIT Women's League
Robert Campbell (Architecture Critic, The Boston Globe)

Spring 2011

"Saucier + Perrotte: Recent Work"
Gilles Saucier (Architect, Saucier Perrotte, Montreal)

"PoPs: Prototypes of Prefabrication"
Antón García-Abril and Débora Mesa-Molina (Ensamble, Madrid)

"Working Grounds: Recent Projects in Lebanon"
Sponsored by The Lebanese Club at MIT
Hashim Sarkis (Aga Khan Professor of Landscape Architecture and Urbanism, Harvard)

"Rients Dijkstra (Maxwan): a balancing act"
Rients Dijkstra (Maxwan Architects, Rotterdam)

"Activating the Mundane"
Walter Hood (Hood Design, Oakland, Professor of Landscape Architecture, Berkeley)

"architecture & environment"
The 22nd Arthur H. Schein Memorial Lecture
Ryue Nishizawa (SANAA / Office of Ryue Nishizawa, Tokyo)

"Atlas of Fabrication"
The 17th Pietro Belluschi Lecture
Régine Leibinger (Barkow Leibinger, Berlin)

"Art, Science and Structures: Cyril Stanley Smith and Design"
The 5th Goldstein Lecture in Architecture, Engineering and Science
Guy Nordenson (Guy Nordenson and Associates, New York City)

Fall 2010

BOS / "On Curating"
Amanda Reeser Lawrence & Ashley Schafer (Praxis Journal), Mark Pasnik & Chris Grimley (pinkcomma gallery, Boston)

STAKES / "Global Critical"
Alexander D'Hooghe, Yung Ho Chang, Hashim Sarkis, Kapil Gupta, Ralph Nelson, Xiangning Li

TRICKS
MIT Students Present
Organized by Architecture Student Council

IN PROGRESS / "Urban Recycling: Two Projects"
Cristina Parreño (MIT; Architect, Madrid)

STAKES / "What is at Stake? Roundtable"
Mark Jarzombek, John Fernandez, Takehiko Nagakura, Caroline Jones, Nader Tehrani, Andrew Scott, Nasser Rabbat, Andrea Frank, Arindam Dutta
(MIT Department of Architecture Discipline Groups Faculty)

BOS / "On Activating"
Sheila Kennedy (Kennedy Violich Architecture, Boston), Carlo Ratti (Director, MIT Senseable City Lab)

IN PROGRESS / "MOS"
Michael Meredith (MOS, Cambridge and New Haven)

Spring 2011

IN PROGRESS / "Queer"
S. Jane Cee (Cee Architects)

STAKES / "Trajectories for Fabrication & Technology in Architecture"
Mark Goulthorpe & Larry Sass (MIT)

IN PROGRESS / "What urban design can do"
Georgeen Theodore (Interboro, Brooklyn)

IN PROGRESS / "Looped"
David Benjamin (The Living, Director, Living Architecture Lab, Columbia GSAPP, New York)

TRICKS / "Architecture About Architecture"
MIT Students Present

IN PROGRESS
Florian Idenburg (SO-IL, Brooklyn)

BOS / "Homemade"
Hansy Better (Studio Luz Architecture, Boston) & Beth Whittaker (Merge Architects, Boston)

IN PROGRESS / "Architecture and Anthropophagy: Lucio Costa et al."

AGA KHAN PROGRAM / AKPIA

Fares el-Dahdah (Rice University, Houston)

Spring 2009
"Islamabad: The Making of a 'City of the Future' 1959-1963"
Ahmed Zaib Khan Mahsud (AKPIA@MIT Post-Doctoral Fellow)

"Arabian Nights Architecture: The Adoption of Fantasy Middle Eastern Design in Constructing Indonesian and Malaysian Identities"
Sarah Moser (AKPIA@MIT Post-Doctoral Fellow)

"Planning Jerusalem: Between Ottoman and Colonial Modernity"
Salim Tamari (AKPIA@MIT Post-Doctoral Fellow)

Zehra Ali "Study of Innovations in Building Energy Efficiency in Northern Pakistan"; Zameer Basrai "A Study in Architectural Identity of Ismaili Philanthropic Institutions in Contemporary Bombay";
Christian Hedrick "German-Austrian Influences in 19th Century Cairo";
Anneka Lenssen "Pioneers and Primitives: Painting from Syria, 1960-1970";
Alexa Rosenberg "Managing Evolution in a Prominent African NGO: Lessons from Enda Tiers Monde in Dakar, Senegal";
2008-09 Aga Khan Travel Grant Presentations
MIT Students Recipients of the Travel Grant Award

Fall 2009
Building New Campuses In the Islamic World

"KAUST–King Abdullah University for Science and Technology–A Step into the Future"
William Odell (HOK Architects)
Ammar Alnahwi, (Global Collaborative Research, KAUST US)

"Education for All–Education City, Doha, Qatar"
Kevin Underwood (EDAW | AECOM)

"Drawing on Islamic City-Building Traditions to Create a 21st Century Community of Learning"
David Dixon (Goody, Clancy & Associates)

"Palmettes, Arches, Geometrical Patterns: Ornaments in the Marble Carvings from Medieval Afghanistan"
Martina Rugiadi (AKPIA@MIT Post-Doctoral Fellow, Sapienza Università di Roma)

Spring 2010
"Preservation of Architectural Monuments in Kazakhstan: Policies and Methods"
Gulnara Kamalova (Head of the Research Department at the Kazakhstan Restoration Agency–Kazrestoration)

"Harar, a Muslim City in Ethiopia"
Philippe Revault (Fulbright Visiting Professor, Wentworth Institute of Technology)

"Revisiting the Trope of 'Unity and Variety' in Islamic Art"
Gülru Necipoglu (Aga Khan Professor of Islamic Art, Harvard University)

"The Architecture of Migration: Translation and Creative Synthesis in the Mosques of Tamil, Hadhrami and Chinese Peranakan Communities in the Emporia of Nusantara"
Imran Bin Tajudeen (AKPIA@MIT Post-Doctoral Fellow)

"Urbanization, Poverty and Land-Use in the Megacities of South Asia"
Elizabeth Dean Hermann (Rhode Island School of Design)

"Interrupting the Archive: Indigenous Interventions to Colonial Categories of Indian Heritage"
Mrinalini Rajagopalan (AKPIA@MIT Post-Doctoral Fellow)

"Breaching the Walled Cities of Bilâd al-Shâm"
Nicolas Prouteau (AKPIA@MIT Post-Doctoral Fellow)

Bernadette Baird-Zars, "Developing Heritage: Constructed Visions in the Decision-Making Process of Property Regulation in Aleppo, Syria"
Charles Curran, "Retrofit + Shrink-wrap Dubai // An Urban Recovery Plan"
Azra Dawood,
Igor Demchenko, "Ahmad Yasawi Mausoleum in Russian Empire: 1864-1917"
Laura Lee Schmidt, "Looking at the Book of Secrets in the Absence of Wonder"
2009-2010 Aga Khan Travel Grant Presentations
MIT Students Recipients of the Travel Grant Award

AUC Cairo Lectures
"Arabic Culture and the Problem of Modernity" (in Arabic)
"How Mamluk Architecture Co-opted the Streets of Cairo" (in English)
Nasser Rabbat (Aga Khan Professor of Islamic Architecture, MIT)

Fall 2010
"Adventures in Arabia and Beyond"
Chad Oppenheim (Oppenheim Architecture + Design, Miami, Florida)

"Mughal Monuments and the Politics of Memory"
Saleema Waraich (AKPIA@MIT Post-Doctoral Fellow)

"Reviving the Invented: The Neo-Achaemenid from Parsi Bombay to Qajar Tehran"
Talinn Grigor (Brandeis University)

Spring 2011
"Islamic Military Architecture in the Near East and Egypt at the Time of the Crusades"
Benjamin Michaudel (Post-Doctoral Fellow, AKPIA@MIT Institut Français du Proche-Orient, Syria)

"The Islamic Paradise Garden: Myths and Realities"
Laura E. Parodi (Post-Doctoral Fellow, AKPIA@MIT Independent Scholar)

"Detranscendentalizing: [Secularism, Economy, Politics, Science]"
Arindam Dutta (History, Theory and Criticism, MIT)

"The Portuguese Architectural Heritage and the Islamic World: The Gulbenkian Project"
Presented by Faculty from the University of Evora, Portugal
Filipe Themudo Barata (Professor of Mediterranean and Heritage History)
Fernando Branco Correia (Assistant Professor of Islamic History and Archeology João Rocha)

"The Global Architect in the Free Trade Age"
"Re-territorializing the Global: Differential Approaches to Tourism in Morocco"
Aziza Chaouni (University of Toronto, Bureau E.A.S.T.)
"Selling Brand Dubai"
Deeba Haider (Consultant/ Writer/ Architect, LA, Associate Editor at International Journal of Islamic Architecture)
"Same Same but Different; The Global Trade in Architecture"
Kevin Mark Low (smallprojects, Kuala Lumpur, Malaysia)
"Jet Planes / Concrete Planes"
Todd Reisz (Architect and Editor, Al Manakh, Amsterdam, The Netherlands)
Moderated by Nasser Rabbat (MIT)

BUILDING TECHNOLOGY

Spring 2009

"Applications of Information Technology"
Jim Butler (Cimetrics)

"AI-based Building Energy Management Systems: University of Miami Case Study"
Dr. Mahling (Consumer Powerline, NY)

"Spatial Archeology: The Gothic Cathedral Revealed by Laser"
Andrew Tallon (Vassar)

"The Transformation of the Design and Construction Professions"
John Tocci (Tocci Construction)

"Center for the Built Environment: Learning from Buildings"
Dr. Gail Brager (UC Berkeley)

Fall 2009
"The Role of Building Performance Simulation in Architectural Education and Practice"
Christoph Reinhart (Harvard GSD)

"Building Science for Historic Buildings"
Brent Gabby (Simpson Gumpertz and Heger)

"Costs and Benefits of Double Skin Facades"
Byron Stigge (Buro Happold)

"Inside the Shoebox: Using Physics-Rich Performance Simulations to Provide Meaningful Design Guidance"
Erik Olsen (Transsolar)

"Structural Sketches: From ActiveStatics to StaticsPad"
Simon Greenwold (MathWorks)

"Sustainable Design: A Collaborative Approach"
Roger Chang (Westlake Reed Leskosky)

Spring 2010
"Computation Optimization in Architecture"
Mario Sassone (Turin Polytechnic)

"The Future of Architecture in a Warming Planet"
Norbert Lechner (Auburn University)

"Glass & Glazing in the 21st Century: Design and Preservation of Contemporary and Historic Architecture"
Conference.

"The Cost Barrier in Achieving Deep Energy Savings in Housing"
Ed Connelly (New Ecology, Inc.)

"Parametric Structural Design: An Intuitive Approach Using Graphic Statics"

Lorenz Lachauer (ETH)

Fall 2010
"High Performance Green Buildings"
Martha VanGeem (CTL Group)

"LEDs and Sustainability in Labs and Architecture: Synergy or Lighting Rivals?"
Thomas Schielke

"The Way Towards ZERO Energy Homes: Energy Efficient Building Technologies Based on European Passive House Technology and Zero Energy Design"
Christoph Buxbaum (Carinthia University, Austria)

Spring 2011
"Sustainability Research at the Fraunhofer Institute for Building Physics"
Klaus Sedlbauer (Fraunhofer Institute for Building Physics, Stuttgart, Germany)

"Some Lessons Learned From Two Decades of Promoting Natural Disaster Risk Reduction"
Brian Tucker (GeoHazards International, Palo Alto, CA)

"Market Response Modeling: Quantifying the Technology and Policies Needed to Drive Global Zero-Carbon-Emission Building Infrastructure"
Kevin Otto (Robust Systems and Strategy LLC, Taunton, MA)

"Lisa Heschong–Creating Consensus on Annual Daylighting Performance Metrics"
Lisa Heschong (Heschong Mahone Group, Inc., Gold River, CA)

"Understanding Thermal Performance of Building Shell Components Containing Blown Fiber Insulations Enhanced with Phase Change Material (PCM)"
Jan Kosny (Fraunhofer Center for Sustainable Energy Systems CSE; Cambridge, MA)

"High Performance Timber Structure"
Ron Anthony (Anthony & Associates, Inc.)

COMPUTATION

Spring 2009
"High-Low Tech: Rethinking Cultural and Material Contexts for Computation"
Leah Buechley (Assistant Professor of Media Arts and Sciences/Dir, MIT Media Lab)

"Constraint and Control: Towards Autonomous Behavior in the Built Environment"
Ziggy Drozdowski (Director of Technology, Hoberman Associates, NY)

"Embedded Intelligence: Design-Driven Computation"
Shane Burger (Associate, Head of Computational Design Unit, GRIMSHAW Associates)

"Engineering structures: art, geometry, mathematics and materials"
Chris Williams (Senior Lecturer, Dept. of Architecture and Civil Engineering, University of Bath)

"PERFORMANCE-Customizing Design"
Jose Luis Gonzalez and Michael Stzivos (architects and designers, SOFTLAB, NY)

"Design Ecology"
David Small (Associate professor, Design Ecology, MIT Media Lab)

"Conceptions of Design in a Culture of Simulation"
Yanni Loukissas (Visiting Lecturer, College of Architecture, Art and Planning, Cornell University)

Fall 2009
"Computational Form and Material Gestalt"
Achim Menges (Professor / Director , Institute for Computational Design Stuttgart University)

"Emergence through Conflict The Multi-Disciplinary Design System (MDDS)"
Anas Alfaris (Research Scientist , Strategic Engineering Group, Engineering Systems Division, MIT)

"Mass Customization: models and algorithms"
Jose Duarte (Associate Professor / Visiting Scientist , Technical University of Lisbon / MIT Design Lab)

"Phrases of the Kinetic: Organicism and Transformation from Robots to Biofuels"
Amanda Parkes (Research Scientist / CTO, Tangible Media Group, MIT Media Lab / Bodega Algae LLC)

"CAD/CAM for Coded Assembly"
Jonathan Bachrach (Principal, Other Lab)

Spring 2010
"I|K investigations"

HISTORY, THEORY, AND CRITICISM

Mariana Ibanez / Simon Kim (I|K studio)

"Built Environment Modeling in practice"
Alvise Simondetti (Architect, Arup)

"Rhino Strategies: the development of Rhinoceros Nurbs Modeling Software"
Bob McNeel (President, Robert McNeel & Associates)

Fall 2010
"Better by Design"
Timothy Prestero (CEO, Design that Matters)

"Mediated Matter"
Neri Oxman (Assistant Professor, Media Arts and Sciences, MIT)

"SURFACE SYMMETRIES: The Smith House Revisited"
Edouard Din (Associate Professor, Tuskegee University)

"Nervous System"
Jessica Rosenkrantz / Jesse Louis-Rosenberg (Co-Founders, Nervous System)

"Epistemological Constructions"
Phillip Anzalone (Director–Building Technology Sequence & Avery Di, Columbia University Graduate School of Architecture)

Spring 2011
"Degrees of Freedom"
Matthew Trimble (Founder, RadLab)

"Emergent mindsets in the digital age: Moving between worlds"
Edith Ackerman (Visiting Scientist, Design Lab, MIT)

"Designing Software Tools at Autodesk Revit"
Lira Nikolovska (Principal Designer, Autodesk)

"Architectural Topologies: Visual Languages and Digital Applications"
Athanassios Economou (Associate Professor / Director of the Shape Computer, Georgia Institute of Technology)

"City and Maps in the Digital Age"
Antoine Picon (Professor, Harvard, GSD)

Spring 2009
HTC Forum:
"How to Write a Critical History of the Venetian City Garden"
John Dixon Hunt (University of Pennsylvania)

HTC Forum:
"Tactics of Ephemerality: Interventionist Public Art in Los Angeles"
Ondine Chavoya (Williams College)

HTC Forum:
"Blogitecture: Architecture on the Internet: The state and influence of architectural criticism in an age of digital networks"
Javier Arbona (UC Berkeley), Mark Jarzombek (MIT), Kazys Varnelis (Columbia)

Fall 2009
HTC Forum:
"The Cool Look of Reasonable Consumption: 'Lifestyle' in Cold War Czech Architectural Discourse"
Ana Miljački (MIT)

HTC Forum:
"Alvar Aalto: Architecture, Modernity and Geopolitics"
Eeva-Liisa Pelkonen (Yale)

HTC Forum:
"Hybridity as Condition + Challenge: Beyond Project Zagreb"
Eve Blau (Harvard GSD)

HTC Forum:
"Seeing Power: Art and Activism in the Age of Cultural Production"
Nato Thompson (Creative Time, NY)

Spring 2010
"Angkor Wat in Cambodian Architecture"
Mark Jarzombek (MIT) and Caroline Jones (MIT)

HTC Forum:
"Can nature be recomposed? A few issues in cosmopolitics"
Bruno Latour (Institut d'Études Politiques de Paris), Introduction by Vincent Antonin Lepinay (MIT), response from Mark Jarzombek (MIT)

HTC Forum:
"Curatorial Models Revisited"
Maria Lind (Bard College) with Ute Meta Bauer (MIT)

HTC Forum:
"On Not Falling to Pieces: A Ballistic History of Paris (September 1792-May 1871)"
Edward Eigen (Princeton)

HTC Forum:
"Free Flight"
Hadas Steiner (University at Buffalo, SUNY)

Fall 2010
HTC Forum:
"Mobility as Archive for Innovation Developing a Video–Photographic Method of Excavating It"
Clapperton Mavhung (MIT), response by Caroline Jones (MIT)

HTC Forum:
"The World Solar Energy Project: Maria Telkes after the Dover Sun House"
Daniel A. Barber (Harvard GSD), response by Arindam Dutta (MIT)

HTC Forum:
"Episodes in the History of Architecture and the Senses: Paris circa 1750"
Rodolphe El-Khoury (University of Toronto, MIT)

HTC Forum:
"Monumental Snapshots of a Soviet Future"
Juliet Koss (Scripps College), response by Ana Miljački (MIT)

Spring 2011
HTC Forum Beischer Lecture:
"Architecture in Print: How Karl Friedrich Schinkel Invented the Oeuvre complete"
Kurt Forster (Yale), introduction by Mark Jarzombek (MIT), response by Erika Naginski (Harvard GSD)

HTC Forum:
"Sacred Space and/or Informational Projection? San Paolo fuori le mura and the Catholic Church in the 1820s"
Richard Wittman (UC Santa Barbara), Response by Kristel Smentek (MIT)

HTC Forum:
"Archive Agendas: Recent Discursive Platforms in Art and Architecture"
Sean Dockray (Telic Arts Exchange, AAAAARGH), Ana Miljački (MIT), Antoni Muntadas (MIT)

ART, CULTURE AND TECHNOLOGY

Spring 2009
"Energy, Community, Communication"
Jegan Vincent de Paul (Community Grid Project),
Wendy Jacob (research associate at the Center
for Advanced Visual Studies), Jae Rhim Lee (FEMA
Trailer Project)

"Tracking Trash"
Armin Linke (artist, Milan and Berlin) and Carlo
Ratti (designer, engineer, SENSEable City Lab)

"Bio-diversity"
Gediminas Urbonas (MIT) and Joe Dahmen
(architect)

"Brain, Body, Networks"
Sebastian Seung (Department of Physics at the
MIT) and Amber Frid-Jimenez (MIT)

Panel discussion at the MIT Museum
"Inducement of pleasure, fantasy fulfillment, and
the mediation of intimacy in a socially-networked
gaming paradigm such as World of Warcraft
(WOW)"
Panelists: Jean-Baptiste Labrune (MIT Media Lab),
Raimundas Malasauskas (Curator/, Artists Space,
NYC), Marisa Jahn (MIT Media Lab), Steve Shada
(artist collaborator), Cati Vaucelle (MIT Media
Lab), Laura Knott (MIT Museum)

Fall 2009
"Factory City"
Christoph Schaefer (conceptual artist, Hamburg,
Germany)

"Performative City"
Joan Jonas (MIT)

"Public City"
Antoni Muntadas (Artist, MIT)

"Propaganda City"
Mike Bonanno (The Yes Men)

"Protest City"
Ana Miljački (MIT Architecture), Nomeda Urbonas
(Pro-test Lab)

"Porous City"
Krzysztof Wodiczko (CAVS, MIT)

Spring 2010
"Production and Reception of the Visual"
Xavier Le Roy (choreographer, France)
Nell Breyer, moderator (MIT)

"Dance on Top of Everyday Throwaways: Extreme
Simultaneity"
Constanza Macras (choreographer, Argentina)
Jay Scheib, moderator (MIT)

"The Bread and Puppet Theater"
Peter Schumann (Bread and Puppet Theater)
John Bell, moderator (MIT)

"It's Real to Me"
Magda Fernandez (artist, Boston)
Amber Frid-Jimenez, moderator (MIT ACT)

"Stylistic Economies, Reenactments, and
Choreographic Regimes"
Catherine Sullivan (University of Chicago)
Jane Farver, moderator (MIT List Visual Arts
Center)

"Where's the Passion"
Yvonne Rainer (choreographer/dancer, filmmaker,
UC Irvine)
Joan Jonas, moderator (MIT)

"Text: Free and Indirect. A Future Perception"
Eva Meyer (writer, filmmaker, Berlin)
Ute Meta Bauer, moderator (MIT)

Fall 2010
"Climate Changes in Science Fashion"
Elke Gaugele (Academy of Fine Arts, Vienna,
Austria)

"Com(ment)ic: Wondersuits, Fast Skin and Poison
Ivy"
Regina Maria Moeller (Norwegian University of
Science and Technology)

"21st Century Living in the Amazon: In the Order
of Chaos"
Laura Anderson Barbata (Instituto Nacional de
Bellas Artes, México)

"Tierra Brillante"
Bulbo (media collective, Tijuana, México)

"Second Skin Bio-Suit"
Dava Newman (Aeronautics and Astronautics and
Engineering Systems, MIT)

"Soft, Smart & Stealthy"
Sheila Kennedy (MIT, Kennedy Violich
Architecture)

"Build Your Own World"
Steve Dietz (ZERO1)

"Sound Shapes and Ear Dances: A Tribute to
Maryanne Amacher"
Lecture by Anne Hilde Neset (the Wire Magazine),
Roundtable discussion with Neset, Florian Heckler
(Vienna), Kevin Drumm (Chicago), Jessica Rylan
Piper (Los Angeles)

"Metabolic Studio"
Lauren Bon (Metabolic Studio, Los Angeles)

Spring 2011
"Luginsland–(On Art as Research)"
Florian Dombois (Bern University of the Arts,
Bern, Switzerland)

"A Guide to Campo del Cielo"
Guillermo Faivovich & Nicolás Goldberg (Artists,
Buenos Aires, Argentina)

"Science & Fictions"
Laurent Grasso (Artist, Paris, France)

"Parallel/Peripheral: Working at the Intersection of
Art and Other"
Jae Rhim Lee (ACT Research Fellow, MIT)

"Transborder Disturbances: Aesthetics,
Interventions, and Technology"
Ricardo Dominguez (UCSD, San Diego, CA)

"Turning Out the Space"
Attila Csörgö (Artist, Budapest, Hungary)

Cherie Abbanat, Lecturer, Architectural Design (not pictured) / Marilyne Andersen, Visiting Scientist, Building Technology / Stanford Anderson, Professor, History, Theory, Criticism / Ute Meta Bauer, Associate Professor, Art, Culture, and Technology / Julian Beinart, Professor, Architectural Design / John Bell, Lecturer, Art, Culture, and Technology (not pictured) / Mario Caro, Lecturer, Art, Culture, and Technology (not pictured) / Yung Ho Chang, Professor, Architectural Design / Alexander D'Hooghe, Associate Professor, Architectural Design / Michael Dennis, Professor, Architectural Design / Chris Dewart, Technical Instructor, Architectural Design / Rients Dijkstra, Lecturer, Architectural Design / Arindam Dutta, Associate Professor, History, Theory, Criticism / Athanassios Economou, Visiting Associate Professor, Computation (not pictured) / Rodolphe el-Khoury, Visiting Associate Professor, Architectural Design / John Fernandez, Associate Professor, Building Technology / Andrea Frank, Lecturer, Art, Culture, and Technology / Philip Freelon, Professor of the Practice, Architectural Design / David Friedman. Associate Professor, History, Theory, Criticism / Jaime Gagne, Lecturer, Building Technology (not pictured) / Antón García-Abril, Visiting Associate Professor, Architectural Design / Nick Gelpi, Lecturer, Architectural Design / Rania Ghosn, Lecturer, Architectural Design (not pictured) / Leon Glicksman, Professor, Building Technology / Reinhard Goethert, Principal Research Associate, Architectural Design / Mark Goulthorpe, Associate Professor, Architectural Design /Roisin Heneghan, Lecturer, Architectural Design, (not pictured) / Walter Hood, Visiting Professor, Architectural Design / Stephen Intile, Research Scientist, Computation (not pictured) / Mark Jarzombek, Professor, History, Theory, Criticism / El Hadi Jazairy, Lecturer, Architectural Design (not pictured) / Joan Jonas, Professor without Tenure (retired), Art, Culture, and Technology / Caroline Jones, Professor, History, Theory, Criticism / Shun Kanda, Senior Lecturer, Architectural Design / Sheila Kennedy, Professor of the Practice, Architectural Design / Terry Knight, Professor, Computation / Joel Lamere, Lecturer, Architectural Design / Kent Larson, Principal Research Scientist, Computation / Yunxiang (Sam) Liang, Lecturer History, Theory, Criticism (not pictured) / Oliver Lutz, Lecturer, Art, Culture, and Technology (not pictured) / Débora Mesa-Molina, Lecturer, Architectural Design

Photo credit: Standing portraits, Charlotte Hagen-Cazes; All others credit George X. Lin and Hiu Lan Kian Yam.

Ana Miljački, Assistant Professor, Architectural Design / Muntadas, Visiting Professor, Art, Culture, and Technology / Nashid Nabian, Lecturer, Architectural Design (not pictured) / Takehiko Nagakura, Associate Professor, Computation / Adèle Naudé Santos, Professor, Architectural Design, SA+P Dean / Angel Nevarez, Lecturer, Art, Culture, and Technology (not pictured) / Leslie Norford, Professor, Building Technology, Associate Department Head / William O'Brien, Jr., Assistant Professor, Architectural Design / John Ochsendorf, Associate Professor, Building Technology / Laura Parodi, Postdoctoral Fellow, History, Theory, Criticism (not pictured) / Cristina Parreño, Lecturer, Architectural Design / Paul Paturzo, Lecturer, Architectural Design (not pictured) / Shih-Fu Peng, Lecturer, Architectural Design / Nasser Rabbat, Professor, History, Theory, Criticism / Lawrence Sass, Associate Professor, Computation / Gilles Saucier, Lecturer, Architectural Design / Nitin Sawhney, Lecturer, Art, Culture, and Technology (not pictured) / Ashley Schafer, Visiting Associate Professor, Architectural Design / Andrew Scott, Associate Professor, Architectural Design / Andres Sevtsuk, Lecturer, Architectural Design (w/ DUSP) (not pictured) / Dennis Shelden, Associate Professor of the Practice, Computation / Kristel Smentek, Assistant Professor, History, Theory, Criticism / Anne Spirn, Professor, Architectural Design (w/ DUSP) / George Stiny, Professor, Computation / Nader Tehrani, Professor, Architectural Design, Department Head / Filip Tejchman, Lecturer, Architectural Design / Skylar Tibbits, Lecturer, Architectural Design / Marc Tsurumaki, Lecturer, Architectural Design / Corinne Ulmann, Lecturer, Architectural Design / Gediminas Urbonas, Associate Professor, Art, Culture, and Technology / Jan Wampler, Professor, Architectural Design / James Wescoat, Professor, Architectural Design and History, Theory, Criticism / J. Meejin Yoon, Associate Professor, Architectural Design

RESOURCES

Libraries:

The Rotch Library, housed in an award-winning building by Schwartz / Silver Architects, is one of the nation's premier resources in architecture and planning. The collection offers extensive depth in architecture, building technology, art history, photography, environmental studies, land use, urban design and development, housing and community development, regional planning and development, urban transportation and real estate.

Rotch Visual Collections, an adjacent branch library, holds 350,000 visual images including the Kepes-Lynch collection, the Kidder Smith Collection and the Aga Khan Visual Archive. Both Rotch libraries are part of the MIT Library System, with more than 2.6 million printed volumes, 17,000 journal subscriptions, 275 online databases and over 3800 electronic journal titles licensed for MIT access.

Access to other libraries is provide through the *Boston Library Consortium*, a cooperative association of nearly 20 academic and research libraries in the area.

Graduate students are also eligible for borrowing privileges at the **Harvard College Libraries** and at the **Loeb Library** at the Harvard Graduate School of Design.

Galleries:

The **Wolk Gallery**, in the School of Architecture + Planning, mounts several shows a year in its exhibition space surrounding Frank Stella's phantasmagorical 3D sculpture **Loohooloo**. Exhibits are curated by the Curator of Architecture and Design at the **MIT Museum**.

The **PLAZmA Digital Gallery** features the work of students and faculty presented on nine large monitors in the school's public areas; the content overlaps with the Online Portfolio. The screens can also be used for student reviews and presentations.

The **MIT Museum** frequently features exhibits on architecture and visual studies in its main galleries at 265 Massachusetts Avenue, as well as in its **Compton Gallery**, located in the heart of campus under the big dome. The **Museum's eGallery**, a virtual exhibition space and archive, features sites designed specifically as virtual exhibitions, spotlighting museum collections as well as exhibitions no longer on display in its galleries.

The **Center for Advanced Visual Studies**, an artists' fellowship program sponsored by the School of Architecture + Planning, maintains a gallery in its space in Building N52-390. A working laboratory for interdisciplinary art practice, the Center commissions and produces new artworks and artistic research, often presenting new work in its gallery space.

The **List Visual Arts Center**, three galleries on the first floor of the Wiesner Building, presents 5-8 shows a year exploring contemporary artmaking in all media. Artists of national and international stature, as well as emerging artists, are featured.

Rotch Library also features exhibits of student, staff and faculty work, as well as shows from its collections, in its space in Building 7.

Online:

Find more information about the department and events at http://architecture.mit.edu.

PUBLICATIONS

Agendas in Architecture is a vehicle for publications and books about student and faculty research at the Department of Architecture. **Testing to Failure** is its third publication.

PLAN is the monthly newsletter of the School of Architecture and Planning. Plan is published both on paper and online at: http://loohooloo.mit.edu/resources/newsletter_plan/

thresholds is the biannual peer-reviewed critical journal of architecture, art and media culture produced by editors in the Department of Architecture at MIT. **thresholds** editors produce one independently themed journal a year. The best submissions from fine arts, design, graphics, media arts and sciences, film, photography, architecture and theory are selected based on their holistic fit around the given theme. Graphic and pictorial works play as strong a role in each journal as do works of critical writing. The **thresholds** advisory board is composed of internationally recognized figures in various fields of visual culture.

The Board provides intellectual support for theme development, and brings forth a large amount of high quality submissions for each issue. As a result, the work of many important international figures has been featured. (See: Alexandra Daisy Ginsberg and Timothy Hyde in Journal #38, Beatriz Colomina and Miranda July in Journal #37, Eric Höweler and Kazys Varnelis in Journal #36, John McMorrough in Journal #35, and many many more.)

thresholds is held within 150 university art and architecture libraries around the world (ISSN #1091-711x), and is available for sale at 40 locations in the US. *thresholds* issues can be acquired individually or on a subscription basis. The cover price is $10 ($13 outside the US).

http://thresholds.mit.edu

Archived issues can be read and downloaded at:

http://www.archive.org/details/thresholds332007mass

little t, or a little thresholds, is a student-run series of quick and dirty interventions in architectural broadcasting. Projects have included broadsheet publications on theses as they are being produced, a photography-in-architecture series titled **SnAP**, and a graphic-novel broadsheet about the Glass House.

THANK YOU

Arindam Dutta

Nader Tehrani

Lindsay Anmuth

Curtis Roth

Jonathan Crisman

Nadya Volicer

Kyle Barker

Rebecca Chamberlain

Jack Valleli

Anne Simunovic